UNLOCKING THE POTENTIAL OF FINTECH IN CENTRAL ASIA

DECEMBER 2025

CAREC
Central Asia Regional Economic Cooperation Program

ADB

6 ADB Avenue, Mandaluyong City, 1550 Metro Manila, Philippines
Tel +63 2 8632 4444; Fax +63 2 8636 2444
www.adb.org

ISBN 978-92-9277-489-9 (print); 978-92-9277-490-5 (PDF); 978-92-9277-491-2 (e-book)
Publication Stock No. SPR250432-2
DOI: http://dx.doi.org/10.22617/SPR250432-2

Notes:
1. In this publication, "$" refers to United States dollars, "¥" refers to yen, "AZN" refers to Azerbaijan manats, "GEL" refers to lari, "MNT" refers to togrog, "PRs" refers to Pakistan rupees, and "TJS" refers to somoni.
2. ADB recognizes "China" as the People's Republic of China; "Hong Kong" as Hong Kong, China; "Korea" and "South Korea" as the Republic of Korea; "Kyrgyzstan" as the Kyrgyz Republic; "Macao" as Macau, China; and "Vietnam" as Viet Nam.
3. Effective 1 February 2021, ADB placed a temporary hold on sovereign project disbursements and new contracts in Myanmar.

Cover design by Jan Carlo Dela Cruz.

CONTENTS

TABLES, FIGURES, AND BOXES

TABLES

FIGURES

BOXES

ABOUT THE EDITORS

Minsoo Lee

Minsoo Lee is a senior economist at the Asian Development Bank (ADB), currently serving in the Central and West Asia Department. Since joining ADB in 2011, he has held several senior positions, including senior economist in the Economic Research and Regional Cooperation Department and head of the Economics Unit at the People's Republic of China (PRC) Resident Mission. In these roles, he has led high-level policy dialogues with government counterparts, contributed to the formulation of national development strategies, and managed regional technical assistance programs.

M. Lee has been a key contributor to ADB's flagship knowledge publications, particularly the *Asian Development Outlook*, authoring theme chapters on energy policy, low-carbon growth, and public–private partnerships. His work has supported regional cooperation frameworks and economic diversification initiatives across Central and West Asia.

Prior to joining ADB, M. Lee was a full professor and associate dean at Peking University HSBC Business School in Shenzhen, PRC, where he taught economics and finance and led academic program development.

George Kvirikashvili

George Kvirikashvili is an experienced development consultant, former prime minister of Georgia (2015–2018), and seasoned professional with over 3 decades of experience across banking, government, and international development.

He currently serves as lead international consultant for the Asian Development Bank, supporting fintech-driven cross-border cooperation in the CAREC region. From 2018 to 2022, he was international advisor to the European Bank for Reconstruction and Development in Uzbekistan, where he helped establish the Foreign Investors Council.

As prime minister, he led Georgia's European integration agenda, introduced corporate tax reforms, and launched the Pillar II pension system. His prior public roles include vice prime minister, foreign minister, minister of economy, and head of the Parliamentary group on Georgia's World Trade Organization accession.

With more than 15 years of executive experience in banking and consultancy, G. Kvirikashvili brings deep expertise in financial sector reforms, pension systems, and capital market development. He also serves on the board of Humo, a Gojo-backed microfinance institution in Tajikistan.

Kiyoshi Taniguchi

Kiyoshi Taniguchi is currently the regional lead economist for the Central and West Asia Department of ADB. Prior to this role, he served as country economist at the Pakistan Resident Mission, focusing on the economies of both Afghanistan and Pakistan. In that capacity, he led the preparation of the Pakistan Country Partnership Strategy 2021–2025 and made significant contributions to ADB's economic knowledge work in the region.

During his tenure at ADB, he has conducted economic analysis for the Pacific Department and the Private Sector Operations Department, and served at the Uzbekistan Resident Mission, where he led a team of economists covering Central Asia and the South Caucasus.

Before joining ADB, K. Taniguchi worked at the World Bank's Indonesia Country Office and began his career as an economist at the Food and Agriculture Organization of the United Nations in Rome, Italy. He has also taught development economics at the International University of Japan, Westminster International University in Tashkent, and the University of the Philippines Diliman.

He holds a doctorate and a master's degree in economics from the Ohio State University, United States, and earned his bachelor's degree in economics with honors from the University of Oregon, United States, and Chiba University, Japan.

FOREWORD

The countries in the Central Asia Regional Economic Cooperation (CAREC) Program have made remarkable strides in developing their infrastructure, connectivity, and regional value chains. To ensure that their people and businesses fully benefit from global advancements, strengthening regional cooperation and integration in finance, trade, investment, and institutional frameworks is essential.

Technological innovation is driving transformation worldwide. In the CAREC region, financial technology (fintech) has great potential to reshape financial services—improving access, delivery, and regulation. By enabling banking, insurance, investment, and electronic commerce (e-commerce) for previously unserved communities, fintech creates unprecedented opportunities for financial inclusion, efficiency, and economic growth. Innovations such as mobile payments and digital wallets reduce barriers to financial access, fostering entrepreneurship, enhancing financial literacy, and supporting sustainable development within and across borders.

Fintech's advantage lies not merely in technological innovation, but also in encouraging collaboration in building a cohesive regional financial ecosystem. By leveraging shared expertise and resources, fintech unlocks new opportunities for growth in the CAREC region. This book explores its transformative potential, emphasizing the role of cooperation and innovation in overcoming barriers. It serves as a guide and inspiration for policymakers and stakeholders to shape a more inclusive financial future for CAREC in an increasingly interconnected global economy.

Through regional cooperation, CAREC nations can build a resilient, inclusive, and future-ready financial ecosystem that benefits all stakeholders and ensures accessibility for people at all income levels. However, achieving a fully integrated and robust fintech ecosystem across the diverse economies of Central Asia presents challenges. Each emerging fintech market has distinct financial priorities and regulatory frameworks, yet the interconnected global economy demands a unified approach. By fostering dialogue and cooperation, Central Asian nations can collectively address shared challenges, including limited access to financial services, the lack of robust digital infrastructure, and financial crime.

The journey ahead requires a shared vision, open dialogue, and a commitment to change—guided by the well-structured road map outlined in this book to accelerate progress. Through collective effort and the spread of innovation, whether homegrown or shared, CAREC's emerging fintech markets can harness fintech's potential to drive sustainable development, enhance regional connectivity, and create opportunities for businesses and communities to thrive in an increasingly digital world.

PREFACE

The transformative potential of financial technology (fintech) is increasingly obvious across the world. However, as this book highlights, Central Asian countries have yet to develop a coherent collective strategy to fully harness its potential. While these economies vary in size and structure, they are also at different stages of adopting technological advancements. This book aims to foster dialogue and collaboration, paving the way for a regional cooperative framework to enhance and expand the delivery of financial services across diverse applications.

A regional cooperative fintech community can serve as a platform for the exchange of knowledge, policy harmonization, and the development of innovative financial solutions tailored to the region's specific needs. It can also enable governments, financial institutions, fintech providers, and civil society to work as a cooperative community in shaping an inclusive, resilient, and future-ready financial ecosystem —one equipped to navigate and capitalize on rapid changes shaping the global economy.

Central Asia's unique position as a historical crossroads of East–West trade and culture—now revitalized by the strategic Middle Corridor linking Europe and Asia—underscores its growing economic significance. As this corridor facilitates the flow of goods, services, and ideas, it also presents an opportunity for CAREC countries to integrate their financial ecosystems, fostering cross-border collaboration and innovation. Key factors supporting this growth include favorable demographics, broad support for improving financial inclusion, vibrant investment ecosystems, rising internet access, and strong government interest in advancing the sector.

Since its establishment in 1997, the Central Asia Regional Economic Cooperation (CAREC) Program has focused on four key areas: improving transport infrastructure; facilitating trade; enhancing energy security and connectivity; and developing economic corridors to drive investment and growth across the region. Supported by the Asian Development Bank (ADB), which acts as its Secretariat, CAREC aims to foster regional cooperation and economic integration.*

With its emphasis on capacity building and knowledge sharing, CAREC is well positioned to support regional financial integration within a more diverse, versatile, and decentralized international finance model. By advancing new capital market settlement mechanisms and regional payment systems, CAREC can facilitate seamless cross-border transactions and expand financial opportunities to a wider range of people, helping to bridge financial access gaps between rich and poor, and between men and women. This includes the more than half of all adults across the region who remain unbanked.

* The Central Asia Regional Economic Cooperation (CAREC) Program is a partnership of 11 countries working together to promote development through cooperation, leading to accelerated economic growth and poverty reduction. These countries include Afghanistan, Azerbaijan, the People's Republic of China, Georgia, Kazakhstan, the Kyrgyz Republic, Mongolia, Pakistan, Tajikistan, Turkmenistan, and Uzbekistan. ADB placed its regular assistance to Afghanistan on hold, effective 15 August 2021, but has continued supporting the Afghan people through a special financing arrangement with United Nations agencies since 2022.

Increasing demand for digital payment methods, including central bank digital currencies and stablecoins, stems from their ability to enable faster and cheaper cross-border transactions, including the remittance of wages crucial to many economies in the region. Digital platforms could establish regionally connected payment and settlement systems, promoting trade and global economic integration. Greater fintech adoption could improve correspondent banking relationships by improving transparency, transaction speed, and information tracking.

Developing an integrated fintech ecosystem remains a complex undertaking, as regulatory frameworks in CAREC countries remain underdeveloped. While most have implemented fintech regulations, mutual recognition agreements are needed to enhance regional financial cooperation. Given the borderless nature of fintech, governments, professional associations, and nongovernment organizations must collaborate with international and regional regulatory bodies to effectively manage risks. Regulation should balance financial stability and consumer protection with the flexibility needed to foster innovation. In addition, regulators must shift from controlling market outcomes to enabling entrepreneurial growth, ensuring that regulation supports rather than stifles technological progress.

Key areas of focus should include open banking and open finance, which can drive greater financial inclusion and innovation by allowing third-party providers to access financial data and offer new services. Interoperability between different financial systems and platforms is crucial for seamless cross-border transactions and integration. Establishing a cross-border regulatory sandbox can provide a controlled environment in which fintech companies can assess new products and services, fostering innovation while ensuring regulatory compliance.

This book aims to foster deep engagement with policy issues, encourage knowledge sharing among CAREC countries, and ignite policy dialogue—thereby leading to a set of common goals. It seeks to bridge infrastructure and digitization gaps while shaping policies that drive economic growth, enhance financial connectivity, and accelerate digital transformation in the region's emerging fintech markets.

Chapter 1 introduces a framework for assessing fintech progress across CAREC's emerging fintech markets, developing indicators to evaluate financial sector maturity, digital and financial infrastructure development, regulatory and business environment strength, and regional cooperation in fostering fintech growth and innovation. Chapter 2 lays the ground for transitioning from nation-centered imperatives to a regionwide road map, emphasizing collaboration between public and private sector stakeholders in shaping a shared fintech vision. In Chapter 3, Georgia, the smallest CAREC economy, presses the case for its strong potential as a center of fintech innovation, arguing that its embrace of advanced concepts such as open finance qualifies it as a strong contender for driving innovation in the region.

Chapter 4 explores key fintech-driven service areas for capital market development in CAREC, focusing on how policymakers can encourage innovation to harness regional financial integration. It outlines a well-structured road map for generating knowledge solutions and implementing policy recommendations. Chapter 5 examines how the private sector can leverage fintech services, and highlights the crucial role of regulators in maximizing benefits while mitigating the risks of fintech disruption. Chapter 6 shifts the discussion to fintech's impact on the growth of electronic commerce (e-commerce), emphasizing the need for cross-border market expansion, given the limited size of domestic markets. It stresses fintech's substantial contribution to economic growth, and by comparing fintech-driven e-commerce in member countries of the Association of Southeast Asian Nations (ASEAN), makes the case for a regional digital strategy that integrates both fintech and e-commerce.

Chapter 7 spotlights Pakistan, CAREC's biggest emerging fintech market. It shows the evolution of Pakistan's fintech ecosystem; the role of key players; and the development of regulatory, technological, and cross-sector initiatives that are expected to spur growth, deepen regional cooperation, and widen financial inclusion.

The final two chapters advance the discussion toward fostering regional dialogue regarding a cooperative fintech community by examining developments in national fintech markets. Chapter 8 showcases private sector fintech innovations and highlights the range of government support that could strengthen fintech ecosystems, drive further development, and promote inclusive regional economic growth. Chapter 9 reviews best practices in payment systems that have facilitated fintech adoption in other regions, and assess the applicability of regulatory reforms within the CAREC context. The chapter then explores strategies for building consensus around mechanisms to create deeper and more frequent dialogue among key stakeholders in a regional cooperative fintech community.

Building a thriving fintech ecosystem in CAREC will come with challenges, requiring open dialogue, adaptability, and a shared vision for the region's economic future. This book offers insights, case studies, and practical recommendations for stakeholders at all levels. Through collaboration, CAREC countries can unlock the potential of fintech, paving the way for a more prosperous and interconnected region.

ACKNOWLEDGMENTS

This book was made possible through the valuable support and collaboration of many individuals and institutions.

We extend our sincere gratitude to Leah Gutierrez, director general of the Central and West Asia Department and Yevgeniy Zhukov, director general of the Climate Change and Sustainable Development Department at the Asian Development Bank (ADB), for their guidance and encouragement throughout the development of this book.

We are also grateful to Lyaziza Sabyrova, regional head at ADB, for her strategic insights and coordination support, which helped shape the structure and direction of this initiative.

We gratefully acknowledge the many ADB colleagues whose insightful and constructive feedback greatly enriched this work. In particular, we thank Mohd Sani Mohd Ismail, director; Lisette Cipriano, principal digital financial specialist; Andrew McCartney, senior financial sector economist; and Kijin Kim, senior economist, for their valuable input and engagement.

Special thanks go to the participants of the Regional Workshop on Fintech Development in the Central Asia Regional Economic Cooperation (CAREC) Region, held in Tbilisi, Georgia, in February 2024. Their active participation and thoughtful feedback significantly enhanced the policy discussions and research outputs—helping advance the region's efforts to harness the transformative power of digitalization in the finance sector.

We especially acknowledge Ghulam Samad, chief of the Research Division at the CAREC Institute, for his valuable contributions to the workshop, book launch, and for his continued collaboration.

We also wish to thank Rene Cris Rivera, Eliot John Avena, Marie Rose Rollan, Maria Citadel Gabatin, and Sarah Cueno for their tireless support throughout the production process.

We also deeply appreciate the contributions of the chapter authors. Their expertise and commitment to regional knowledge sharing form the foundation of this book.

Finally, we would like to recognize James Unwin for his critical editorial oversight, coordination, and dedication in bringing this book to completion.

ABBREVIATIONS

ADB	Asian Development Bank
AFAQ	Arabian Gulf System for Financial Automated Quick Payment Transfer
AFIN	ASEAN Financial Innovation Network
AFSA	Astana Financial Services Authority
AI	artificial intelligence
AIFC	Astana International Financial Centre
AML/CFT	anti-money laundering/combating the financing of terrorism
API	application programming interface
APN	Asian Payment Network
ASEAN	Association of Southeast Asian Nations
B2B	business-to-business
B2C	business-to-consumer
BIS	Bank for International Settlements
CAREC	Central Asia Regional Economic Cooperation (Program)
CBDC	central bank digital currency
CIBA	Client-Initiated Backchannel Authentication
CNIC	Computerized National Identity Card (Pakistan)
CPMI	Committee on Payments and Market Infrastructures (BIS)
CRM	customer relationship management
CSD	central securities depository
DeFi	decentralized finance
DGA	Digital Governance Agency
DLT	distributed ledger technology
DPI	Digital Public Infrastructure
e-commerce	electronic commerce
e-money	electronic money
e-payment	electronic payment
e-wallet	electronic wallet
ECB	European Central Bank
eKYC	electronic Know Your Customer
EMI	electronic money institution
EU	European Union
EUDIW	EU Digital Identity Wallet
FAPI	financial-grade API

FMU	Financial Monitoring Unit (Pakistan)
FPS	fast payment system
FTA	free trade agreement
GCC	Gulf Cooperation Council
GDP	gross domestic product
GDPR	General Data Protection Regulation
GFIN	Global Financial Innovation Network
GITA	Georgia's Innovation and Technology Agency
GMV	gross merchandise value
ICO	initial coin offering
ICT	information and communication technology
ID	identification
IFC	International Finance Corporation
IoT	Internet of Things
IPC	Interbank Processing Center (Kyrgyz Republic)
IPO	initial public offering
IPS	Instant Payment System (Azerbaijan)
ISO	International Organization for Standardization
IT	information technology
ITU	International Telecommunication Union
KYC	Know Your Customer
Lao PDR	Lao People's Democratic Republic
MAS	Monetary Authority of Singapore
Mbps	megabits per second
MDITC	Ministry for the Development of Information Technologies and Communications (Uzbekistan)
ML	machine learning
MNO	mobile network operator
MOESD	Ministry of Economy and Sustainable Development (Georgia)
MoITT	Ministry of Information Technology and Telecommunication (Pakistan)
MOU	memorandum of understanding
MSMEs	micro, small, and medium-sized enterprises
NADRA	National Database and Registration Authority (Pakistan)
NAPP	National Agency of Perspective Projects (Uzbekistan)
NBFI	nonbank financial institution
NBG	National Bank of Georgia
OECD	Organisation for Economic Co-operation and Development
P2P	peer-to-peer
POS	point-of-sale

PRC	People's Republic of China
PSD_2	Payment Services Directive (revised) (EU)
PTA	Pakistan Telecommunication Authority
QR	Quick Response (code)
RCI	regional cooperation and integration
RTGS	real-time gross settlement
RTP	real-time payment
SBP	State Bank of Pakistan
SECP	Securities and Exchange Commission of Pakistan
SEPA	Single Euro Payments Area
SMEs	small and medium-sized enterprises
STO	security token offering
STZA	Special Technology Zones Authority (Pakistan)
UAE	United Arab Emirates
UK	United Kingdom
UNCTAD	United Nations Conference on Trade and Development
UNDP	United Nations Development Programme
US	United States
VASP	virtual asset service provider

PART I

A COLLABORATIVE APPROACH TO FINTECH

1

Measuring Fintech Progress in Central Asia

Peter Lovelock

INTRODUCTION

Growth in financial technology (fintech) has been phenomenally rapid in some Central Asian markets, while others are poised for significant expansion in the coming years, driven by an emphasis on financial access and digital adoption. Growth is accelerating because of factors such as favorable demographics, a low initial base of financial inclusion, vibrant investment ecosystems, rising internet access, and regulatory authorities that recognize their crucial role in developing the sector. Innovation hubs and regulatory sandboxes for start-ups are helping to increase the scale, scope, and reach of the fintech sector, enabling it to benefit larger populations.

To examine the sector's strengths and weaknesses, and identify opportunities to facilitate fintech growth at the national level and cooperation at the regional level, it is critical to evaluate conditions in those Central Asia Regional Economic Cooperation (CAREC) countries where fintech market data are available and progress is possible. This chapter assesses the conditions through a series of indicators across four pillars: finance, technology, capability, and regional cooperation. These are compared with conditions in member countries of the Association of Southeast Asian Nations (ASEAN) and in mature economies such as India, Japan, and the Republic of Korea. Lessons and next steps are the focus for nine emerging CAREC fintech markets with development potential.[1] While data from the People's Republic of China (PRC) are included, the PRC is a clearly a more developed fintech market, and an outlier in size and usage of fintech in everyday lives.

The spread and efficacy of fintech across the nine economies are both supply-facilitated, through banks and nonbank financial institutions (NBFIs) that adopt and promote fintech applications, and demand-driven, as customers use those fintech applications (for example, through mobile banking apps).

The four types of services and products most relevant across the emerging fintech markets in CAREC are payments, lending, insurance, and investment and financial advice. The adoption rates in the PRC are touching 87% (ADB 2021, EY 2019), but the four types are also being adopted across emerging fintech markets in CAREC, with both user demand and the capacity of mobile operators and payment platforms to meet that demand now major drivers. For instance, in Kazakhstan, market leaders such as Kaspi Bank operate payment platforms that enable customers to make online, in-store,

1 The emerging fintech markets of CAREC are Azerbaijan, Georgia, Kazakhstan, the Kyrgyz Republic, Mongolia, Pakistan, Tajikistan, Turkmenistan, and Uzbekistan. They represent the countries for which e-commerce market data are available, excluding the dominant People's Republic of China (PRC) market.

and peer-to-peer (P2P) payments, providing merchants with point-of-sale (POS) solutions that enable interoperability. In the Kyrgyz Republic, digital lending solutions seeing increased adoption are provided by telecommunications business offshoots that are leveraging customer bases, and are offered in partnerships with banks to offer short-term microloans.

Fintech holds significant potential to improve the economic status of the more than half the adult population in the region who remain unbanked and thus excluded from the financial system.[2]

Indicators for CAREC's Fintech Economies

This chapter presents a framework for assessing progress in CAREC's emerging fintech markets. Across the four pillars—finance, technology, capability, and regional cooperation—indicators have been identified from third-party sources such as the World Bank, and created by research by Access Partnership, to assess finance sector maturity, the development level of the digital and financial infrastructure, the strength of the regulatory and business environment, and the extent of cooperation within the region to promote fintech growth and innovation.

Table 1.1 summarizes the performance of each emerging CAREC fintech market and the fintech market in the PRC across the four pillars. Kazakhstan and Mongolia score highest across all categories. At the other end are countries significantly below the regional average, signifying challenges in financial access and adoption, inadequate technological infrastructure, a less-than-conducive policy and regulatory environment, and limited capacity for regional cooperation initiatives. Others, such as Pakistan and Tajikistan, face similar challenges, especially in the strength of their finance sectors and digital infrastructure.

Table 1.1: Summary of CAREC Fintech Progress

(%)

Country/Region	Finance	Technology	Capacity	Regional Cooperation
Azerbaijan	21.7	55.9	81.8	33.3
People's Republic of China	53.0	68.8	78.5	100.0
Kazakhstan	42.1	50.6	71.2	66.7
Kyrgyz Republic	25.0	24.9	54.9	66.7
Mongolia	63.0	54.3	54.5	44.4
Pakistan	12.8	36.2	58.5	44.4
Tajikistan	21.2	21.5	53.4	66.7
Turkmenistan	27.7	0.04	50.0	11.1
Uzbekistan	33.3	46.3	66.7	22.2
CAREC	**31.8**	**36.5**	**60.2**	**45.5**

CAREC = Central Asia Regional Economic Cooperation, fintech = financial technology.
Note: The values represent the percentage.
Source: Access Partnership.

[2] Author's calculations. Also see World Bank (2021).

Understanding the scale and scope of fintech adoption across the region's finance sector is crucial for maximizing the region's economic potential and for promoting financial integration. It is critical to assess fintech's progress in financial inclusion and financial services delivery, as well as where fintech can produce greater cross-sector benefits within and across nations. Comprehensive data evaluation will provide an assessment of the contribution of the digital and financial infrastructure, the regulatory and business environments, and regional cooperation initiatives. It may also provide insights into the comparative strengths and weaknesses of finance sectors and identify areas where policy and regulatory efforts should be directed. An understanding of the regional fintech landscape could also support cross-border cooperation by removing barriers and bringing about an alignment on regulatory frameworks and international standards, thereby facilitating fintech growth and enhancing competitiveness at the international level.

PILLARS OF FINTECH PROGRESS

As fintech evolves—for example, from barcodes to Quick Response (QR) codes, or from plastic swipe cards to online digital identities and transactions—so does the structure of and services offered by the finance sector. New customer-facing fintech innovations are of two types: (i) digital services that simply replace analog services, such as the use of mobile phones to transfer money (P2P) and make payments (person-to-consumer, person-to-business, or person-to-government); and (ii) digital services that are themselves innovative, such as crowdsourcing, the use of QR codes, and online products, such as insurance and budget-management apps.

Regarding payments, lending, insurance, and investment and financial advice, the focus across CAREC's emerging fintech markets has primarily been on payment services and, to an extent, on lending (Figure 1.1).

Figure 1.1: Prominent Types of Fintech Products and Services

Payments: Digital payments from one account to another, including remittances, using a variety of payment methods (credit and debit cards, prepaid cards, bank transfers, and mobile wallets).

Lending: Digital credit tailored to user needs and offered to MSMEs and consumers.

Insurance: Digital insurance products—including life, health, travel, and vehicle insurance—to meet the specific needs of consumers.

Investment and financial advice: Digital platforms that provide financial advice on the stock market, mutual funds, bonds, and more based on algorithms—also known as "robo-advisors."

fintech = financial technology; MSMEs = micro, small, and medium-sized enterprises.

Source: Access Partnership.

Fintech solutions are also building on the larger financial services ecosystem, where different types of financial institutions offer a variety of financial products and services either to mass markets or to specific customer groups. They include the following:

- **Commercial banks.** They offer a range of modern services and products, including checking and savings accounts, debit and credit cards, automated teller machines (ATMs), electronic funds transfer at point of sale (EFTPOS), internet banking, mobile banking, and salaries crediting.
- **Microfinance institutions.** There are licensed institutions in the region offering services that include different types of accounts (savings, checking, fixed deposit, and special savings), as well as a range of lending options.
- **Savings and loan cooperatives.** These are member-owned institutions whose core business is to collect savings from members, use the funds to provide loans to members at affordable interest rates, and train members in financial literacy. Most savings and loan cooperatives are farmer- and welfare-based societies that are small and not connected to the National Payment Switch system.
- **Nonbank institutions.** They offer services not provided by banks and specialize in certain sectors or target groups. They may include insurance companies, venture capital firms, electronic money (e-money) institutions, foreign exchange firms, and pawn shops.
- **Postal services.** Post offices may offer a range of services, including domestic remittance, check cashing, bill payment processing, and small loans.

Overall, fintech growth is accelerating in several of the nine CAREC markets. In digital banking, even as leading commercial banks have digitalized some aspects of their services, fintech development in the region is still nascent—with inconsistent strategies and regulations, a lack of foreign investment, and low mobile phone and internet penetration (Mynbayev and Aushev 2020). At the same time, reduced access to trained staff and experts who understand digital technologies and how best to implement them, as well as a weak financial infrastructure that imposes constraints due to underdeveloped payment systems, limits both the scale and security of transactions.

For the many developing countries in CAREC, there is a leapfrog opportunity. However, this is subject to the availability of enabling infrastructure such as broadband internet, bank branches, ATM networks, mobile wallets, and online instant-payment systems. Fintech nevertheless has a significant potential to improve the economic status of a vast number of people.

Besides the fact that more than half of the adult population is unbanked, further disparities exist between rich and poor, and men and women. In Georgia, among the poorest 40% of the population, only 62% have a bank account, compared with 76% for the richest 60% (Chapter 3). In Pakistan, among the poorest 40%, as of 2021, only 18% had a bank account, compared with 23% for the richest 60% (Chapter 7) (World Bank 2021).

This section presents the framework for assessing fintech progress and shares evidence and insights, identifying the successes, challenges, and barriers that need to be addressed. Detailed analysis is presented below, covering all four pillars.

Finance

Selected indicators in Table 1.2 measure progress in financial access, adoption, and usage. Financial inclusion is seen as a foundational driver of fintech development in the region, hence its presence in the finance indicator.

The data show significant regional variation; for instance, financial institution account ownership, indicating the extent of financial inclusion, is close to 16% in Pakistan, but 98% in Mongolia. This impacts the adoption and use of digital payments. While usage has generally accelerated since the coronavirus disease (COVID-19) pandemic (World Bank 2022b), it remains highest in countries with greater financial inclusion. Financial inclusion and digital payments are likely to be driven by similar factors, such as national economic growth (Figures 1.2 and 1.3). This is also true for ownership of debit and credit cards and the ability to make utility payments and receive wages in financial institution accounts. Evidence suggests that mobile money has accelerated throughout CAREC's emerging fintech markets (World Bank 2022a), but data on ownership of mobile money accounts are limited.

Table 1.2: CAREC Progress in Fintech Finance

(%)

Country/Region	Has Financial Institution Account (15+ years of age)[a]	Has Mobile Money Account (15+ years of age)[a]	Made or Received a Digital Payment (15+ years of age)[a]	Received Wages in a Financial Institution Account (15+ years of age)[a]	Owns a Debit or Credit Card (15+ years of age)[a]	Made a Utility Payment Using an Account (15+ years of age)[a,b]	Firms Using Banks for Investment Capital	Firms Using Banks for Working Capital	MSMEs Reporting Financial Gap[c]	Firms Reporting Finance as Major Constraint[c]
Azerbaijan[d]	29	...	25	9	27	9	24	19	99	41
PRC	89	...	86	35	78	22	15	22	32	41
Georgia	70	8	62	20	46	28	35	32	60	20
Kazakhstan	81	...	78	31	63	32	14	13	87	48
Kyrgyz Republic	41	11	39	11	28	11	17	19	83	48
Mongolia	98	59	97	49	87	44	48	38	39	55
Pakistan	16	9	18	3	8	7	8	9	91	53
Tajikistan	39	2	33	9	16	14	8	13	95	30
Turkmenistan[d]	41	...	34	25	38	0	...	...	...	...
Uzbekistan	44	...	42	13	36	16	27	24	92	13
CAREC	**51**	**15**	**48**	**18**	**39**	**17**	**20**	**20**	**78**	**40**

... = data not available; CAREC = Central Asia Regional Economic Cooperation; MSMEs = micro, small, and medium-sized enterprises; PRC = People's Republic of China.

[a] This refers to the percentage of persons at least 15 years of age in 2021.

[b] This refers to persons who had made a utility payment using an account at a financial institution or a mobile money account.

[c] The extent of reporting varied from 2012 to 2019.

[d] The latest available data for Azerbaijan and Turkmenistan are from 2017.

Sources: International Finance Corporation (IFC). 2017. *MSME Finance Gap: Assessment of the Shortfalls and Opportunities in Financing Micro, Small and Medium Enterprises in Emerging Markets*; World Bank. n.d. *Global Financial Development Report 2019/2020: Bank Regulation and Supervision a Decade after the Global Financial Crisis*. https://www.worldbank.org/en/publication/gfdr/data/global-financial-development-database; and World Bank. 2022. Global Findex Database 2021: Financial Inclusion, Digital Payments, and Resilience in the Age of COVID-19. https://www.worldbank.org/en/publication/globalfindex (accessed 16 November 2022).

The types of fintech adopted and promoted by banks and NBFIs can be broadly categorized as (i) inward-facing in terms of bank administrative procedures, such as those concerning clearing systems, capital assets, and loan risk management; and (ii) customer-facing in terms of assessments of customers' needs and credit worthiness, accounting for the wide variation among individual customers; micro, small, and medium-sized enterprises (MSMEs); and corporate business clients.

Financial Exclusion Remains a Challenge Across the Region

Central Asia is home to a large majority of the globally unbanked and faces many challenges in providing safe, timely, and affordable financial services. Poor and marginalized segments of society, such as older people and women, tend to be more widely excluded from formal financial services, stifling their opportunities to progress up the economic ladder. Moreover, large access and utilization disparities persist for financial services of all kinds. While bank account ownership is nearly universal in developed economies, only about one in 10 people have access to financial accounts in the emerging fintech markets of CAREC. Within these countries, access to financial services can also be unevenly distributed.

Despite this, financial inclusion rates have improved. For instance, in the Kyrgyz Republic, financial account ownership rose from 4% in 2011 to 41% in 2021 (Figure 1.2). Similarly, in Tajikistan, these figures increased from 3% to 39% over the same period. For Tajikistan, efforts to narrow the financial access gap between men and women have also made progress. In 2014, financial account ownership rates stood at 14% for men and 9% for women; but by 2021, they had increased to 38% for men and 39% for women (World Bank 2021).

Income and financial account ownership have a positive association. As shown in Figure 1.2, there is a positive correlation between gross domestic product (GDP) per capita and account ownership. In addition, Figure 1.3 shows a positive correlation between mobile penetration and account ownership. This suggests that as income rises, so does the incentive to use a bank or NBFI featuring a mobile wallet; and as mobile penetration increases, partly due to smartphones and other mobile devices falling in price (both nominal and real) and increasing in gigabyte capacity, their correlation with account ownership becomes stronger.

Figure 1.2: Correlation Between Gross Domestic Product Per Capita and Account Ownership

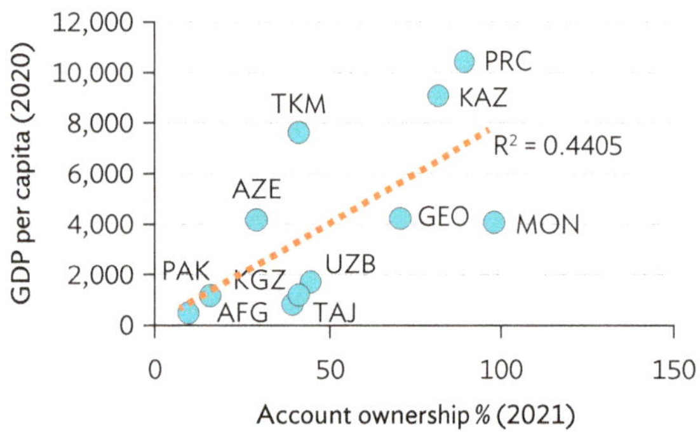

Figure 1.3: Correlation Between Mobile Penetration and Account Ownership

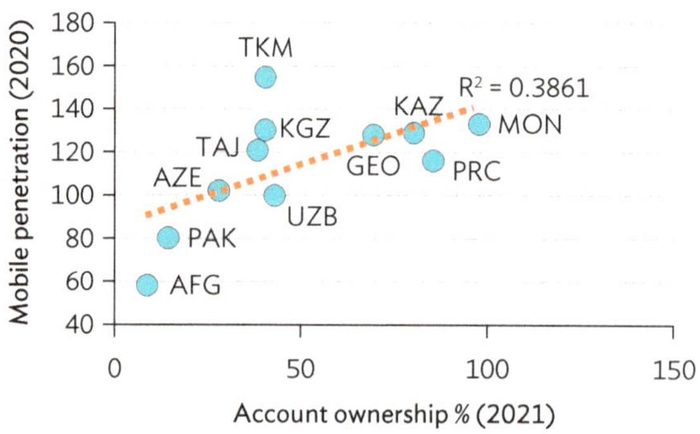

AFG = Afghanistan, AZE = Azerbaijan, GDP = gross domestic product, GEO = Georgia, KGZ = Kyrgyz Republic, MON = Mongolia, PAK = Pakistan, PRC = People's Republic of China, TAJ = Tajikistan, TKM = Turkmenistan, UZB = Uzbekistan.

Note: The correlation between per capita GDP and account ownership, as shown in Figure 1.2, is 0.66; and the correction between mobile penetration and account ownership, as shown in Figure 1.3, is 0.62.

Sources: Access Partnership team analysis; and World Bank. https://data.worldbank.org/indicator/FX.OWN.TOTL.ZS.

In the 1990s, high-tech industries globally were increasingly driven by the demands of consumers, including business customers, equipped with affordable mobile digital devices and growing computing power, a process that became known as "consumerization" (Gartner 2022). The data suggest that fintech has also been driven by consumer demand using mobile devices. On the supply side, digital web-based platforms accessible by mobile devices have proliferated.

However, for most of CAREC's emerging fintech markets, until 2018, the provision of financial accounts on alternative financing platforms—that is, platforms managed by nonbank entities such as electronic commerce (e-commerce) websites, crowdsourcing, and P2P lending sites—trailed more advanced economies such as Japan, the Republic of Korea, the United Kingdom (UK), and the United States (US) (Figure 1.4).

Figure 1.4: Alternative Finance Market Sizes and Platforms in CAREC and Other Countries, 2018

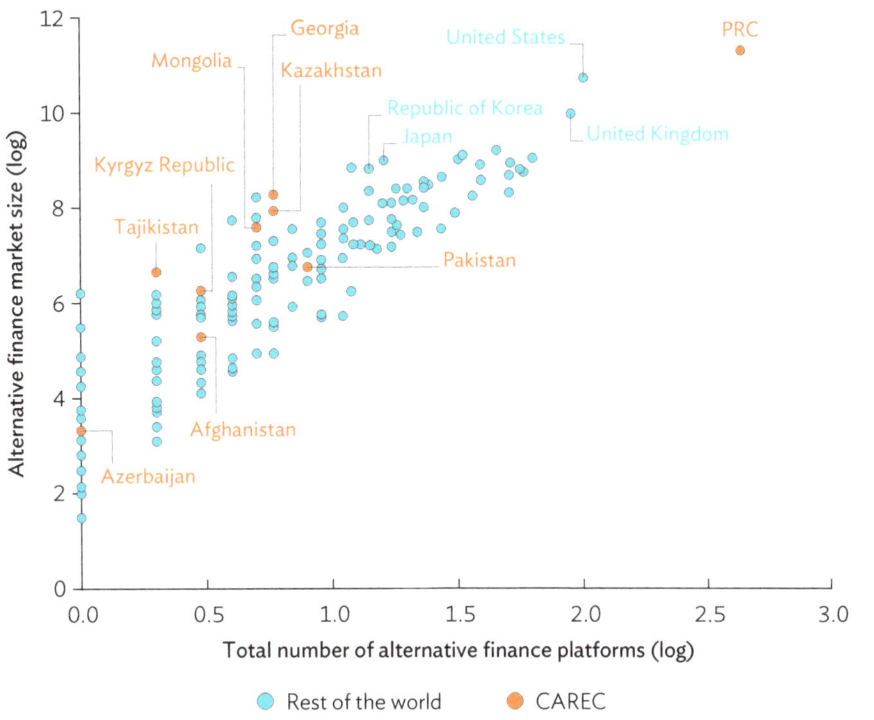

CAREC = Central Asia Regional Economic Cooperation (program), log = logarithm, PRC = People's Republic of China.

Source: M. Lee et al. 2021. Leveraging Fintech for Central Asia's Trade Financing Needs: Supporting Underserved Micro, Small, and Medium-Sized Enterprises. *ADB Briefs*. No. 193. Asian Development Bank. https://www.adb.org/publications/fintech-central-asia-trade-financing-needs.

Alternative finance platforms are designed to scale up and represent a stage of development beyond the online transactions offered by individual banks, mobile operators, or third parties. The second stage in their development is their interoperability and transformation into international platforms (Figure 1.4). Most emerging fintech markets in CAREC countries are slowly evolving toward the second stage. However, Figure 1.4 does not show the dominance of particular platforms within a country.

In larger economies, such as the PRC, the UK, and the US, the market is well developed, as all the banks and mobile operators, as well as many third-party payment platforms, compete for financial business. An example comes from the PRC, where the Ant Group, using its "310" artificial intelligence (AI) online lending model, had served 29 million small and medium-sized enterprises (SMEs) by 2021, while maintaining a nonperforming loan ratio of under 2%, even during the peak of the pandemic (Lee et al. 2021). While Georgia, Kazakhstan, Mongolia, and Pakistan are more second stage, their banking and finance sectors are either highly concentrated or oligopolies, even though occasional digital banks do enter the market.

Digital Payments Segment Dominates the Regional Fintech Markets

Digital payments is the largest segment in terms of total transaction value in CAREC's emerging fintech markets, compared with segments such as alternative financing, alternative lending, digital investment, digital assets, and digital banking. A paper by the CAREC Institute and Islamic Development Bank on six of the region's lowest-income economies supports this view, reporting that "the countries demonstrate closer results in most sub-indicators of digital payments within the range of 45 percent to 54 percent (the average for the selected six countries is 50.7 percent) except for the 'volume of cashless payments,' which is the weakest point (33.3)" (CAREC Institute and Islamic Development Bank 2022).

The pandemic accelerated the digitalization of payments and, in turn, created opportunities for start-ups in Central Asia to offer innovative apps in sectors such as e-education, digital health, and smart energy.[3] Taking the example of the shift to e-commerce, ADB-published data on online shopping transaction values that can be converted to show the propensity to shop online (Chapter 6).[4] The data show Kazakhstan (86%), Azerbaijan (81%), the PRC and Mongolia (78%), and the Kyrgyz Republic (75%) leading the way; followed by Georgia (67%), Turkmenistan (50%), Uzbekistan (40%), and Tajikistan (37%), with Pakistan (14%) well behind. Propensity to shop online grows with internet access, which indicates a combination of "learning by doing" and growing financial literacy, as well as an environment of online e-commerce platforms supported by the local logistics necessary for home deliveries. However, where access to mobile networks is limited, the lack of access can be regarded as a major obstacle to fintech deployment (CAREC Institute 2021).

Banks Are Slow to Adopt Fintech

Banks across Central Asia have been slow to adopt fintech (Kim et al. 2021). In banking operations, fintech is limited to certain tasks such as digital filing and transmission (42%) and electronic signature platforms (28%), while firms use them primarily for digital record keeping and accounting (20%), as shown in Figure 1.5.

As reported in the 2021 ADB Trade Finance Gaps, Growth, and Jobs Survey, which spanned 79 banks in 43 countries, the major constraint cited by banks was the high cost of technology (56%). Others included lack of technological expertise (20%) and insufficient connection or interoperability (18%) across financing platforms (Kim et al. 2021). These constraints are also frequently noted by banks in Central Asia.

[3] The CAREC program for start-ups sponsored by the Republic of Korea provides examples of start-up initiatives in Azerbaijan, Georgia, and Mongolia during COVID-19 (CAREC Program 2021a).

[4] "Propensity to consume" measures those who had the means to shop online, and the percentage of those that did so (ADB News and Events 2022).

Figure 1.5: Fintech Adoption in Bank and Business Operations

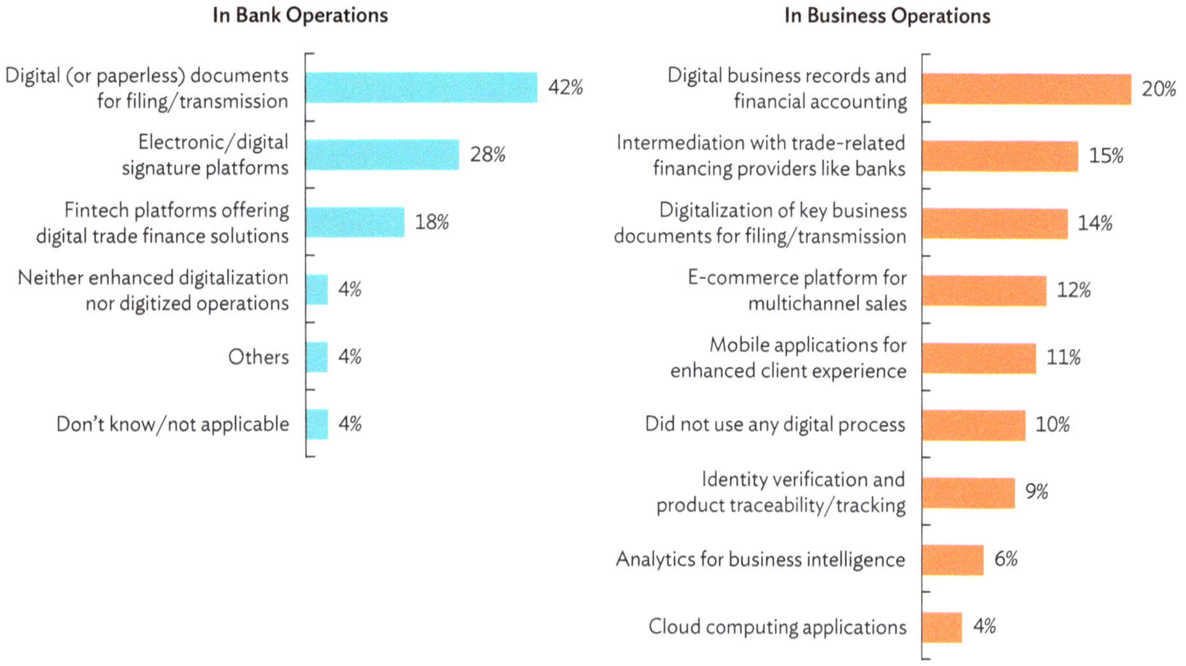

fintech = financial technology.

Note: Each bar represents the percentage of banks or businesses that have engaged in the specified operation.

Source: K. Kim et al. 2021. 2021 Trade Finance Gaps, Growth, and Jobs Survey. *ADB Briefs*. No. 192. Asian Development Bank. https://www.adb.org/publications/2021-trade-finance-gaps-growth-jobs-survey.

Firms Face Capital and Financing Constraints

Gaps in banking services and in their ability to provide adequate capital to business customers, which fintech could help solve, are illustrated by the indicators in this chapter. Azerbaijan, the PRC, Georgia, Mongolia, and Uzbekistan exhibit significant bank support for firms needing capital investment and working capital, while financing gaps in Azerbaijan, Georgia, and Mongolia have been noted as a major constraint on business.

Capital market financing of the financiers is also an issue. For example, although Kazakhstan ranks 13th among Asia and the Pacific countries in the Global Fintech Index Rankings, as the chief economist of the National Bank of Kazakhstan points out, "Almost 70% of start-ups are self-funded. In this regard, one of the main constraints on the rapid development of the FinTech market in Kazakhstan is the lack of free access to financing" (Yerzhan 2022). This situation was made far worse by COVID-19 and Russia's war in Ukraine, according to the CAREC Senior Officials' Meeting in June 2022, which proposed the creation of a Capital Markets Regulators Forum (CAREC Program 2022).

MSMEs comprise over 90% of businesses in most CAREC countries, and often account for 50% or more of employment and sources of income. Financing their role in supply chains is, therefore, important for securing their sustainability (ADB Institute 2021). The general financing gap for MSMEs is below 40% only in the PRC and Mongolia. In five countries, it exceeds 90% of reported needs. Trade finance is especially important to MSMEs, as their revenues reflect their ability to sell. However, as the report noted, rejections of trade finance for MSMEs across the entire region in 2018 reached 57%, compared with 33% in the rest of Asia.

This highlights the challenges in the "Know Your Customer" (KYC) framework and the lack of digital IDs among MSMEs. Fintech, such as AI, "can allow financial service providers to reduce the cost of analyzing MSMEs' financial information and make credit decisions without formal documentation" (Morgan and Yoshino 2021).

The ADB survey also found that lack of information about digital platforms for alternative financing (39%) and lack of expertise in managing these types of technology (18%) are the key factors preventing enterprises from embracing digital or web-based platforms (Lee et al. 2021). While more and better training can help SMEs leverage innovative financing options, the availability of these alternatives is often constrained by banks' legacy systems and outdated processes. An example is their cumulative investment in branches and ATM networks (Figure 1.6; Umar 2021).

Figure 1.6: Commercial Bank Branches and ATMs in the CAREC Region
(number per 100,000 adults)

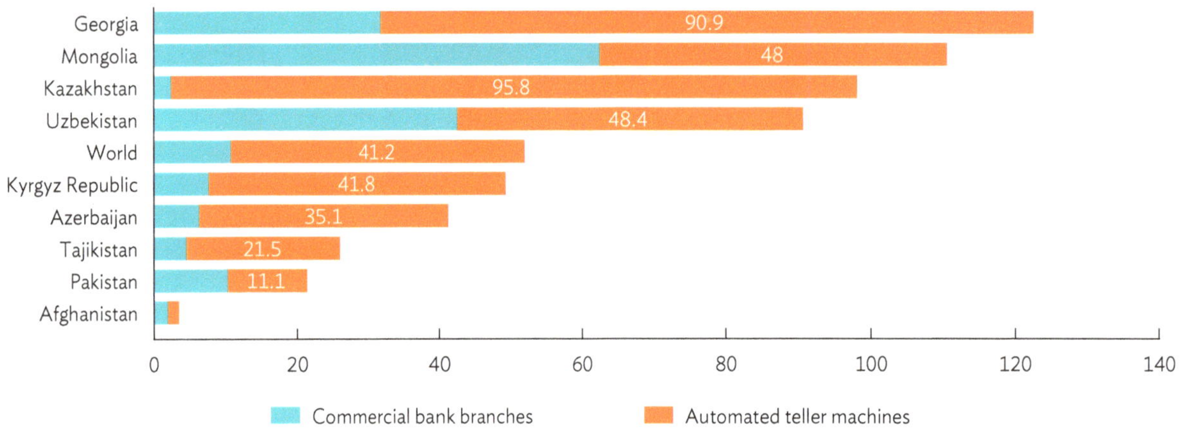

Notes:
1. Data for Turkmenistan are not available, and the data for the rest of the countries are for the year 2020.
2. The values shown in the bars represent only the number automated teller machines per 100,000 adults.

Sources: World Bank. Automated teller machines (ATMs) (per 100,000 adults). Data. https://data.worldbank.org/indicator/FB.ATM.TOTL.P5 (accessed 12 November 2022); and World Bank. Commercial bank branches (per 100,000 adults). Data. https://data.worldbank.org/indicator/FB.CBK.BRCH.P5 (accessed 14 November 2022).

Bank Access for Small and Medium-Sized Enterprises Hampered by Poor Infrastructure

Without adequate financial infrastructure, access to banking has been restricted, especially outside major urban centers. However, as mobile devices such as smartphones and tablets proliferate, the shift toward mobile-centric banking and digital apps involves a costly replacement (amortization) of this infrastructure and its back-end support by new technologies. This involves additional costs, ranging from servers and database software to AI apps, blockchains, cloud, and/or distributed-edge computing—sometimes referred to as the "ABCD" of fintech—and to other frontier technologies that exploit access to growing sources of data (AlAji 2018). The technical and managerial skill sets involved are also challenging.
The comparatively slow development of the supply side is, therefore, unsurprising, not least in developing CAREC economies. The drive toward fintech will mostly come from consumers, for services such as m-payments, mobile wallets, mobile banking, and financial apps.

Digital Banking Leverages Fintech Growth

When permitted by the authorities, digital banking has emerged as a growth area. Digital banking is limited and experimental, but it is being encouraged in some economies, such as Pakistan and Uzbekistan, as a path toward fintech innovation (chapters 7 and 8). While a nascent development, digital banking platforms are spurring other financial institutions in the ecosystem to expand their reach to customers. Post offices are traditionally important for rural and semi-urban areas, fulfilling functions such as domestic remittance, check cashing, and bill-payment processing; and it could become important as digital banking services are being developed.

Technology

This section examines the second pillar: Technology (which includes infrastructure). Selected indicators in Table 1.3 measure progress in the access to and adoption of digital infrastructure; the development of financial infrastructure, such as fast-payment systems, which facilitate interoperable payments; the implementation of soft infrastructure, such as national digital identification (ID) systems; and investment in emerging technologies, such as AI and blockchain.

Table 1.3: CAREC Progress in Technology

Country/ Region	Internet Users, 2020[a] (%)	Mobile Broadband Subscriptions, 2020[b] (per 100 inhabitants)	Fixed Broadband Speed, May 2022[c] (download Mbps)	Fast Payment Systems (0–3)[d]	National Digital Identities (0–3)[d]	Adoption of and Investment in Emerging Technologies[e]
Azerbaijan	85	70	21	2	3	45
PRC	70	95	182	2	3	46
Georgia	73	82	20	1	2	19
Kazakhstan	86	95	36	2	2	26
Kyrgyz Republic	80	119	46	0	1	14
Mongolia	63	109	49	3	2	24
Pakistan	25	41	10	3	1	41
Tajikistan	32	25	20	2	0	27
Turkmenistan	52	15	2	0	0	...
Uzbekistan	71	94	40	2	1	...
CAREC	**61**	**69**	**39**	**1.5**	**1.4**	**30**

... = data not available, CAREC = Central Asia Regional Economic Cooperation, Mbps = megabits per second, PRC = People's Republic of China.

Note: The latest data available were used for each indicator.

[a] International Telecommunication Union (ITU) ICT [Information and Communication Technology] Indicators Database. Internet Users. https://www.itu.int/en/ID/Statistics/Documents/statistics/2021/December/PercentIndividualsUsingInternet.xlsx (accessed 23 November 2022).

[b] ITU ICT Indicators database, Mobile broadband subscription (accessed 17 Novermber 2022).

[c] Speedtest Global Index, Fixed broadband speed (accessed 22 Novermber 2022).

[d] Access Partnership analysis and research. The 0–3 range is the scoring system for these indicators in the ITU ICT Indicators Database, representing the levels of progress made in the development of fast-payment and national-digital-identity systems (with "3" representing the most progress). See the Appendix, Pillar 2 for a description of the meaning of each score for each indicator.

[e] Network Readiness Index, Emerging Technologies (accessed 16 November 2022).

Source: Author.

Among the basic requirements for furthering fintech growth is improving access to the internet; mobile connectivity; and access to corresponding devices, such as mobile phones or computers, on the user side; as well as enhancing an enabling financial infrastructure on the supply side. While the CAREC countries average is 61.3% for internet users and 69.4% for mobile broadband subscriptions, significant gaps in some countries, such as Pakistan and Tajikistan, highlight cost and geographical constraints (Figure 1.7). Similarly, the adoption of emerging technologies remains limited to advanced economies, though the rates of adoption are higher where enabling policies and private sector investment have been encouraged, as in Azerbaijan and Pakistan. Progress in upgrading payment infrastructure, as well as investments in digital identity programs, remains low; but governments are becoming more interested.

Figure 1.7: Access to Internet and Mobile Broadband, 2020

(%)

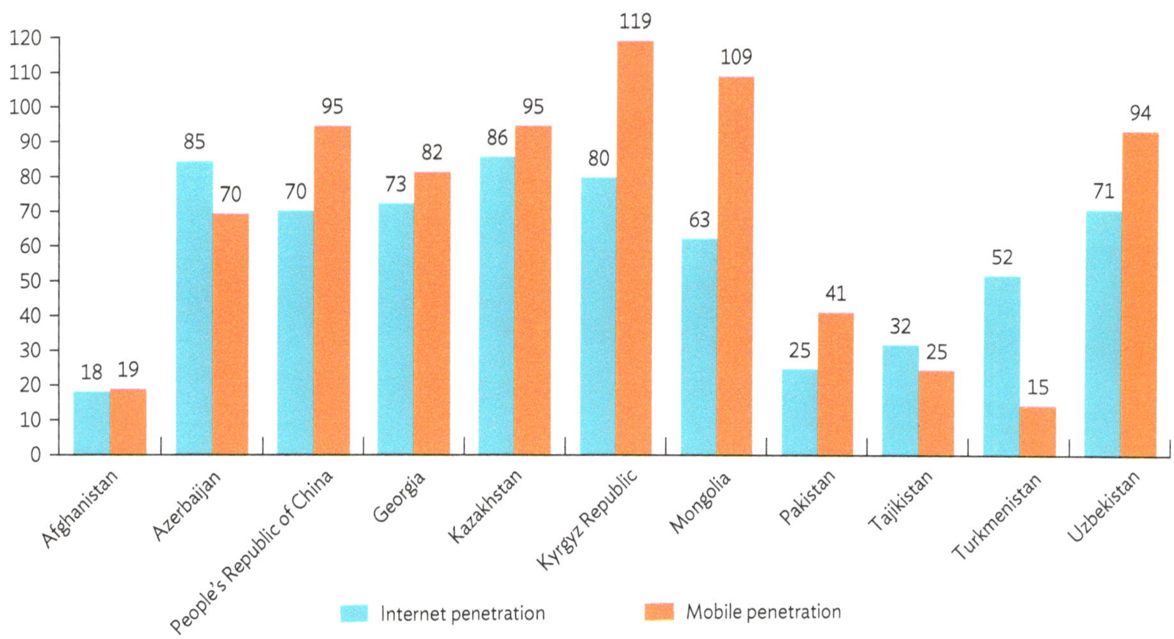

Source: International Telecommunication Union. 2020. ICT Indicators.

Investments in Improving Internet Access

Lack of coverage, high costs (relative to income), and lack of digital literacy are key barriers to increasing internet access. Some economies have succeeded in reducing the gap between urban and rural internet access through initiatives such as "broadband access to every village."

To address this gap, emerging fintech markets in CAREC have strategies to provide universal access to digital technologies, including for those with special needs, and to address the gender divide. They have also accelerated their efforts to promote the development of their digital economies. For example, Georgia has a state program on Broadband Infrastructure Development, 2020–2025; Kazakhstan has the Digital Kazakhstan Program, 2018–2022; and the Kyrgyz Republic has Digital Kyrgyzstan, 2019–2023.

Some governments in Central Asia have demonstrated the ability to move fast when digital infrastructure is necessary. For example, Uzbekistan almost doubled its fiber optic infrastructure, from 36,600 kilometers in 2019 to 68,600 kilometers in 2020, enabling an accelerated rollout of mobile networks (Buruncuic 2021). Similarly, Kazakhstan has set a goal of ensuring 100% coverage with high-quality internet and 95% with home broadband access networks by 2025 (Satubaldina 2022).

Remaining Obstacles Against Increased Mobile Broadband Access

Wireless networks and mobile broadband are the fastest modes to achieve widespread internet penetration. While 2G penetration is ubiquitous across the region, coverage for 4G networks lags, with a median of 69%. The 4G network is necessary for providing consumers and businesses with access to a faster and more reliable internet that can facilitate fintech adoption.

Obstacles to increasing access to 4G networks include lack of access to an internet-enabled device, the inability of consumers to pay, and the need for most mobile operators to recover their investment in 3G before upgrading. Across the Kyrgyz Republic, Pakistan, and Tajikistan, the cost of mobile broadband and the lack of access to infrastructure have proven to be the greatest impediments. At the other end of development, Georgia and Kazakhstan still have significant potential for improvement in digital access, infrastructure, quality, and security.

Slow Pace of Initiatives for Delivering High-Speed Internet

Internet speed remains a concern. The average speed in CAREC countries is under 40 megabits per second (Mbps), which drops to 24 Mbps if the PRC is excluded. Some factors leading to lower speed are weak national backbone infrastructure (i.e., legacy technology, such as copper access infrastructure), constrained international transit, and inadequate domestic internet exchange capacity. Lack of competition in wholesale markets, which creates bottlenecks upstream, is a concern in some countries.

Regional programs have been introduced to overcome these issues. For example, the Asia-Pacific Information Superhighway is an ongoing initiative to improve regional broadband connectivity through a dense web of open-access cross-border connectivity. The Information Superhighway will provide both intraregional and intercontinental access through a cohesive regional network of optic fiber. This will help drive international bandwidth prices down, increasing resilience by offering redundancy to submarine cables and decreasing latency across the region.

A paradigm shift in speed could come from 5G technology, especially in urban and industrial settings. This could help with high-speed low-latency use cases, such as the Internet of Things (IoT), e-commerce, health care, and education. This has been highlighted as a concern in CAREC's emerging fintech markets. Fast and reliable online access is crucial for achieving the CAREC Digital Strategy 2030 mission of creating a data-driven digital economy. Investing in it can provide leapfrogging opportunities for mobile internet speeds (CAREC Program 2021b).

Advancements in Payment Systems

Fast payment systems (FPSs) enable end-to-end payments among individuals, businesses, and governments. Payments are settled in real time or near real time and 24/7—or as close to 24/7 as possible. Such features give FPS-enabled payment settlements a near cash-type characteristic that can foster end-user confidence in digital-payment methods and encourage adoption. Beyond this, FPSs also support innovation in the wider digital-payments landscape. For example, FPS transactions can be made through a variety of interfaces, such as mobile applications from third-party providers, and initiated through new methods, such as QR codes.

Membership in an FPS is typically broader than in traditional payment systems, in which nonbank payment service providers participate directly or indirectly. In turn, this can encourage interoperability and drive innovation and integration among payment providers, improving the consumer experience and boosting the adoption of digital payment methods. In addition, the use of aliases such as phone numbers or e-mail addresses as proxies for bank account numbers has made it more convenient to access FPS services, further promoting uptake.

The introduction of FPSs in CAREC's emerging fintech markets is relatively recent. Economies that have successfully introduced FPSs as part of their national payments infrastructure include Azerbaijan (Instant Payment System), Kazakhstan (Instant Payment System), Mongolia (Automated Clearing House Plus, or ACH+), Pakistan (Raast), Tajikistan (Automated Transfer System, or ATS), and Uzbekistan (Instant Payment System). These FPSs are operated by the central banks. Georgia has announced plans to introduce an FPS or similar real-time system with 24/7 features to its national payments infrastructure to encourage interoperability and innovation in the retail payments space.

Membership in most FPSs in the region is only open directly to banks, except for Pakistan's Raast (Chapter 7) and Mongolia's ACH+. The Mongolian FPS allows nonbank financial institutions (NBFIs), including e-money providers and nonbank payment service providers, to connect directly to the system. It is an upgraded version of the central bank's automated clearing house payments system. The upgrade, undertaken with ADB support, improved the efficiency of the national payment system by increasing the number of payment-system participants; and it is connected to key public infrastructure for security, privacy, and protection (Anudari 2018).

Tajikistan is another economy that has upgraded its existing national payment system. In 2019, the National Bank of Tajikistan introduced its ATS, which includes an updated real-time gross settlement system, an automated clearing house (ACH), a central securities depository (CSD), and an instant funds transfer (IFT) system. The ATS covers aspects of payments and securities operations processing; and it offers liquidity management facilities, multicurrency support, and statistical analysis, among other services; and it enables the use of new, advanced methods for cashless money transfers, including transfers to accounts, cross-border payments, mobile payments, and QR-based money transfers. As of 2020, all banks, deposit-taking microfinance organizations, and the Ministry of Finance were connected to the updated system (CMA 2019; World Bank 2020a).

Growing Interest in National Digital Identities

Digital identities refer to a set of digital attributes and credentials claimed by an individual or entity that can be authenticated remotely over digital channels. Unlike physical identity cards that can be easily stolen, duplicated, or lost, and that display only a fixed amount of information at any given time, digital identities have the potential to be more secure and flexible in terms of the information incorporated within the identity. Digital identities also give owners more control over the information shared in a transaction and they make online transactions easier, improving the overall user experience. For many advanced and developing economies, government-verified digital identities, or national digital identities, are increasingly seen as a key public good for advancing national agendas. They can help accelerate the digital transformation of governments and industries, contribute to data portability and personal data rights, and unlock long-term economic value by enabling more inclusive access to finance, health care, and education. Digital identities are also key to fostering the growth of the digital economy and digital trade, as they can streamline and ease the transaction process between buyers and sellers across one or multiple channels; remove the potential for human error; and assist in efforts to combat criminal activities, such as fraud, theft, and money laundering.

Within CAREC's fintech markets, Azerbaijan, the PRC, Georgia, Kazakhstan, and Mongolia have each successfully launched versions of national digital identities, allowing users to access a variety of government services. For example, Mongolia launched its e-Mongolia digital identity app, which allows citizens access to over 181 government services. To encourage adoption, e-Mongolia app users were not charged for data used while accessing the app during a period of time agreed to by the government and local mobile broadband service providers (Choi 2022). Uses for the Azerbaijan version are described in Box 1.1, below. By contrast, economies like the Kyrgyz Republic, Pakistan, Tajikistan, Turkmenistan, and Uzbekistan are at various stages of developing and implementing national digital identities.

Some economies, like the Kyrgyz Republic and Mongolia, have formed strategic agreements with other countries to receive assistance for the development of their national digital identities and of their wider digital transformation strategies. In April 2022, the Kyrgyz Ministry of Digital Development signed a memorandum of understanding (MOU) with the Korea Minting, Security Printing and ID Card Operating Corporation (KOMSCO) for assistance with its digital cooperation efforts, including the digitizing of government-issued documents (e.g., identity cards), authentication technology, and certificates of tax payments (Yoon 2022). Mongolia has a similar arrangement with Estonia, which assists with its digital government transformation efforts (Choi 2022).

Box 1.1

Case Study—National Digital Identities in Azerbaijan

Azerbaijan's national mobile electronic identification (eID) system, Asan İmza, enables financial institutions, mobile network operators, and government agencies to digitally verify a user's identity; and enables e-signatures for users of digital services, such as online banking. Based on a public–private partnership model, its key stakeholders include the Asan Certification Services Centre (ASXM), the country's certification authority; a service provider (B.EST Solutions); mobile operators (Azercell, Azerfon, Bakcell); end users; and end-user service providers, such as government agencies and banks.[a]

Asan İmza's implementation has increased efficiency and reduced administrative costs. For instance, 90% of tax declarations, 100% of labor contracts, and 100% of customs declarations can now be completed online. In addition, 100% of business-to-business invoices are now issued online, and a firm can be set up in 5 minutes.[b] All major banks use Asan İmza for customer identification, which has helped streamline know-your-customer and anti-money-laundering efforts.

As a result, the government has achieved an estimated annual savings of 2% of gross domestic product (GDP). Every digital signature from a person in the workforce will help the country save €1 and 5 days per year. The mobile eID solution has also bridged the digital and financial access and literacy gaps in Azerbaijan. For instance, taxpayers can submit tax declarations to a dedicated helpline without needing a computer or the internet. Similarly, users can access a range of financial services and prove their identity over the phone to their providers.[a]

[a] J. Krimpe. 2019. *Digital Trade Hub of Azerbaijan: The PPP Initiative for Cross-Border e-Trade & e-Services*. Presentation prepared for the Subregional Workshop on Non-Tariff Measures in Azerbaijan and North and Central Asia, organized by the United Nations Economic and Social Commission for Asia and the Pacific (UNESCAP) and the Food and Safety Agency of the Republic of Azerbaijan. 9–11 December 2019, Baku, Azerbaijan. https://www.unescap.org/sites/default/files/Session.8.%20Digital%20Trade%20Hub.pdf.pdf.

[b] International Telecommunication Union (ITU). 2022. Asan İmza: Azerbaijan National Mobile eID and Legally Binding e-Signature. https://www.itu.int/net4/wsis/archive/stocktaking/Project/Details?projectId=1515503655.

Source: Author.

Growing Adoption of and Investment in Emerging Technologies

Across Central Asia, the investment trend toward emerging technologies is increasing—especially for software. Azerbaijan and Tajikistan have started their national AI journeys. Tajikistan held its first AI development forum in August 2021 to accelerate the country's development and industrialization, while Azerbaijan has integrated a national plan for AI into its "Industry 4.0" national framework. Kazakhstan has made a significant investment in IoT technology, and has indicated the need to regulate AI with its "Concept for a Legal Policy until 2030." Pakistan, on the other hand, has invested in new tech zones that have the potential to double its IT industry to $6 billion in 2 years (*Express Tribune* 2021).

Capability

This section examines the third pillar: Capability. Selected indicators in Table 1.4 examine progress across two dimensions: the regulatory and business environments. Across the regulatory environment, foundational enablers such as data protection and privacy, cybersecurity, and e-signature legislation, are examined. The ability of regulatory frameworks to keep pace with digital disruption and the new business models that emerge from digital transformation is examined. "Fit for purpose" and clear regulations help ease business uncertainty and facilitate the growth and use of innovative fintech products and services. CAREC countries are at similar levels, averaging 3.8 for the regulatory environment and 3.9 for the business environment. Fintech-specific regulations also play a key role in creating an enabling environment for banks and NBFIs to drive initiatives. On average, the region's emerging fintech markets have introduced two or three targeted regulations on specific fintech products or services, such as e-money, electronic payments (e-payments), and anti-money laundering.

Table 1.4: CAREC Progress in Regulatory and Business Environments

Country/Region	Laws Relating to ICTs, 2016 (1-7)[a]	Adaptability of Legal Frameworks, 2019 (1-7)[a]	Fintech-Focused Regulations, 2021 (0-6)[a]	Fintech Innovation Initiatives, 2021 (0-6)[a]	Digital Skills, 2021 (1-7)[a]
Azerbaijan	4.9	4.6	6.0	6.0	5.1
People's Republic of China	4.2	4.6	6.0	6.0	4.7
Georgia	3.8	4.1	4.0	4.0	3.6
Kazakhstan	4.6	4.0	4.0	6.0	4.7
Kyrgyz Republic	3.0	3.0	4.0	4.0	3.9
Mongolia	3.0	2.9	4.0	4.0	3.8
Pakistan	2.9	4.1	4.0	4.0	4.2
Tajikistan	3.6	3.6	4.0	2.0	4.4
Turkmenistan	...	...	4.0	2.0	...
Uzbekistan	...	...	4.0	4.0	...
CAREC average	**3.8**	**3.9**	**4.4**	**3.8**	**4.3**

... = data not available, CAREC = Central Asia Regional Economic Cooperation, fintech = financial technology, ICT = information and communication technology.

[a] Under the scoring systems, with the ranges of 0–6 or 1–7, the higher the score, the greater the coverage or progress with regard to each indicator. The indicators are described in the Appendix, under Pillar 3.

Source: Access Partnership.

Along with enabling regulations, the creation of a supportive business environment through initiatives and policy mechanisms, such as regulatory sandboxes and innovation hubs, has been emphasized (Table 1.4). Given the importance of digital and financial literacy in encouraging user adoption, the presence of initiatives to promote digital skills is also examined.

Supporting and enabling regulations and initiatives play a critical role in fintech growth. They facilitate innovative technologies and user adoption by unlocking opportunities for growth through tiered regulations, through such means as the Know Your Customer (KYC) framework, regulatory sandboxes, innovation offices, and others, while mitigating risks by implementing customer-protection mechanisms.

Importance of Establishing Foundational Frameworks

Some governments in emerging CAREC fintech markets have implemented foundational policies and regulations to facilitate access to and the adoption of digital financial services, encouraging innovation and competition, and safeguarding individuals and businesses. These include regulatory guidelines for outsourcing, consumer protection, and data management and governance. For instance, the National Bank of Kazakhstan published an open banking report (National Bank of Kazakhstan 2022), and Georgia has introduced an open banking framework to encourage fintech innovation in banking. The average regional score for passing laws relating to information and communication technology (ICT) is 3.8, highlighting the presence of some foundational regulations, especially on data protection and privacy. However, gaps around data-sharing frameworks, competition law, and consumer protection persist across almost all CAREC countries; and open banking is still a work in progress (CAREC Institute 2021).

Azerbaijan, Georgia, Kazakhstan, and the Kyrgyz Republic have developed foundational legislative frameworks for personal data protection and cybersecurity (Government of Azerbaijan n.d.; Spînu 2020). Others, such as Pakistan, have recently accelerated work on the development of data protection regulations (OneTrust DataGuidance 2021). As the fintech ecosystem grows, cybersecurity poses risks to individual countries, as well as cross-border threats. Cybersecurity regulation remains underdeveloped, so there is scope to strengthen regulations and guidance (World Bank 2020b).

Development of Consumer Protection Mechanisms

The proliferation of digital technologies exposes consumers to data security risks. Without consumer protection mechanisms and safeguards, additional vulnerabilities from the increased number of access points online and exposure to malicious actors may also increase fraud and scams. Clear frameworks and guidelines for consumer protection and dispute resolution are crucial for financial stability. In the PRC, all four finance sector regulatory authorities—the People's Bank of China (PBOC), China Banking Regulatory Commission, China Securities Regulatory Commission, and China Insurance Regulatory Commission—have established internal financial consumer protection departments. In 2014, the revised Law of the PRC on the Protection of Consumer Rights and Interests also came into force, explicitly mentioning the obligations of banking, securities, and insurance providers relating to the disclosure of charges, safeguards, and warnings regarding risks.

Facilitating Know-Your-Customer Measures to Drive Efficiency and Inclusivity

Regulatory authorities play a critical role in facilitating growth in emerging CAREC fintech markets, such as by enabling the entry of payment providers, products, and business models. In particular, financial regulators have streamlined KYC processes or allowed electronic Know Your Customer (eKYC) processes.

This helps simplify registration processes and facilitates the adoption of products and services such as digital banking and payments. In Azerbaijan and Uzbekistan, for instance, regulators have taken steps to facilitate eKYC and customer due diligence. In addition, Azerbaijan issued guidelines in 2019 to permit remote account opening and digital onboarding, while the Kyrgyz Republic has encouraged the use of e-signatures (World Bank 2020c). In Tajikistan, financial services providers have been able to offer digital onboarding to clients for low-risk profiled financial products and services since 2020 (International Finance Corporation 2021).

Regulatory Sandboxes

Regulatory sandboxes play a crucial role in encouraging innovation, collaboration, and partnerships between traditional banking institutions and new market entrants to enhance innovation in products and services. While regulatory sandboxes increase oversight and supervision, they also allow new fintech products and services to be tested on a smaller scale with defined parameters to mitigate risks, encouraging innovation by allowing disruptive technologies the space and flexibility to demonstrate proof of concept. While approaches vary, fintech sandboxes have been implemented in Georgia, Kazakhstan, Pakistan, and Tajikistan. In Kazakhstan, for instance, regulatory sandboxes have been established in the Astana International Financial Centre (AIFC), which is described in Chapter 8 (Box 8.2).

Innovation Offices

Innovation offices facilitate engagement between regulators and fintech industry participants, and can help gather feedback on policies and regulatory reforms; encourage adoption of industry-wide standards, such as open application programming interfaces (APIs); and provide platforms for continuous engagement for the sector's development. In addition, the CAREC program is promoting the use of hackathons (CAREC Program n.d.-a). Several regulators in the region have set up innovation offices within the banks or as separate entities. Others have set up fintech hubs and accelerators.

Fintech hubs and accelerators also serve other important functions, such as enhancing digital literacy, promoting start-up ecosystems, and enhancing support for and investment in priority sectors. Although CAREC countries have implemented IT capacity-building initiatives, digital literacy levels remain low, hindering the region's ability to leverage new IT capacity to develop fintech solutions and increase adoption. There is thus a need to direct resources and policy attention toward designing complementary initiatives offered by innovation offices and fintech hubs to achieve better outcomes.

Regional Cooperation

This section examines the fourth pillar: Regional Cooperation. Table 1.5 shows selected indicators of cooperation: international commitments in the form of trade agreements and MOUs, cross-border initiatives, and participation in multilateral platforms. Among the three indicators, CAREC scores lowest in international commitments, with only the PRC as part of a key trading agreement. Others in the region have bilateral fintech cooperation agreements in place, but primarily with countries outside the region. For the most part, CAREC's emerging fintech markets have only one or two cross-border initiatives to enhance payment interoperability or harmonize standards, and these are with countries outside the region. Financial regulatory authorities have increased participation in multilateral initiatives to support financial innovation, such as in the Global Financial Innovation Network (GFIN); and digital financial inclusion, such as in the Alliance for Financial Inclusion. Notably, they also participate in region-specific initiatives, including the CAREC Economic and Financial Stability Cluster, to develop and implement agreed common practices (CAREC Program n.d.-b), among other goals. The Cluster organizes events and discussions to promote financial inclusion and enable fintech innovation.

Table 1.5: CAREC Progress in Regional Cooperation
(0–6)[a]

Country/Region	International Commitments, 2022	Cross-Border Initiatives, 2022[b]	Participation in Regional/ International Platforms, 2022
Azerbaijan	4	2	0
People's Republic of China	6	6	6
Georgia	0	4	4
Kazakhstan	4	4	4
Kyrgyz Republic	4	4	4
Mongolia	0	4	4
Pakistan	0	4	4
Tajikistan	4	4	4
Turkmenistan	2	0	0
Uzbekistan	0	0	4
CAREC average	**2.4**	**3.2**	**3.4**

CAREC = Central Asia Regional Economic Cooperation.

[a] The 0–6 scale is the scoring system for the various stages of progress toward the achievement of the indicators, from none (0) to the maximum (6) as defined for each indicator. A description of the scoring system is provided in the Appendix, under Pillar 4.

[b] These initiatives concern such issues as interoperability, e-invoicing, and standards.

Source: Access Partnership.

Regional cooperation can foster the growth of fintech by opening avenues for competition and innovation. Integrating different national (policy and regulatory) approaches, setting up mechanisms for information sharing and cooperation, and encouraging greater cross-border partnerships between industry and academia will accelerate fintech growth and reduce some of the risks, such as cyber fraud, data security, and privacy breaches. The sections below detail some of the key developments in regional cooperation activities.

Growing Opportunities for Cooperation and Information Sharing

Free trade agreements—such as the United States–Mexico–Canada Agreement (USMCA), US–Japan Digital Trade Agreement, Singapore–Chile–NZ Digital Economy Partnership Agreement (DEPA), and Singapore–Australia Digital Economy Agreement (SADEA)—establish rules for cross-border data flows, including flows of financial information. Some, such as the SADEA, have also included separate MOUs on fintech cooperation as part of the overarching agreements. These agreements are binding commitments; as such, they play a key role in furthering cooperation in financial services, including fintech. There are few such agreements in the CAREC region, with only the PRC as part of the Regional Comprehensive Economic Partnership (RCEP). In 2022, however, the DEPA Joint Committee began the accession process for the PRC to join the DEPA (Government of Singapore, Ministry of Trade and Industry 2022).

Economies can also increase cooperation through bilateral and multilateral cooperation agreements, including MOUs, between governments or financial regulators. There is a growing trend of fintech MOUs across the globe; for instance, the PBOC and the Hong Kong Monetary Authority (HKMA) signed an MOU in 2021 on supervision and cooperation for fintech innovation (Moody's Analytics 2021).

While evidence of similar MOUs between CAREC's emerging fintech markets is limited, economies in the region are beginning to follow this trend. That was the case for Azerbaijan, which signed an MOU with Türkiye in April 2022 to enhance cooperation on the expansion of its fintech ecosystem (AZERTAC 2022). Such MOUs represent a first step in fostering broader cooperation among financial regulators by facilitating business market entry and information sharing. It is expected that more CAREC countries will sign fintech MOUs and cooperation agreements to promote innovation in the sector.

Greater Participation in International Platforms

While regulatory cooperation among CAREC's emerging fintech markets is low, their participation in regional and international platforms to enhance fintech innovation and address priorities (e.g., financial inclusion) is indicative of their support for building an enabling environment for fintech development. For instance, central banks and financial regulatory bodies across Georgia, Kazakhstan, the Kyrgyz Republic, Mongolia, Pakistan, Tajikistan, and Uzbekistan are members of the Alliance for Financial Inclusion. Georgia and Kazakhstan are also members of GFIN. Platforms such as these enable new channels for cooperation between financial service regulators and industry, and promote the sharing of new approaches and best practices through capacity-building initiatives, such as policy forums, member trainings, and intercountry dialogues. For instance, the Eastern Europe & Central Asia Policy Initiative, which includes Kazakhstan, Mongolia, Tajikistan, and Uzbekistan, has achieved several milestones, including a regional framework on eKYC and digital ID, as well as a special report with recommendations for promoting the interoperability of cross-border remittance systems between its members (Alliance for Financial Inclusion n.d.-a).

Cross-Border Collaboration Is Nascent

Furthering fintech growth across the region will require greater cooperation. While cooperation agreements have increased in number, there has been only limited development of bilateral and multilateral collaboration mechanisms, such as interoperable cross-border payment systems, harmonization of standards, enablement of data-sharing certification of third-party services, and alignment on money-laundering rules. One potential avenue for encouraging greater cross-border collaboration is the development of financial centers across the region. The success of the AIFC points to the significant potential for collaborative platforms elsewhere. The AIFC, with the primary aim of positioning Kazakhstan as a global center for finance, also functions as a dynamic platform for regional cooperation on fintech innovation and growth (Chapter 8).

Private Sector Cross-Border Initiatives Gain Ground

There are several initiatives aimed at facilitating cross-border payments that are being led by the private sector. For instance, in Tajikistan, Alif Bank has partnered with Visa to develop new cashless payment solutions for the domestic market, and is now expanding to the UK based on this partnership. Similarly, in Pakistan, a partnership between Telenor Microfinance Bank and Valyou of Malaysia has led to the introduction of the country's first blockchain-based cross-border remittance service, with the online payment platform developed by Alipay (Pakistan Remittance Initiative 2019).

BENCHMARKING THE FINTECH JOURNEY

To compare fintech development in Central Asia with that of countries in other regions, data from the ASEAN economies, and from India, Japan, and the Republic of Korea, were compiled for the indicators selected under the four pillars (Table 1.6). This benchmarking exercise not only enabled a comprehensive review and a deeper understanding of the variation in performance across different regions, it also enabled the identification of good international practices and lessons learned from countries farther down the road than the emerging fintech markets of CAREC.

Table 1.6: Benchmarking CAREC Progress in Finance
(%)

Country/ Region	Has a Financial Institution Account, 2021 (15+ yrs of age)	Has Mobile Money Account, 2021 (15+ yrs of age)	Made or Received a Digital Payment, 2021 (15+ yrs of age)	Received Wages Paid into a Financial Institution Account, 2021 (15+ yrs of age)	Owns a Debit or Credit Card, 2021 (15+ yrs of age)	Made a Utility Payment Using an Account, 2021 (15+ yrs of age)	Firms Using Banks for Investment Capital	Firms Using Banks for Working Capital	MSMEs Reporting a Financial Gap	Firms Reporting Lack of Finance as a Major Constraint
CAREC	50.7	14.8	47.5	18.1	39.1	17.0	19.8	19.3	77.5	40.3
ASEAN	56.9	21.6	50.7	19.7	44.7	16.4	18.4	25.1	36.0	12.1
India	77.0	10.0	35.0	7.0	28	7.0	30.3	36.4	34.9	15.1
Japan	98.0	...	96.0	58.0	90	59.0	...	...	...	...
Korea, Rep. of	99.0	...	98.0	60.0	92	69.0	...	...	...	...

ASEAN = Association of Southeast Asian Nations; CAREC = Central Asia Regional Economic Cooperation; MSMEs = micro, small, and medium-sized enterprises; yrs = years.

Sources: World Bank. Global Financial Development Database. Data on MSMEs reporting financial gap and firms reporting finance as a major constraint from the IFC. 2017. *MSME Finance Gap*; and World Bank. Global Financial Development Database 2021: Financial Inclusion, Digital Payments, and Resilience in the Age of COVID-19 (accessed 12 November 2022).

Finance Benchmarking Results

Financial Account Ownership

A comparison of the financial status of various countries showed that the average proportion of the population 15+ years of age with an account at a financial institution is 50.7% in the CAREC region and 56.9% in the ASEAN member states. In Central Asia, Mongolia is the standout—as is the PRC, though to a lesser extent; next is Kazakhstan, some way behind, followed by Georgia. Except for Pakistan, which has low account ownership, the emerging fintech markets in CAREC cluster between 30% and 50% (Table 1.2).

Digital Payments

On average, ASEAN is ahead of CAREC in the adoption and use of mobile money, with an average of 21.6%, compared with 14.8%. However, the gap closes slightly in the use of digital payments, at 50.7% in ASEAN and 47.5% in CAREC. The average gap is even smaller in those receiving salary payments directly into a financial account, with averages of 19.7% in ASEAN and 18.1% across CAREC. In six CAREC countries, this occurs in over 20% of cases, whereas it only occurs in over 13% of cases in three ASEAN countries, suggesting that the CAREC latecomers to digital payment systems are taking more active steps to promote such transfers. ASEAN countries are farther ahead in the ownership of credit and debit cards: on average, 69% compared with 39.1%. This may foretell a future focus on mobile apps and payment systems that do not use plastic cards.

Capital and Financing Constraints

Among firms in CAREC, including fully or partially privately owned establishments with five or more employees, 19.8% on average use banks for capital investment, compared with 18.4% in ASEAN. Those that use banks for working capital are only slightly lower, at 19.3%, while for ASEAN firms the figure is 25.1%.

The spreads are fairly similar, suggesting that access to bank capital reflects the relative strengths of the finance sectors in these countries. This is because four CAREC countries (Azerbaijan, Georgia, Mongolia, and Uzbekistan) and three ASEAN countries (Indonesia, Malaysia, and Viet Nam) use bank investment capital more than the average, while four in CAREC (the PRC, Georgia, Mongolia, and Uzbekistan) and four in ASEAN (Indonesia, Malaysia, Thailand, and Viet Nam) use banks for working capital at a higher than average rate.

On average, 10.8% of the capital investment of firms in CAREC comes from banks (mostly in Azerbaijan, 19%; Georgia, 20%; and Mongolia, 26%), and 7% of working capital (mostly in Georgia, 15%; and Mongolia, 14%). The corresponding figure for ASEAN countries is 9.2%, with the use of banks for working capital occurring at more even rates across ASEAN. The difference between the median and the average is 0.6%, compared with 1.0% for CAREC, indicating less variation among ASEAN economies. This suggests that, in general, ASEAN firms make more use of access to banks for their working capital. This may reflect a reliance of MSMEs in CAREC countries on informal sources of funding or a reluctance of banks to lend to MSMEs without sufficient collateral. Often, the biggest problem for small enterprises is not revenues, however small they may be, but the large number of them, which can lead to a liquidity shortage.

Of the MSMEs in CAREC countries, 77.5% reported facing a financial gap, which suggests difficulties in obtaining loans, while 40.3% reported the lack of financing as a major constraint on their business. Among the ASEAN MSMEs, 36.0% reported financial gaps and 12.1% reported a lack of financing. These data suggest that access to bank finance is a bigger problem in much of CAREC than in ASEAN. Among the ASEAN countries, the widest reported financial gaps were in Indonesia (at 52%) and Thailand (at 55%). This is well below CAREC's 77.5% average; furthermore, relatively few ASEAN firms reported a lack of finance as a serious constraint, suggesting that it is less of a barrier for them.

Technology Benchmarking Results

Internet Access and Adoption

According to statistics from the International Telecommunication Union (ITU), 61% of the CAREC population and 66% of the ASEAN population had access to the internet in 2020 (Table 1.7), which is vital for gaining access to financial services, especially for unbanked consumers. The disparity in internet penetration was higher in ASEAN, ranging from 34% in the Lao People's Democratic Republic (Lao PDR) to 95% in Brunei Darussalam.

In contrast to internet penetration, the average number of mobile broadband subscriptions per 100 inhabitants was much higher in ASEAN (100) than across CAREC (69). Access to the internet and mobile broadband is quite high in both regions, but the quality of access, as measured by fixed broadband download speed, is much lower in CAREC (39 Mbps) than in ASEAN (73 Mbps).

The ASEAN Digital Masterplan 2025 identified improving the quality and coverage of fixed and mobile broadband infrastructure as one of its priority outcomes (ASEAN 2021b). To boost the insufficient cross-border investment in telecom infrastructure, it is important to develop consistent regulations across ASEAN. As the demand for internet bandwidth continues to grow, ASEAN will continue to review the connectivity gaps in a bid to upgrade international fiber links.

Table 1.7: Benchmarking CAREC Progress in Technology

Country/ Region	Internet Users, 2020[a] (%)	Mobile Broadband Subscriptions, 2020[b] (per 100 inhabitants)	Fixed Broadband Speed[c] (download Mbps)	Fast Payment Systems (0–3)[d]	National Digital Identities (0–3)[d]	Adoption of and Investment in Emerging Technologies[e]
CAREC	61.3	69.4	38.9	1.5	1.4	30.1
ASEAN	66.3	100.3	73.0	2.4	1.5	41.5
India	43.0	52.5	47.9	3.0	3.0	35.0
Japan	90.2	202.3	137.2	2.0	2.0	72.2
Korea, Rep. of	96.5	116.9	109.7	3.0	3.0	63.4

ASEAN = Association of Southeast Asian Nations, CAREC = Central Asia Regional Economic Cooperation Program, Mbps = megabits per second.

Note: The latest data available were used for each indicator.

[a] International Telecommunication Union (ITU) ICT [Information and Communication Technology] Indicators Database. Internet Users (accessed 22 November 2022).

[b] ITU ICT Indicators Database, Mobile broadband subscription (accessed 22 October 2022).

[c] Speedtest Global Index. Fixed broadband speed (accessed 11 December 2022).

[d] Access Partnership analysis and research. The 0–3 range is the scoring system for these indicators in the ITU ICT Indicators Database, representing the levels of progress made in the development of fast-payment and national-digital-identity systems (with "3" representing the most progress). See the Appendix, Pillar 2 for a description of the meaning of each score for each indicator.

[e] Network Readiness Index 2024, Emerging Technologies (accessed 12 December 2022).

Source: Author.

Emerging Technology Adoption and Investment

This indicator measures the extent to which countries have adopted emerging technologies (e.g., AI, big data analytics, cloud computing, robot density), the extent to which firms are investing in these technologies, and the firms' spending on software as a percentage of GDP. While the indicator does not specifically measure the use of emerging technologies in the financial sector, it gives a general assessment of how widespread the adoption of emerging technologies is across an economy, as well as the firms' willingness to invest in them.

Overall, the adoption rates of new technologies are lower in the emerging fintech markets of CAREC than they are in ASEAN markets. CAREC investment in software and emerging technologies also trails investment in ASEAN and other Asian countries, such as India. A CAREC Institute report from 2021 references the *Cisco Global Digital Readiness Index 2021* scores for readiness regarding technology infrastructure, technology adoption, and government and business investment, noting that "none of the CAREC countries is categorized as 'amplify,' which means countries have made significant progress in achieving digital maturity" (Umar 2021). To address this problem, under the auspices of the CAREC Program, the PRC in 2023 launched the Innovation Decoded initiative "to provide South–South learning and networking opportunities for the start-up ecosystem players in the CAREC region" (CAREC Program 2023).

Singapore leads the pack among the ASEAN countries, with notable investments in advanced technologies and the widespread adoption of technologies such as machine learning (ML) and the Internet of Things (IoT), as well as a high robot density of 100 per 10,000 employees in the manufacturing industry.

On fintech adoption by consumers, a survey conducted in 2021 by United Overseas Bank (UOB), PricewaterhouseCoopers Risk Services (PwC Singapore), and the Singapore FinTech Association showed that 60% of consumers in the six largest ASEAN economies had used electronic wallets (e-wallets), with 20% using them to make overseas transfers. Digital tools such as robo-advisors and online brokerage platforms have been used by 60% of retail investors.

National Digital Identities

As in CAREC, ASEAN economies recognize the importance of building a trusted digital ID system that facilitates the authentication of a person's identity on demand, given the benefits it brings in accelerating financial inclusion, enabling the provision of e-government services and a comprehensive social safety net. Nevertheless, the stages of implementation vary quite widely. The digital ID systems in Singapore and Thailand not only enable users to access government services, but also to private sector services, such as setting up a bank account.

Singapore Personal Access (Singpass), which has evolved from a national authentication system into a digital ID, allows access to over 2,000 government and private sector digital services. The Monetary Authority of Singapore (MAS) has been working with the Smart Nation and Digital Government Office (SNDGO) and the Government Technology Agency (GovTech) to enhance the functions of Singpass and its mobile app through initiatives such as the Singapore Financial Data Exchange (SGFinDex) (MAS 2024b). Financial institutions can streamline customer onboarding, and customers can access their financial information from different government agencies and financial institutions, and digitally sign documents by using Sign with Singpass (Government of Singapore 2025). In addition to expanding the use of a government digital payment service, GovWallet (Government of Singapore 2022), to disburse funds securely and conveniently, Singapore is working with other countries to enhance the cross-border interoperability of digital IDs to facilitate digital transactions, trade, travel, and employment (Government of Australia n.d.; Government of the UK 2022).

In Thailand, the National Digital ID platform (NDID) has been deployed for government services such as the electronic filing of taxes, and for private sector services such as opening a bank account and applying for credit online (National Digital ID Co. n.d.). With 30 million registered users, the system processed more than 9 million identity verification requests in 2021. Other Asian countries, including India and the Republic of Korea, have fully implemented their digital ID systems. The Republic of Korea has adopted a decentralized approach to identity and personal-data management, as opposed to a centralized national ID system. The use of blockchain technology reduces the security risks arising from forgery and identity theft, as the personal data are encrypted and stored in the user's mobile device (Lim 2021).

Aadhaar, India's national digital ID system, which currently covers 99.7% of India's adult population (Dutta 2021), has been leveraged to boost financial access and mobile communications penetration through the Jan Dhan program since 2014. With the use of digital IDs, financial institutions can fulfill the eKYC requirements, while reducing the costs of onboarding new customers. It is estimated that Aadhaar has directly led to the opening of over 150 million new bank accounts, thereby contributing to financial inclusion. The digital ID system is also linked with the beneficiary databases for public service and verification purposes, while the Aadhaar Payments Bridge System is used to deposit money (Gelb and Mukherjee 2019).

Other ASEAN countries, including Cambodia, Indonesia, the Lao PDR, Malaysia, Myanmar, the Philippines, and Viet Nam, are either in the planning or early implementation stage of developing their digital ID systems, through the issuance of relevant laws and regulations to provide a legal basis for managing and using e-identification and authentication services. The Government of the Philippines has made significant progress in its push to establish a nationwide identification system. The Philippine Identification System (PhilSys) had received more than 90 million registrations as of December 2024 (Government of the Philippines, Philippine Statistics Authority 2025). According to the Philippine Statistics Authority (PSA), PhilSys has improved financial inclusion, as over 8 million unbanked Filipinos signed up for an account at Land Bank.

In April 2022, the PSA unveiled an authentication program, PhilSys Check, for verifying the authenticity of ePhilIDs through QR codes to enable transactions between individuals and between the public sector and private firms. PhilSys Check was piloted in collaboration with 13 financial institutions (PSA 2022).

Fast Payment Systems

Within ASEAN, most countries have already established real-time fast-payment systems to drive the development of digital payments; and those systems in Cambodia, Indonesia, Malaysia, the Philippines, Singapore, and Viet Nam are accessible by nonbank financial institutions (NBFIs) and payment service operators (Table 1.8). In Singapore, NBFIs licensed as payment institutions under the Payment Services Act, 2019 have been able to connect directly to Fast and Secure Transfers (FAST) and its overlaying service, PayNow, since February 2021 (Association of Banks in Singapore 2022; Association of Banks in Singapore, n.d-b.; MAS 2020). FAST and PayNow both feature 24/7 availability and instant payment settlement. Moreover, retail customers can initiate or receive payments with a mobile number, Singapore National Registration Identity Card, Foreign Identification Number, a Virtual Payment Address (VPA), or a passport number. The transfer limit is capped at S$200,000 ($145,216) per transaction. PayNow Corporate was launched in 2018 to extend the service to entities such as corporations, government agencies, and associations.

Table 1.8: Fast Payment Systems in ASEAN and Other Asian Economies

Country	Fast Payment System	Year of Launch	Features
Brunei Darussalam	In the planning stage		
Cambodia	Retail Pay[a]	2021	• Real-time retail fund transfers through QR codes or mobile payments • Transfers possible in riels or US dollars • Enables digital payments of rent, utility bills, maintenance fees
Indonesia	Bank Indonesia Fast Payment[b]	2021	• Individual credit transfer services • Operational 24/7 • Real-time service at the bank and customer levels • Open to both bank and nonbank players
Lao PDR	Not yet developed		

continued on next page

Table 1.8 *continued*

Country	Fast Payment System	Year of Launch	Features
Malaysia	Real-time RPP[c]	2018	• 24/7 service • Instant credits or P2P payments • Supports Request-to-Pay service for mobile commerce and e-commerce • Direct access to RPP for nonbank payment service providers
Myanmar	CBM-NET2[d]	2020	• 24/7 payroll transfers • Domestic kyat remittance allowed • ATM withdrawals to pay taxes and utility bills
Philippines	InstaPay[e]	2018	• Enabling real-time, low-value electronic fund transfer and retail transactions • Consumers able to pay for goods and services at partner stores and other businesses nationwide displaying the QR PH code • Accessible 24/7 through mobile apps and internet banking facilities provided by participating bank and nonbank e-money issuers[f]
Singapore	FAST[g]	2014	• Real-time interbank payments • Instant P2P fund transfers from bank or e-wallet accounts • Merchant payments and bill payments supported by FAST • Eligible NBFIs able to access FAST as direct participants
Thailand	PromptPay[h]	2016	• Real-time electronic fund transfer system • Operates on 24/7 basis • Supports bulk payments, bill payments, merchant payments, Request to Pay, and eDonation • Nonbank payment service providers allowed indirect access to the system
Viet Nam	NAPAS 247 Quick Transfer[i]	2021	• Real-time fund transfers available anytime, anywhere • Customers allowed to use bank cards, bank accounts, e-wallets, and QR codes to send and receive funds through online banking and e-wallet applications • Banks and payment intermediaries able to access system to provide payment services
India	UPI[j]	2016	• 24/7 real-time fund transfer system, available 365 days a year, linking multiple bank accounts into a single mobile application • Enables round-the-clock instant payments using a Virtual Payment Address created by the customer • Banks, NBFIs, and third-party processors allowed to participate
Japan	Zengin Moretime System[k]	2018	• Allows instant 24/7 fund transfer across banks • Transfers of salaries, bonuses, and funds over ¥100 million excluded from the system • Participation in the Zengin System, currently limited to banks, soon to allowed for fund transfer service providers

continued on next page

Table 1.8 *continued*

Country	Fast Payment System	Year of Launch	Features
Republic of Korea	EBS K-cash Network[l]	2001 2000	• Accessible on a 24/7 basis • Supports individuals and firms making instant fund transfers • K-cash Network designed for the settlement of electronic money transactions • Both banks and NBFIs given direct access to the retail payment systems

CBM-NET2 = Central Bank of Myanmar Financial Network System 2, e-commerce = electronic commerce, e-wallet = electronic wallet, EBS = Electronic Banking System, FAST = Fast and Secure Transfers, Lao PDR = Lao People's Democratic Republic, NAPAS = National Payment Corporation of Viet Nam, NBFI = nonbank financial institution, P2P = peer-to-peer, QR = Quick Response, RPP = Retail Payments Platform, UPI = Unified Payments Interface.

Note: A blank cell indicates that the column head does not apply.

[a] C. Sok. 2021. NBC Launches New Payment and Transfer System. *Khmer Times*. 27 January. https://www.khmertimeskh.com/50807469/nbc-launches-new-payment-and-transfer-system/.

[b] Bank Indonesia. 2021. Bi Launches Bank Indonesia Fast Payment. News release. 21 December. https://www.bi.go.id/en/publikasi/ruang-media/news-release/Pages/sp_2333421.aspx.

[c] PayNet. n.d. Real-time Retail Payments Platform. https://paynet.my/fi-rpp.html.

[d] Japan International Cooperation Agency (JICA). 2020. Central Bank of Myanmar (CBM) Launches New Payment and Settlement System (CBM-NET2). 16 November. https://www.jica.go.jp/myanmar/english/office/topics/press201116.html.

[e] Bangko Sentral ng Pilipinas. n.d. InstaPay FAQ Sheet. https://www.bsp.gov.ph/PaymentAndSettlement/FAQ_Instapay.pdf.

[f] InstaPay. 2022. More Banks and E-Money Issuers Now InstaPay Partners. https://www.instapayph.com/more-banks-and-e-money-issuers-now-instapay-partners/.

[g] World Bank. n.d. *World Bank Fast Payments Toolkit: Case Study; Singapore*. https://fastpayments.worldbank.org/sites/default/files/2021-10/World_Bank_FPS_Singapore_FAST_Case_Study.pdf.

[h] World Bank. n.d. *World Bank Fast Payments Toolkit: Case Study; Thailand*. https://fastpayments.worldbank.org/sites/default/files/2021-09/World_Bank_FPS_Thailand_PromptPay_Case_Study.pdf.

[i] *Viet Nam News*. 2023. Cashless Payment Promoted in Remote Areas. 1 August. https://vietnamnews.vn/economy/1551915/cashless-payment-promoted-in-remote-areas.html.

[j] World Bank. n.d. *World Bank Fast Payments Toolkit: Case Study; India*. https://fastpayments.worldbank.org/sites/default/files/2021-10/World_Bank_FPS_India_IMPS_and_UPI_Case_Study.pdf.

[k] Zengin System. 2019. *Zengin System: The Zengin Data Telecommunication System*. https://www.zengin-net.jp/en/zengin_net/pdf/pamphlet_e.pdf.

[l] Bank of Korea. 2017. *Payment and Settlement Systems Report 2016*. https://www.bok.or.kr/eng/bbs/E0000866/view.do?nttId=229218&menuNo=400047&pageIndex=1.

Source: Author.

In Malaysia, NBFIs—including approved issuers of e-money, issuers of designated payment instruments, and registered merchant acquirers—are allowed to access PayNet, which operates real-time retail payment and clearing systems, after fulfilling the requirements stipulated in the prescreening application and the qualification processes (Association of Banks in Singapore n.d.-a). Like PayNow in Singapore, DuitNow, which is offered through PayNet, enables instant and secure fund transfers using identifiers such as mobile phone numbers, national ID numbers, and passport numbers.

To facilitate seamless payments and remittances between Singapore and Malaysia, a phased linkage between PayNow and DuitNow was launched in November 2023. A similar partnership was forged between the MAS and the Reserve Bank of India through the latter's real-time payment system, Unified Payments Interface (MAS 2021b). All these regional initiatives enable low-cost cross-border fund transfers on a reciprocal basis without the need to get onboarded onto the other payment systems, paving the way for connecting payment systems across ASEAN at scale in the future.

Likewise, the Philippines' InstaPay, governed and managed by the Philippine Payment Management Inc., allows a real-time low-value electronic fund transfers between customers of participating banks, supervised by the Bangko Sentral ng Pilipinas (BSP) and nonbank e-money issuers in the country (BSP 2025).

Indonesia's first real-time digital payment system, BI-FAST, implemented by Bank Indonesia and ACI Worldwide, is open to both bank and nonbank players. Participating institutions can provide real-time credit transfers with instantaneous settlement at the bank and customer level in the initial phase. To join BI-FAST, institutions need to meet financial-performance and technical-capability criteria, on top of being able to contribute to the development of finance and of the digital economy (*Jakarta Post* 2021).

Cambodia has also made good progress toward the establishment of interoperable payment systems to promote e-payments. The National Bank of Cambodia (NBC) unveiled the national Retail Pay system in early 2021 to promote efficient, secure, and timely trade settlements, with the financial and technological support of the Korea International Cooperation Agency (KOICA). The blockchain-based Bakong System, which connects financial institutions and payment service providers under a single payment platform and allows cash transfers between e-wallets, requires the use of a smartphone (UNCDF 2021).

Thailand's real-time payment system, PromptPay, was established in 2017 to enable more than 56 million registered users to receive and transfer funds instantly using ID or mobile numbers, and to receive personal income tax returns or welfare payments from the government. In terms of collaborative cross-border payment systems, Thailand and Singapore have linked their retail payment systems to enable daily fund transfers of up to the equivalent of about $700 across the two countries. Despite this, access to PromptPay is only open to established banks in Thailand or through partnering with them, as financial institutions need to meet stringent regulatory and security requirements to join the service (United Overseas Bank 2021).

Capability Benchmarking Results

Table 1.9: Benchmarking CAREC Progress in Capability

Country/ Region	Laws Relating to ICTs, 2016[a] (1–7)[b]	Legal Framework's Adaptability to Digital Business Models, 2019[c] (1–7)[b]	Fintech-Focused Regulations, 2021[d] (0–6)[b]	Fintech Innovation Initiatives, 2021[e] (0–6)[b]	Digital Skills Among the Population, 2021[f] (1–7)[b]
CAREC	3.8	3.9	4.4	3.8	4.3
ASEAN	3.9	4.1	3.4	3.4	4.6
India	4.2	4.5	4.0	4.0	4.4
Japan	4.8	4.2	6.0	6.0	4.4
Republic of Korea	5.1	4.3	6.0	6.0	5.0

ASEAN = Association of Southeast Asian Nations, CAREC = Central Asia Regional Economic Cooperation, e-money = electronic money, fintech = financial technology, ICT = information and communication technology, P2P = peer-to-peer.

[a] Examples include laws on electronic commerce (e-commerce), digital signatures, and consumer protection.

[b] Under the scoring systems, with the ranges of 0–6 or 1–7, the higher the score, the greater the coverage or progress with regard to each indicator. The indicators are described in the Appendix, under Pillar 3.

[c] These models concern such areas as commerce, the sharing economy, and fintech.

[d] The regulations cover such areas as payments, e-money, and P2P.

[e] Such initiatives might include regulatory sandboxes, innovation hubs, and accelerators.

[f] The digital skills could include, among others, computer skills, basic coding, and digital reading.

Source: Access Partnership.

An Enabling Legal Framework

To benchmark capacity for promoting the development of fintech activity with other countries, we examine whether foundational laws related to the use of ICTs have been put in place. Legislation will address consumer protection, data privacy, e-commerce, and digital signatures that facilitate financial transactions and protect the integrity of signed contracts and documents. CAREC as a region (3.8) fares similarly to ASEAN (3.9), but lags developed countries like Japan (4.8) and the Republic of Korea (5.1) (Table 1.9). Great diversity within both regions is also observed, with Azerbaijan and Kazakhstan as the clear leaders in CAREC, and Singapore and Malaysia as the top ASEAN scorers.

Data Protection and Privacy Regulations

To strengthen personal data protection, an ASEAN Framework on Personal Data Protection, intended to guide regional and national policies, was adopted in 2016 (ASEAN 2016). In accordance with the principles of the Framework on Personal Data Protection, the ASEAN Data Management Framework and Model Contractual Clauses for Cross Border Data Flows were then developed by the Working Group on Digital Data Governance, led by Singapore (ASEAN 2021b, 2021c). While the Data Management Framework provides a step-by-step guide for businesses seeking to establish a data-management system with data governance structures and safeguards, the Model Contractual Clauses lay out templates that reduce negotiation and compliance costs and time, especially for small and medium-sized enterprises (SMEs).

Among the ASEAN countries, a personal data protection law has been enacted in Indonesia, Malaysia, the Philippines, Singapore, and Thailand, while Brunei Darussalam and Viet Nam are revising draft legislation after public consultations.

Financial Consumer Protection

Every ASEAN country has consumer protection laws to safeguard the well-being and interests of consumers (ASEAN 2021d). It is common for legislation that governs banking and financial institutions to include provisions on issues related to banking services and the provision of consumer credits and loans.

In Singapore, consumers can file complaints against financial institutions that have subscribed to the independent Financial Industries Disputes Resolution Centre, and seek mediation and adjudication for disputes regarding financial products and services. The Bank of Thailand's Financial Consumer Protection Centre handles inquiries and complaints about financial products and services, and coordinates with providers to resolve consumer issues.

Regional collaborative efforts to promote consumer protection in ASEAN began with the establishment of the intergovernmental ASEAN Committee on Consumer Protection (ACCP) in 2007. An ASEAN Capacity Building Roadmap for Consumer Protection 2025 was also formulated to assess and enhance the capacity of consumer authorities (ASEAN 2020). In addition, a framework of cross-border cooperation was established to strengthen collaboration among consumer protection authorities in the region.

Adaptability of Legal Frameworks to the Digital Economy

ASEAN performs slightly better than CAREC's emerging fintech markets with regard to legal framework adaptability. While Azerbaijan, Georgia, and Kazakhstan score higher than the regional average, the Kyrgyz Republic, Mongolia, and Tajikistan are at the other end of the spectrum. Across ASEAN, adaptability varies markedly, with Indonesia, Malaysia, and Singapore topping the list. The scores of the remaining ASEAN countries are well below the regional average, and there is room for improvement regarding the flexibility of regulatory frameworks to accommodate the rapid evolution of the digital economy.

Fintech-Focused Policies and Regulations

Malaysia and Singapore lead, with comprehensive regulations covering all major enabling technologies and addressing both the positive and negative impacts that these technological advancements can bring about. For example, both countries have laid out policies for legal certainty regarding blockchain technology, to promote its deployment in areas such as smart contracts. Similarly, Malaysia and Singapore have formulated policies to encourage financial institutions to adopt cloud computing. On AI governance frameworks, the Monetary Authority of Singapore (MAS) released the *Principles to Promote Fairness, Ethics, Accountability and Transparency (FEAT) in the Use of Artificial Intelligence and Data Analytics (AIDA) in Singapore's Finance Sector* in 2018 (MAS 2018a). These foundational guidelines enable financial institutions to operationalize the FEAT Fairness Principles Assessment Methodology, and it provides an open-source software toolkit to strengthen the capacity of financial institutions to develop responsible AI (Veritas 2022).

Thailand's Ministry of Digital Economy and Society has also published its National AI Ethics Guideline, which sets boundaries for the ethical deployment of AI technologies through six aspects of AI ethics: competitiveness and sustainability development; laws, ethics, and international standards; transparency and accountability; security and privacy; fairness; and reliability.

In Malaysia, instead of issuing a separate framework to govern the ethical use of AI, machine learning (ML), or other forms of predictive algorithms in the finance sector, guidelines are included in the policy document on eKYC (Bank Negara Malaysia 2020), which aims to facilitate the online process of identifying and verifying customers of financial institutions.

In terms of regulations that govern the operation of different fintech services, ASEAN countries have enacted licensing requirements for the provision of digital payment services and the issuance of e-money, due to the proliferation of e-payment services.

Fintech Innovation Initiatives

Innovation Hubs and Accelerator Programs

To foster the development of a fintech ecosystem and assist start-ups in building their capacity for research and applications, Indonesia, Malaysia, and Singapore have set up innovation centers dedicated to the finance sector, while other ASEAN countries, such as Brunei Darussalam, Cambodia, Myanmar, the Philippines, Thailand, and Viet Nam, have accelerator initiatives geared toward IT capacity building and the promotion of digital innovations.

The Indonesian Financial Services Authority, Otoritas Jasa Keuangan (OJK), established the Innovation Centre for Digital Financial Technology (OJK Infinity) in 2018 as a fintech business incubator and education center, in collaboration with academics, industry associations, and the private sector. Singapore's financial regulator encourages financial institutions and consultancy firms to establish their own innovation labs to spur service solutions and act as start-up accelerators. The country has about 40 innovation labs, some focusing specifically on disruptive technologies such as ML, blockchain, and robotic process automation (MAS 2024a).

With a grant of $2.7 million from KOICA, the National Incubation Center of Cambodia (NICC) opened in March 2024 to provide digital training and mentoring for start-ups. To drive digital technologies and nurture talent, the National Institute of Posts, Telecommunications, Information, and Communication Technology (NIPTICT) was expanded to become the Cambodia Academy of Digital Technology (CADT) in 2021 (CADT 2021).

Regulatory Sandboxes

Sandboxes enable the collaborative efforts of regulatory authorities, fintech companies, financial institutions, and investors to support innovative projects and business models. Countries that adopt a regulatory sandbox approach tend to attract more technology firms, talent, and investment. Among the ASEAN countries, Brunei Darussalam, Indonesia, Malaysia, Singapore, and Thailand have already introduced regulatory sandboxes. In Cambodia, the regulatory sandbox is restricted to mobile payment solutions only, which could limit the development of financial services that cut across different regulated sectors (DFDL 2021). The development of a regulatory sandbox in the Philippines and Viet Nam is still being considered. Regulatory sandboxes offer many benefits; not only to the fintech innovators, but also to regulators and consumers (chapters 2, 3, 7, and 8).

With the enactment of the Special Act on Support for Financial Innovation in April 2019, the Government of the Republic of Korea launched its financial regulatory sandbox program to remove regulatory obstacles and promote innovation among fintechs and start-ups in the financial industry, while protecting consumers. In further support for the development of digital finance, the government announced plans to smooth the way for fintech firms' applications and allow them to pilot their innovations virtually through a digital sandbox (Government of the Republic of Korea 2021).

India finalized a framework for a regulatory sandbox in August 2019 to allow fintech firms to test new products and services in a live environment subject to regulatory oversight (Reserve Bank of India 2019). To cater to the proliferation of cross-sector, hybrid financial products, and in response to a call for an interoperable framework, the Reserve Bank of India has further issued a standard operating procedure for its interoperable regulatory sandbox, as innovative fintech has fallen under the remit of more than one regulator since October 2022. The FinTech Department of the Reserve Bank of India is the coordination group for applications (Reserve Bank of India 2022).

Digital Skills Among Populations

As indicated by the measurements of a population's digital skills (e.g., computer skills, digital reading, basic coding) under the Global Competitiveness Index, the level of such skills is higher in ASEAN countries than in emerging fintech markets of CAREC. However, significant disparity exists in both. Setting aside the PRC, Azerbaijan leads and Kazakhstan scores well above the average of 4.3, while Georgia, the Kyrgyz Republic, and Mongolia lag far behind. Data on Tajikistan and Turkmenistan are not available for comparison.

Across ASEAN, Malaysia, the Philippines, and Singapore are top performers, while digital skill levels in emerging market economies such as Cambodia, the Lao PDR, and Viet Nam trail. The relatively high digital literacy rate among Filipinos could be attributed to the Digital Philippines Strategy and to initiatives by the Department of Information and Communications Technology (DICT) to boost ICT competency among citizens. The ICT Academy has focused on improving digital skills through both online platforms and over 4,000 nationwide physical Technology Empowerment for Education, Employment, Entrepreneurship, and Economic Development (Tech4ED) centers. Digital-skills-development initiatives, such as the Digital Workforce Upskilling Pilot Project and Cybersafe Learning Project, have been implemented for different target groups, including technical people, teachers, and learners. Digital skills in the Republic of Korea are on par with those of high-performing ASEAN countries, while India and Japan trail the region. ICT has been integrated into all levels of the education system in the Republic of Korea to ensure that its working population has strong digital skills. However, the digital gap between generations, as indicated by the share of people aged 55–65 lacking basic digital skills, is also high (OECD 2021).

Regional Cooperation Benchmarking Results

Compared with ASEAN as a whole and the three Asian economies shown in Table 1.10, regional cooperation in CAREC is relatively limited, especially in international or regional commitments and cross-border fintech initiatives.

Table 1.10: Benchmarking CAREC Progress in Regional Cooperation
(0–6)[a]

Country/Region	International Commitments, 2022	Cross-Border Initiatives, 2022[b]	Participation in Regional/ International Platforms, 2022
CAREC	2.2	2.9	3.1
ASEAN	3.4	4.4	3.2
India	4.0	4.0	4.0
Japan	6.0	6.0	4.0
Republic of Korea	6.0	6.0	4.0

ASEAN = Association of Southeast Asian Nations, CAREC = Central Asia Regional Economic Cooperation.

[a] The 0–6 scale is the scoring system for the various stages of progress toward the achievement of the indicators, from none (0) to the maximum (6) as defined for each indicator. A description of the scoring system is provided in the Appendix, under Pillar 4.

[b] These initiatives concern such issues as interoperability, e-invoicing, and standards.

Source: Access Partnership.

International Commitments

Advanced Asian economies like Japan, the Republic of Korea, and Singapore have been proactive in forging partnerships and formulating cooperative agreements with their trading partners to accelerate digital economy development and promote innovations, cross-border digital transactions, and financial services.

In 2019, Japan reached a digital trade agreement with the US to ensure that data could be transferred across borders by financial service suppliers and to prohibit data-localization measures that imposed restrictions on where financial data can be stored and processed. The agreement also promotes cross-border digital trade and transactions by allowing the use of electronic signatures for authentication (United States Trade Representative 2019). Under the European Union (EU)–Japan Economic Partnership Agreement, a Joint EU–Japan financial regulatory forum was established to provide a framework for cooperation between the EU's Directorate-General for Financial Stability, Financial Services and Capital Markets Union and Japan's Financial Services Agency.

Similarly, the Republic of Korea has concluded a Digital Economy Partnership Agreement with Singapore (Government of Singapore, Ministry of Trade and Industry et al. 2021) to deepen cooperation in the digital economy, promote interoperability between digital systems, and prohibit data localization that requires data to be stored in-country. With trusted data flows, cross-border digital transactions will be enhanced, and opportunities for e-payments and digital financial services can be created.

Singapore's Digital Economy Partnership Agreement with the Republic of Korea was its first one signed with another Asian economy; previous ones had been established with Chile and New Zealand (Government of Singapore, Ministry of Trade and Industry 2019), Australia (Government of Australia n.d.), and the UK.

These agreements encompassed collaborations on technology, data innovations, and regulatory sandboxes, while covering personal data protection, digital identities, and digital trade standards, which are pivotal to regional fintech development. Other ASEAN countries, including Indonesia, Malaysia, and Thailand, have also started engaging in regional cooperation.

Cross-Border Fintech Initiatives

Enhanced cross-border payment system interoperability has accelerated the adoption of digital payments and digital remittances across ASEAN, and contributed to financial inclusion. ASEAN economies stand out in their efforts to advance payment system interoperability through the ASEAN Payment Connectivity Initiative, launched in 2019. Cross-border QR codes enable consumers and merchants to improve efficiency; they also lower the cost of cross-border payments and facilitate intra-ASEAN trade. Thailand is one of the most interconnected ASEAN member countries, with cross-border QR payment linkages already established with Cambodia, Indonesia, the Lao PDR, Malaysia, Singapore, and Viet Nam (Bank of Thailand 2020; Bank Indonesia 2021; RYT9 2019; Bank Negara Malaysia 2021; Bank of Thailand 2021; PYMNTS 2021). To facilitate cross-border financial payments and boost tourism growth as international travel gradually resumed, the MAS and Bank Indonesia started working on a cross-border payment linkage initiative by making Indonesia's Quick Response Indonesian Standard (QRIS) code and Singapore's NETS QR standard interoperable (Bank Indonesia 2022).

Collaboration among the MAS, the Bank of Thailand, payment system operators, and participating financial institutions have resulted in the world's first real-time retail payment system linkage to allow bank account holders to transfer funds using a mobile number (MAS 2021a). The initiative enhances cross-border remittances through the provision of faster fund transfers and greater transparency of remittance charges.

Regional and International Platform Participation

In terms of participation in multilateral platforms that foster closer international or regional collaboration, the emerging fintech markets of CAREC are on par with the markets in ASEAN member countries. Central banks and financial regulatory institutions in Kazakhstan, the Kyrgyz Republic, Mongolia, Pakistan, Tajikistan, and Uzbekistan are principal members of the Alliance for Financial Inclusion (Alliance for Financial Inclusion n.d.-b), which provides a knowledge-exchange platform for regulators, international organizations, and the private sector to drive financial inclusion at the country, regional, and broader international levels. However, only the National Bank of Georgia and Kazakhstan's Astana Financial Services Authority (AFSA) have joined global platforms like the Global Financial Innovation Network (GFIN) to promote regional fintech innovation (Global Financial Innovation Network n.d.).

While both regions score similarly on this aspect, Singapore's MAS, together with the International Finance Corporation (IFC) and the ASEAN Bankers Association, has established an ASEAN-specific platform designed for intraregional cooperation, especially for less developed markets in the region. The mission of the ASEAN Financial Innovation Network (AFIN) is to foster innovation and cooperation among financial institutions, including microfinance institutions, NBFIs, and fintechs. To help the participating firms test their cross-border fintech applications and solutions, an API Exchange (APIX) platform was set up to enable pilots using a cloud-based architecture (API Exchange n.d.; MAS 2018b). In addition to APIX, AFIN also launched a global fintech registry for financial institutions in ASEAN to identify and assess fintech firms for collaboration. AFIN has also partnered with an enterprise-blockchain software provider to enable banks and fintechs to create and test central bank digital currency (CBDC) applications (Regulation Asia 2021).

In addition, Asian countries such as Japan and the Republic of Korea are members of the Bank for International Settlements (BIS) Innovation Network. Japan has also joined forces with the Bank of Canada, Bank of England, European Central Bank, US Federal Reserve, Sveriges Riksbank, and Swiss National Bank to experiment with retail CBDCs, which could help to facilitate international or cross-border payments through improvements in system interoperability (BIS 2021).

UNPACKING FINDINGS AND LESSONS

This chapter concludes by analyzing the progress achieved in areas that will be fundamental for building an innovative, competitive, and resilient ecosystem encompassing the emerging fintech markets of CAREC. Despite the unevenness of growth across the region, progress in payment development, financial inclusion, and digital connectivity can be seen. Enabling regulatory frameworks have been put into place gradually, and fintech centers are also being established to encourage innovation and regional collaboration.

In terms of fintech technologies and regional cooperation, Mongolia and Kazakhstan frequently occupy the first and second positions, while Azerbaijan leads in capacity building. Georgia and the Kyrgyz Republic are rarely far behind, while Mongolia leads in financial inclusion. Pakistan, the biggest potential market, trails the rest. Yet the challenges are often the same across the CAREC countries. For example, the region has the highest concentration of unbanked households among emerging market economies globally. On the other hand, the gap between men and women with financial accounts has narrowed. Among the key drivers of increased numbers of financial accounts are GDP growth, which has been interrupted, and the spread of mobile phone ownership, which has not.

Two other important drivers—and constraints—are digital literacy among households and the training of staff at banks, NBFIs, and private enterprises in the use of fintech technologies. Banks have been particularly slow to adopt fintech, partly because of the cost of acquiring the new technology and the costs of making the transition, for example, from branch banking and ATMs to mobile banking apps. Furthermore, advances such as the use of AI to assess risk management for small borrowers, which has been successfully deployed in the PRC, are still not widely used across the CAREC region's emerging fintech markets. This may hinder financial inclusion. Evidence exists that micro, small, and medium-sized enterprises (MSMEs), which account for about 90% of output and 50% of employment in CAREC, are frequently short of funds, but tend not to access banks for investments or working capital.

Where fintech has been more successful is in the rise of financial centers across CAREC (Chapter 8). Georgia and Kazakhstan, for example, have venture-capital and start-up accelerators. Fintech has also been successful among enterprises concentrated in emerging platform businesses. In most of CAREC, fintech development is between stage one, when a business has an online presence; and stage two, when the business trades through a third-party platform. In this landscape, electronic payments stand out as the most developed, followed by digital investments. The use of fast payment systems (FPSs), such as QR codes, has been especially dynamic. One stream of payments is remittances, which are especially important, accounting for over 38% of Tajikistan's GDP and more than 17% of Uzbekistan's GDP in 2023, according to the World Bank. One estimate suggests that, had remittances to Europe and Central Asia in 2018 been facilitated by fintech, users could have collectively saved $1.59 billion. Furthermore, as remittance payments across Sharia-compliant fintech platforms grow, Central Asia is set to become a global leader in Sharia-compliant fintech (Kurbanov and Rahmatulloev 2022).

One more significant driver of fintech seems to be the innovations encouraged by regulators, ranging from regulatory sandboxes to legislation enabling digital banks, although these are mostly at a nascent stage. In Azerbaijan and Pakistan, state policy and private investment have encouraged the emergence and diffusion of digital financial technologies. Most encouraging are the relatively high scores for digital literacy among many of CAREC's emerging fintech markets and the growing awareness of the need for digital frameworks that cover areas such as data privacy and protection, cybersecurity and digital signatures, connectivity for fast and secure digital transfers, digital IDs and KYC rules, and a growing interest in green finance. These are equally necessary for domestic and cross-border transactions; but CAREC is weaker for not having robust, comprehensive regional cooperation. In this regard, its emerging fintech markets would benefit from more detailed data on financial flows and the benefits arising from strengthening cross-regional cooperation.

The following recommendations, which are elaborated on in subsequent chapters, highlight the potential value of having emerging fintech markets come together to further enable fintech growth in the region:

- **Foster policy and coordination mechanisms.** With the fintech market poised for growth, CAREC countries will benefit from ensuring that initiatives are not undertaken in silos, but through a coordinated approach involving relevant government departments and financial regulators. This will give policymakers and other stakeholders a broader, more holistic picture of the goals of financial inclusion, in addition to revealing challenges and gaps in cross-sector areas of development and economic growth. In turn, this will enable the development of policy tools that inform the requirements of regulatory frameworks, payment infrastructure, and interoperable platforms, among other benefits.
- **Track progress through measurement and evaluation.** CAREC countries should accord high priority to developing comprehensive and coherent data measurement and evaluation systems. These systems may track aspects such as the performance of payment providers, the type and level of utilization, whether and what user needs are being met, and the impact of the providers. This evaluation could assist in making timely adjustments to initiatives and feed into relevant policy reforms.
- **Develop an enabling and harmonized regulatory environment for fintech growth.** CAREC countries should prioritize financial inclusion. For this, a legal and regulatory environment that promotes consumer and data protection, financial literacy, and user awareness is required, with the aim of minimizing risks and safeguarding the interests of all stakeholders in the market. For an inclusive fintech ecosystem, incorporating proportionality will help integrate the concept of a tiered approach into anti-money laundering/combating the financing of terrorism (AML/CFT) for lower-risk users. Although a wide variation in regulatory approaches is expected, depending on the current market state and priorities regarding financial inclusion, some harmonization will help in setting up interoperable payment systems *across* the region and *with* other regions.
- **Establish a commitment to responsible digital finance practices that protect consumers and data.** Policymakers and regulators in CAREC's emerging fintech markets must establish comprehensive approaches to ensure consumer and data protection (e.g., against cybersecurity threats) and to address AML/CFT considerations. These efforts will involve strengthening the capacity of public sector agencies and other stakeholders to develop and implement such initiatives for financial products and services and new and emerging technologies, with particular emphasis on "uneconomic" groups. Such approaches will be useful in minimizing risk, enhancing user trust, and reducing a barrier against demand, the benefits of which accrue to payment providers that are dependent on the scalability of services to get returns on investment.

- **Develop and enable Digital ID adoption across the region.** Robust, inclusive, and secure digital ID systems are key building blocks for a fintech ecosystem. They are also essential for governments, financial services, and other sectors of the economy to increase efficiency, enhance effectiveness, and promote innovation. CAREC countries should develop digital ID and customer identity systems to register populations, thereby facilitating access to financial services, and widening the scope of digital and financial inclusion. An interoperable digital ID could also be a shared goal that countries could pursue together. This may produce benefits for all member countries; for example, the ability to open bank accounts in other jurisdictions, hassle-free travel, and convenience (as well as an expanded regional market) for consumers and merchants.

REFERENCES

ADB News and Events. 2022. Four Ways to Boost E-Commerce in Central Asia. 25 May. https://www.adb.org/news/features/four-ways-boost-e-commerce-central-asia.

AlAji, F. T. 2018. ABCD's Driving FinTech. *Medium*. 28 July. https://medium.datadriveninvestor.com/abcds-driving-fin-tech-db0986b1ddee.

Alliance for Financial Inclusion. n.d.-a Eastern Europe & Central Asia Policy Initiative (ECAPI). https://www.afi-global.org/activities/regional-initiatives/eastern-europe-central-asia-policy-initiative-ecapi/.

———. n.d.-b. Members. https://www.afi-global.org/about-afi/members/.

Anudari, M. 2018. Automated Clearing House System for Low-Value Transactions to be Introduced. *MONTSAME (Mongolian News Agency)*. 4 June. https://montsame.mn/en/read/135364.

API Exchange (APIX). n.d. About: Collaborate to Innovate. https://apixplatform.com/about-us.

Aronia, G. 2021. Space: First-Ever International Georgian Fintech by TBC Group: Interview with Nika Kurdiani. *Forbes*. 24 November. https://forbes.ge/en/spheisi-thibisi-jguphis-pirveli-saerthashoriso-qarthuli-phinteqi-interviu-nika-qurdianthan/?fbclid=IwAR21NwtBes1tesJNU4mCusnHeM-sRPvGNEGX5CUHPIBecASAhu8W51kLt80.

Association of Banks in Singapore. 2022. Fast and Secure Transfers—Fact Sheet. https://abs.org.sg/docs/library/fast-fact-sheet.pdf.

———. n.d.-a. 4 Steps to Participate in RPP. DuitNow. https://www.duitnow.my/pdf/Admission_to_RPP.pdf.

———. n.d.-b. PayNow. https://www.abs.org.sg/consumer-banking/pay-now.

Association of Southeast Asian Nations (ASEAN). 2016. *ASEAN Telecommunications and Information Technology Ministers Meeting (TELMIN): Framework on Personal Data Protection*. https://asean.org/wp-content/uploads/2012/05/10-ASEAN-Framework-on-PDP.pdf.

———. 2020. *ASEAN Capacity Building Roadmap for Consumer Protection 2020–2025*. https://asean.org/wp-content/uploads/2021/08/Final-ASEAN-Capacity-Building-Roadmap-2020-2025-3Mar20.pdf.

———. 2021a. *ASEAN Data Management Framework: Data Governance and Protection Throughout the Data Lifecycle*. https://asean.org/wp-content/uploads/2-ASEAN-Data-Management-Framework_Final.pdf.

———. 2021b. *ASEAN Digital Masterplan 2025*. https://asean.org/wp-content/uploads/2021/09/ASEAN-Digital-Masterplan-EDITED.pdf.

———. 2021c. *ASEAN Model Contractual Clauses for Cross Border Data Flows*. https://asean.org/wp-content/uploads/3-ASEAN-Model-Contractual-Clauses-for-Cross-Border-Data-Flows_Final.pdf.

———. 2021d. *Handbook on ASEAN Consumer Protection Laws and Regulations*. 2nd ed. https://aseanconsumer.org/file/post_image/2nd%20Edition%20of%20The%20ASEAN%20Consumer%20Protection%20Handbook%20-%208Nov21.pdf.

Azerbaijan State News Agency (AZERTAC). 2022. Azerbaijan's Central Bank, Turkish Finance Office Sign MOU. 1 April. https://azertag.az/en/xeber/Azerbaijan_039s_Central_Bank_Turkish_Finance_Office_sign_MoU-2075183.

Bangko Sentral ng Pilipinas (BSP). 2025. InstaPay ACH Participants. https://www.bsp.gov.ph/PaymentAndSettlement/Instapay%20Participants.pdf.

Bank for International Settlements (BIS). 2021. *Central Bank Digital Currencies*. Executive Summary. https://www.bis.org/publ/othp42.pdf.

Bank Indonesia. 2021. Indonesia and Thailand Launch Cross-Border QR Payment Linkage. News release. 17 August. https://www.bi.go.id/en/publikasi/ruang-media/news-release/Pages/sp_170821.aspx.

———. 2022. Indonesia and Singapore to Pursue Cross-Border QR Code Payments Connectivity and Explore Promoting the Use of Local Currencies for Bilateral Transactions. News release. 29 August. https://www.bi.go.id/en/publikasi/ruang-media/news-release/Pages/sp_2423322.aspx.

Bank Negara Malaysia. 2020. *Electronic Know-Your-Customer (eKYC)*. https://www.bnm.gov.my/documents/20124/948107/e-KYC+Policy+Document+300620.pdf/af752210-02e5-d2a4-e2ee-04b00c731a91?t=1594085248675.

———. 2021. Launch of the Cross-Border QR Payment Linkage Between Malaysia and Thailand. Press release. 18 June. https://www.bnm.gov.my/-/cross-border-qr-payment-linkage-between-malaysia-and-thailand.

Bank of Thailand. 2020. The Launch of Interoperable QR Payment Linkage Between Cambodia and Thailand. Press release. 18 February. https://www.bot.or.th/content/dam/bot/documents/en/news-and-media/news-pdf/2020/n0963e.pdf.

———. 2021. Cross-Border Payment Connectivity.

Burunciuc, L. 2021. How Central Asia Can Ensure It Doesn't Miss Out on a Digital Future. *World Bank Blogs*. 21 June. https://blogs.worldbank.org/europeandcentralasia/how-central-asia-can-ensure-it-doesnt-miss-out-digital-future.

Cambodia Academy of Digital Technology (CADT). 2021. NIPTICT Officially Rebranded to CADT. News release. 8 November. https://www.cadt.edu.kh/news/announcement-niptict-national-institute-rebranded-to-cambodia-academy-of-digital-technology-cadt/.

Central Asia Regional Economic Cooperation (CAREC) Institute. 2021. Participation in Astana Finance Days. News release. 1 July. https://www.carecinstitute.org/news/participation-in-astana-finance-days/.

CAREC Program. 2021a. *Startups in the CAREC Region*. https://www.carecprogram.org/newsletters/issues/20210702/.

———. 2021b. *CAREC Digital Strategy 2030: Accelerating Digital Transformation for Regional Competitiveness and Inclusive Growth*. Asian Development Bank. https://www.carecprogram.org/uploads/MC-2021-Docs-2-CAREC-Digital-Strategy-2030-20211711-EN.pdf.

———. 2022. *CAREC Economic and Financial Sustainability Cluster Progress Report and Work Plan: July 2021–June 2022*. Reference document prepared for the Senior Officials' Meeting on CAREC 2030: Economic & Financial Sustainability; July 2021–June 2022. 28 June. https://www.carecprogram.org/uploads/SOM2022-1_Economic-and-Financial-Stability-Cluster-EN.pdf.

———. 2023. CAREC Innovation Decoded—The People's Republic of China Episode. https://www.carecprogram.org/?event=carec-innovation-decoded-china-episode.

———. n.d.-a *CAREC Hackathon Concept Note*. https://www.adb.org/sites/default/files/linked-documents/54341-001-sd.pdf.

———. n.d.-b Economic and Financial Stability Cluster. https://www.carecprogram.org/?page_id=13243.

Choi, T. 2022. Estonia to Support Mongolia's Transition to Digital Government: Digital Identity Among Focusses of Collaboration. *BiometricUpdate.com*. 15 April. https://www.biometricupdate.com/202204/estonia-to-support-mongolias-transition-to-digital-government.

CMA. 2019. National Bank of Tajikistan Launches Automated Transfer System. 2 December. https://www.cma.se/news/national-bank-of-tajikistan-launches-automated-transfer-system.

DFDL Cambodia. 2021. Navigating the Fintech Revolution—Cambodia.

Dutta, S. 2021. Over 100 Crore Aadhaar Cards Issued in India so far, Says UIDAI CEO. *Hindustan Times*. 16 December.

Ernst & Young (EY). 2019. *Global FinTech Adoption Index 2019*. https://eyfinancialservicesthoughtgallery.ie/wp-content/uploads/2019/09/ey-global-fintech-adoption-index.pdf.

European Commission. 2018. Agreement Between the European Union and Japan for an Economic Partnership. https://policy.trade.ec.europa.eu/eu-trade-relationships-country-and-region/countries-and-regions/japan/eu-japan-agreement/eu-japan-agreement-chapter-chapter_en.

Express Tribune. 2021. Pakistan Seeks to "Double IT Industry in Two Years through Tech Zones." 23 June. https://tribune.com.pk/story/2306849/pakistan-seeks-to-double-it-industry-in-two-years-via-tech-zones.

Gelb, J. and A. Mukherjee. 2019. CDG Note: Building on Digital ID for Inclusive Services: Lessons from India. *Center for Global Development*. 13 September. https://www.cgdev.org/publication/building-digital-id-inclusive-services-lessons-india.

Global Financial Innovation Network (GFIN). n.d. Members. https://www.thegfin.com/members.

GOV.UK. 2022. UK-Singapore Digital Economy Agreement: Final Agreement Explainer. https://www.gov.uk/government/publications/uk-singapore-digital-economy-agreement-explainer/uk-singapore-digital-economy-agreement-final-agreement-explainer.

Government of Australia, Department of Foreign Affairs and Trade. n.d. Australia-Singapore Digital Economy Agreement. https://www.dfat.gov.au/trade/services-and-digital-trade/australia-and-singapore-digital-economy-agreement.

Government of Azerbaijan. n.d. Criminal Code of the Azerbaijan Republic, Section 1, Chapter 1 (unofficial translation in English). World Intellectual Property Organization. https://www.wipo.int/edocs/lexdocs/laws/en/az/az017en.pdf.

Government of the Philippines, Philippine Statistics Authority. 2022. PSA Unveils PhilSys Check, a PhilID Verification System. https://psa.gov.ph/content/psa-unveils-philsys-check-philid-verification-system.

———. 2025. Philippine Identification System. https://www.philsys.gov.ph/.

Government of the Republic of Korea, Financial Services Commission (FSC). 2021. Digital Finance Meeting Discusses Ways to Improve Rules for Fintechs and Big Techs. 9 February. https://www.fsc.go.kr/eng/pr010101/75353.

———. 2024. Fintech Innovation Fund Worth KRW500 Billion Planned for 2024–2027. Press Release. 9 April. https://www.korea.net/Government/Briefing-Room/Press-Releases/view?articleId=82093&insttCode=A260302&type=N.

Government of Singapore. 2022. GovWallet. Singapore Government Developer Portal. https://www.developer.tech.gov.sg/products/categories/platform/govwallet/overview.html.

———. 2025. Integrate Your Digital Services with Singpass. Singpass (Dev.). https://developer.singpass.gov.sg/.

Government of Singapore, Ministry of Trade and Industry. 2019. Singapore Leads the Way in New Digital Economy Partnership Agreement with Chile and New Zealand. Press release. 17 May. https://www.mti.gov.sg/Newsroom/Press-Releases/2019/05/Singapore-leads-the-way-in-new-Digital-Economy-Partnership-Agreement-with-Chile-and-New-Zealand.

———. 2022. Digital Economy Partnership Agreement Joint Committee Commences Accession Working Group for China. Press release. 18 August.

Government of Singapore, Ministry of Trade and Industry, Ministry of Communications and Information, and Infocomm Media Development Authority. 2021. Singapore and the Republic of Korea Conclude Negotiations on a Digital Economy Agreement. Press release. 15 December. https://www.mti.gov.sg/-/media/MTI/Newsroom/Press-Releases/2021/12/Singapore-and-the-Republic-of-Korea-conclude-negotiations-on-a-Digital-Economy-Agreement.pdf.

Government of Thailand, Ministry of Digital Economy and Society. 2021. *Digital Thailand: AI Ethics Guideline* (in Thai). https://www.etda.or.th/getattachment/9d370f25-f37a-4b7c-b661-48d2d730651d/Digital-Thailand-AI-Ethics-Principle-and-Guideline.pdf.aspx?lang=th-TH.

Government of the United Kingdom, Department for International Trade. 2022. UK-Singapore Digital Economy Agreement: Final Agreement Explainer. https://www.gov.uk/government/publications/uk-singapore-digital-economy-agreement-explainer/uk-singapore-digital-economy-agreement-final-agreement-explainer.

International Finance Corporation (IFC). 2021. IFC and Alif Bank to Boost Digital Finance in Tajikistan. Press release. 31 May. https://www.ifc.org/en/pressroom/2021/ifc-and-alif-bank-to-boost-digital-finance-in-tajikistan.

International Telecommunication Union (ITU). n.d. Asan İmza: Azerbaijan National Mobile eID and Legally Binding e-Signature. https://www.itu.int/net4/wsis/archive/stocktaking/Project/Details?projectId=1515503655.

ITU, Digital Transformation Centres. 2020. Issue 03. *DTC News*. June–July. https://academy.itu.int/sites/default/files/media2/file/DTC%20News%20-%20Issue%203.pdf.

Jakarta Post. 2021. Bank Indonesia Launching BI-Fast in December 2021 to Offer Fast and Low-Cost Transactions. 3 November. https://www.thejakartapost.com/adv/2021/11/03/bank-indonesia-launching-bi-fast-in-december-2021-to-offer-fast-and-low-cost-transactions.html.

Japan International Cooperation Agency (JICA). 2020. Central Bank of Myanmar (CBM) Launches New Payment and Settlement System (CBM-NET2). 16 November. https://www.jica.go.jp/myanmar/english/office/topics/press201116.html.

Kim, K. et al. 2021. 2021 Trade Finance Gaps, Growth, and Jobs Survey. *ADB Briefs*. No. 192. Asian Development Bank. https://www.adb.org/publications/2021-trade-finance-gaps-growth-jobs-survey.

Krimpe, J. 2019. *Digital Trade Hub of Azerbaijan: The PPP Initiative for Cross-Border e-Trade & e-Services.* Presentation prepared for the Subregional Workshop on Non-Tariff Measures in Azerbaijan and North and Central Asia, organized by the United Nations Economic and Social Commission for Asia and the Pacific (UNESCAP) and the Food and Safety Agency of the Republic of Azerbaijan. 9–11 December 2019, Baku, Azerbaijan. https://www.unescap.org/sites/default/files/Session.8.%20Digital%20Trade%20Hub.pdf.pdf.

Kurbanov, A. and Z. Rahmatulloev. 2022. How Is Fintech Transforming Banking in Central Asia? *Wealth and Finance*. 8 July. https://www.wealthandfinance-news.com/how-is-fintech-transforming-banking-in-central-asia/.

Lee, M. et al. 2021. Leveraging Fintech for Central Asia's Trade Financing Needs: Supporting Underserved Micro, Small, and Medium-Sized Enterprises. *ADB Briefs*. No. 193. Asian Development Bank. https://www.adb.org/publications/fintech-central-asia-trade-financing-needs.

Lim, J. 2021. South Korea's Brilliant Decentralized Approach to Citizen Identity Management. *TechWire Asia*. 25 June. https://techwireasia.com/2021/06/koreas-decentralized-identity-approach-to-identity-management/.

Monetary Authority of Singapore (MAS). 2018a. *Principles to Promote Fairness, Ethics, Accountability and Transparency (FEAT) in the Use of Artificial Intelligence and Data Analytics in Singapore's Financial Sector*. https://www.mas.gov.sg/~/media/MAS/News%20and%20Publications/Monographs%20and%20Information%20Papers/FEAT%20Principles%20Final.pdf.

———. 2018b. World's First Cross-Border, Open-Architecture Platform to Improve Financial Inclusion. Media Release. 17 September. https://www.mas.gov.sg/news/media-releases/2018/worlds-first-cross-border-open-architecture-platform-to-improve-financial-inclusion.

———. 2020. Non-Bank Financial Institutions to Have Access to FAST and PayNow. Media release. 30 November. https://www.mas.gov.sg/news/media-releases/2020/non-bank-financial-institutions-to-have-access-to-fast-and-paynow.

———. 2021a. Singapore and Thailand Launch World's First Linkage of Real-Time Payment Systems. Media release. 29 April. https://www.mas.gov.sg/news/media-releases/2021/singapore-and-thailand-launch-worlds-first-linkage-of-real-time-payment-systems.

———. 2021b. Singapore's PayNow and India's UPI to Link in 2022. Media release. 14 September. https://www.mas.gov.sg/news/media-releases/2021/singapores-paynow-and-indias-upi-to-link-in-2022.

———. 2024a. FinTech Innovation Labs. https://www.mas.gov.sg/development/ fintech/ fintech-innovation-labs.

———. 2024b. Singapore Financial Data Exchange (SGFinDex). https://www.mas.gov.sg/development/fintech/sgfindex#_about-sgfindex.

Moody's Analytics. 2021. HKMA and PBC Sign Cooperation Agreement on Fintech Innovation. https://www.moodysanalytics.com/regulatory-news/oct-21-21-hkma-and-pbc-sign-cooperation-agreement-on-fintech-innovation.

Morgan, P. J. and N. Yoshino, eds. 2021. *Leveraging SME Finance Through Value Chains in CAREC Landlocked Countries*. Asian Development Bank Institute. https://www.adb.org/sites/default/files/publication/672041/adbi-book-leveraging-sme-finance-through-value-chains-carec.pdf.

Mynbayev, B. and K. Aushev. 2020. *Overview of Fintech Development in Central Asia: Kazakhstan, Kyrgyzstan, Uzbekistan, Tajikistan*. KPMG. https://assets.kpmg/content/dam/kpmg/kz/pdf/2020/12/Overview-of-Fintech-Development-in-Central-Asia.pdf.

National Bank of Kazakhstan. 2022. *Development of Open API, Open Banking and Ecosystem of Digital Financial Services in the Republic of Kazakhstan*. https://nationalbank.kz/en/page/Digital-Financial-Infrastructure.

National Digital ID Co., Ltd. (Thailand). n.d. About NDID. https://ndid.co.th/en/about-us-en/.

OneTrust DataGuidance. 2021. Pakistan Personal Data Protection Bill, 2021. https://www.dataguidance.com/legal-research/personal-data-protection-bill-2021-august.

Organisation for Economic Co-operation and Development (OECD). 2021. OECD Skills Strategy Implementation Guidance for Korea: Strengthening the Governance of Adult Learning. https://www.oecd.org/en/publications/oecd-skills-strategy-implementation-guidance-for-korea_f19a4560-en.html.

PYMNTS. 2021. Thailand, Vietnam Launch QR Code Link for Cross-Border Payments. 5 April. https://www.pymnts.com/news/payment-methods/2021/thailand-vietnam-launch-qr-code-link-for-cross-border-payments/.

Razzaq, A. et al. 2022. *Digital CAREC: Analysis of the Regional Digital Gap; Phase 1*. CAREC Institute / Islamic Development Bank. https://www.carecinstitute.org/publications/digital-carec-analysis-of-the-regional-digital-gap/.

Regulation Asia. 2021. AFIN, R3 Partner to Launch CBDC Sandbox on APIX Platform. 17 June. https://www.regulationasia.com/afin-r3-partner-to-launch-cbdc-sandbox-on-apix-platform/.

Reserve Bank of India. 2019. *Enabling Framework for Regulatory Sandbox*. https://www.rbi.org.in/Scripts/PublicationReportDetails.aspx?UrlPage=&ID=938#5.

———. n.d. *Inter-Operable Regulatory Sandbox: Standard Operating Procedure*. https://www.rbi.org.in/scripts/bs_viewcontent.aspx?Id=4196.

RYT9. 2019. Thanachart Bank and BCEL Joint Initiative for Cross-Border QR Payment. Press release. 4 April. https://www.ryt9.com/en/prg/225390.

Satubaldina, A. 2022. Building a Digital Kazakhstan: Kazakhstan Seeks to Provide 100 Percent of Population with Internet by 2025. *Astana Times*. 11 August. https://astanatimes.com/2022/08/building-a-digital-kazakhstan-kazakhstan-seeks-to-provide-100-percent-of-population-with-internet-by-2025/.

Spînu, N. 2020. *Azerbaijan Cybersecurity Governance Assessment*. Geneva Centre for Security Sector Governance. https://www.dcaf.ch/sites/default/files/publications/documents/AzerbaijanCybersecurityGovernanceAssessment.pdf.

Statista. n.d. Payments – Worldwide (database). https://www.statista.com/outlook/fmo/payments/worldwide?currency=USD (accessed 18 November 2022).

Umar, K. 2021. *Working Paper: Financial Inclusion and Fintech in CAREC; Constraints and Prospects*. CAREC Institute. https://www.carecinstitute.org/publications/working-paper-financial-inclusion-and-fintech-in-carec-constraints-and-prospects/.

UNCDF (United Nations Capital Development Fund). 2021. Cambodia Financial Inclusion Refresh. https://www.uncdf.org/Download/AdminFileWithFilename?id=16788&cultureId=127&filename=4-4-2022map-diagnostic-refresh-for-cambodiapdf.

United Overseas Bank (UOB). 2021. FinTech in Thailand 3Q 2021: Thailand 4.0 Plots Way Forward. https://www.uobgroup.com/techecosystem/news-insights- fintech-in-thailand-3q-2021.html.

UOB, PricewaterhouseCoopers Risk Services (PwC Singapore), and the Singapore FinTech Association (SFA). 2021. *FinTech in ASEAN 2021: Digital Takes Flight*. UOB, PwC Singapore, SFA. https://www.uobgroup.com/techecosystem/news-insights- fintech-in-asean-2021.html.

United States Trade Representative. 2019. Agreement Between the United States of America and Japan Concerning Digital Trade. https://ustr.gov/sites/default/files/files/agreements/japan/Agreement_between_the_United_States_and_Japan_concerning_Digital_Trade.pdf.

Veritas. 2022. *Veritas Document 3: FEAT Principles Assessment Methodology*. https://www.mas.gov.sg/-/media/MAS-Media-Library/news/media-releases/2022/Veritas-Document-3---FEAT-Principles-Assessment-Methodology.pdf.

World Bank. 2020a. *Implementation Completion and Results Report on a Grant in the Amount of SDR 6.5 Million to the Republic of Tajikistan for the Private Sector Competitiveness Project*. https://documents1.worldbank.org/curated/en/872161594308781646/pdf/Tajikistan-Private-Sector-Competitiveness-Project.pdf.

———. 2020b. FinTech in Europe and Central Asia: Maximising Benefits and Managing Risks. Open Knowledge Repository. https://openknowledge.worldbank.org/bitstream/handle/10986/33591/fintech-in-Europe-and-Central-Asia-Maximizing-Benefits-and-Managing-Risks.pdf?sequence=1&isAllowed=y.

———. 2020c. *Fintech in Europe and Central Asia: Maximizing Benefits and Managing Risks*. Fintech Note No. 4. https://documents1.worldbank.org/curated/en/640021585934004225/pdf/Fintech-in-Europe-and-Central-Asia-Maximizing-Benefits-and-Managing-Risks.pdf.

———. 2022a. Account Ownership at a Financial Institution or with a Mobile Money Service Provider (% population ages 15+). *Global Findex Database*. https://data.worldbank.org/indicator/FX.OWN.TOTL.ZS.

———. 2022b. COVID-19 Drives Global Surge in Use of Digital Payments. Press release, 29 June. https://www.worldbank.org/en/news/press-release/2022/06/29/covid-19-drives-global-surge-in-use-of-digital-payments.

———. n.d. Global Findex Database 2021: Financial Inclusion, Digital Payments, and Resilience in the Age of COVID-19. https://www.worldbank.org/en/publication/globalfindex (accessed 22 November 2022).

Yerzhan, I. 2022. *Kazakhstan's Fintech Landscape*. National Bank of Kazakhstan. https://www.kiep.go.kr/aif/issueFileDownload.es?brdctsNo=332778&brdctsFileNo=82772.

Yoon, J. 2022. KOMSCO Signs MOU with Kyrgyzstan for Digitization. *Korea Times*. 6 April. https://www.koreatimes.co.kr/www/biz/2022/06/126_326868.html.

2

Foundations of Regional Fintech Cooperation

George Kvirikashvili

INTRODUCTION

The footprint of financial technology (fintech) in the Central Asia Regional Economic Cooperation (CAREC) region remains extremely limited, even within national markets that have established their own ecosystems or clusters for fintech advancement. Lack of regional cohesion is notable for two critical aspects: the regulatory framework governing fintech entry, and the establishment of standardized protocols for cross-border operations. Instead, firms seeking to penetrate CAREC's emerging fintech markets, whether based in the region or not, face challenging tasks as they adapt to various sets of government regulations (where they exist) and differing technical specifications in each country.

The removal of these barriers to market entry and cross-border operations is pivotal for nurturing a genuinely regional fintech capacity. This approach can harness economies of scale and other efficiencies, reduce costs, and lead ultimately to more affordable access for consumers. To realize this objective, it is imperative for emerging fintech markets in CAREC to foster collaboration that prioritizes connectivity and financial integration, while capitalizing on the existing financial infrastructure of each economy.

The Development Need for Fintech Collaboration

An effective regional cooperation mechanism is necessary for building functional and harmonized regulatory standards and surveillance systems for fintech to (i) boost opportunities for scaling up national fintechs; (ii) ensure regional cohesion and clarity of the rules of the game for non-regional fintech players interested in entering its markets; and (iii) prevent further risks involving drug trafficking, money laundering, terrorism financing, cybercrime, fraud, and concerns regarding the breach of intellectual property rights, personal data, and privacy. Fintech has the potential to move economies and financial systems in the region toward a common development goal. It offers innovative solutions that could mobilize finance for efficient and inclusive intermediation, create new forms of cross-border financial flows, and introduce new instruments for conducting capital market transactions across borders.

Fintech is transforming international capital flows by breaking down information barriers and more effectively aligning savings with investments, thereby diversifying and decentralizing financial services. The increased use of digital payments will result in cross-border transactions that will not only be cheaper and faster, but also more transparent. This can deepen global economic integration while fostering financial inclusion and sustainable development.

The level of fintech development and sophistication differs widely across the region, given that the architecture in the People's Republic of China (PRC) is advanced, while fintech activities in other member countries remain mostly led by payments. The electronic-commerce (e-commerce) revenue generated by CAREC's nine emerging fintech markets amounted to $13.9 billion in 2022, with fintech accounting for about of half of payments (Castro 2024). That was a sharp increase from the $325 million in transaction value in 2018. By comparison, e-commerce revenue generated by fintech in the member countries of the Association of Southeast Asian Nations (ASEAN), which has about double the population, exceeded $60 billion, about 8.5 times more than in CAREC's emerging fintech economies. In 2022, CAREC had 84 million fintech users, a significant increase from the 63 million users in 2019.

The legal and regulatory environment remains weak, as does the capacity to develop modern regulatory frameworks and jurisdictions essential for expanding fintech solutions. Regional and global dialogues are crucial for supporting effective data frameworks, especially considering the cross-border and global accessibility nature of platforms.

Most CAREC member countries have rules and regulations for developing fintech. However, the rules and regulations need to be supported by mutual recognition agreements to harness the potential of fintech for deeper regional financial cooperation (ADB 2022a). CAREC also trails benchmark regions in promoting collaborative regional fintech communities, which could offer a timely opportunity for regional collaboration among regulators and other fintech players.

The road map for accelerating fintech adoption and for harmonizing national fintech ecosystems is driven by the benefits of deeper regional economic and financial cooperation. The goal is to foster a collaborative regional fintech community with interoperable national clusters that facilitate trade, financial exchange, and inclusive economic growth.

Toward a Regional Fintech Consensus

The initial and critical step in pursuing this overarching objective involves enhancing communication among stakeholders in both the public and private sectors. This approach aims to facilitate a smooth transition to regional schemes and systems. At the same time, these discussions and decisions should be rooted in a shared vision for the nature of fintech. In this regard, we can consider two broad scenarios:

- Scenario 1 involves identifying the most developed existing fintech cluster within CAREC's emerging fintech markets and nurturing it as the primary center of fintech innovation. Subsequently, other clusters and jurisdictions would merge into this leading center.
- Scenario 2 focuses on establishing seamless interoperability among existing fintech clusters and jurisdictions to create opportunities for cross-border expansion. This approach would harness competition among the clusters, thus accelerating innovation and shaping a collaborative regional fintech community.

After a comprehensive evaluation of both scenarios—considering the primary objectives of removing barriers to entry into the fintech market and encouraging efficient cross-border operations—Scenario 2 emerged as the better course of action. It would entail the development of a strategic plan to foster interoperability among multiple fintech-advanced jurisdictions or clusters. Subsequent phases would concentrate on expanding this initiative to involve more CAREC countries. This approach would not include the PRC, given the significant gap between PRC's advanced fintech development level and the overall fintech capacity of CAREC's other members.

In the context of national efforts, a series of critical policy decisions pertaining to collective action in CAREC's emerging fintech markets has been proposed. Among them are actions covered in this book to regionalize payment systems, harmonize open banking and finance, encourage innovation, use fintech to drive cross-border e-commerce and trade finance, and promote the development of regionalized capital markets.

An action-specific road map was developed for accelerating the adoption of fintech within the region, thereby creating deeper regional economic and financial integration. Core tasks were to assess the feasibility of adopting compatible regulatory frameworks and operating protocols and standards to ease cross-border activities, and to create a collaborative fintech community to further develop expertise and drive innovation in the finance sector regionally. Out of this work came suggestions for the next steps to implement these goals.

KEY PILLARS FOR FINTECH IN CAREC

Five key "pillars" represent the most critical areas of focus for enhancing regional fintech capabilities in CAREC (Figure 2.1):

- Pillar 1: establishing cross-border digital payments infrastructure and fast payment systems (FPS);
- Pillar 2: cultivating an application programming interface (API) ecosystem to ensure interoperability, paving the way to cross-border open banking, financial services, and data sharing;
- Pillar 3: promoting collaboration and cooperation in the field of innovation;
- Pillar 4: advancing fintech-led cross-border business-to-consumer (B2C) e-commerce and trade finance solutions; and
- Pillar 5: exploring opportunities for fintech-driven cross-border capital market integration, aiming at the regionalization of CAREC's capital market.

Figure 2.1: Suggested Strategic Framework for Developing a CAREC Collaborative Fintech Community

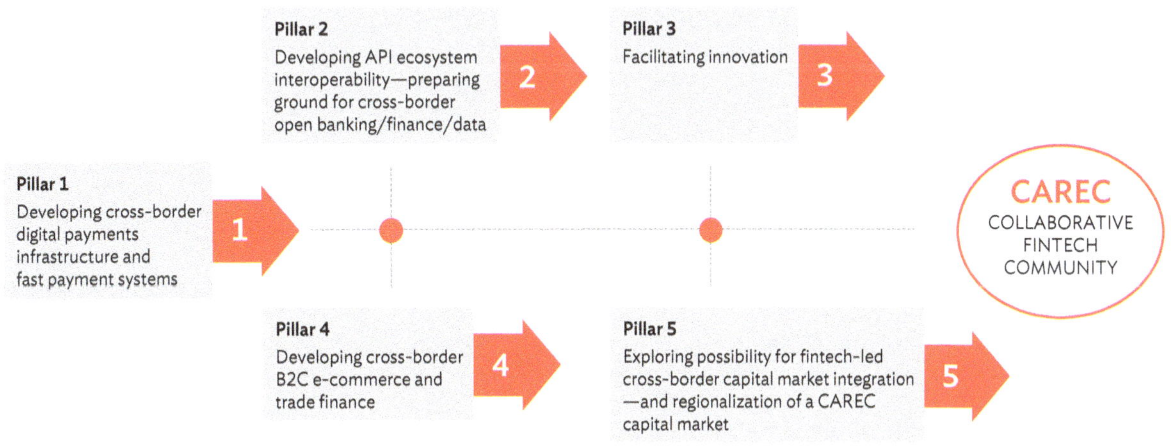

API = application programming interface, B2C = business to consumer, CAREC = Central Asia Regional Economic Cooperation, fintech = financial technology.

Source: CAREC Institute.

These pillars support the proposed strategic approach to bolstering CAREC's capabilities in the fintech realm, and they are instrumental in achieving the project's overarching goals. After an examination of the pillars, some overarching recommendations emerge that can be considered for inclusion in the regional framework for action.

Pillar 1: Payment Systems

It is imperative that the approach to payment systems ensure the following, to foster a collaborative and efficient payment-system framework for the CAREC region:

- **Governance framework.** Member countries should work to harmonize their legislation governing payment system entry and operations. For example, the feasibility of adopting a regionally harmonized passporting system for payment system licenses, based on rules similar to those in the European Union (EU) Single Rulebook, should be carefully explored.
- **Balanced economic incentives.** Members must conduct a thorough comparison of the economic incentives, if any, currently offered by their respective public sectors, with the objective of harmonizing these incentives across national borders.
- **Safe and reliable operations.** The adoption of a standardized technology to govern payment-system operations, one that is recognized and guaranteed to ensure safety and reliability, is paramount.
- **Information exchange.** Consideration should be given to establishing a system for the exchange of information pertaining to cybersecurity, data privacy, and protection, which are essential for compliance and enforcement.
- **Interoperable digital IDs.** The establishment of interoperable digital identification (ID) and digital corporate ID could be an important point to be considered by the members, as this would significantly enable interoperability.

In the lead-up to addressing the attainment of safe and reliable operations, CAREC members should assess and deliberate upon the potential creation of a system similar to the Arabian Gulf System for Financial Automated Quick Payment Transfer (AFAQ) for all member countries, with a focus on fulfilling cross-border and regional requirements.

Pillar 2: Open Banking and Open Finance Systems

The following entities should be established under Pillar 2 to help establish a robust foundation for open-banking and open-finance systems, thereby promoting cross-border compatibility and efficiency among CAREC member countries:

- **harmonized legal frameworks:** the establishment of compatible laws for adoption by each member country to govern open banking and open finance, or the necessary amendments to existing laws to ensure harmonization across the region;
- **standardized technical protocols:** the selection of standardized technical protocols to be applied in the domain of open banking and open finance, including
    - an **identity protocol**, perhaps using OpenID Connect 1.0;[5]

[5] OpenID Connect 1.0 is an authentication layer built on top of the OAuth 2.0 protocol. It allows clients (such as web applications or mobile apps) to verify the identity of end users based on the authentication performed by an authorization server.

- a **security profile**, perhaps using the OAuth-based API and financial-grade API (FAPI) 1 or 2,[6] and Client-Initiated Backchannel Authentication (CIBA);[7]
- a **trust management framework**, possibly managed by the banking regulator, and possibly using one of the established vendors; and
- **standardized API specifications and data models**; and

- a **coordinating and standard-setting body:** modeled after the EU's Berlin Group or the Financial Data Exchange (FDX) in the United States (US) and Canada, to standardize technical protocols.

Pillar 3: Facilitating Innovation

These following initiatives under Pillar 3 would be geared toward fostering a culture of innovation and entrepreneurship within the region, promoting collaboration and supporting the growth of the CAREC fintech ecosystem.

- **Regional regulatory sandboxes.** This would entail converting existing domestic regulatory sandboxes into regional operations, capitalizing on the advantages of harmonized regulatory laws and standards established under the other pillars. CAREC members could leverage ADB's Digital Innovation Sandbox Program, which is designed to offer an environment for experimenting with innovative solutions, while mitigating the risks associated with creation, innovation, and implementation (fundsforNGOs 2023).
- **Empowered accelerators and innovation centers.** Governments could enhance the role of existing accelerators and innovation centers through various initiatives, including (i) organizing fintech contests, and cultivating international teams; (ii) building a directory of start-ups and diverse communication channels to assist start-ups in fundraising; and (iii) organizing exhibitions or forums.
- **Fintech co-creation platforms.** Dedicated arenas could facilitate and advance tasks related to fintech development.

Pillar 4: Developing Fintech-Led Cross-Border E-Commerce and Trade Finance

These following strategies under Pillar 4 would aim to enhance and streamline cross-border B2C e-commerce and trade finance, leveraging fintech innovations to boost efficiency and facilitate international trade operations within the CAREC region (Chapter 6):

- **fintech-powered working capital solutions:** selecting a suitable fintech solution from the existing vendor landscape to provide working capital to international trade entities;
- **harmonized domestic B2C e-commerce and trade finance laws:** aligning domestic laws within CAREC related to B2C e-commerce and trade finance when conducted in the fintech domain, to ensure compatibility across member countries; and

6 The API security profile defines how parties are authenticated, how the authorization and the data request and response are secured, and how message integrity is preserved. The governing entity must determine the standard for the API security profile. The majority of open ecosystems for banking, finance, and data have chosen the OAuth-based financial-grade API (FAPI). In some countries, FAPI Client-Initiated Backchannel Authentication (CIBA) is used for decoupled authentication across channels. This global adoption has allowed multiple vendors to provide support for FAPI and has reduced the costs of adoption. Most live ecosystems (e.g., Brazil, United Kingdom) operate on FAPI 1.0, while others (e.g., Norway, Australia) have started implementing FAPI 2. FAPI 2 simplifies the security profile, especially for data consumers (clients), and adds common building blocks (Grant Management, Pushed Authorization Requests, and Rich Authorization Requests) to improve functionality and increase interoperability in the area of fine-grained consent capture and management.

7 CIBA is one of the latest standards from the OpenID Foundation. It is used to define new authentication and authorization flows, which are categorized as "decoupled flows," compared with the traditional OAuth OpenID Connect "redirect flows." CIBA enables new ways of obtaining an end user's consent, which can significantly improve customer experience.

- **promoting digital trade insurance:** encouraging the adoption of digital trade insurance instruments through tailored programs designed to facilitate and support regional and cross-border trade transactions facilitated by fintech.

Pillar 5: Developing Regional Linkages of Member Capital Markets

The following actions should be taken under Pillar 5 to encourage the development of stronger regional linkages within member capital markets, fostering financial stability and efficiency through collaborative efforts and innovative technologies (Chapter 4):

- **ensuing central securities depository (CSD) sustainability:** investigating whether financial sustainability concerns could serve as catalysts for potential mergers or collaboration among member countries' CSDs, considering both operational and ownership perspectives;
- **utilizing distributed ledger technology (DLT):** exploring the implementation of DLT as an information technology (IT) system for the purposes of clearance, settlement, and record keeping within the capital markets (ADB 2022b);[8] and
- **harmonizing legal frameworks:** adopting a compatible legal framework to govern the operations of CSDs that would ensure consistency and interoperability among the member countries.

Given the requirements of the five pillars as described above, several essential actions must be taken to advance the overall fintech landscape:

(i) Policymakers and financial regulators should adopt a unified and coordinated approach to promoting fintech development, and enhance financial inclusion.

(ii) Member countries should collaboratively establish a regulatory environment that is conducive to fintech growth, and is harmonious across borders.

(iii) Member countries, in consultation with industry stakeholders, should embrace consistent operational protocols and standards, or at the very least, compatible ones. This alignment would facilitate seamless cross-border operations.

(iv) Within these established protocols and standards, regulators must prioritize responsible digital financial practices to ensure consumer protection and data privacy.

(v) Similarly, within the framework of protocols and standards, the industry, with support from the public sector, should work toward the secure and interoperable adoption of digital IDs throughout the region.

(vi) To gauge progress effectively, there should be a commitment to ongoing and consistent measurement and evaluation of fintech advancements in the region, using the framework and results described in Chapter 1 of this book.

These actions will ensure a clear understanding of the impact and effectiveness of the implemented initiatives.

[8] In this regard, CAREC member countries should consider proposals or ideas generated under a recently launched ADB project to make cross-border securities transactions in Asia and the Pacific more efficient and secure through the use of blockchain technology. Applications of technological advancements described in a 2022 ADB report *Recent Technological Advances in Financial Market Infrastructure in ASEAN+3* could be especially useful. The report examines how disruptive technologies such as blockchain, artificial intelligence (AI), and the Internet of Things (IoT) could play a revolutionary role in the establishment of a modern cross-border securities transaction architecture by creating regional CSDs and real-time gross settlement linkages that would regionally powered by such technologies (ADB 2022b).

NEXT STEPS TO A CAREC STRATEGIC APPROACH

The central question for turning the recommendations associated with the five pillars into a more concrete road map will revolve around a determination of the next steps. Having assessed CAREC's position in terms of fintech development, having embraced the analytical framework for advancing interoperability, and having identified the nature of tasks required, stakeholders and analysts now face the question: How should emerging fintech markets in CAREC collectively progress toward realizing the potential of fintech on a regional basis?

The next logical step will entail fostering consensus among stakeholders and securing their commitment to specific thematic actions. Crafting a multiyear, intricate road map may not yet be feasible, primarily because agreement on the strategic goals has yet to be reached. While it is possible to outline a road map featuring suggested actions within each pillar (strategic recommendations), it remains unfeasible to allocate responsibilities and establish timelines (in other words, make tactical decisions) with the approval of CAREC member countries.

Instead, the identification of the next steps will hinge on the feedback and inputs received from a **pan-CAREC public–private dialogue platform** and from the engagement of a diverse spectrum of stakeholders from the member countries. Such stakeholder engagement will likely be instrumental in refining our understanding of the process and transforming the proposed road map into an actionable plan, thus raising fintech capabilities within the CAREC region to a significantly higher standard.

Throughout these discussions, it will be important to align conceptualization with the digital-development strategies and state programs of the CAREC countries. In some instances, based on outcomes of this dialogue, there may be a need to respond by proposing modifications or introducing new elements to the existing country strategies. As indicated by the findings from national expert studies and open sources, it is evident that the majority of national governments have already adopted or are in the process of formulating digital strategies to various extents. A detailed review is set out in the Appendix.

Models for a Collaborative Fintech Ecosystem

After the actions needed to develop CAREC fintech have been broadly defined, the most pressing question becomes: How should the efforts of the stakeholders (and the support from the donor community) be organized to generate the best chances for practical, substantial progress?

Fortunately, significant guidance for answering this question already exists. As explained in Chapter 9, in a globalized world, successful models and best practices are plentiful and readily available. CAREC's emerging fintech economies can learn from them, and take the opportunity to tailor those models and practices to their own financial systems.

Two models provide guidance for structuring the CAREC effort. The first is the broader approach adopted by ASEAN to overall financial integration within its membership (Table 2.1). That matrix identifies six areas of "financial integration challenges" (i.e., eliminating "friction") and the steps needed to overcome them (Figure 2.2).

Table 2.1: ASEAN Approaches to Financial Integration

ASEAN Financial Integration Challenge	Recommendations
Internal disparities constraining single market scaling opportunities	• Review disparities among the ASEAN member states, identifying the enablers of inclusive and equitable growth in the region. • Initiate policies to reduce the current divide between the LCMVB and ASEAN-5 markets.[a]
Dependence on external payment intermediation	• Monitor commercial flows and external payment intermediation for ASEAN and individual markets. • Establish action plans for increasing the settlement of domestic commercial flows within respective ASEAN markets. • Formalize agreements among ASEAN markets for greater flexibility in the settlement of trade and investments in local currencies.
Underserved and under-engaged corporations	• Study the needs of corporations in ASEAN markets from a regional and individual market perspective. • Ensure a balanced and deeper engagement of the private sector in ASEAN integration initiatives.
Slow financial infrastructure modernization, particularly in payment systems	• Establish an action plan for adopting ISO 20022 standards across ASEAN payment-market infrastructures.[b] • Review specific payment-market infrastructure development needs, and align the payment market modernization road map accordingly. • Formalize a regional governance body to lead the action plan for regional payment-system integration, including a balanced inclusion of the public and private sectors and an initial pilot "proof of concept."
Low digital competency	• Engage a strong public–private partnership to develop a digital-economy framework and trade-digitalization programs. • Initiate ISO 20022 adoption plans in ASEAN markets for regional and domestic financial messaging flows. • Implement strong cybersecurity frameworks at the market level, adopting global best practices and engaging with global programs.
Stakeholder alignment	• Identify market-level champions accountable for regional initiatives. • Formalize the governance and cooperation models used by these ASEAN champions. • Establish deeper and more regularized collaboration mechanisms at the regional, subregional, and market levels.

ASEAN = Association of Southeast Asian Nations; ISO = International Organization for Standardization; LCMVB = Lao People's Democratic Republic, Cambodia, Myanmar, Viet Nam, and Brunei Darussalam.

[a] "ASEAN-5" refers to Indonesia, Malaysia, the Philippines, Singapore, and Thailand.

[b] ISO 20022 standards refer to the handling of data in the financial services industry.

Source: SWIFT. 2017. *Achieving Financial Integration in the ASEAN Region*. SWIFT Discussion Paper.

The ASEAN material shows that the obstacles to financial system integration in the ASEAN region are largely similar to those facing CAREC members with regard to fintech. At the same time, ASEAN's financial integration approach is too broad for use in the more limited space of fintech development and regional integration. A more tailored and incisive framework is needed. That said, parts of the ASEAN rubric could be borrowed for developing the analysis and recommendations for CAREC, and included in a suggested strategic framework for CAREC.

The second set of guidance derives from the Group of Twenty (G20) and its approach to facilitating cross-border payments. To some degree, this rubric is the opposite of ASEAN's, in that it focuses on the narrow aspect of cross-border payment systems that relates to fintech development.[9]

The beginning point for the G20 approach is derived from a Stage 1 report of the Financial Stability Board (FSB 2020), which identified seven areas of friction, as shown in Figure 2.2.

Figure 2.2: Seven Frictions in Developing a CAREC Cross-Payment System

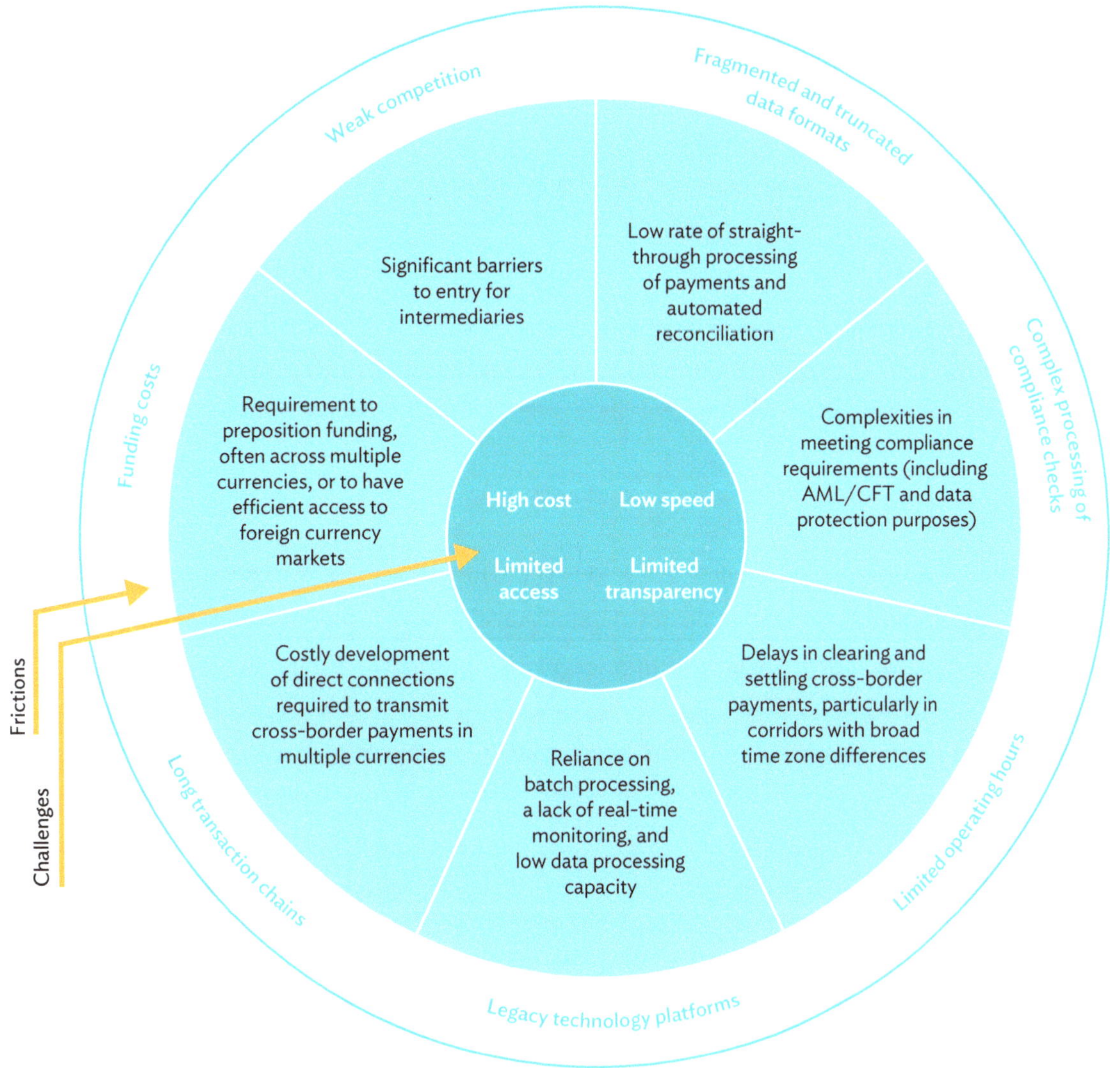

AML/CFT = anti money laundering/combating the financing of terrorism.

Source: Bank for International Settlements, Committee on Payments and Market Infrastructures. 2020. *Enhancing Cross-Border Payments: Building Blocks of a Global Roadmap*. Stage 2 Report to the G20. https://www.bis.org/cpmi/publ/d193.pdf.

[9] The G20 framework is geared not only to new fintech solutions, but also to traditional payment systems. Thus, it is aimed at both current and new systems and technologies, and in this sense, its boundaries are not coextensive with those of pure fintech considerations.

It can, therefore, be seen that all of the obstacles identified by the G20 regarding cross-border payments are almost identical to (but perhaps stated differently from) those facing CAREC fintech development.

To address these issues, in 2020, the G20 endorsed a road map setting out the responsibilities and timelines for a comprehensive G20 cross-border payments program that sought to address the four "challenge areas" shown in Figure 2.3 (Arner et al. 2022).

Figure 2.3: Challenges to Cross-Border Payments Identified by the G20

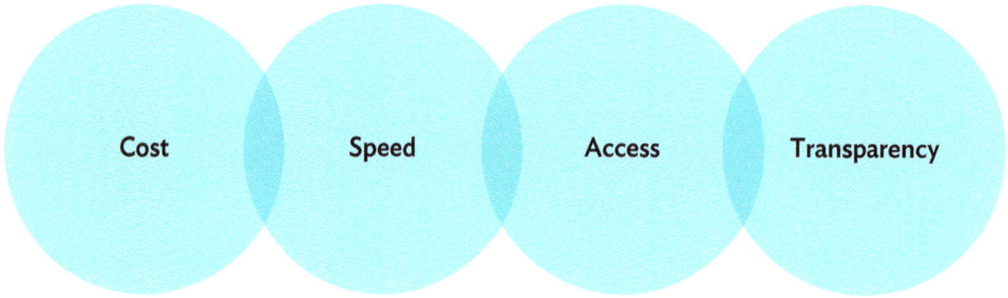

G20 = The Group of Twenty.

Source: D. Arner et al. 2022. Building Regional Payment Areas: The Single Rule Book Approach. *BIS Working Papers*. No. 1016. Bank for International Settlements. https://www.bis.org/publ/work1016.htm.

Within each challenge, the road map had specific goals:

- **cost:** reducing costs to 1% of the value of cross-border payments, and to 3% of remittances;
- **speed:** crediting the payment (wholesale, retail, remittance) within 1 hour of payment initiation;
- **access:** increasing access for financial institutions and for individual and small-business end users to every type of payment system, including for wholesale, retail, and remittance payments; and
- **transparency:** enhancing payment providers' accountability to payees and payers concerning transaction costs, currency exchange rates, conversion charges, expected time for fund delivery, payment status tracking, and terms of service.

In 2020, the Bank for International Settlements (BIS) Committee on Payments and Market Infrastructures (CPMI) submitted a Stage 2 report to the G20, as a follow-up to the Stage 1 report submitted by the Financial Stability Board (FSB) earlier that year. The Stage 2 report identified 19 building blocks and grouped them into five focus areas where joint public–private efforts could enhance cross-border payments and mitigate identified problems (BIS 2020). As illustrated in Figure 2.4, the five focus areas include

- a commitment to a joint public–private sector vision for enhancing cross-border payments and driving meaningful, coordinated change over a sustained period;
- regulatory, supervisory, and oversight framework coordination to mitigate critical challenges arising from the multijurisdictional nature of cross-border payments, by advancing consistent international rules and standards without compromising individual jurisdictional discretion or lowering standards;
- improving existing payment infrastructures and arrangements to support the requirements of the cross-border payments market, focusing on technical and operational improvements in existing domestic and international payment infrastructures that cross-border payments depend upon;

Figure 2.4: G20 Approaches to Improving Cross-Border Payment Systems

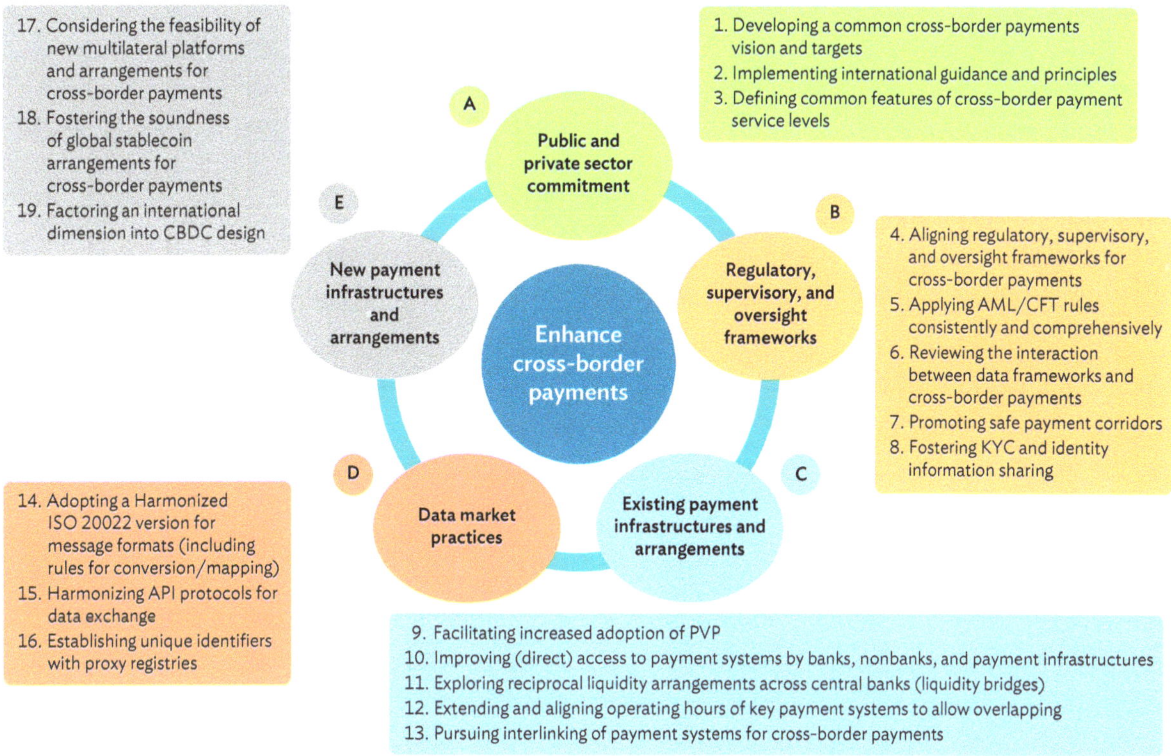

AML/CFT = anti-money laundering and combating the financing of terrorism, API = application programming interface, CBDC = central bank digital currency, G20 = The Group of Twenty, ISO = International Organization for Standardization, KYC = Know Your Customer, PVP = payment versus payment.

Source: Bank for International Settlements, Committee on Payments and Market Infrastructures. 2020. *Enhancing Cross-Border Payments: Building Blocks of a Global Roadmap*. Stage 2 Report to the G20. https://www.bis.org/cpmi/publ/d193.pdf.

- increasing data quality and straight-through processing by enhancing data and market practices, to maximize the positive impact of the technical, operational, and regulatory process changes being advanced in [certain] focus areas (with the potential to improve compliance processes and address data handling issues); and
- exploring the potential role of new payment infrastructures and arrangements, particularly the potential of new multilateral cross-border payment platforms and arrangements, and central bank digital currencies (CBDCs) to enhance cross-border payments.

Even as the CPMI report was being presented to the G20 audience, direct connections could be drawn to CAREC's challenges. Distributed ledger technology (DLT) applications are useful in this regard, given that they can be applied to three areas of cross-border payments: back-end processes, compliance, and means of payment (Chapter 4).

The question remains: Are the G20's and CPMI's rubrics applicable to CAREC's fintech efforts? The G20's focus on areas of friction applies, but they are only part of the overall challenges that CAREC faces. However, the G20's focus on cross-border payment obstacles could be incorporated into the CAREC framework.

A STRATEGIC FRAMEWORK FOR CAREC

In light of the available approaches, the challenge is to adapt those aspects of the G20 and ASEAN strategic frameworks that are applicable to the CAREC context, and then to fill in the remaining gaps. Given the findings, along with a consideration of the applicable literature, it appears that the five-pillar approach is best suited to CAREC. The details of a proposed comprehensive strategic framework for CAREC (Figure 2.1) can now be explained in greater detail for each of the five pillars.

Pillar 1: Developing Cross-Border Digital-Payment Infrastructure and Fast Payment Systems

One of the key enablers for financial integration in the CAREC region is the modernization of the domestic payments and settlements through **applications of new payment systems** and the formulation of an infrastructure for regional payments. This includes building domestic systems, as well as integrating cross-border interoperability.

In terms of CAREC's current status and promise for future progress, this may be the most important pillar. The development of **fast payment systems** (FPSs) is already a focus within CAREC, and when completed will serve as the "blood and vessels" base layer for the construction of other types of fintech products.

Developing FPSs requires (i) modernizing existing national systems, (ii) building domestic interoperability among national payment systems, and (iii) building regional payment infrastructure by building cross-border interoperability.

The road map for achieving interoperability for cross-border payment systems can be borrowed from the work of Alice Negre and Will Cook, who have created the schematic overpage (Negre and Cook 2021) that outlines the process of achieving payment system interoperability, based on fulfilling three main preconditions:

- Governance rules are in place.
- Economic incentives are balanced.
- Safe and reliable operations are designed.

The upper part of Figure 2.5 shows the benefits of improving payment system interoperability.

The recommendation of this author is to use this rubric as the road map for developing cross-border digital payment infrastructure and FPSs under Pillar 1.

The Arabian Gulf System for Financial Automated Quick Payment Transfer (AFAQ) provides a case study that is applicable to CAREC as a model for multilateral cross-border real-time gross settlement (RTGS) payment cooperation.[10] AFAQ offers a common regional platform that connects the RTGS systems of all the Gulf Cooperation Council (GCC) member states, whereby financial transfers between GCC states are

[10] AFAQ was launched 10 December 2020. The system has been operated by the Gulf Payment Company (GPC), based in Riyadh, since the GCC's Supreme Council decision to build and operate the RTGS system. The company is owned and managed by the central banks of the six GCC countries: Bahrain, Saudi Arabia, Kuwait, Qatar, Oman, and the United Arab Emirates (https://www.gulf-payments.com/en/). See Chapter 9.

executed by the end of the day, including gross settlements. It also supports cross-border multilateral net settlement instructions submitted by various regional clearing systems. AFAQ executes money transfers in the local currencies of the GCC countries and in other currencies in a short time, at a low cost for customers and dealers, and within a safe and stable environment. The AFAQ payment system adopted the latest technologies in a way that has improved efficiency and reduced dependence on financial systems and external transfer networks. Thus, an AFAQ-like solution for cross-border RTGS transactions may exist for emerging fintech markets in CAREC if the proper regulatory and protocol changes are adopted.

Figure 2.5: Road Map for Achieving Pillar 1

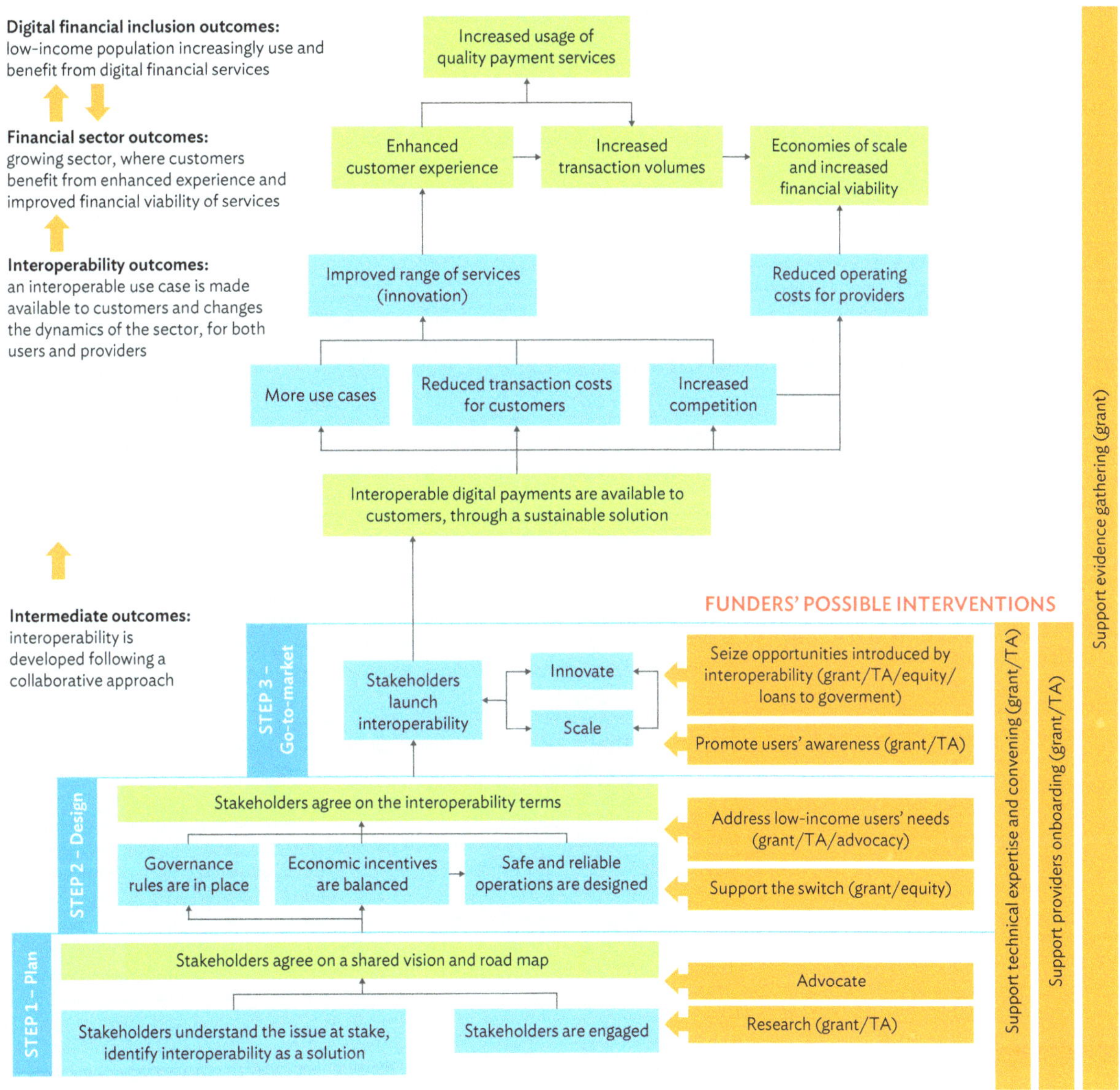

TA = technical assistance.

Source: A. Negre and W. Cook. 2021. *Interoperability in Digital Financial Services: Emerging Guidance for Funders*. Technical Note. Consultative Group to Assist the Poor (CGAP). https://www.cgap.org/sites/default/files/publications/2021_01_Technical_Note_Interoperability_Digital_Financial_Services.pdf.

Initial Policy Recommendations for CAREC Pillar 1 Deliberations

As part of the public–private dialogue recommended in this report, the participants must agree on the following key policy points:

- The regionalization approach for payment systems will ensure that (i) the proper governance framework is in place, (ii) the economic incentives offered by the public sector within each member country are balanced (do not skew development), and (iii) the overall system will possess safe and reliable operations.
    - With regard to point (i), the member countries will harmonize their laws governing payment system entry and operations.
    - With regard to point (ii), the members will compare and contrast the economic incentives (if any) currently offered by their public sectors, with the goal of harmonizing them across boundaries.
    - With regard to point (iii), the members will adopt a standardized technology to govern payment systems operations, which should be recognized, with their safety and reliability ensured.
- As a preliminary step to point (iii), the members will decide whether creating a system similar to AFAQ for all member countries would meet cross-border and regional needs.

Pillar 2: Open Banking, Finance, and Data in an Application-Programming-Interface Ecosystem

To achieve a cross-border open banking capacity within the CAREC, the elements of an application programming interface (API) ecosystem must be established. This allows data retrieval and transmission within the system participants, and its use as authorized by customers. Without it, there can be no migration of information to "sew together" the various institutions possessing customer information.

To set up an API ecosystem, CAREC will need to determine its technical standards and define its business and legal rules, so it can ensure a compatible, interoperable, and secure process for all participants. A typical API ecosystem setup also requires technical building blocks, as is shown in Figure 2.6.

Figure 2.6: Technical Building Blocks Required for an Application-Programming-Interface Ecosystem Setup

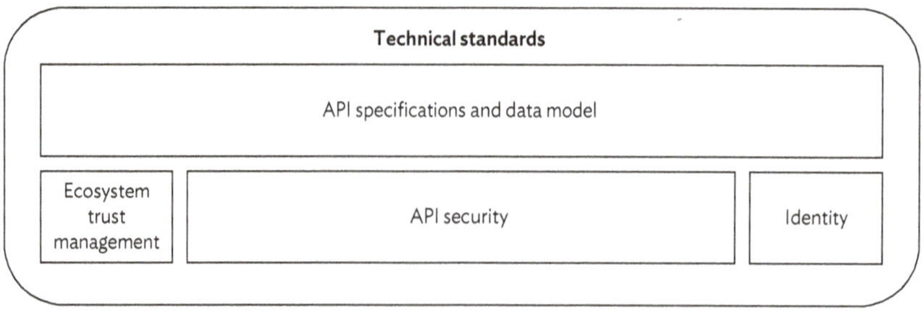

API = application programming interface.

Source: D. Postnikov. 2022. Open Banking and Open Data: Ready to Cross Borders? *Open ID*, First Editor's Draft, 29 July. https://openid.net/wordpress-content/uploads/2022/07/OIDF-Whitepaper_Open-Banking-Open-Data_1st-Editors-Draft_2022-07-29.pdf.

Within this figure, the identity protocol defines how identity information is transferred from a data provider to a data consumer with end-user consent. Most ecosystems across the globe have adopted OpenID Connect 1.0. This end-user authentication OAuth 2 extension has been an industry standard, with broad vendor support.

The API security profile defines how parties are authenticated, how the authorization and the data request and response are secured, and how message integrity is preserved. One key step the governing entity must take is to determine the standard for the API security profile.

Each ecosystem is still local or regional, and limited to its jurisdiction, but the majority of open-banking, open-finance, and open-data ecosystems have chosen the OAuth-based financial-grade API (FAPI) as their API security profile. Also, in some countries, FAPI Client-Initiated Backchannel Authentication (CIBA) is used for decoupled authentication across channels. This global adoption has allowed multiple vendors to provide support for FAPI and reduce the costs of adoption.

While most live ecosystems (e.g., Brazil, United Kingdom) operate on FAPI 1.0, others (e.g., Norway, Australia) have started with FAPI 2 implementation. FAPI 2 simplifies the security profile, especially for data consumers (clients), and adds additional common building blocks (Grant Management, Pushed Authorization Requests, and Rich Authorization Requests) to improve functionality and increase interoperability in the area of fine-grained consent capture and management.

A trust management framework is required to establish a minimum trust level among participants. How do you know whom to trust and who is allowed to do what? There is almost no standardization in this area. To date, every jurisdiction has had to develop a trust management framework on its own, and determine key issues, such as which data holders and relying parties merit access to the ecosystem, how to ensure their conformance, and how to maintain the registry of participants.

In private ecosystems, trust establishment among the participants is simple, customary, and controlled by one entity, usually the private entity itself or the entity's delegated service provider. In open banking and open finance, trust management is usually done through the central registry, typically managed by the regulator or by an entity authorized by the regulator. In some cases, especially in open finance and open data, there are multiple ecosystem regulators involved.

Given that establishing an open banking framework across the globe is a repetitive task, a new breed of vendors has appeared on the market: ecosystem providers. For example, companies like Raidiam are industrializing the setting up of open banking ecosystems, based on its experience in the United Kingdom (UK), Brazil, and other countries.

Standardized API specifications and data models provide a common understanding of the data moving between data providers and data consumers. In regard to API data models, there is a degree of standardization, as some ecosystems—such as the Berlin Group and the Open Banking Implementation Entity (OBIE)—have opted for data models based on International Organization for Standardization (ISO) 20022 (where available), but other implementations have deployed custom data models. When looking at variances among open-banking implementations, the greatest divergences are found among the standardized functional API specifications controlled by local governing bodies.

There have been only a few efforts to develop API specifications and data-model ecosystems, such as the Berlin Group (in 10 European countries) and the Financial Data Exchange (FDX), in the US and Canada. Every other jurisdiction has had to produce its own API blueprints.

With regard to the possible development of open banking within the CAREC (more specifically, of an API ecosystem to support it), the need for standardization within these areas cannot be overemphasized (Postnikov 2022). A successfully implemented API ecosystem would provide

- proven technology,
- secure operations,
- cost savings and vendor support, and
- conformance testing and certifications.

For CAREC, the adoption of open banking would be only a first step toward enhanced services by banks and other financial institutions. Figure 2.7 reflects the vision of the National Bank of Georgia (NBG) regarding how "open banking extensions" could add value to the core service. The figure also describes key benefits and challenges, lists the steps to open data, specifies the important infrastructure needed for each extension, and discusses the possibilities and benefits of the cross-country use of open data.

Achieving these open-banking and data-sharing goals will require a great deal of collaboration on their implementation and governance. At the initial stages, participant central banks or bank associations could help by creating working groups (with tasks such evaluating the current standards of their national ecosystems) and by working toward compatibility and interoperability through piloting open-banking use cases. As for the future governance of the API ecosystem, oversight structures, such as the Joint Regulatory Oversight Committee (JROC) in the UK, or the Southern African Development Community (SADC) Payment System Oversight Committee (PSOC) might prove to be useful models.

The benefits of open banking can be realized within the CAREC member countries if they possess the proper API ecosystem, as outlined in Chapter 3.

Initial Policy Recommendations for CAREC Pillar 2 Deliberations

As part of the public–private dialogue regarding regional open banking, the participants must agree to

- create compatible laws for adoption in each member country governing open banking and open finance, or amending existing laws to achieve harmonization;
- select standardized technical protocols to apply to the open banking and open finance areas, including
    - an identity protocol, perhaps using OpenID Connect 1.0;
    - a security profile, perhaps using OAuth-based FAPI and FAPI 1 or 2 CIBA;
    - a trust management framework, possibly managed by the banking regulator, and perhaps using one of the established vendors; and
    - standardized API specifications and data models; and
- with regard to technical protocols, establish a coordinating and standard-setting body modeled after the Berlin Group (EU) or FDX (US and Canada).

Figure 2.7: Extensions of Open Banking to Open Finance and Open Data

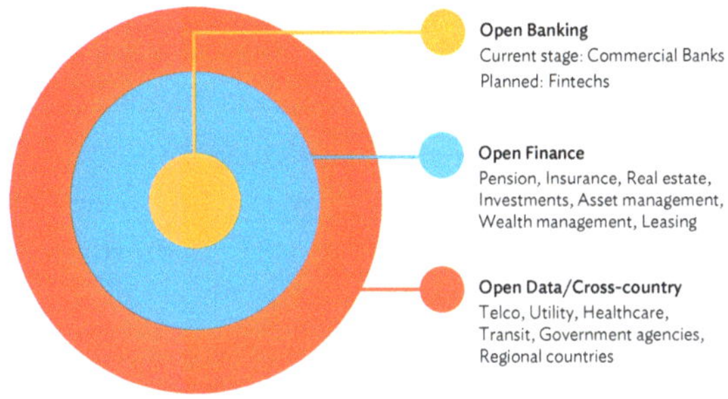

Next steps – Possible Open Banking extensions

VRPs for Sweeping
Form of payment instruction that can be set up and used to make a series of future payments

Event Notifications
Functionality to allow a TPP to receive Event Notifications

Savings Accounts
To give the Third-Party Providers access to the information on a Savings Accounts

Loan Details
To give the Third-Party Providers access to the detailed information on the consumer's Loans

Credit Limits in Balances
To give the Third-Party Providers access to the information on a Credit Line and Overdraft limits

Open Banking KPIs
- Measurement of PISP response times
- Measurement of AISP response times
- API Performance statistics

Road toward an Open Finance

Key Benefits
- More transparency for lenders and customers
- Greater data volume
- Better data control
- The centralization of services
- Wiser financial decisions
- Financial data-driven automation

Key Challenges
- Distrust of the customers stakeholder awareness
- Data safety
- Technological readiness
- Lack of legal regulation

Future plan for OF
- QR Codes Payments
- Creating a cross-cutting consumer data right
- Creating a clear liability framework
- Berlin Group Open Finance framework
- Develop an enabling infrastructure
- Broadening the license scope for third-party providers
- Letting the market build open finance infrastructure

Infrastructure that might encourage OF

Enabling Technology	Project Timeline
Cloud Computing	Cloud Computing Model Guide at the end of 2022 (by NBG)
Privacy Enhancing Technology for Data-sharing	In a research phase (within a year, by NBG)
E-KYC	Within a year (by MOESD)
CDI (Corporate Digital ID)	In a research phase (currently unknown)
AI/ML	New AI/ML tools are developed every year by the NBG
Regulatory Sandbox	Already in place

Open Data/Cross-country – Final Stage

Open Data possibilities
- Stimulate economic growth and spur innovation
- Help address societal challenges with the development of innovative solutions such as in healthcare or in transport
- Increase efficiency in public adminstrations
- Increase the transparency of government

Cross-country data benefits
- Access to the wide range of goods and services
- Enables companies to use common infrastructure to serve multiple markets

AI = artificial intelligence, AISP = account information service provider, CAREC = Central Asia Regional Economic Cooperation, CDI = corporate digital identity, eKYC = electronic Know Your Customer, ID = identification, KPI = key performance indicator, ML = machine learning, MOESD = Ministry of Economy and Sustainable Development (Georgia), NBG = National Bank of Georgia, PISP = payment initiation service provider, QR = Quick Response, TPP = third-party provider, VRPs = variable recurring payments.

Source: National Bank of Georgia. Financial Technologies Georgia for BSFH Concept. Unpublished.

Pillar 3: Facilitating Innovation

To facilitate fintech-related innovation within CAREC Pillar 3, five main tasks need to be undertaken:

- Enhance the role of existing accelerators and innovation centers in the CAREC region as platforms for communication on fintech issues and cross-agency collaboration.
- Hold fintech contests, select and cultivate international teams, and strengthen connections with the international community.
- Build a directory of start-ups and diverse communication channels to assist start-ups in fundraising and in pitch and match.
- Organize fintech exhibitions or forums to increase the visibility of fintech development in CAREC.
- Propose the establishment of co-creation platforms to assist in the promotion of fintech development-related tasks.

Fintech development-related tasks would include improving supervisory technology; building capacity; organizing contests and awards; selecting international teams; recruiting and selecting fintech image ambassadors, as well as advertising and promotion staff; and assisting in the promotion of the industry's achievements.

As noted in Chapter 4, the concept of regulatory sandboxes can be used to advance CAREC's fintech efforts in two ways.

The first way is to expand a regulatory sandbox from the domestic level to the regional level. There are two good examples. The Global Financial Innovation Network (GFIN) is an international alliance of government regulators led by the UK's regulatory body, with the aim of providing financial firms with an environment for testing cross-border solutions. The ASEAN Financial Innovation Network (AFIN) is a cloud-based marketplace for the distribution of fintech solutions to financial institutions located in multiple jurisdictions.

Regarding the second way, if a regional regulatory sandbox is agreed upon by the CAREC countries, it becomes much easier for regional fintech firms to test the viability of innovative concepts in multiple jurisdictions in the region, with the granting of licensing exemptions and conditional relief from regulatory requirements (Chapter 5).

Several case studies apply. One concerns the efforts of the United Nations Development Programme (UNDP) in Singapore. Its Global Center for Technology, Innovation and Sustainable Development has worked with other UNDP offices to bring Nordic fintech start-ups to Singapore to support cross-border collaboration and the exchange of technology and innovations, aiming to fast-track commercially scalable and sustainable impact-oriented ventures in ASEAN. Local start-ups tackling some of the world's most urgent challenges, as well as program partners, were also involved to help foster new partnerships and even stronger ties between the two regions.

Initial Policy Recommendations for CAREC Pillar 3 Deliberations

As part of the public–private dialogue regarding the facilitation of innovation, the participants need to agree to

- convert existing domestic regulatory sandboxes into regional operations, taking advantage of the benefits of compatible regulatory laws and standards to be executed under the other pillars;
- enhance the role of existing accelerators and innovation centers, including, for example by (i) organizing fintech contests and cultivating fintech international teams, (ii) building a directory of start-ups and diverse communication channels to assist start-ups in fundraising, and (iii) organizing fintech exhibitions or forums;
- establish fintech co-creation platforms to assist in the promotion of fintech development–related tasks; and
- determine how to leverage these efforts with effective capacity building; science, technology, engineering, math (STEM) education; and human capital development.

Pillar 4: Developing Fintech-Led Cross-Border E-Commerce and Trade Finance

Chapter 6 focuses on cross-border business-to-customer (B2C) e-commerce in CAREC's emerging fintech markets. It emphasizes the pivotal role that an expansion of B2C e-commerce could play in increasing consumer welfare; inclusion of micro, small, and medium-sized enterprises; and gender equity. And the chapter offers valuable insights on how to make the ASEAN experience in applying fintech to cross-border B2C e-commerce and trade finance a useful source of expertise, given suitable adaptations to the CAREC landscape.

In addition, analysis of cross-border trade finance needs in CAREC and the success thus far in meeting them can be set out clearly. Although trade and supply-chain finance underpins as much as 90% of global trade, it fails to meet the needs of small firms in developing economies that lack collateral and viable credit histories, while lenders struggle with high compliance costs for smaller transactions (Kim et al. 2021).[11]

Fintech solutions offer promising ways to address these challenges, with blockchain technology streamlining processes and improving information flows. Lending systems powered by artificial intelligence (AI) have been successful. For example, Ant Group's "310" model processes loans in minutes with low default rates, while serving millions of small businesses in the People's Republic of China (PRC). Similar innovations in digital banking across Southeast Asia, supported by the Asian Development Bank (ADB), are expanding financial access for previously underserved enterprises.

In view of these points, CAREC's focus in Pillar 4 would appear to be not only a necessary component to the overall program, but also a timely one. Consider the following:

- Unmet demand for international trade finance amounted to $1.5 trillion in 2021, and could reach $2.4 trillion by 2025 if effective solutions are not in place (Kim et al. 2021).
- The gap is $3 trillion and widening. The consulting firm Accenture estimated that demand for trade finance will reach $6.1 trillion by 2027, according to the World Bank.
- Supply chains have also come under pressure, hitting small supplier companies. The coronavirus disease (COVID-19) pandemic and Russia's war in Ukraine have restricted the movement of goods globally, compounding the problem of suppliers receiving payments on time.

Initial Policy Recommendations for CAREC Pillar 4 Deliberations

As part of the public–private dialogue regarding the development of cross-border B2C e-commerce and trade finance, the participants must agree to

- adopt, from among the existing vendors, a fintech IT solution to provide working capital to international trade entities;
- adjust the domestic laws of the CAREC countries governing B2C e-commerce and trade finance, so they are implemented in a compatible manner; and
- promote the use of digital trade insurance instruments through specially designed programs to facilitate and enable regional trade powered by fintech.[12]

Pillar 5: Fintech-Led Regionalization of CAREC Capital Markets

The levels of capital market development within the CAREC region vary widely, as pointed out in Chapter 4. One reason is the differing histories of the members' financial systems. A number of CAREC members were part of the former Soviet Union, while others were (are) part of the nonaligned group of countries. More importantly, the sizes and makeups of the members' economies vary dramatically, hence the need for their own (sustainable) local capital markets. "Scale" is an often-encountered challenge for the domestic-only capital markets in smaller economies.

[11] M. Lee et al. (2022) expand on this theme.

[12] A useful example is ADB's Trade and Supply Chain Finance Program (TSCFP). https://www.adb.org/what-we-do/trade-supply-chain-finance-program. A similar insurance program could be designed specifically for cross-border trade operations involving fintech.

Some emerging capital markets have sought to solve the "scale" problem by linking with nearby exchanges. This has followed a various models, such as (i) neighboring markets that are completely integrated under common ownership (Estonia, Latvia, and Lithuania); (ii) overlapping ownership and IT systems (Budapest, Vienna, Ljubljana, and Prague); and (iii) the cross-border routing of orders via SEE Link, which connects the Bulgaria, Macedonia, and Zagreb stock exchanges. Other models include common regulatory standards across a region where different central securities depositories (CSDs) clear and settle trades (e.g., the Central Securities Depository Regulation, mandatory for all EU members), and global custodial networks that allow foreign investors to hold assets in local markets (Clearstream and Euroclear). The applicability of these models to the emerging fintech markets in CAREC is explored in Chapter 9 and in Box 4.1.

Initial Policy Recommendations for CAREC Pillar 5 Deliberations

As part of the public–private dialogue regarding regional linkages of the member capital markets, the participants must agree to

- explore whether financial sustainability issues can serve as drivers for potential combinations of the members' CSDs, from an operational or ownership viewpoint;
- consider the use of distributed ledger technology (DLT) as an IT system for clearance, settlement, and record-keeping;
- determine the level of interest in participating in an ADB project that is considering DLT for CSDs within ASEAN+3;[13] and
- adopt a compatible legal framework for CSD operations, regardless of whether a CAREC or ASEAN+3 scope is used.

TOWARD A FINTECH ROAD MAP

The chapters that follow are integral to the story of how the foundations of a workable road map for fintech development can be developed for the CAREC region. Each helps to pin down the work needed for advancing the interoperability of services and innovations, and for identifying and setting the direction of tasks required to move toward this common goal.

The second part of the book focuses on key service areas for fintech-driven capital market development in CAREC, and on the role of policymakers in encouraging the spread of innovations that will support this, with chapters 4 and 5 detailing the conditions needed to advance innovation in CAREC capital markets. It also underscores the significant role of fintech in bolstering B2C e-commerce and in spreading its benefits (Chapter 6).

This forensic focus continues in Chapter 7, which zeros in on the strategic challenges involved in expanding and deepening the fintech ecosystem, going into greater detail on the market development challenges in Pakistan—the biggest national market in CAREC outside the PRC. The last two chapters throw the spotlight on the policy efforts needed to move the road map forward, by means of support for innovation and a strengthening of the relevant institutional arrangements, along with the promotion of emerging fintech use cases with the potential to be scaled up through regional cooperation.

[13] ASEAN+3 includes the 10 member states of the Association of Southeast Asian Nations plus the PRC, Japan, and the Republic of Korea.

Meanwhile, the next chapter describes the elements of the road map, using developments in Georgia, CAREC's smallest emerging fintech market. Through its push toward open finance, support for start-ups, outward-looking approach, and desire to be a regional fintech center, Georgia is driving ideas that could be incorporated into national strategies for building a collaborative regional fintech community.

REFERENCES

Arner, D. et al. 2022. Building Regional Payment Areas: The Single Rule Book Approach. *BIS Working Papers*. No. 1016. Bank for International Settlements. https://www.bis.org/publ/work1016.htm.

Asian Development Bank (ADB). 2021. *Technical Assistance for Financial Technology for Regional Cooperation in Central Asia Regional Economic Cooperation Countries*. https://www.adb.org/projects/55122-001/main.

———. 2022a. *Fintech Policy Tool Kit for Regulators and Policy Makers in Asia and the Pacific*. https://www.adb.org/sites/default/files/publication/780806/fintech-policy-tool-kit-regulators-policy-makers.pdf.

———. 2022b. *Recent Technological Advances in Financial Market Infrastructure in ASEAN+3: Cross-Border Settlement Infrastructure Forum*. https://www.adb.org/publications/technological-advances-financial-market-infrastructure-asean3.

———. 2022c. ADB to Develop Prototype for Cross-Border Securities Transaction System Using Blockchain. News release. 26 January. https://www.adb.org/news/adb-develop-prototype-cross-border-securities-transaction-system-using-blockchain.

Bank for International Settlements (BIS), Committee on Payments and Market Infrastructures (CPMI). 2020. *Enhancing Cross-Border Payments: Building Blocks of a Global Roadmap*. Stage 2 Report to the G20. https://www.bis.org/cpmi/publ/d193.pdf.

BIS et al. 2023. *Exploring Multilateral Platforms for Cross-Border Payments.* BIS. https://www.bis.org/cpmi/publ/d213.pdf.

Castro, L. 2024. *Fintech and B2C E-Commerce: Lessons for CAREC.* Paper prepared for the ADB Regional Workshop on FinTech Development in the CAREC Region. 21–22 February. https://estore.carecinstitute.org/wp-content/uploads/2024/02/ENG_Final-Version_FinTech_B2C-E-Commerce_LPC_ML_Feb2024.pdf.

Financial Stability Board (FSB). 2020. *Enhancing Cross-Border Payments.* Stage 1 Report to the G20. https://www.fsb.org/uploads/P090420-1.pdf.

fundsforNGOs. 2023. ADB's Digital Innovation Sandbox Program. https://www2.fundsforngos.org/information-technology/adbs-digital-innovation-sandbox-program/.

IBM Industry Academy. 2020. *Global Open Banking Landscape.* IBM Corporation. https://uploads-ssl.webflow.com/5f09129bc08517c75c0103d5/5f0a3631c085172f7502bcd3_aot-globalopenbankinglandscapev1-200621043820-compressed.pdf.

International Telecommunication Union (ITU), ITU-T Focus Group Digital Financial Services. 2016. *Payment System Oversight and Interoperability*. Focus Group Technical Report. ITU. https://www.itu.int/en/itu-t/focusgroups/dfs/documents/10_2016/itufgdfs_report%20on%20payment%20system%20oversight%20and%20interoperability.pdf.

Kim, J.-K. et al. 2021. Financial Inclusion in the CAREC Region: Promoting Fintech to Meet Underserved Needs in Trade Finance. *KDI School Working Paper Series*. No. 21-06. KDI School of Public Policy and Management. https://papers.ssrn.com/sol3/papers.cfm?abstract_id=3995027.

Lee, M. et al. 2022. Financial Inclusion in the CAREC Region: Promoting Fintech to Meet Underserved Needs in Trade Finance. In I. Abdullaev et al., eds. *COVID-19 and Economic Recovery Potential in the CAREC Region*. CAREC Institute / Asian Development Bank Institute. pp. 52–102. https://www.adb.org/sites/default/files/publication/784141/adbi-covid-19-and-economic-recovery-potential.pdf.

National Bank of Georgia. Financial Technologies Georgia for BSFH Concept. Unpublished.

Negre, A. and W. Cook. 2021. *Interoperability in Digital Financial Services: Emerging Guidance for Funders*. Technical Note. Consultative Group to Assist the Poor (CGAP). https://www.cgap.org/sites/default/files/publications/2021_01_Technical_Note_Interoperability_Digital_Financial_Services.pdf.

Postnikov, D., ed. 2022. *Open Banking and Open Data: Ready to Cross Borders? Open ID*. 1st editor's draft. https://openid.net/wordpress-content/uploads/2022/07/OIDF-Whitepaper_Open-Banking-Open-Data_1st-Editors-Draft_2022-07-29.pdf.

SWIFT. 2017. *Achieving Financial Integration in the ASEAN Region*. SWIFT Discussion Paper. https://www.swift.com/sites/default/files/documents/swift_payments_white_paper_asean_regional_financial_integration.pdf.

PART II

FINTECH-DRIVEN ROAD MAPS TO COOPERATION

3

Georgia's Vision of Collaborative Fintech

Varlam Ebanoidze

INTRODUCTION

Historically, Georgia has served as a bridge between Western and Eastern cultures, facilitating the exchange of knowledge and inventions. Trade through the Silk Road has connected Asia and Europe for about 1,500 years; and Georgia, with its strategic location on the Black Sea, has positioned itself as a center for modern financial innovation.

Georgia has many positive attributes that qualify it for a leading role in the push to develop the regulatory and technological conditions for a collaborative regional financial technology (fintech) community. It is in a strong position to promote fintech among the Central Asia Regional Economic Cooperation (CAREC) economies, with the potential to deliver innovative financial services and deepen financial inclusion. Its GMT+4 time zone and cultural affinity for the West offer distinct advantages for connecting financial markets and services.[14] Moreover, as a small economy, Georgia lacks the market capacity to scale domestically, so it is focused on promoting a model of fintech development that emphasizes international cooperation.

Fintech investors typically look for a supportive regulatory environment that encourages innovation. Therefore, the central bank, the National Bank of Georgia (NBG), tries to create regulatory frameworks that are transparent, flexible, and responsive to the needs of the fintech industry. The NBG is taking an open approach to attracting investment to fintech, including by establishing a basic infrastructure and developing a supportive environment for testing innovative ideas. Fintech investors typically look for a regulatory environment that encourages innovation.

Another strong motivation for encouraging fintech in Georgia is to use innovation to promote domestic competition and help private firms arrange financing, thereby disrupting a finance sector in which, as of 2024, banks accounted for more than 90% of the market.

The creation of fintech platforms is underpinned by a national desire to enable data democratization (breaking down institutional barriers that restrict data access and analysis), foster new business models, and draw fintech firms (foreign and domestic) into the market. In addition, fintech investors are often attracted to regions that have a thriving innovation ecosystem.

[14] "GMT" refers to Greenwich Mean Time, with +4 indicating that Georgia is 4 hours ahead.

Georgia's fintech sector development has three government champions: the NBG; the Ministry of Economy and Sustainable Development (MOESD); and the Digital Governance Agency (DGA), under the Ministry of Justice. Other institutions and agencies participate in fintech development, but the role of these three institutions is dominant.

Crucially, the NBG plays a central part in the conversation about creating a regional community for fintech development. It has developed various supervisory approaches and facilitated the creation of a basic infrastructure for fintech operations, which consists of two vectors: the financial infrastructure and the supervisory framework.

Examples of the financial infrastructure include open banking, standardized application programming interface (API), a fast payment system, and the Digital Lari project (Box 3.2). The NBG tries to lead infrastructure projects with the maximum involvement of the private sector, and operates a public–private partnership scheme.

The NBG is focused on finding the optimal balance between innovation and risk in regulatory development. It can support the growth of a collaborative regional fintech community, which can attract investment and create a vibrant community of entrepreneurs, investors, and other stakeholders. Overall, fintech investors are looking for fintech firms whose innovative products and services have been tested in a secure environment and already address real-world problems.

THE CASE FOR GEORGIA'S REGIONAL LEADERSHIP

To offer constructive suggestions on best practices regarding fintech-enabled regional cooperation,[15] it may be necessary to start with those CAREC countries that already have unique resources and capabilities needed to develop the fintech ecosystem.

Georgia has developed one of the most technologically advanced financial systems in the region. The country has attracted numerous fintech start-ups, given that it is known for having a progressive regulatory framework. Besides that, Georgia has a high level of internet penetration (approximately 80%) and a supportive ecosystem for digital innovation.

The case for Georgia taking an active role in promoting a collaborative regional fintech community focuses on the strategic vision of a forward-looking regulator, strong policies, favorable conditions for business, and the experience of Georgian banks in markets outside the country. As a regulator, the NBG supports the disruption of finance-sector entry barriers by acting as an enabler of open banking and open finance; it has also supported the development of a central bank digital currency (CBDC) as an "ecosystem" for payments. In addition, Georgia supports the testing of innovative ideas in the market, with a view to creating common standards for "cross-border regulatory sandboxes" that can reduce the time it takes to put worthwhile use cases into the hands of businesses and consumers across the region.

[15] The emerging fintech markets of CAREC are Azerbaijan, Georgia, Kazakhstan, the Kyrgyz Republic, Mongolia, Pakistan, Tajikistan, Turkmenistan, and Uzbekistan. They represent the countries for which e-commerce market data are available, excluding the dominant People's Republic of China (PRC) market. No data are available for Afghanistan. The Asian Development Bank (ADB) placed its regular assistance to Afghanistan on hold effective since 15 August 2021, and has supported the Afghan people through a special financing arrangement with United Nations agencies since 2022.

Georgia has the same goals as other CAREC economies: to enable fintech to encourage competition and to help private companies arrange financing (Figure 3.1). As noted above, banks accounted for more than 90% of Georgia's financial system in 2024, and during that year, they rejected about one-fifth of loan applications from small and medium-sized enterprises (SMEs). The main obstacles to getting bank credit include the lack of collateral (banks on average require 191% of the loan amount), lack of a credit history, difficulty in forecasting and managing risks, and the low quality of business plans. Fintech technologies, including artificial intelligence (AI) technologies developed in Georgia, have the potential to solve some of these issues.

Figure 3.1: Strengthening Fintech in the Service of Micro, Small, and Medium-Sized Enterprises

Access to finance is one of the biggest challenges for MSMEs.

Bank financing plays a crucial role in the MSME sector.

MSMEs receive a disproportionately small share of credit.

Alternative sources of finance should cover underexplored instruments and technologies.

Objective: Explore the potential of alternative financial instruments and financial technologies in Georgia.

fintech = financial technology; MSMEs = micro, small, and medium-sized enterprises.
Source: National Bank of Georgia.

Georgia's banking legislation is being harmonized with that of the European Union (EU), with the regulations concerning open banking and digital banking based on the guidelines of the European Central Bank. Also, the NBG has links to EU research resources, including association status at Horizon Europe, a research and innovation funding program with a budget of euros (€)93.5 billion for 2021–2027. In the World Bank's ranking for ease of doing business, Georgia came in seventh in 2023—after the United States (US), but before the United Kingdom (UK)—and ranked second (after New Zealand) for ease of starting a business.

Among other factors that make Georgia attractive for accelerating regional cooperation among CAREC emerging fintech economies is that its banks have built internal processes from scratch using information technology (IT) solutions, rather than being burdened with legacy systems. This has made them agile and able to absorb innovation. Banks and talented Georgian bankers already have their success stories, and have exported their "know how" to the rest of the region. TBC Bank launched the first digital bank in Uzbekistan (Chapter 8), while outside of the region, the Bank of Georgia has acquired the largest bank in Armenia. That these banks have flexibly integrated with new markets underscores the innovative nature of the technology and services they are exporting abroad along with their banking expertise. Both banks are also listed on the London Stock Exchange, which highlights their credibility. In addition, at the national level, Georgia has experience with regional cooperation through its collaboration with Armenia and Azerbaijan.

Georgia's location as a gateway between Europe and Asia also counts, as does the Government of Georgia's aspirations to make the country a major destination for fintech entrepreneurs under its Fintech Vision. In addition, the electronic commerce (e-commerce) and IT sectors in Georgia have a double-digit growth potential through 2035. In 2020, e-commerce represented just 1.1% of total retail sales, showing the scale of the potential, while information and communication technology (ICT) has been the fastest-growing industry in Georgia since 2022 (Bochorishvili, Shengelia, and Peranidze 2021; Bochorishvili, Samkurashvili, and Okropiridze 2024).

Investment in fintech needs to be encouraged since its fall from $33.4 billion in 2022 to $12.5 billion in 2023 has forced companies and investors to reassess their strategies and priorities (Thompsett 2024). Regional collaboration, therefore, becomes more important, whether for generating government backing for innovation or for doing more to attract private investors and promote the spread of innovation by emerging fintech economies in CAREC, allowing foreign firms to enter their fintech markets.

The local banking sector has developed significant talent in the past 3 decades and welcomed tech talent from elsewhere in the region. A survey in 2023 found that relocated IT professionals considered Georgia to be an attractive destination, in part because firms there were offering relatively high salaries, averaging $3,179 a month. Programming was the main field, and IT professionals were mostly employed through international companies. Of these professionals, 31% worked as freelancers, although 34% said they would consider working for a local IT company, and 45% were interested in the potential for residency status (Staske 2023). Georgia is also becoming the next favorite destination for "digital nomads."

REGIONAL FINTECH COOPERATION AND THE "MIDDLE CORRIDOR"

In the context of Georgia's promotion of a collaborative regional fintech community, discussion has focused on what the NBG refers to as "Middle Corridor" momentum. The Middle Corridor, also known as the "China–Central Asia–West Asia Economic Corridor," encompasses CAREC's emerging fintech economies. It is a multimodal land and sea transport route that starts in the People's Republic of China (PRC), crosses Central Asia and the Caspian Sea, and extends into the South Caucasus and Türkiye before reaching Europe. The Middle Corridor is part of the PRC's broader Belt and Road Initiative, which seeks to improve global trade and stimulate economic growth across Asia. As such, it offers an alternative trade route to the Russia-dominated Northern Corridor and to traditional maritime routes across the Indian Ocean. A decreased dependency on trade routes through Russia has become crucial for Azerbaijan, Georgia, and Kazakhstan because of Russia's war in Ukraine; and the Middle Corridor has received strong support from the international community.

A 2023 World Bank study predicts that by 2030, freight volumes along the Middle Corridor will triple, with travel times expected to halve. The surge in trade among Azerbaijan, Georgia, Kazakhstan, and Europe is the primary driver of this demand. In addition, modeling forecasts a 37% increase in trade among Azerbaijan, Georgia, and Kazakhstan, along with a 28% rise in trade between these nations and the EU by 2030.

A developed Middle Corridor has the potential to foster fintech growth across borders, increase trade flows, and deepen economic integration. For the corridor to achieve digitalization, arrangements for cross-border data exchange and digital infrastructure governance will be needed, matched by timely coordination and a cross-sector approach. Mutual recognition of licenses would be helpful, and could be allied with the approach embodied in the mBridge and Aperta projects for cross-border trade finance and cross-border open banking (both involving Georgia, and explored in Chapter 9).

Georgia's payment strategy involves seeking membership in the EU's Single Euro Payments Area (SEPA), while simultaneously working to establish a Middle Corridor fast payments system, which would connect Central Asian and other nations. SEPA currently enables fast, low-cost cross-border payments across 36 European countries, processing more than 40 billion transactions a year.

In the interim, Georgia has leveraged its relationship with Paysera, a digital bank that operates through its Lithuanian entity, to provide Georgian clients access to SEPA payments at significantly reduced costs—charging €7, compared with the €30 that Georgian banks typically charge for SWIFT transactions. The strategic decision to grant Paysera a digital banking license has created an effective bridge to European payment systems, though full SEPA membership would eventually extend these benefits to all Georgian banks and fintech firms.

By pursuing integration both within and outside the CAREC region, Georgia aims to create direct links to real-time gross settlement systems, potentially transforming itself into a key payments gateway between the EU and Central Asia.

The significant role that Georgia could acquire through these and other opportunities would be in line with the NBG's "Beyond Georgia" concept. This promotes the NBG, not only as a basic fintech infrastructure enabler and facilitator for finance sector disruption at home, but also as a supporter of ongoing trends in the real economy, with new fintech infrastructure motivating others within the region. Georgia organizes its thinking around this concept through a learning-by-doing philosophy—one that also encompasses support for goals such as open banking and open finance, a CBDC as an ecosystem, and a "cross-border regulatory sandbox" for fintech-enabled services. In this sense, the NBG sees regional cooperation on fintech development more as a flexible process that takes account of the sector's dynamism than as a set destination.

The NBG also recognizes that Beyond Georgia is not completely selfless: part of the goal is to build on existing national attributes and deepen Georgia's first-mover advantage in finding a niche position for promoting its fintech industry—a value proposition for creating jobs in financial services driven by the sector's development (Figure 3.2).

In other integration developments, the NBG has signed several memoranda of understanding (MOUs) for knowledge exchange with foreign authorities and other international counterparts, and has taken on a convening role in the region. In the context of open banking, examples include MOUs with the Central Bank of the Republic of Türkiye and the Korea Financial Telecommunications and Clearings Institute.

Figure 3.2: The Georgian Fintech Vision of Regional Cooperation

fintech = financial technology.
Source: National Bank of Georgia.

Regarding CBDC experiments, Georgia has signed MOUs with the Bank for International Settlements (BIS) Innovation Hub, Ripple, and Elevandi. Serving as an observer of the Innovation Hub's Project mBridge,[16] the NBG sees it as a potential model for emerging fintech economies in CAREC, providing a way for them to accelerate trade growth through a multi-CBDC platform. The NBG is set to continue implementing new regulatory policies, developing innovative fintech infrastructure, and forging international partnerships to enhance financial innovation. It also participates in Project Promissa.[17]

International collaboration is a growing and vital part of Georgia's fintech strategy, and the priority means for achieving its fintech goals (Figure 3.3). It allows firms to operate across markets and access larger markets, thereby supporting the growth of "homegrown" fintech and attracting foreign firms to the country. In addition, it capitalizes on Georgia's strengths to drive regulatory and technical harmonization, as well as policy alignment in the region, building on the active international role of the NBG and other authorities and stakeholders through priority actions. Fintech also represents an opportunity to enhance trade flows under the Middle Corridor agenda, though this role is not yet fully recognized.

[16] Project mBridge aims to develop a multi-central bank digital currency (m-CBDC) platform shared by participating central banks and commercial banks; it intends to use DLT to enable instant cross-border payments and settlements. The project is the result of extensive collaboration starting in 2021 involving the BIS Innovation Hub, the Bank of Thailand, the Central Bank of the United Arab Emirates, the Digital Currency Institute of the People's Bank of China, the Hong Kong Monetary Authority, and the Saudi Central Bank. *BIS*. 2024. Project mBridge Reached Minimum Viable Product Stage. 11 November. https://www.bis.org/about/bisih/topics/cbdc/mcbdc_bridge.htm.

[17] Project Promissa is a joint experiment of the BIS Innovation Hub Swiss Centre, the Swiss National Bank, and the World Bank that aims to build a proof of concept for a platform for digital "tokenized" promissory notes. The International Monetary Fund (IMF) is participating in the project as an observer. *BIS*. 2025. Project Promissa: Tokenisation of Promissory Notes. 23 April. https://www.bis.org/about/bisih/topics/fmis/promissa.htm.

Figure 3.3: Priority Actions for Fintech Development in Georgia

1. INSTITUTIONAL ARRANGEMENTS AND GOVERNANCE

- Establish institutional arrangements (e.g., fintech committee/ working group, and others) with operating rules and procedures.

2. INFRASTRUCTURE

- Design FPS to allow broad access for various entities and support overlay services.
- Evaluate the discharge of open banking arrangements and ensure broad stakeholders' inputs.
- Increase the independence of the working group responsible for the technical standard of Open Banking/Finance/Data.
- Assess feasibility of shared platforms applications for e.g., SMEs lending or RegTech.
- Issue the digital identity wallet in the financial sector.

3. INNOVATION SUPPORT

- Revise sandbox access criteria to enable participation of unregulated entities.
- Evolve toward a "one-stop shop" connecting sandbox entities to financial support.

4. REGULATION, OVERSIGHT, AND SUPERVISION

- Develop a staggered approach to broadening the scope of open banking.
- Issue a call for evidence on P2P lending and securities crowdfunding to guide a regulatory proposal.
- Design a regulatory road map on crypto-assets/services, with a focus on consumer/investor protection.
- Explore and operationalize AI uses for fraud detection and prevention.
- Enhance cooperation in cybersecurity, expanding supervision, and strengthening fraud management and product suitability frameworks for complex fintech products.

5. INTERNATIONAL COLLABORATION

- Promote common principles on open banking by relevant regional fora.
- Work with regional authorities for establishing a cross-border sandbox.
- Identify fintech-related enablers and actions under the Middle Corridor road map.

AI = artificial intelligence, fintech = financial technology, FPS = fast payment system, P2P = peer-to-peer, SMEs = small and medium-sized enterprises.

Source: National Bank of Georgia.

GEORGIA'S FINTECH DEVELOPMENT STRATEGY

Georgia's Fintech Development Strategy aims to provide an enabling environment and a modern infrastructure for fintech to drive responsible innovation and competition in financial services, domestically and across borders.[18] As of early 2025, the NBG had disseminated its plans, received feedback from stakeholders in the Georgian fintech ecosystem, and was working to gain government approval of the strategy.

Key Objectives

The strategy can be broken down into six objectives, of which half are distinctly ripe for inclusion in any initiative to build a collaborative regional fintech community:

- **Support Georgia's digital economy.** This aspect involves putting in place safe, reliable, fast, and convenient payment services. It entails promoting fast payments across a wide range of transaction channels and use cases, including at the point of interaction and for large-volume, recurring payment streams and third-party initiation of payments in synergy with open banking.
- **Leverage innovation for small business.** The aim is to reduce the financing gap for micro, small, and medium-sized enterprises (MSMEs) and to address the needs of underserved segments (e.g., remittance recipients). This includes promoting asset-based financing solutions and evaluating alternative financing models, as well as building upon open finance to reduce information asymmetries and improve credit decisions.

[18] Georgia's Fintech Development Strategy, described in this chapter, was prepared by the NBG's Fintech and Suptech Development Department, with support from the World Bank. A draft of the strategy was released for public consultation on 4 November 2024 (NBG 2024b).

- **Expand the fintech-driven market.** There should be increased participation by new players in the market for financial services, to foster competition. This goal builds on reforms to remove regulatory barriers by enabling access to key infrastructure and data assets, while also strengthening the competition framework in light of platform models.
- **Foster regional collaboration on fintech issues.** The goal is to promote regulatory harmonization and technical standardization, with a view to improving cross-border payments and facilitating the provision of innovative services across borders. At the same time, cooperative oversight will have to be effective.
- **Facilitate the Middle Corridor agenda.** This would be achieved by creating the enabling conditions for the provision of innovative financial services for cross-border trade and e-commerce.
- **Attract fintech solutions to Georgia.** The goal is to grow the fintech ecosystem and talent pool, raising the international profile of Georgia as a focal point for a collaborative regional fintech community.

There are three dimensions for fintech development, and they are very much interlinked: policy; infrastructure; and the ecosystem, specifically, the Beyond-Georgia fintech ecosystem (Figure 3.4). It should also be noted that there are three ways to make progress on the ecosystem, and they are related to each other: (i) fostering the principles and practices of regional collaboration, (ii) encouraging and supporting the Middle Corridor agenda, and (iii) attracting fintech solutions to Georgia. The success of Georgia's fintech strategy will depend on how well the country can facilitate innovations driven by overlapping regulatory and technological advances.

Figure 3.4: The Three Dimensions of Georgia's Fintech Development Strategy

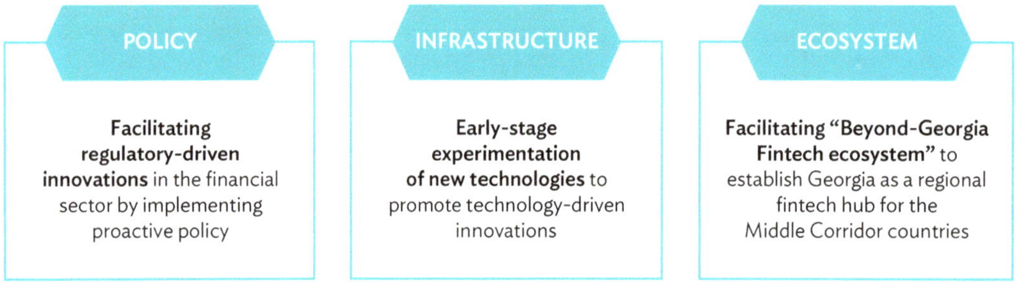

fintech = financial technology.

Source: National Bank of Georgia.

Dimension 1: Facilitating Regulatory-Driven Innovations

Georgia has sound institutions, and the public sector has shown varying degrees of support for innovation. Authorities have generally embraced a pro-innovation stance across sectors and government agencies, resulting in several initiatives that collectively benefit the fintech ecosystem.

An assessment of the legislative barriers to innovation revealed that, under Georgian legislation and NBG decrees, 25% of business models are partially or fully restrictive, while 75% could be implemented.

The regulatory framework is complicated, especially for fintech start-ups. To support fintech innovations and the fintech sector, the NBG created an Innovation Office, where regulated and unregulated entities and individuals can receive support and consultations.

Another tool established by the NBG is the Regulatory Sandbox, which helps the bank's regulated entities test innovative services and products in a controlled environment. This forms the basis of testing cross-border innovations, a priority action that is explored later in this chapter. In early 2020, the NBG started work on its open-banking project. The regional opportunity for this technological advance is explored in detail later in this chapter.

In 2019, the NBG introduced digital-bank-licensing principles to reduce entry barriers for new market players. As a result, the NBG has launched three digital banks so far, including one that enables seamless transactions with the EU economic zone and with the world's first programmable bank, based in Singapore. These banks are expected to enhance cross-border payments and accelerate growth in trade volumes.

In 2022, the NBG also officially applied for membership in SEPA to enhance Georgia's financial connectivity and position it as a crucial transactional gateway between other Middle Corridor countries and the EU. Within Georgia itself, digital payments have been a driver of financial inclusion (World Bank 2023).

In addition, the NBG is working on structuring a regulatory and legal framework for smart contracts that will facilitate the integration of delivery-versus-payment and payment-versus-payment use cases in financial and legal systems.

The next steps will be to accelerate reforms, strengthen coordination between authorities, and develop harmonized approaches to new fintech developments, with the goals of (i) formulating a cohesive response to the next wave of innovation and (ii) increasing efficiency and effectiveness. This will require establishing adequate cooperation arrangements and working methods. The fintech strategy could provide a platform for combining all relevant agencies under shared governance and a common vision.

Dimension 2: Early-Stage Experimentation with New Technologies

Georgia has several elements of a strong infrastructure foundation in place, with others in the process of being developed or upgraded. The country benefits from high levels of mobile-broadband penetration and mobile phone ownership—despite gaps in rural access—as well as nearly universal coverage of citizens by a national digital identification (ID) system. The NBG is also developing a fast payment system (FPS) that will complement and modernize Georgia's retail payment infrastructure, as well as broaden acceptance of electronic payments. The standardization of application programming interfaces (APIs), a key precondition for widespread participation in open banking, is being carried out by the Banking Association of Georgia.

Georgia sees blockchain as a technology-driven innovation in the finance sector, and the goal is to make it accessible as a public good. This is why NBG has started early-stage experimentation with a retail CBDC as a platform for powering innovations, with a focus on the value-adding functionalities of blockchain, such as programmability and smart contracts.

Initiatives on platforms for asset-based lending and supply-chain financing are in the early stages of conceptualization. Work is ongoing under the leadership of the Ministry of Justice to develop a digital identity wallet, which can be used for identity verification and authentication in financial transactions. Financial and other supporting infrastructure is a key component of the fintech strategy, as it provides a sound foundation for inclusive and sustainable digital financial services.

Dimension 3: Facilitating the "Beyond-Georgia" Fintech Ecosystem

Georgia's focus on international cooperation as a way to scale up fintech revenues explains why the NBG is participating in Project mBridge, which aims to enhance international trade and connectivity between central and commercial banks through wholesale CBDCs. Besides viewing the project as a promising opportunity to accelerate trade growth along the Middle Corridor, the NBG regards it as having the potential to address inefficiencies in current international settlement systems by eliminating intermediaries.

In addition, the NBG aims to become an observer member of the BIS Project Aperta, which seeks to reduce global financial friction and costs by connecting interoperable APIs in open-finance ecosystems (BIS 2024).

In the domestic context, Georgia has seen a sustained rise in fintech-related activity in recent years. As an indicator of the size of the market, Georgia's fintech association has around 30 members. Fintech developments in Georgia have primarily focused on payments. Several electronic money (e-money) providers are active in the market, even though they account for only a fraction of card transactions.

Banking plays a leading role as a provider of digital financial services. Banks have been instrumental in expanding access to transaction accounts and in making card payments available to the general population. Customer experience is the main way they try to outcompete one another, which has recently led to a commercial focus on developing all-inclusive banking apps and digital ecosystems. In parallel, incumbent banks are partnering with fintech firms to develop innovative products and services. Microfinance institutions are digitizing their internal operations and enabling digital channels for transactions. In the insurance field,[19] sales origination and claim management are highly digitized. By contrast, fintech developments in the capital market are almost nonexistent.

The chapter now turns to an assessment of the regulatory support for the three dimensions in the context of Georgia's objectives for fintech development—both within its domestic finance sector and across CAREC's emerging fintech economies. It then considers how this support contributes to the formulation of directions for priority actions that could promote the creation of a collaborative regional fintech community.

REGULATORY ENABLERS OF FINTECH GROWTH

Georgia has already taken steps to articulate a regulatory and supervisory approach to fintech. In particular, the NBG has issued regulations on payment service providers and open banking; developed principles for digital bank licensing; and established a registration regime for virtual asset service providers (VASPs), among others. The regulatory framework underpins digital financial services and fintech by addressing risks such as cybersecurity, data protection and privacy, and consumer protection. The NBG's scope of oversight and supervision perimeter have gradually expanded. Appropriate regulation, oversight, and supervision are an important focus when creating an environment for encouraging the growth of digital financial services and fintech while managing risks.

With regard to the active regulatory approach, the NBG has implemented several projects that need additional development and support (Figure 3.5).

[19] Many commercial banks in Georgia own insurance companies.

Figure 3.5: A Proactive Policy for Regulatory-Driven Innovation in Georgia

REGULATORY SANDBOX Allows regulated financial entities to test innovative services and products like remote ID verification, digital forex, escrow services, credit bureau platforms, and crypto-backed loans.	**OPEN BANKING/FINANCE** Introduced in 2020, open banking became available to all regulated entities by May 2023. The next strategic goal is the transition to open finance.
INNOVATION OFFICE Consults fintech organizations and startups in understanding the NBG's regulatory requirements.	**DIGITAL BANK LICENSING PRINCIPLES** Unveiled in 2019, the Digital Banking Licensing Principles paved the way for three Digital Bank license issuance by 2024.
VASP REGISTRATION REGIME Introduced in 2023, the VASP registration regime regulates VASPs operating in Georgia for AML/CFT compliance.	**SMART CONTRACTS LEGAL FRAMEWORK** In cooperation with USAID, the NBG is preparing the regulatory and legislative framework draft for smart contracts.

AML/CFT = anti-money laundering/combating the financing of terrorism, fintech = financial technology, forex = foreign exchange, ID = identification, NBG = National Bank of Georgia, USAID = United States Agency for International Development, VASP = virtual asset service provider.

Source: National Bank of Georgia.

Building on existing foundations, the fintech strategy aims to support a comprehensive and forward-looking regulatory agenda aligned with international best practices.

In 2019, the Financial and Supervisory Technologies Development Department was established to ensure that the NBG remained at the forefront of industry advancements. Then, in 2020, the NBG embarked on a series of strategic initiatives, including joining the Global Financial Innovation Network (GFIN), and establishing the Innovation Office and the NBG's Regulatory Sandbox.

The NBG has led several efforts to modernize the legal and regulatory framework. It developed principles of digital bank licensing; and in 2022, the first digital bank was licensed. Other NBG-led key regulatory reforms include an amendment to the Law on Payment Systems and Payment Services in alignment with the EU revised Payment Services Directive (PSD2), and the VASP registration regime.

The promotion of fintech development features in the NBG's 2023–2025 supervisory strategy. This strategy outlines the NBG's supervision principles and vision regarding innovation, and sets out five supervisory priorities, including the "promotion of financial innovation and development of supervisory technologies" (NBG 2024a).

As part of this priority, the NBG strategy aims to support (i) the adoption of open banking and its development, and a transition to open finance; (ii) the upgrade of the regulatory sandbox; and (iii) the facilitation of the development of suptech at the NBG.[20]

[20] Suptech is the type of technology used by financial supervisory agencies to automate and optimize supervisory tasks such as data collection, standardization, and supervision, and to improve productivity and efficiency in regulatory workflows.

In addition to the NBG, several other government agencies play a role in the digital delivery of financial services and fintech development, and in overseeing cross-cutting issues. Below are the descriptions of the most notable ones:

- The Insurance State Supervision Service is exploring and building institutional capacity for insurtech (insurance technology).
- The Ministry of Economy and Sustainable Development (MOESD) is tasked with (i) promoting access to finance within the country, elaborating on strategies and action plans, and proposing new legislation related to capital market and private saving pension reform; (ii) managing and overseeing Enterprise Georgia (the entrepreneurship development agency) and Georgia's Innovation and Technology Agency (GITA), and; (iii) participating in the elaboration and implementation of state policy in the fields of electronic communications, information technologies, and postal services, among others. The MOESD issued the SME Development Strategy of Georgia, 2021–2025 and the Capital Market Development Strategy, 2023-2028, along with its Action Plan, 2023–2024; and it is finalizing a digital strategy for the country that includes a pillar on digital financial services.
- The Digital Governance Agency (DGA), under the Ministry of Justice, leads the development of Digital Georgia. This encompasses Georgia's e-governance strategy, data exchange infrastructure (the Georgian Government Gateway "3G" platform), and the government portal (my.gov.ge), among others. Trust services and cybersecurity critical-information infrastructure for the private sector also fall under the scope of the DGA. The agency is developing a framework for open government data; this framework would articulate uniform rules and standards for data sharing between government agencies and private entities.
- The State Inspector's Service is an independent state authority that, as a legal successor to the Office of the Personal Data Protection Inspector, has been operating in Georgia since May 2019 with a mandate to oversee the implementation of the data protection legislation, handle citizens' complaints, and monitor the lawfulness of data processing in Georgia. In June 2023, the new Law of Georgia on Personal Data Protection, replacing the Data Protection Act, 2011, brought the country in line with the EU's General Data Protection Regulation (GDPR).
- The National Security Council is a consultative body directly under the Prime Minister of Georgia. Through its Department of Information and Cybersecurity, the National Security Council oversees national-level cybersecurity strategies and coordination.
- While the NBG's mandate extends to applications of competition law in the financial sector, the Georgian National Competition Authority maintains its role as competition watchdog when other sectors are involved.

Closer coordination between such government-led efforts (under the MOESD and GITA) and NBG's own mechanisms to support fintech could help leverage resources to realize the vision for the fintech ecosystem in Georgia.

This section has described the growing policy and regulatory framework for Georgia's fintech strategy, from which fintech firms can benefit. It should be noted that fintech strategy is not directly concerned with the broader innovation support, but it does depend on the presence and development of enabling infrastructure to achieve its strategic objectives. Only then can the strategy increase the range and functionality of fintech, deepen trust and acceptance, and put useful products into the hands of people throughout the emerging fintech economies in CAREC.

TECHNOLOGICAL INNOVATION: FROM OPEN BANKING TO OPEN DATA

The NBG sees itself as an "infrastructure enabler" for new entrants into the financial services sector. This focuses the discussion squarely on the approach Georgia is taking to facilitate open banking, data democratization, and infrastructure development through regulations supporting the creation of technology-driven innovation—under which the NBG could offer open banking data and APIs, procedures for easily obtaining credit information (with customer consent), and a credit registry as tools that fintech start-ups could experiment with through its regulatory sandbox. In that sense, the NBG is an enabler of the kind of efficiency that will smooth the path from open banking to a future of open finance.

Open Banking to Open Finance

Georgia has laid out a comprehensive regulatory framework for open banking. The open policy-driven approach to promoting the development of fintech firms entails the NBG implementing measures to establish a basic fintech infrastructure, remove barriers to fintech firms entering the market, and put supervisory policies in place.

The framework allows NBG to take a "bottom-up" approach that in May 2023 saw open banking extended from commercial banks to all regulated third-party providers of financial services. The potential for open banking to create disruption in Georgia has not yet fully been realized; and though Georgia already has a fully functional open banking system, an instant payment system that could provide extra momentum has yet to be launched. However, the NBG has put together an expansive list of opportunities, ranked by complexity, impact, and the customer value they would create. This value curve of use cases reflects the interests and needs of fintech firms and end users (Figure 3.6).

Figure 3.6: Open Finance Opportunities and Prioritization Matrix

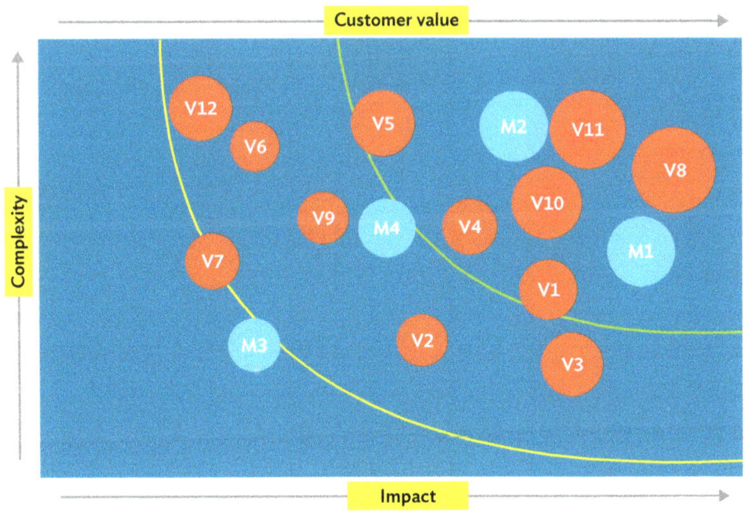

V Value-driven use cases

1. Comparison tools for provider switching
2. Online brokerages that provide financial products with the best value
3. Tailored financial offers
4. Personal finance and wealth management
5. Alternative credit scoring methods
6. Digital tools to assess the ESG profile
7. BaaP
8. KYC and digital ID services for faster customer onboarding
9. Embedded finance
10. QR code payments
11. FX exchange platforms
12. Cloud accounting and sophisticated cash flow management

M Potential marketplace

1. Retail
2. SMEs
3. Agriculture
4. Travel and transport

BaaP = Banking as a Platform; ESG = environmental, social, and governance; FX = foreign exchange; ID = identification; KYC = Know Your Customer; QR = Quick Response; SMEs = small and medium-sized enterprises.

Source: National Bank of Georgia, Fintech and Suptech Development Department.

As a part of its open finance strategy, NBG held targeted meetings with microfinance organizations, foreign-currency exchange platforms, and start-ups supported by GITA and private incubators, along with insurance companies, payment service providers, and brokerage firms. They were all provided with concrete value-added use cases and detailed information about how they could use open banking effectively.

The NBG offers interested parties the opportunity to function as a financial services platform by registering with the country's credit information bureau, CreditInfo Georgia. Registration allows fintech firms to access the data they need to offer innovative products and services. The development of better credit-scoring models by these platforms can help small and medium-sized enterprises (SMEs) gain more access to financing and reduce the cost of borrowing.

With commercial banks having added electronic Know Your Customer (eKYC) information to their API, fintech firms with a payment initiation service provider (PISP) or an account information service provider (AISP) license can use this service for customer onboarding. API offerings are mostly concentrated at the two biggest banks, the Bank of Georgia and TBC Bank. Nonbanks and fintech firms currently have little in the way of market shares or offerings, as they have yet to identify a compelling business case for engaging in open banking services.

By the end of 2024, two PISPs had been licensed: Keepz, the first nonbank financial institution (NBFI) in Georgia to receive an open banking license, in September; and Money Movers, which obtained its license in November. Six others had officially submitted applications. Similarly, QR code–enabled payment acceptance is limited.

Digital Banking Delivery

Through the development of digital banking, Georgia is seeking to foster innovative business models, enhance financial product diversity, and optimize the utilization of big data, while also reducing market entry barriers.

This model strives to cultivate a customized, user-friendly, efficient, and cost-effective digital financial ecosystem by leveraging technological infrastructure, maximizing the efficiency of cloud services, streamlining integration with tech firms, and establishing a banking model for a wholesale market service. Besides these advantages, digital banking promotes the entry of new technology players and bolsters competition within the financial sector.

Since the creation of a digital banking license in 2023, three digital banks—operated by Paysera, Pave Bank, and Hash—have obtained authorization (Figure 3.7), with a focus on specialized services for specific segments (e.g., cross-border payments, business-to-business-to-customer services).

Besides these developments, fintech has yet to make inroads into factoring, reverse factoring, or alternative financing models. However, entities engaged in crypto-asset services and activities are quite active: As of July 2024, there were 15 registered VASPs and several registration applications.

The Banking Association of Georgia is currently leading API standardization through the Berlin Group standard (NextGenPSD2). This critical step, taken to ensure adoption, will require broad stakeholder participation and inputs, as well as effective oversight.

Figure 3.7: Licensed Digital Banks in Georgia

Paysera Bank Georgia JSC functions as a digital bank centered around integration with the EU's financial system through SEPA, offering remote services to clients without physical branches.

Pave Bank Georgia JSC plans to function as a digital bank, merging financial products with digital assets and programmable accounts. The focus is on catering to technology-driven companies, with the aim of becoming the world's first programmable bank.

Hash Bank JSC plans to function as a digital bank, with a focus on guiding both traditional and technology-driven customers through a transition to a digital strategy, emphasizing personalized financial solutions, technology, and a unique user interface and experience.

EU = European Union, JSC = Joint Stock Company, SEPA = Single Euro Payments Area.

Notes:

1. Paysera, Pave, and Hash Bank operate as licensed digital banks, while others, such as TBC Bank and Bank of Georgia, operate under regular bank licenses and have good digital bank value propositions.
2. SEPA is a European Union payment-integration initiative aimed at simplifying euro-denominated bank transfers within Europe. SEPA covers not only the 27 EU countries, but also non-EU countries, including Iceland, Liechtenstein, Norway, and Switzerland. The National Bank of Georgia (NBG) applied for SEPA membership in 2022.

Source: National Bank of Georgia.

The NBG regulatory approach to open banking is to closely mirror PSD2 and European technical standards. The Open Banking Committee, set up with the Banking Association of Georgia, is responsible for developing a common open banking standard, whereas final approval and endorsement rests with the NBG. The scope of the standard has increased over time, from "basic" PSD2 services to include bulk payments and, starting in November 2024, account information extensions (savings and credit accounts) and "value-added" payment initiation services, such as variable recurring payments (Box 3.1).

As a full-service regulator covering banking, payments services, and capital markets, the NBG has the advantage of being able to take a holistic approach to financial regulation. This can help ensure that the different policy objectives of each area are balanced, and that the regulatory framework is comprehensive and consistent across the financial sector. For example, where a fintech firm is offering a product or service that could be classified as both a banking and payment service, having one regulator overseeing both areas could help ensure that the appropriate regulations and protections are in place.

That said, balancing the different policy objectives of each area can still be a challenge for any regulator, and requires careful consideration of the potential impacts of regulatory decisions on each sector.
In addition, it is important for regulators to strike a balance between promoting innovation and competition, while also ensuring that consumer protection and financial stability are not compromised by data democratization in the move toward open finance.

Box 3.1

Case Study—Adoption of Open Banking in Georgia

The experience of Georgia in creating open banking and a more organized and secure information web can serve as a case study for adoption by the emerging financial technology (fintech) economies of the Central Asia Regional Economic Cooperation (CAREC) member countries. The two figures below depict how the system in Georgia has been transformed since 2005 from a web of interrelationships into a centrally operated system. Since 2022, the body managing data exchanges, operated by the Ministry of Justice, has been the Data Governance Agency.

The Before Picture, 2005

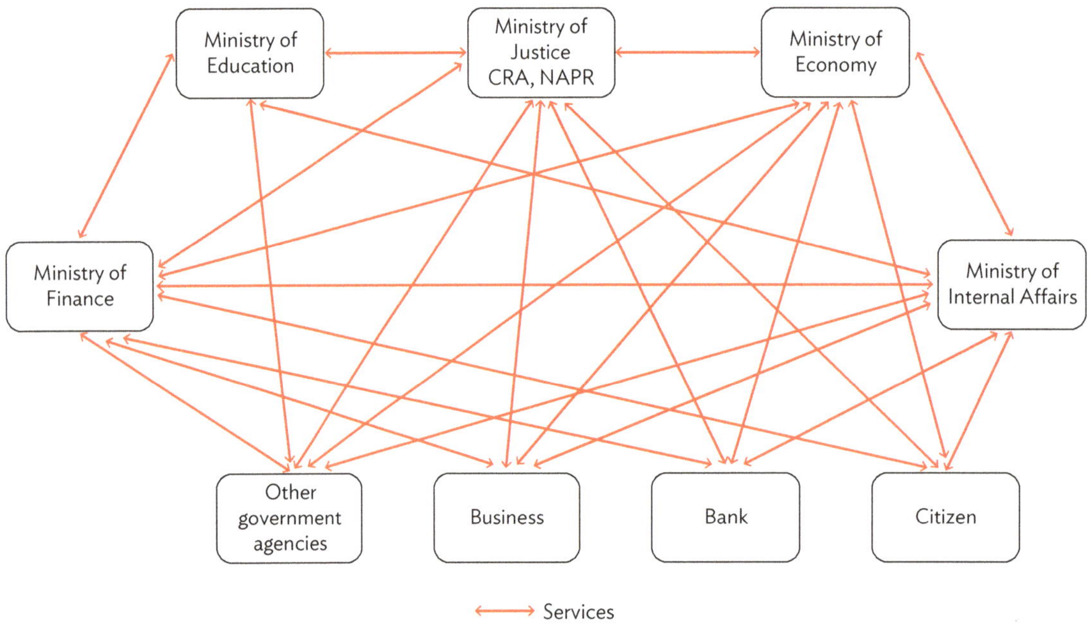

CRA = Civil Registry Agency, NAPR = National Agency of Public Registry.

Source: I. Gvenetadze. 2014. *Georgia's Successful Journey to E-Government: E-Government Development in Georgia*. Government of Georgia, Ministry of Justice.

To take advantage of this centralized system, Georgia has implemented three recent measures to capture more value. The National Bank of Georgia (NBG), which is the central bank, and the Ministry of Economy and Sustainable Development (MOESD) have

- agreed to expand from open banking to open finance;
- started an outreach effort to explain the added value of open banking and the central bank digital currency to the Georgia Innovation and Technology Agency (GITA) tech start-ups and small and medium-sized enterprises; and
- expanded open banking use cases to telecommunications, insurance, and retail by common efforts.

continued on next page

Box 3.1 *continued*

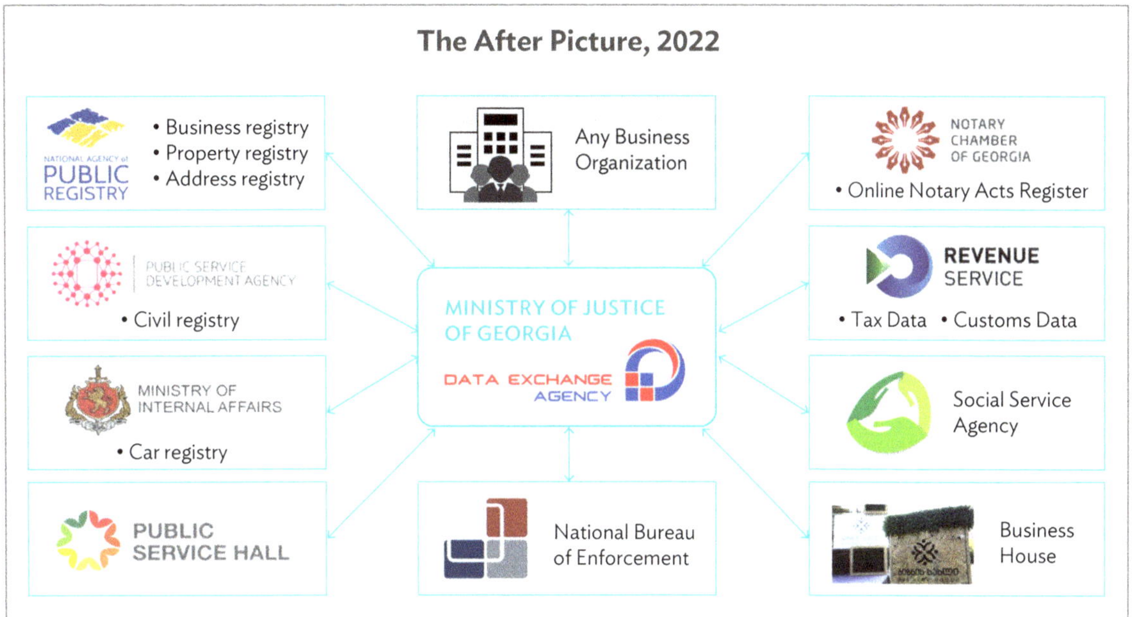

Source: N. Goderdzishvili and N. Gagnidze. 2017. *Development Path of Digital Georgia: From eGovernance Frameworks to eGovernment Initiatives*. Presentation prepared for the 3rd Asia Pacific Public Electronic Procurement Network Conference. 2–4 October.

Much of this is driven by NBG analysis of the business processes that can be opened by moving from open banking to open finance. Even at the first level of expansion, the activities would include

- account aggregation,
- budgeting,
- financial and nonfinancial product matching,
- financial coaching,
- tax calculations,
- Know Your Customer (KYC) compliance,
- peer-to-peer lending and matching,
- third-party referrals,
- savings,
- identity providers, and
- receipt management.

The economic sectors that could benefit include retail, e-commerce, agriculture, and travel and transportation. CAREC's emerging fintech economies could realize all these open banking benefits if they possess the proper application programming interface (API) ecosystem.

Source: Author.

DATA DEMOCRATIZATION

A necessary part of the development of commercial services through open finance is the expansion of open API standards and the integration of bank services, where personal data can be shared securely and standards and principles can be applied to other sectors.

Open finance must obsessively guard personal data with the highest technical protections, and ensure high standards when it is shared across systems. Hence, the NBG has formulated regulations to enforce compliance with the General Data Protection Regulation (GDPR), protecting general data through a "GDPRization" process.

In the regional context, the importance of cross-border data flows is reflected in the G20 cross-border payments road map and the recent publication of a Financial Stability Board consultative report on how to promote interoperability across data frameworks for cross-border payments (FSB 2024). Increasing the veracity of personal data in the public and private sector will require the free movement of data with the consumers' consent.

There is an opportunity to broaden the NBG open finance framework to nonfinancial entities (e.g., mobile network operators, utilities), but the commercial model is not clear. It is also unclear how the data governance framework—under the leadership of the DGA—would interact with the framework, and the extent to which entities other than government agencies might be affected. Notwithstanding these concerns, the parameters for moving toward an open finance model can be defined as an expansion of API standardization and the spread of data standards to sectors beyond banking.

Acceleration and Incubation Support

The Financial Innovation Office

The Financial Innovation Office is designed for individuals and organizations entering the fintech and regulatory-technology (regtech) markets,[21] particularly those with business models that could transform financial services. It aligns with the NBG's aim to enhance financial stability by balancing sector development with risk management, particularly for fintech start-ups. The mission is to promote responsible innovation while helping fintech start-ups understand NBG regulations. The NBG sees it as an important task to encourage innovators with fintech ideas and to support the transformation of these ideas into sustainable financial models.

The Financial Innovation Office serves as a communication bridge to fintech innovators, facilitating the transformation of innovative ideas into sustainable financial models. The technologically neutral supervisory approach taken by the office is intended to give innovators equal opportunities to demonstrate their value and improve the financial market. It does this through three main services, which it offers at no charge: (i) general information to help start-ups navigate the regulatory frameworks and public documentation essential for implementing their ideas, (ii) direct communication by providing a channel for timely responses to inquiries about supervisory approaches to fintech, and (iii) tailored feedback based on the specific needs of each innovator. These services are not intended for intermediaries, legal, or consulting firms.

21 Regtech is the use of IT to enhance regulatory monitoring, reporting, and compliance.

Georgia Innovation and Technology Agency

Government support for start-ups comes mainly through mentorship, financing, and connections with international partners of GITA.

Its goal is to create an effective system for developing innovation and technology, as well as to promote the commercialization of innovative knowledge to enable the incorporation of new technologies into all economic sectors and to create the necessary platform for innovative development. Facilitating the growth of investment capital and encouraging private businesses to increase research on the commercialization of innovations are also important parts of GITA's work.

GITA prioritizes investing in the development of infrastructure needed for innovation, opening technoparks, innovation centers, and industrial laboratories along the way. The agency is responsible for implementing the Georgia National Innovation Ecosystem (GENIE) Project, which focuses on increasing innovative activities and participation in the digital economy, including widening internet access for small businesses. GENIE's Startup Matching Grants Program provides funding to innovative start-ups, with 20 start-ups receiving up to lari (GEL)100,000 ($36,610) in funding in 2021, awarded by a committee of venture capital experts that included Silicon Valley investors. Supporting Commercialization of Scientific Projects: in collaboration with the European Union and the World Bank, GITA has also supported the commercialization of scientific projects.

Private Incubators

A major private sector incubator in Georgia is 500 Global. This US venture capital firm, with $2.3 billion in assets under management as of March 2024, invests in fast-growing technology firms in markets where technology, innovation, and capital can unlock long-term value and drive economic growth.

Through 500 Global in Eurasia, a Georgia-based accelerator and investment program, 500 Global (which is based in Palo Alto, California) joined with GITA and the Bank of Georgia to establish the 12-week 500 Global Accelerator Program in Eurasia for start-ups with the potential to scale globally. As of May 2024, it had trained 70 start-ups from 10 countries.

The mission of 500 Global is to nurture a thriving tech hub in Georgia while attracting talented entrepreneurs from neighboring countries such as Azerbaijan, Kazakhstan, and Uzbekistan; and to open up to eastern European countries and other CAREC emerging fintech economies: the Kyrgyz Republic, Tajikistan, and Turkmenistan. The program covers areas vital for transforming ideas into revenue, such as customer discovery, marketing, sales, cross-border expansion, and fundraising.

FINTECH ECOSYSTEM PARTNERSHIPS

The Regulatory Sandbox

Approaches to innovation are aimed at eliminating entry barriers for fintech firms, and at supporting the digital transformation of financial services. The concept of the regulatory sandbox is a significant catalyst for bringing private sector innovations to market, in part by enabling the testing of new products and services from regulated fintech firms within a controlled environment. In Georgia, the NBG's Regulatory Sandbox is a special legal regime and a useful tool for facilitating the safe access of fintech to new markets, but it is currently limited to supervised entities and their partners.

The main aim of the sandbox is to expand market access and help identify the need for new or updated regulations, with a view to supporting the expansion of the fintech sector.

The final phase of the regulatory laboratory entails conducting tests in the "real environment." A small number of projects are being tested on a limited number of users under NBG supervision (Table 3.1).

The NBG's Regulatory Sandbox has focused on remote-identification and ID-verification services, such as facial recognition and liveness checks and information extraction. To gain a holistic view and determine the strategic focus, the NBG initiated the Fintech Business Model Mapping project, which analyzed diverse fintech business models worldwide to understand their key value for the Georgian financial ecosystem and to determine the regulatory barriers to innovation. The study revealed that, under Georgian legislation, 9 out of 36 business models were partially or fully restrictive. Different variables were used to prioritize business models for the open-banking, open-finance, and central bank digital currency (CBDC) projects. Notably, the models are transferable, and can be upscaled by other emerging fintech economies in CAREC.

Table 3.1: Real Environment Test Cases for the Georgian Regulatory Sandbox

Organization	Project Description
JSC Credit Information Bureau, CreditInfo Georgia (ID 204470740)	CreditInfo Georgia offers an identity-provider (authentication) service based on an existing and operating service (MyCreditinfo) by introducing additional technical solutions. The main technical component of this service is Red Hat Single Sign-On, which was purchased from partner company Orient Logic Ltd. The partner company can integrate users into the MyCreditinfo system, which is needed for accessing the identity provider service. This service, which allows users to identify clients, is available for remote access by organizations that either lack the resources to implement their own identification solution or want an alternative method of identification.
LTD Kursi.ge (ID 405031040)	LTD Kursi.ge is an online currency-conversion service for individuals and legal entities. This easy-to-use service offers competitive currency conversions remotely on the website https://kursi.ge/.
LTD Credit Information Bureau, Platform Ranko (ID 406337593)	This digital platform, accessed through https://ranko.ge/, helps users to connect with credit organizations and get the best offers for their desired credit products. With the user's consent, Platform Ranko collects credit information bureau and other additional data necessary for the analysis of the user's creditworthiness, and shares it with partner lending organizations to find the best loans for the user.
LTD "Digital Platform" (ID 405449625)	"Digital Platform" gives individuals the opportunity to obtain an innovative product: a loan secured by a virtual asset.
LTD Rico Express (ID 205034639)	Rico Express is an online currency-conversion service for individuals and legal entities. The service offers currency conversion remotely, easily, and under competitive conditions through the website www.ricofx.ge.

ID = identification, JSC = Joint Stock Company, LTD = Limited.

Source: National Bank of Georgia.

A Sandbox Pivot and Open Banking

In response to market demand, NBG has pivoted the sandbox focus toward digital foreign-currency-exchange transactions, based on two new business models: (i) credit information bureau platforms, and (ii) crypto loans.

Foreign conversions in Georgia are mainly done in cash by currency exchange offices offering more competitive rates than banks or other financial institutions. Their turnover is entirely in cash, and increasing every year, from about GEL2.3 billion ($842 million) in 2020 to nearly GEL4.3 billion ($1.6 billion) in 2022. Currency exchange offices are not yet authorized to provide digital foreign-exchange-conversion services. However, digitization is encouraged to simplify the end user's experience, reduce the need for cash, promote financial inclusion, and improve anti-money laundering procedures.

Credit information bureau platforms and crypto loans are both innovative models, and were chosen because they fit the end user-oriented approach, can improve inclusion, and offer tailored financial services.

Besides the regulatory sandbox concept, the NBG has launched the first Open Banking Technical Sandbox in the region, which has allowed selected fintech and other nonbank firms, including those in the telecommunications sector, to experiment with new open banking APIs. The same approach was extended to open finance APIs in an international finance corporation-backed project, and the first was ready at the end of 2024. In collaboration with the World Bank, the NBG has also been working on implementing instant payments, which are expected to be available by the end of 2025.

The NBG's proactive digital transformation initiatives through the regulatory and technical sandboxes can be redesigned to facilitate cross-sector cooperation, taking a lead from practices in other parts of the world (Table 3.2).

Table 3.2: Redesigning the Regulatory Sandbox for Cross-Sector Cooperation

Economies	Regulated Entities	Nonregulated Entities	Regulated Entities with Nonregulated Products
Saudi Arabia	The regulated entities include SAMA-licensed innovators wishing to test a solution covered by existing SAMA permissions, or those wishing to enter SAMA's Regulatory Sandbox to test an innovative solution. Examples of firms in this category include banks, insurance companies, financial service firms, and currency exchanges.	These are unlicensed local and international fintechs and start-ups, including those developing new fintech solutions with a view to deploying them in Saudi Arabia. Nonregulated entities can take part in the regulatory sandbox by (i) partnering with a fully licensed firm or (ii) obtaining sandbox permission through a letter of application.	Regulated entities can develop nonregulated products if they are within the entities' scope of activities.

continued on next page

Table 3.2 *continued*

Economies	Regulated Entities	Nonregulated Entities	Regulated Entities with Nonregulated Products
UK	FCA-regulated financial services include firms engaged in activities that are directly regulated, or firms that are looking to help regulated firms follow the rules.	"As the UK's financial services regulator, our remit is FCA-regulated financial services. This includes firms that are doing activities that we directly regulate, or firms that are looking to help regulated firms follow our rules."	Regulated entities can develop nonregulated products if such products are within their scope of activity. In particular, all activities should be within the scope of activities regulated by the FCA.
Singapore	Regulated entities can submit an application with or without the involvement of a technology company.	This includes any firm that is looking to apply technology in an innovative way, to provide new financial services that are regulated.	The Monetary Authority of Singapore does not limit applications according to the products.
Hong Kong, China	The FSS, launched by the HKMA in 2016, allows banks and their partnering technology firms to conduct pilot trials of their fintech solutions involving a limited number of participating customers, without having to comply fully with the supervisory requirements.	Interested tech firms and their partnering banks should jointly submit a proposal and information on their trial projects to the HKMA for an assessment of "fitness for public objective."	Regulated entities can develop nonregulated products, if they are within their scope of activities.
Georgia	Regulated entities can submit an application with or without the involvement of a technology company.	Nonregulated entities are not eligible for the NBG's Regulatory Sandbox.	Regulated entities can develop nonregulated products, if they are within their scope of activities.

FCA = Financial Conduct Authority, fintech = financial technology, FSS = Fintech Supervisor Sandbox, HKMA = Hong Kong Monetary Authority, NBG = National Bank of Georgia, SAMA = Saudi Central Bank, UK = United Kingdom.
Source: National Bank of Georgia, Fintech and Suptech Development Department.

Among the next steps for developing the NBG's Regulatory Sandbox is the revision of access criteria for unregulated entities. In many economies around the world, regulatory sandboxes are open to innovative business models, products, and processes, whether regulated, unregulated, or slated for possible future regulation. Typically, the firms that apply for entry into a regulatory sandbox have already developed an offering, and wish to test its viability in the market. Authorities often apply a risk-based approach in determining the most appropriate form of regulatory support (e.g., the extent of relaxation of specific legal or regulatory requirements) to facilitate experiments in the sandbox.

Another step is to push the sandbox toward a "one-stop shop" approach that would include connecting sandbox entities with financial support. With any subsequent moves into exploring opportunities for regional cooperation, one viable option would be a niche value proposition for open banking that would feature mutual recognition of licenses among CAREC's emerging fintech economies.

Cross-Border Regulatory Sandbox Initiatives

The NBG is promoting the idea of a "cross-border regulatory sandbox" to support ongoing trends in the real economy through the use of new fintech infrastructure, and has taken a number of successful steps to realize the concept. Its efforts could motivate other emerging fintech economies to test fintech solutions in controlled environments across multiple jurisdictions. This setup would enable firms to test and scale new technologies, products, or business models in different countries simultaneously or consecutively.

The goals of a cross-border regulatory sandbox, besides offering a safe space for innovation, also include promoting cooperation among regulators from different countries, so they can harmonize their regulatory approaches and share best practices, thereby reducing regulatory hurdles for firms looking to expand their innovative solutions internationally. Another goal is to ensure that new financial products and services are tested thoroughly to protect consumers from potential risks.

Given that the cross-border sandbox is a only nascent idea in the CAREC region, the Global Financial Innovation Network (GFIN) provides an example of a cross-border regulatory sandbox, also known as the "global sandbox," that can enable firms to test and scale up new technologies, products, or business models across different countries, consecutively or concurrently, with the GFIN experiment offering coordinated responses from regulators. The first official trial, which started in October 2020, involved 35 regulators from 21 jurisdictions (GFIN 2024).

A sandbox approach might provide a temporary solution to data-related friction that can affect cross-border payments and, more broadly, the provision of financial services across borders, particularly (i) different and jurisdiction-specific data framework requirements, and (ii) outright restrictions on the flow of data across borders (e.g., data localization requirements). However, without a standing cross-border regulatory coordination arrangement, or a mechanism for transitioning from a testing to the live environment, a sandbox alone is unlikely to provide a definitive solution. Privacy-enhancing technologies and techniques have recently emerged as a potential solution for facilitating cross-border data flows while ensuring regulatory compliance.

A good example of cross-border collaboration comes from the Uzbekistan capital market sandbox. In 2024, the country's National Agency for Prospective Projects welcomed the Bank of Georgia as its inaugural participant. This meant that the Bank of Georgia was primed to serve as a conduit for large institutional investors seeking exposure to Uzbekistan's capital market (Daryo 2024).

Beyond Georgia and Into the Future

It bears emphasizing again that real world initiatives are at the heart of Georgia's efforts to build a fintech ecosystem domestically and to facilitate a collaborative regional fintech community. The NBG and its counterparts in Azerbaijan and Uzbekistan, with intermediation from the Asian Development Bank (ADB), have already had calls to explore collaboration on fintech. The Central Bank of the Republic of Uzbekistan (CBRU) and the NBG are working on a partnership for a fintech project to be developed for private sector financial institutions in Uzbekistan, and for the start of knowledge sharing between the two central banks. This partnership has already produced the following promising results:

- In 2019, Georgia's TBC Bank created its first fully digital banking platform, called "Space International." The CBRU–NBG partnership assisted the TBC Bank in building a scoring model based on data analytics. This, in turn, strengthened Space International's capacity to give micro-borrowers more access to finance and increase its outreach to women borrowers in general. Since then, the digital bank has attracted more investors, growing in size to meet latent demand. In addition to capital injections in 2021 and 2022, TBC Bank Group in 2023 joined the European Bank for Reconstruction and Development (EBRD) and the International Finance Corporation (IFC) to coinvest $28.3 million of additional capital into Space International. These injections have contributed to the further digitalization of the Uzbekistan's banking sector.

- Georgia's open-banking infrastructure and regulation sandbox may be of interest to fintech firms in the CAREC emerging fintech economies, specifically for their data-driven experiments, business model development, and other initiatives.

Taking this idea one step further toward knowledge sharing regarding the regulatory framework for open banking, there is the potential for seamless cross-border cooperation between national open banking infrastructures in future, provided that coordination on the architecture and design elements can be worked out.

Another initiative with a potential for regional cooperation is that concerning Georgia's CBDC (Box 3.2). With Georgia on the verge of launching use cases for the NBG-issued digital lari, the central bank has expressed a willingness to share its experiences, challenges, and future strategies, and to learn from its counterparts in CAREC's emerging fintech economies.

Box 3.2

Central Banks Break the Mold with Digital Currencies

The Promise and Challenges of Central Bank Digital Currencies

Central bank digital currencies (CBDCs) put governing bodies in the unusual position of having to be innovators, which tends to be outside their conservative comfort zones. However, CBDCs offer countries the option to become frontrunners in technology, something required for moving forward. The struggle to break the mold is one reason many central banks have had lengthy CBDC research phases.

Effective implementation must focus on the actual problems that CBDCs can solve. Otherwise, there is a risk of being attracted to new technologies that add no value. This situation presents a start-up dilemma: Is a CBDC a solution for nonexistent problems or for ones that have already been addressed? Is it a panic response to the rise of cryptocurrencies? And can a CBDC tackle existing issues that current infrastructure cannot resolve?

Fortunately, CBDCs offer more benefits than merely being another payment method. Even countries with advanced digital payment systems can explore additional use cases such as smart contracts and wallet programmability. Recognizing that existing financial services primarily serve the general public, the National Bank of Georgia (NBG) designed a CBDC to address specific, contextualized use cases. This approach seeks to determine whether CBDCs can solve specific problems, rather than being drawn to new technologies like a moth to a flame.

The NBG has focused on specific design features (programmability, smart contracts) and use cases (real estate transactions, cross-border payments). Its CBDC project has entered the pilot stage in partnership with Ripple. A white paper was expected to be published after the conclusion of a pilot in the in the first quarter of 2025. The NBG, in collaboration with the United States Agency for International Development (USAID), has also concluded a legal review of smart contracts.

continued on next page

Box 3.2 *continued*

Georgia does not expect to make giant strides with a CBDC, as banking services are widely used. However, the NBG aims to simplify and reduce the costs of some services. It has identified use cases that can only be realized with CBDCs. Despite extensive research, CBDCs remain a relatively new concept, and many unknowns persist.

Based on this, the NBG will proceed with a "learning-by-doing" approach, participating in global efforts to address policy and technology challenges, facilitating mutual knowledge and experience exchange, and preparing for the timely introduction of CBDCs.

Although CBDCs present a challenge, their innovation risks can be minimized without overlooking their benefits. The NBG has adopted a modular approach, breaking down CBDC initiatives into deliverables and milestones. Each completed milestone allows for the addition of new components, which can be gradually introduced to the public, ensuring adequate risk management and flexibility.

The NBG sees the potential for CBDCs to evolve beyond mere payment methods. Strategic priorities focus on use-case-by-use-case implementation. Four use cases have been identified for a limited-access pilot project to test technology capabilities and assess the practical utility of CBDCs, encouraging financial technology (fintech) firms to develop innovative solutions on this foundation.

One example is the use of smart contracts for real estate transactions. The National Agency of Public Registry is working to implement smart contracts that enable seamless ownership changes. Indeed, using CBDCs for smart contracts could eliminate intermediaries and simplify transactions. However, current technology limits automation, requiring bank reserves in multiple commercial banks for timely transactions.

Common Questions About Central Bank Digital Currencies, and the National Bank of Georgia's Responses

Will we need incentives to encourage CBDC wallet adoption?

We view a CBDC as a complement to current systems, not a replacement. Intense incentives or compulsion are unnecessary. The added value of a CBDC should encourage user uptake, aided by the gamification of popular products.

How can we balance data objectives with privacy concerns?

Privacy is crucial. We are exploring ways to balance safety and privacy, such as using Zero-Knowledge Proofs. Privacy will match or exceed current banking standards, potentially enhancing security.

What limits should wallets have for individuals and corporations?

We believe that there should be limits, especially during the early stages of a CBDC. We will study the implications before determining specific limits.

Can citizens from other countries have wallets? Is dollarization a concern?

Dollarization is a concern for developing countries. Allowing foreign citizens to use local currency could help combat this. Timely action is critical to ensure that local CBDCs have appealing features to prevent citizens from adopting external currencies.

How will cross-border payments between digital currencies be made?

Central banks must consider this in CBDC design. Establishing international standards for communication between different countries' CBDCs would facilitate cross-border transactions.

Source: Author.

Innovators Opening Doors Abroad

Notable fintech firms in Georgia have emerged from acceleration and incubation programs, and leveraged unique products to tap into markets in neighboring countries and beyond. By offering tailored digital solutions and fostering cross-border partnerships, these firms are helping to spread innovation and spur fintech growth and acceptance.

Payze and Kernel are two Georgian fintech firms that have successfully expanded internationally after receiving support from Georgia's Innovation and Technology Agency (GITA). Payze, a financial transactions platform for receiving payments online, was founded in 2020 by Giorgi Tsurtsumia and Kakha Gelashvili. It gained recognition by winning the Visa Everywhere Initiative for the Central and Eastern Europe, the Middle East and Africa in 2021. This award provided the firm with the resources and visibility needed to scale operations beyond Georgia. The firm is represented in Azerbaijan, Kazakhstan, and Uzbekistan, and serves about 1,000 companies. Besides cross-border payments, it offers multicurrency support and advanced fraud prevention (Payze n.d.).

Kernel, an invoicing automation fintech company with a platform that digitizes day-to-day operations for small businesses and freelancers, has expanded from Georgia into markets in the Philippines and India. It plans to scale into Pakistan and Nigeria and build on its range of its simple, user-friendly digital financial tools. In 2022, the company raised $30,000 through an appearance on the US television show Shark Tank, where entrepreneurs present their ideas to a panel of investors, or "sharks," who decide whether to invest in their companies (Palchynska 2022).

Payme specializes in providing digital payment solutions, and has quickly built a significant position in Georgia's fintech sector, where the transaction value of digital payments has reached about $2.9 billion a year, and is expected to grow about 25% a year through 2029 (Statista n.d.). The firm, founded in 2014, reached a significant milestone when it was acquired by TBC Bank Uzbekistan in 2019. This acquisition validated Payme's innovative approach to financial services, but also facilitated its entry into the Uzbek market, where it continues to grow. The company offers a range of services, including online payments, mobile payments, and electronic wallets (e-wallets)—all aimed at simplifying and securing transactions for both businesses and consumers (Payme n.d.).

Overall, the most successful entrepreneurial tech start-up story from Georgia so far is in the artificial intelligence (AI) domain. Pulsar AI, founded in Tbilisi in 2016, has developed an AI platform designed to enhance customer communications. Pulsar AI leverages machine-learning models and natural language processing (NLP) to enable personalized, two-way conversations with online shoppers. The platform helps clients speed up response times and improve the quality of the answers the receive, making customer interactions more efficient and engaging. In 2021, Pulsar AI was acquired by Impel AI, a Silicon Valley productivity software company that saw its products as beneficial for industries such as auto dealerships, where it can automate appointment scheduling; follow up on leads; and provide 24/7 conversational support through e-mail, text messaging, or web chats (Impel AI 2021).

GEORGIA'S NEXT STEPS TOWARD REGIONAL FINTECH COOPERATION

This chapter has laid out common principles that Georgia follows with regard to open banking. These principles could be taken further in regional forums as a first step toward cross-border interoperability. The NBG is seeking to work with other central banks and authorities in the CAREC region to explore the establishment of a cross-border sandbox and cross-border payment systems using QR codes. In the first phase, the cross-border sandbox could serve as a framework for testing innovative products and services in multiple jurisdictions participating in the framework. It would offer the possibility of making the test results visible, without prejudice to the application of country-specific sandbox rules. Online knowledge-sharing platforms could encourage the dissemination of best practices and lessons learned from regulatory sandboxes, and promote discussions on the technical, regulatory, and operational aspects of cross-border payment systems and CBDCs.

Using its position as the sole CAREC participant in Project mBridge, Georgia could utilize this experience to enhance the region's international trade potential and support connections among central banks. The NBG views mBridge as a compelling model for the region's emerging fintech economies of how to accelerate trade. The project's framework could even serve as a benchmark for evaluating each country's current capabilities and readiness to develop similar systems for improving payment infrastructures across the region. More details and examples are presented in the last chapter of this book.

As a final note, it is important to highlight Georgia's calling card for steering the regional fintech revolution: the NBG is willing to take the lead in articulating the specifics of driving regulatory and technical innovations and infrastructure development, while also identifying how to adapt the Beyond Georgia fintech ecosystem so it can function as a vital part of a collaborative regional fintech community.

REFERENCES

Bochorishvili, E., K. Samkurashvili, and M. Okropiridze. 2024. *IT Sector in Georgia*. Galt and Taggart. https://api.galtandtaggart.com/sites/default/files/2024-05/report/it-sector-in-georgia_may-2024_eng.pdf.

Bochorishvili, E., B. Shengelia, and N. Peranidze. 2021. *E-Commerce in Georgia*. Galt and Taggart. https://api.galtandtaggart.com/sites/default/files/2021-07/report/e-commerce-in-georgia_july-2021_eng.pdf.

Daryo (the Uzbek Press and Information Agency). 2024. Bank of Georgia Enters Uzbekistan's Capital Market Sandbox—NAPP [National Agency for Prospective Projects]. News release. 28 February. https://daryo.uz/en/2024/03/01/bank-of-georgia-enters-uzbekistans-capital-market-sandbox-napp.

Financial Stability Board (FSB). 2024. *Recommendations to Promote Alignment and Interoperability Across Data Frameworks Related to Cross-Border Payments*. Consultant's report.

Global Financial Innovation Network (GFIN). 2024. *GFIN One Year On Report: The Global Financial Innovation Network Reflects on Its First Year*. https://www.thegfin.com/publications/gfin-one-year-on-report.

Impel AI. 2021. Impel Acquires Pulsar AI. News release. 11 May. https://impel.ai/newsroom/impel-acquires-pulsar-ai/.

National Bank of Georgia (NBG). 2024a. *Supervisory Strategy 2023–2025*. https://nbg.gov.ge/en/page/supervisory-strategy.

———. 2024b. The National Bank of Georgia Releases the First Draft of the National Fintech Development Strategy. News release, 4 November. https://nbg.gov.ge/en/media/news/the-national-bank-of-georgia-releases-the-first-draft-of-the-national-fintech-development.

Palchynska, L. 2022. How Georgian Fintech Conquers Indian and Philippine Markets: Interview with Kernel Co-founder. *AIN*. 6 July. https://en.ain.ua/2022/07/06/interview-with-kernel-co-founder.

Payme. n.d. News (mostly in Georgian and Russian). https://payme.uz/home/news.

Payze. n.d. Unlimited Ways to Receive Online Payments. https://payze.io/en.

Staske, S. 2023. *Relocation of People from Russia and Belarus to Georgia: Results of Survey Among IT Professionals*. Policy Briefing: Georgia. German Economic Team. https://www.german-economic-team.com/wp-content/uploads/2023/03/GET_GEO_PB_01_2023_en.pdf.

Thompsett, L. 2024. The Fintech Funding Landscape: Navigating Turbulent Waters. *FinTech Magazine*. 31 October. https://fintechmagazine.com/articles/the-fintech-funding-landscape-navigating-turbulent-waters.

World Bank. 2023. Digital Payments in Georgia: Bolstering the Regulatory Environment and Developing Infrastructure for an Inclusive Future. News, Feature Story. 2 October. https://www.worldbank.org/en/news/feature/2023/10/02/digital-payments-in-georgia-bolstering-the-regulatory-environment-and-developing-infrastructure-for-an-inclusive-future.

4

A Road Map for Fintech-Led Capital Market Development

Hee-Yul Chai and Yeongseop Rhee

INTRODUCTION

Regional cooperation is important not only for creating a prosperous financial technology (fintech) ecosystem, but also because openness to the spread of technological advances and the removal of barriers to innovation will have significant impacts on the development of efficient capital markets. Market integration, initially in the real sector and eventually in the finance sector, is among key strategies for promoting economic development in many emerging economies. Market integration brings benefits while also generating new risks. Regional cooperation is thus essential for reaping the benefits and preventing the risks of integration.

This chapter sketches out a way forward for promoting Central Asia Regional Economic Cooperation's (CAREC's) capital market development through regional cooperation and fintech. A well-structured road map is needed to generate policy-relevant knowledge solutions and to implement policy suggestions, but it should account for the features specific to the region.

The first feature to consider is that CAREC countries on average have low fintech and capital market development, so it would be desirable to prepare a road map and implement development strategies step by step, rather than trying to achieve a benchmark country level all at once. In addition, the gaps among the CAREC countries in the development of fintech and capital markets are significant. Thus, while it is important to improve the development level of fintech and capital markets in the region as a whole, the road map should also be used to mitigate intraregional gaps.

Second, CAREC should simultaneously pursue capital market development and regional integration through fintech. While many countries in the region have rules and institutions for capital market development, stronger mutual recognition agreements are needed to harness the potential of fintech to deepen regional financial integration. The strategy of pursuing capital market development and regional integration at the same time is likely to have a big impact on integration and intensify the shock of structural reform. These dual shocks may be too much for some countries to withstand, and thus may require an adjustment period aligned with the strategy laid out in a road map.

The path to capturing fintech efficiencies for developing capital markets through regional cooperation becomes clear for at least two reasons: First, capital markets struggle in isolation; and second, collaboration on fintech innovation also spurs market growth.

Capital market depth (size and liquidity) and efficiency can hardly be achieved in an inward-looking national capital market. The regional integration of national capital markets would effectively contribute to improving depth and efficiency. That is why many countries in Europe, East Asia, and elsewhere have been taking steps to integrate capital markets in their regions. It is now time for the CAREC countries to seriously work on integrating their capital markets through multilevel cooperation—in institutional, regulatory, and technical areas. Many problems inherent in integrating national markets will be avoided if policymakers consider the international dimension while designing domestic market institutions and infrastructures.

The ongoing expansion of fintech in CAREC will make it more important for financial regulators to coordinate effectively with peers and countries beyond the region. Fintech companies want to work across borders, and their activities positively promote market development and integration. However, where regulations fail to keep up with these changes, regulatory arbitrage behaviors or regulatory fragmentation may arise. Regulatory and supervisory authorities must advance fintech and integrate markets while addressing the challenges of these changes. All policy efforts will require close regional and international cooperation.

In line with the focus of this book, which is to promote actionable change, this chapter lays out a clear road map and strategies for capital market development in CAREC through fintech. For the road map to demonstrate value, the question of how capital markets in the region can be developed through the practical implementation of fintech advances will have to be answered. It will also be necessary to examine the policy areas where cooperation will need to apply international standardization and best practices, institutional harmonization for market integration, and actions to minimize the negative impact of market integration on the effectiveness of regulations.

THE REGIONAL CASE FOR CAPITAL MARKET DEVELOPMENT AND INTEGRATION

Realization of Micro and Macro Benefits

The World Bank (2014) presents macro benefits and micro benefits as two broad classes of advantages of regional financial integration. External macro benefits include the following: expansion of trade and investment flows among CAREC countries for deeper integration, attraction of external investment capital to the region, diversification of trade concentration and capital exposure of CAREC countries across larger market areas, and the enhancement of the depth and width of regional financial markets through enlarged market liquidity (World Bank 2014). Internal micro benefits include the following: lower user costs for individuals, businesses, and public administrations; lower end-to-end transaction costs for financial firms; improved and broader cross-border access to financial services with faster, more reliable, and simpler transaction processes; lower financial development and operating costs for individual participating members through broader cost sharing in regional financial arrangements; and improved risk management, greater risk reduction, and stronger financial stability through a widespread utilization of legal and technical standards and best-practice risk-management designs and procedures (World Bank 2014). These benefits are not automatically guaranteed, but will instead require collective effort. Thus, regional cooperation, first of all, is needed for realizing the benefits of integration.

There are various approaches for opening capital markets to financial integration. The unilateral approach is to act independently to open financial markets, usually through a process of financial reform. The bilateral or regional approach is to effect financial opening through negotiations, such as free trade agreements among concerned countries. In the case of the multilateral approach, financial opening is implemented following multilateral negotiations.

Once a country decides to liberalize its capital markets, financial integration becomes quite a different process, depending on the nature of the approach. With a multilateral approach, negotiations take place on issues of common interest to most countries, but it is hard to reflect the specific interests and peculiarities of individual countries. Since financial integration through a multilateral approach is based on general rules, these may be appropriate for some regions, but not for others. In the bilateral or regional approach, the issues of interest are pertinent to the concerned countries in a region, and negotiations can reflect their specific characteristics, as well as the global trends addressed in the multilateral approach. The financial integration of national markets at the regional level would more effectively reflect the specific features and connectivity of regional economies, and contribute more to improving the development of the region's capital markets. That is why many regions, including Europe and East Asia, have been making region-based efforts to integrate national capital markets.

The case for regional integration of capital markets in the CAREC countries is strong. Unlike in advanced economies, capital markets in CAREC's developing and emerging market economies are limited by having only a small number of listed companies, few market participants, and low capitalization and trading volumes. Figure 4.1 shows the wide disparities in financial development among the CAREC countries.

Figure 4.1: Financial Sector Development Scores for CAREC Countries, 2006–2019
(0–1 points)

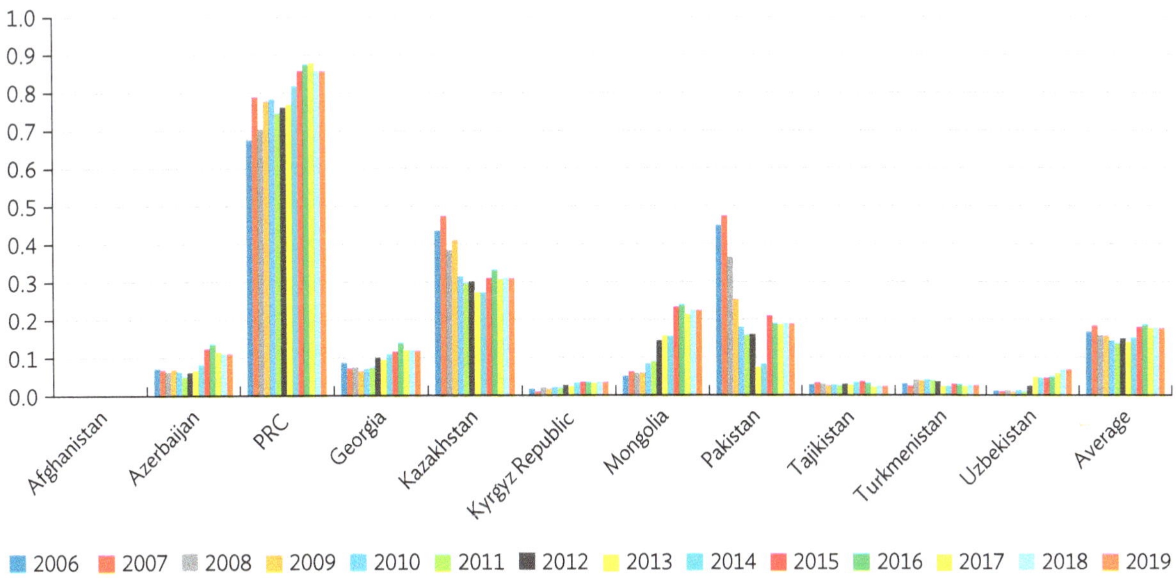

CAREC = Central Asia Regional Economic Cooperation, PRC = People's Republic of China.

Note: No data were available for Afghanistan.

Source: CAREC Institute. 2021. *CAREC Regional Integration Index: Some Progress, but New Push Required*. https://www.carecinstitute.org/wp-content/uploads/2021/02/CRII-edited-10-Feb-2021_HK3.pdf.

While the index score is over 0.8 for the People's Republic of China (PRC), it is well below 0.1 for the Kyrgyz Republic, Tajikistan, and Turkmenistan.[22] Even excluding the PRC, wide disparities exit.

Protection Against Risks and Crises

Regional cooperation is also needed to cope with the potential risks of financial integration. Aside from bringing benefits, financial integration always comes with potential problems. One risk is that a country may become more vulnerable to external shocks. These days, international capital flows are large enough to dwarf the economy of any country. Once financial markets are more open and internationally integrated, the risk from exposure to world financial markets increases, and financial integration raises the likelihood of cross-border spillovers of financial distress and contagion.

Another negative effect of financial globalization is that it can amplify a boom–bust cycle. An increase in private capital inflows provides additional liquidity that allows banks and nonbank financial intermediaries to increase lending. As the lending boom proceeds, their portfolios will get riskier. Hence, credit booms after financial globalization amplify the boom–bust effect. Financial integration may also reduce the effectiveness of monetary and fiscal policies because the international movement of capital tightly constrains domestic policymaking. If domestic policy changes make prices in financial markets more volatile, capital flows could be large enough to nullify the intended policy effects.

Four main layers of financial safety nets provide insurance against crises by mitigating their impact: the countries' own international currency reserves, bilateral swap arrangements under which central banks exchange currencies to provide liquidity to financial markets, regional financial arrangements under which countries pool their resources during a crisis to leverage financing, and global safety nets from international financial organizations such as the International Monetary Fund (IMF) or the World Bank. In the case of developing and emerging countries, international reserves and bilateral swaps are not so available, whereas crisis arrangements and global safety nets may be possible.

That said, regional peculiarities and past experiences of financial crises suggest that both regional and global arrangements are needed. Once their financial markets are open and liberalized, developing and emerging countries in the CAREC region may tend to suffer most from international financial crises, regardless of the origin (whether internal or external). The main reason these countries may become so vulnerable to capital flows is the effectiveness of financial intermediation. They have not accumulated enough capital to support regional economic activities, and will thus need to turn to international markets for finance.

Even though the region may have a high savings rate and run a current account surplus after regional financial integration, these extra savings may not be adequately and effectively channeled into regional investments in a manner conducive to ensuring monetary and financial stability, unless regional financial markets are developed enough to absorb excessive money. This problem would arise where inefficient financial systems in the region inhibit the flow of long-term savings into long-term investments.

[22] The CAREC Institute has developed the CAREC Regional Integration Index (CRII). The dimension of money and finance is measured by the following variables: the financial institutions depth index, financial markets access index, financial markets depth index, and the financial markets efficiency index. As the CAREC Institute (2021) explains, these variables are used to measure this dimension within the respective countries, rather than on a regional basis, due to data limitations for other indicators.

The underdevelopment of financial markets in the region has produced an unhappy consequence: vulnerability to external factors from the "original sin" hypothesis.[23] CAREC countries need financial cooperation to avoid this intrinsic problem and to eradicate the possibility of a crisis.

A large body of literature argues that regional cooperation is also needed because of the financial contagion that can result from a crisis. A financial shock starting in one country tends to spread to neighboring countries. Capital flows into different countries in the same region are synchronized through various channels of contagion. A crisis in one country often leads to a generalized increase in risk aversion on the part of international investors, who will try to reduce their exposure to many other markets. It is important to have a clear grasp of the potential contagion and spillover risks brought on by integrated financial markets. Once these risks are identified, strong policy cooperation at the regional level is needed to properly manage the risks.

A fundamental question regarding the implementation of collective action for self-protection against crises is whether there is a role for a regional financial arrangement separate from a global one. The experience of East Asia provides clear arguments that support the necessity of a regional financial arrangement. The first argument is that international responses are not nimble enough nor sufficient to contain a crisis, whereas a regional institution can allocate resources more efficiently than one bound by global rules and prior experiences that may not be appropriate for local circumstances (Moon and Rhee 2012).

Harmonization of Real and Financial Sector Development

Another big reason for regional cooperation is the need to harmonize development in the real and finance sectors. It is widely believed that real economic development tends to go hand in hand with financial development because financial markets enable capital to efficiently flow into the economy in ways that facilitate capital accumulation and the production of goods and services.

In the CAREC countries, however, the underdevelopment of financial systems may aggravate the risks of a financial opening, unless regional financial integration deepens. CAREC countries also need to integrate regional markets for financial development. As financial integration proceeds regionally as well as globally, the drivers of the benefits of financial globalization for developing countries are "not just the capital inflows themselves, but what comes along with the capital inflows" (Kose et al. 2006, p. 31). To enjoy the assumed benefits of financial globalization, countries must satisfy certain threshold conditions—high-quality institutions, good governance, sound macroeconomic policies, trade integration, and so on.

It is widely accepted that financial openness can be good for a country in terms of delivering benefits and reducing risks when threshold conditions are met. But there are plenty of instances when the premature opening and liberalization of financial markets, without well-prepared threshold conditions, led to a financial crisis through sudden stops or reversals of capital flows. Thus, it is desirable for the CAREC countries to work together to improve their threshold conditions, so that financial openness can in principle and reality be good for the CAREC member countries by virtue of being regionwide.

[23] Original sin is a situation in which developing and emerging market economies are not able to borrow internationally in their own currency. This term in economics literature was originally proposed by Eichengreen and Hausmann (1999).

As important as it is for regional integration, finance sector development needs to be implemented in tandem with the integration of the real sector. If financial integration is to have any meaningful implication for regional development, regional financial markets should be closely integrated, and "a regional rather than a global factor should be a main element in the integration process" (Moon and Rhee 2012, p. 101). In East Asia, the progress of regional financial integration is attributed more to the simple opening of its markets to the world than to deepening regionalism. Rhee and Chai (2006) showed the real sector in East Asia is more regionalized through intraregional trade and investment, while the finance sector is more globalized and strongly tied to the United States (US) market.

Thus, financial markets cannot adequately reflect the movements of the real economy,[24] and financial integration will not necessarily generate its assumed benefits. If the financial links are weak among countries in the region, but rather strong with external financial centers, such as those in the US and European Union (EU), then the shock of external financial markets could easily spill over into CAREC countries, especially when their markets are more open. If the financial shock is too big to be confined to the finance sector, it may consequently spread to the real sector in the region. Thus, to prevent problems caused by the disharmony between CAREC's real sector regionalization and finance sector globalization, and to reap the benefits of financial openness, regional cooperation is further needed for regional financial integration.

TASKS FOR REGIONAL FINTECH COOPERATION

Fintech can amplify both the benefits and risks of financial integration, while regional cooperation on fintech is essential for reaping further benefits and reducing the problems arising from financial integration. Since fintech not only changes the way business is done, but also the way daily lives are led (Hendershott et al. 2021), the impact that fintech innovations have on traditional financial services and products is simply described as a "disruption" of financial systems (Kagan 2024).

Finance is regarded as an industry that is vulnerable to disruption by these innovations, as financial services are intangible products, rather than tangible goods (Wikipedia 2025). As fintech develops, not only do the benefits of financial integration increase, but also the risks caused by the expanded capital flows. Concerns about fintech development and financial integration are wide-ranging. Besides cyberattacks, money laundering, and terrorist financing, they include the need to protect consumers and investors, the question as to whether regulatory and legal frameworks can be consistently applied, the possible inadequacy of the safety nets, and the potential threats to financial integrity (IMF and World Bank 2018). Like foreign banks in opened financial markets, fintech firms frequently operate beyond the scope of existing financial regulations and supervision, upsetting the competitive balance among traditional financial institutions. This regulatory gap can heighten financial stability risks, particularly as fintech's influence continues to grow (Word Bank 2020).

24 A problem due to the disharmony between real regionalization and financial globalization has been observed in the movement of exchange rates. For example, the yen depreciated against the United States (US) dollar between 2000 and 2006, before the global financial crisis, although it was the US, not Japan, that had a massive current account deficit. Similarly, the won appreciated strongly against the yen, even though the Republic of Korea was continuously running a trade deficit with Japan. Thus, financial prices can easily disrupt not only the operation of financial markets, but also the real sector (Kim and Rhee 2010).

The adoption of fintech innovations may pose transition challenges. Policy responses need to be nimble, innovative, and cooperative to capture the full benefits while minimizing problems. Policymaking also needs to strike the right balance between enabling financial innovation, on the one hand, and, on the other, addressing new and extended risks to the market, financial integrity, consumer protection, and financial stability. The right balance is important for delivering the welfare benefits of financial innovation and for ensuring that it continues to reach the underserved (IMF and World Bank 2018). Close international cooperation is needed not only to balance the efficiency and risk effects of fintech innovations, but also to avoid unnecessary friction in international transactions.

However, there are several reasons why it would be more desirable for CAREC countries to promote cooperation on fintech development at the regional level, rather than at the global level. One can think of four main categories of obstacles to financial integration through the adoption of new technologies: cultural, economic, technical, and legal.

As seen in different experiences of economic development, psychological and cultural barriers are more serious impediments to financial integration than the level of economic development. Moreover, those barriers are much larger between CAREC and other regions than they are among the CAREC countries, especially when it comes to differences in digital and financial literacy.

Also, there is an overly wide disparity in economic and financial development between the CAREC countries and advanced economies. A better approach would be to promote financial development and integration directly by adopting technologies that could help expand financial access in an appropriate manner for a developing or emerging economy, than by adopting complicated technologies that would better fit a traditional advanced financial system.

The feasibility and commercial viability of different technologies depend not only on a country's level of technical development, but also on its general infrastructure; one example is electricity, as all technological solutions depend on reliable sources of power (Davidovic et al. 2019). In contrast to advanced economies, what the CAREC countries need most to enable fintech adoption is the development of both technological and general infrastructure, which should be jointly promoted in the region.

The successful adoption of technological solutions also depends on a sound regulatory environment, with all the competitors operating under the same rules. The variations in laws and regulations throughout CAREC suggest that it would be easier and more valuable to prepare an adequate legal framework at the regional level. Moreover, as fintech activities increase in the region, intraregional cooperation among financial authorities will be key to monitoring the macro-financial risks that can emerge from unsupervised and unchecked financial activities involving fintech applications.

Regional cooperation on the adoption of fintech innovations could accelerate capital market development, and a regional approach could facilitate knowledge sharing and strengthen the integration of CAREC countries into the global financial system, especially given the potential of fintech to shift CAREC economies and financial systems toward a common development goal (ADB 2021).

Nurturing the Conditions for Regional Financial Integration

The transmission channels through which fintech leads to capital market development are summarized in Figure 4.2.[25] These channels can be broadly divided into two categories: a simple channel (channel 1 in the figure), and the integration channels (the others). The simple channel shows that fintech development will cause a "disruption" in financial systems, generating draconian changes in the industry. The integration channels indicate that fintech innovations will promote financial market integration and eventually lead to capital market development.

Within the integration channel in Figure 4.2, there are two types of subchannels through which fintech could promote regional financial integration: direct (channel 2) and indirect (channels 4 and 5). The direct channel implies that the growth of the fintech industry will encourage the cross-border flow of capital and boost the international activities of financial institutions in foreign countries, so that national financial markets could be integrated more with one another. The indirect channels imply that the innovations generated by the fintech companies will improve and strengthen the basic conditions for regional financial integration.

Figure 4.2: Transmission Channels

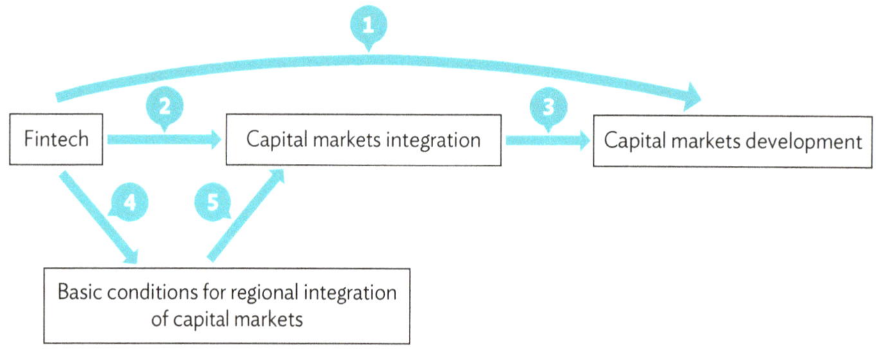

fintech = financial technology.
Source: Authors.

The experiences of the EU and other regional groupings point to three types of basic conditions for regional financial integration: technical, economic, and legal. For example, the integration policies of the EU had the explicit aim of removing barriers to cross-border activities and building the necessary technical infrastructure (Tumpel-Gugerell 2010).

First, if fintech is to make its expected contribution to financial integration and financial development, a basic requirement would be to improve the technological and general infrastructure, as they make dependable, modern, and scalable technology work. Thus, CAREC countries should invest heavily in modern information technology (IT) infrastructure throughout the region to support innovations and accelerate the adoption of more sophisticated fintech applications.

[25] All the channels operate in both directions, but in this section, the focus is only on the one-way directions shown in Figure 4.2.

Second, the literature on monetary and financial integration suggests that the following economic conditions are needed for regional integration (Moon and Rhee 2012): openness and economic interdependence, symmetry of shocks, factor mobility, and similarity of policy objectives. When a national economy is open and deeply integrated with other regional economies and when shocks to countries in the region are symmetrical, the benefits from regional integration will be high. Also, if labor mobility and capital mobility are high, it will be easy to redress macroeconomic imbalances arising from shocks, and the conditions for integration will improve. Finally, similar policy objectives will make it easier to cooperate toward a common goal, and the conditions for integration will improve due to the lower possibility of policy conflicts. To improve economic conditions, CAREC countries thus need to deepen their linkages and promote close policy cooperation.

Third, the successful adoption of technological solutions relies on a sound regulatory and market environment and on equal market treatment. Fintech projects in developing economies have succeeded when an enabling regulatory environment is supported by clearly defined roles and close collaboration (IMF 2019a). However, the legal systems differ among the CAREC countries, and the quality of regulation and supervision of the finance sector varies widely across the region, but is very low overall. CAREC countries need to upgrade their national standards first, and then harmonize the upgraded standards at the regional level.

The selection of strategies to promote fintech cooperation and regional financial integration in CAREC countries is based on two principles: flexibility and harmonization. First, flexible approaches are desirable, given the large disparities in the levels of financial and fintech development between CAREC and the advanced regions and among the CAREC countries themselves. Some experiments (e.g., sandboxes) supported by special flexible legislation would establish a controlled environment for market participants and regulators alike to test innovations. Second, regional cooperation requires the harmonization of dissimilar policies. Since fintech tends to expand and decentralize, it is necessary to find an application through which the harmonization of national policies can be promoted in the region and disparities in the levels of fintech development reduced.

In suggesting fintech cooperation strategies, the authors regroup financial service categories into three categories: fintech cooperation on payments and settlements, fintech cooperation on capital market activities, and fintech cooperation on legal systems. While fintech can have positive effects across the whole range of financial services, cross-border payments and settlements are the most relevant for CAREC countries and regional cooperation, so they warrant a closer focus.

Fintech Cooperation on Cross-Border Payments and Settlements

In CAREC countries, a high percentage of the population still relies on cash payments. Fintech could have positive effects on financial services and improve the efficiency of payment systems. Thus, fintech could help the region overcome the pervasive problem of payments, encouraging cross-border real and financial transactions and make not only domestic, but also international payments more efficient (World Bank 2020). Several technological models could improve the efficiency of payment systems, including mobile money, mobile payments, modernized interbank settlement systems, and fintech applications for cross-border payments and remittances.

Cross-border payments are especially ripe for fintech applications because there are substantial inefficiency problems that need to be solved. Cross-border payment chains from sender to recipient are composed of four segments, each with a different function (He et al. 2017): capturing, which involves interfacing directly with clients on the sending end; messaging, which involves handling payment instructions; settlement, which involves the transfer of funds across borders, usually by correspondent banks; and disbursement, which entails interfacing again, this time with clients on the receiving end. Along the chain, traditional payments are routed through many intermediate banks before they reach their destination. Thus, traditional cross-border transfers are costly, slow, cumbersome, opaque, and not transparent. The shortcomings of inefficiency and opaqueness arise from the technology, regulations, and market structure.

Impediments to cross-border payments are particularly significant in CAREC because remittances are one of the main sources of income for the region's population, as they are in other developing regions. In the Kyrgyz Republic and Tajikistan, international remittances account for more than 30% of gross domestic product (GDP), and are also high in Georgia, Pakistan, and Uzbekistan (Table 4.1). Remittances are sent home typically by using banks or money transfer operators, and these traditional channels for moving money across borders come with very high costs. According to the World Bank (2020), the average cost of remittance services in countries in Europe and Central Asia was 7.18% of the remittance value in the first quarter of 2019.[26]

Fintech applications could hugely lower the costs and enhance the transparency of international remittances in the CAREC countries. They could save around half of the costs, and combine all the costs and fees into one charge that would be easy for consumers to follow and compare across providers (World Bank 2020). Thus, fintech could work as a key instrument for overcoming the structural problems of payments and for encouraging intraregional trade and financial transactions in the region.

Table 4.1: International Remittances in the CAREC Region

	Remittance Inflows, 2023		Remittance Outflows, 2022	
Country	Amount ($ million)	Share of GDP (%)	Amount ($ million)	Share of GDP (%)
Azerbaijan	2,800	3.6	812	1.0
PRC	49,500	0.3	18,256	0.1
Georgia	4,500	15.0	290	1.2
Kazakhstan	440	0.2	2,373	1.1
Kyrgyz Republic	2,600	20.5	1,224	10.5
Mongolia	440	2.3	129	0.8
Pakistan	24,000	7.0	208	0.1
Tajikistan	5,700	48.2	224	2.1
Turkmenistan	...	...	...	...
Uzbekistan	16,100	17.8	625	0.8

... = no data available, CAREC = Central Asia Regional Economic Cooperation, GDP = gross domestic product, PRC = People's Republic of China.

Source: D. Ratha et al. 2023. Leveraging Diaspora Finances for Private Capital Mobilization. *Migration and Development Brief 39*. World Bank and KNOMAD. https://documents1.worldbank.org/curated/en/099740408142422676/pdf/IDU-84dfd61b-e135-4242-a202-3728b2e8fa86.pdf.

26 The countries covered by this World Bank report include eastern European and CAREC countries. Russia is included, but the People's Republic of China (PRC) is not.

Various ideas for fintech innovations in remittance services are underway, and the World Bank (2020) shows four examples: digital-only new entrants, white-label front-end options,[27] white-label back-end platforms,[28] and blockchain-based models. Among them, the blockchain-based models will be the most useful because distributed ledger technology (DLT) has the potential to disintermediate payments and improve efficiency by lowering the costs related to traditional intermediaries.[29]

DLT can be applied to three aspects of the cross-border payment process: back-end processes, compliance, and means of payment. First, regarding back-end processes, the many traditional players still participating in the payment process could resolve many shortcomings of cross-border payments if they were to use DLT applications. For example, SWIFT is planning DLT utilization to improve the speed, transparency, and end-to-end tracking of cross-border payments (*Economist* 2021). Traditional correspondent banks also participate in a shared permissioned DLT platform to automate the tracking of payments and optimize liquidity and risk management: Payments settled through correspondent banks hence become more transparent and traceable (He et al. 2017).

Second, DLT can be used to lower the cost of compliance when such costs are high for remittances in the CAREC region, as compliance with programs on anti-money laundering/combating the financing of terrorism (AML/CFT) is expensive, and transaction sizes tend to be small. Compliance requires banks to verify the identity of customers, monitor suspicious transactions, and provide regular reporting. The application of DLT to Know-Your-Customer (KYC) utilities and digital identity will facilitate the sharing of customer information, record keeping and data management, and the verification and tracking of payments, which can improve the detection and reporting of suspicious financial transactions. DLT will disintermediate the payment process and further lower costs related to traditional intermediaries. The elimination of intermediaries will allow for cost- and time-efficient payment systems, simplifying the processing of international transactions.

Third, DLT can be used to develop a new means of payment. Two applications of DLT for settling transactions are relevant for cross-border payments; first, a privately run hub-and-spoke payment network and, second, central bank digital currencies (CBDCs) (He et al. 2017).[30] In the first application, customers exchange fiat money for DLT-based tokens held in digital wallets through traditional means of payments or online interfaces (spokes); these tokens are then transferred across borders through the virtual currency's secure network (the hub) to the payee's digital wallets, and tokens are exchanged for foreign fiat money through spokes. In the second application, central banks develop their own digital currencies and utilize them as a novel means of payment. It is recommended that CAREC countries investigate the design and scope of CBDCs, taking into account their own national situations. When CAREC countries explore the use of national CBDCs, they will need to select a shared design among various alternatives, as a way to promote regional integration.

27 "White-label" refers to services in which a specialized provider offers the service and other companies use the service, often through outsourcing arrangements and under their own brands.

28 For white-label back-end platforms, the companies establish banking partnerships and linkages across several countries, and the link platform is offered to other banks and smaller money transfer operators in CAREC countries where they do not have a direct distribution network (World Bank 2020).

29 DLT applications for cross-border payment systems could also resolve the interoperability problem. Interoperability allows customers to transact outside the network created by their own financial service provider. In the absence of interoperability, customers must go through complicated and costly processes when transacting with users of different service providers. DLT application could easily satisfy one of three key elements for the success of an interoperable system: an operational model, including the technology infrastructure, that safely and reliably connects providers. For more discussion on interoperability issues, see Negre and Cook (2021).

30 For a more detailed explanation of the applications of DLT as a means of payment, refer to He et al. (2017, pp. 24–27).

To improve the channel of cross-border payments and remittances, CAREC countries should ideally focus more on two areas: the back-end process and compliance. And they should launch a CAREC payment and settlement system as part of their regional trade agreement,[31] so that the region's many systems can work better together. Developing a regionally integrated payment system would bring huge benefits. Specifically, digitizing clearing arrangements could reduce transaction times; disintermediation could lower the cost of doing business for financial institutions; a common protocol for electronic transfers would make it easier to integrate innovations into common systems across the region; and an integrated payment system could point the way toward a low-cost, efficient real-time gross settlement system for the region.[32]

Fintech Cooperation on Capital Market Activities

Regional cooperation on fintech can also be promoted as a way to develop regional capital markets. This can be achieved through strategies for improving cooperation on financial services other than payments and settlements. A few such strategies are outlined below.

Identity Verification

Fintech solutions such as digital identifications (IDs) can be used to facilitate the identification process, enhance due diligence when making loans, and improve access to financial services by cutting down on paperwork. Traditional identification systems require the submission of reams of paper documents and long due-diligence times, which is inefficient for both customers and financial institutions. CAREC's huge population has trouble accessing financial services because proper identity documentation is lacking. Digital IDs could be a low-cost alternative for validating customer identity and accessing financial services, which would also improve financial inclusion. Digital ID verification enables CAREC countries to build national digital ID systems into financial products and applications, ensuring that banks and digital finance providers "comply with identification requirements" (Davidovic et al. 2019, p. 8). If CAREC can establish a well-designed and robust digital ID system through fintech cooperation, these benefits will easily expand throughout the region. A robust digital ID system could also pave the way for sophisticated regional credit scoring and information sharing.

Credit Scoring and Information Sharing

The lack of information about creditworthiness is one of the most serious impediments to financial market development in the CAREC countries. It needs to be addressed as soon as possible to improve financial services. The absence of high-quality credit information about customers obstructs due diligence and lending decisions, increasing financial institutions' exposure to risks, and reducing lending capacity. Banks in the CAREC countries, therefore, often rely on government-guaranteed loan programs to make lending decisions, but these programs underestimate credit risk and hinder the lenders' credit-assessment and risk-management skills. Fintech solutions can encourage the collection and sharing of consumer financial information and behavior, and thus underpin the development of national and regional credit bureaus and registries.

---

[31] For an account of the issues surrounding the development of a CAREC regional trade agreement, refer to CAREC Institute and ADB (2019).

[32] S. Davidovic et al. (2019) emphasizes that regional integration of payment system will also be beneficial for both financial sector development and regional trade. "Developing the capacity for real-time gross settlement is an opportunity to improve the existing Fintech infrastructure through the design and building of systems that facilitate regional integration and could complement other Fintech developments."

Data on customer behavior and payment history from traditional and alternative sources, such as social media and mobile phones, could be consolidated into a single database; digital financial profiles could be developed based on this data, and then used for credit modeling purposes. By employing DLT, fintech solutions can help financial institutions build consumer data protection into their products and services.

Fintech solutions for credit scoring and information sharing will provide the basic building blocks for a regional approach to institution building. The ability to develop digital financial profiles using data from various sources will support financial stability and market efficiency at the regional level. Financial institutions can draw on credit reporting systems to screen borrowers and monitor risk profiles across the region. It would be possible for financial regulators to access credit information to improve their understanding of interconnected credit risks and to conduct their national and regional oversight functions.

Trading Systems

Cross-border linkages between stock exchanges have traditionally been made through the cross-listing of securities traded in national exchanges, an arrangement that does not encourage cross-border investment. More sophisticated forms of regional and cross-regional integration among exchanges have emerged since the 1990s. Fintech applications can be applied to the integration of capital markets in CAREC, including through the integration of the trading platforms of national exchanges. There are two possible arrangements. The symmetric arrangement links the trading systems of exchanges in CAREC countries bilaterally through a telecommunications network, but this does not operate on a common platform. In the hub–spoke arrangement, national exchanges are linked based on a central operating facility. It would be desirable for CAREC countries to start with bilateral linkages, move to hub–spoke linkages, and eventually integrate their trading systems into a common platform for settling domestic and cross-border transactions (Box 4.1).

Institutional Advances for Fintech Cooperation

To enhance regional cooperation in fintech, an institution to lead and promote solutions needs to be established. CAREC countries could start with a fintech policy forum managed by a secretariat as a necessary focal point.[33] This would function as a channel for sharing important information and would contribute to regional cooperation through regular meetings and new initiatives for regional integration. The next step would be to set up a financial committee to help facilitate policy coordination and cooperation, including for fintech applications.

These bodies could offer a dedicated point of contact and support for fintech-related issues. They could also help firms to identify opportunities for fintech innovation, provide useful guidance on how innovations could meet regulation requirements, and promote cooperation between public regulators and private innovators. To effectively support fintech cooperation, these bodies would require staff and executive support with technical competency.

As regional integration advances, it could be a new catalyst for development and prosperity, not only for the region, but also for neighboring regions, because the potential for infrastructure development investment in CAREC is huge.

[33] The European Banking Authority (EBA) launched its own Fintech Knowledge Hub to support its fintech initiatives, and the European Commission launched the European Forum for Innovation Facilitators, with a view to improving cooperation and coordination among national regulatory bodies in support of the region's growing fintech economy (World Bank 2020).

Box 4.1

Cross-Border Clearing and Settlement Linkages in Asia and the Pacific

The Cross-Border Settlement Infrastructure Forum (CBSIF), under the Asian Development Bank (ADB), published a report in 2022 that proposed a way to directly link the settlement systems of central banks with central securities depositories (CSDs). Currently, cross-border transactions of securities are processed by custodians and banking networks, a situation that is beset with difficulties such as time lags between trade and delivery and a risk of settlement. The CBSIF, which has central banks and CSDs as members, initiated a CSD–real-time gross settlement (RTGS) linkage. Through this linkage between national CSDs and individual central bank RTGS systems, many problems associated with the current system of cross-border transactions were addressed, and intraregional portfolio investments were more actively promoted.

The report identified six key technologies that are transforming fundamental financial market infrastructure—distributed ledger technology (DLT), artificial intelligence (AI), big data analytics, cloud computing, enhanced cybersecurity technologies, and application programming interface (API)—and assessed how those technologies could be applied to CSD–RTGS linkages. The linkages would be part of a regional settlement intermediary model that connects CSDs and central banks in the region directly. The study concluded that all six new technologies could be deployed using this linkage model. The Cross-Border Settlement Infrastructure Forum (CSIF) is currently engaged in a project exploring the redesign of CSD–RTGS linkages using DLT. The DLT-based linkage model is expected to be more useful and feasible, and to serve as a baseline for any future development by CSIF members of DLT-based market infrastructure.

Source: ADB. 2022. *Recent Technological Advances in Financial Market Infrastructure in ASEAN+3: Cross-Border Settlement Infrastructure Forum*.

Various ideas could be suggested for meeting development financing needs. CAREC could benefit from the financing programs of international financial institutions such as the IMF and the World Bank; indeed, countries in the region need to pursue those sources more aggressively. But the region's development financing needs are too large to be fully met by existing institutions alone. Some of the many ideas for cooperative development-financing mechanisms in Northeast Asia could be applied.[34] Three of these ideas are worth special attention: a CAREC Development Bank (CDB), CAREC Infrastructure Fund (CIF), and a CAREC Development Corporation (CDC).

The CDB would be a multilateral, quasi-commercial bank with ownership shared by national governments in the region and approved international organizations. The CIF would be a well-organized infrastructure investment fund focused on CAREC countries. The CDC would be a joint investment company, or an affiliated firm, supported by contributions of capital, mainly through CAREC government-run banks.

Among the three, the CIF and CDC could be applied. A CAREC Development Bank would not be desirable, as existing multilateral development banks, such as the World Bank and ADB, would regard it as redundant.

[34] For more detailed explanation of these ideas, refer to Chapter 7 of Rhee and Messerlin (2021).

A better idea would be to start with the CIF because it could meet additional financing needs by working with all development stakeholders, including multilateral development banks. Once the CAREC countries have gained experience in running the CIF, they could establish the CDC to raise funds by issuing bonds in intraregional markets, and specialize in investing in regional projects, including fintech infrastructure projects within the region.

Fintech and Cross-Border Supervision in CAREC

Financial transactions involving cross-border fintech solutions will blur the boundaries among financial institutions, activities, and jurisdictions. Since fintech is an international issue, international cooperation will be essential for harmonizing financial regulations to the extent that they align with national priorities. Regulation certainly plays a great role in facilitating market integration. The harmonization of financial regulations imposed on multinational financial companies will provide powerful incentives for cross-border financial activities and operations (Restoy 2019).

Challenges of Regulatory Coordination

Fintech raises new issues for international cooperation on financial regulation. Financial markets are globalized and fintech is disruptive in nature. Therefore, international cooperation is required for fintech regulation, especially for an environment of rapidly evolving technological complexity, where financial regulators will face serious challenges in designing regulatory regimes. Also, many innovative fintech companies will seek to operate in more than one country. When innovative companies try to expand their businesses into multiple jurisdictions, they will navigate different sets of financial regulations, which significantly increases regulatory complexity and uncertainty. Thus, regulators will have to deal with an additional challenge in achieving international regulatory coordination to reduce complexity and uncertainty (Bromberg, Godwin, and Ramsay 2018).

Fintech innovations will be applied to a wide scope of financial services and will be available on a large scale. The rise of multinational fintech companies working across borders demands close collaboration among financial regulators in different jurisdictions to deal with new emerging risks. International cooperation should be focused on balancing the efficiency and risk effects of new forms of global financial flows, and on avoiding friction in international transactions.

Whereas fintech firms operate globally, regulation is conducted largely within national or subnational borders. The local nature of regulation may create challenges regarding cross-border supervision and enforcement; for instance, regulatory inconsistency across jurisdictions increases the potential for regulatory arbitrage. A key challenge in international regulatory cooperation on fintech activities is how to prevent regulatory arbitrage. Financial regulators need to assess whether regulation causes unwarranted discrepancies in the requirements of countries, and to what extent those discrepancies can be justified by differences in their national situations. Even though some discrepancies may be justified, close cooperation among regulatory bodies is required so that regulatory gaps between nations cannot create opportunities for cross-border regulatory arbitrage.

The expansion of fintech in CAREC will make it more important for financial regulators to coordinate effectively with their peers in the region, and in countries beyond. In the region, the legal and regulatory environment remains weak, as does the capacity to develop relevant and modern regulatory frameworks and jurisdictions that are essential for expanding fintech solutions. Regional and global dialogues are widely regarded as crucial for supporting effective data frameworks, especially considering the cross-border and global accessibility of fintech.

Close cooperation at the international level will be especially useful. But a regional approach to fintech applications for financial regulatory frameworks will be essential for overcoming capacity and scalability constraints in the CAREC countries. An effective regional cooperation mechanism is necessary for building functional and harmonized regulatory standards and surveillance systems for fintech, to further prevent money laundering, terrorism financing, cybercrime, and fraud, as well as breaches of intellectual property rights and of personal data and privacy. While most CAREC members have rules and regulations on fintech development, harmonization is needed to harness the potential of fintech to support deeper regional financial integration. The region also needs to trail benchmark regions, so that good experiences in other regions can be emulated in CAREC.

Toward a Fintech-Enabling Legal Framework

Setting up an enabling legal and regulatory framework in each country is a prerequisite for any regional cooperation on financial regulation in CAREC. As noted above, the quality of financial regulation in the region varies across countries, but is relatively low overall. The absence or weakness of legal standards and supervisory functions may discourage some countries from adopting fintech applications, since an adequate legal framework is indispensable for promoting innovations.

Strengthening the national regulatory frameworks is not only necessary for regional cooperation, regional cooperation can help improve the national regulatory frameworks. Each CAREC country—having made the tough decisions to open up and reform its economy, and to adopt high standards and a transparent regulatory process—will become an advocate for these policies, and will try hard to satisfy the standards. For instance, if CAREC countries without cybersecurity and consumer protection legislation were to agree on regional cooperation on legislation, they would be obliged to establish matching domestic legislation.

Two points are noteworthy. First, to achieve the regional harmonization of fintech regulations, the initial step should be a comprehensive review of the existing legal and regulatory framework in each country. This review would be necessary for (i) identifying any existing regulations regarding fintech services, and (ii) figuring out how a country's legal and regulatory framework should be adjusted to handle fintech developments and foster fintech innovations. Second, it would be more desirable to follow flexible approaches to building a fintech-enabling regulatory framework.

The laws and regulations regarding fintech are rather weak in CAREC, with large disparities among countries. It will thus be necessary to spur CAREC countries to develop or strengthen their legal frameworks, and to encourage the harmonization of regulatory standards across the region, though with flexible approaches to regulation and supervision. This would balance the objective of ensuring rigorous standards with the reality of existing weak legal frameworks.

In addition to setting up a fintech-enabling legal framework, CAREC countries should make efforts to improve the regulators' skills and knowledge of fintech developments. Knowledge exchange through regulation coordination among CAREC countries and through international standard-setting bodies can help enhance their knowledge of cross-cutting issues. The suggested CAREC fintech policy forum could drive this capacity building and knowledge exchange among national regulatory bodies. Developing collaboration models, training curricula, and exchange programs—both among regional members and with international organizations—can help close the knowledge gap.

Regional Regulatory Communities and Sandboxes

Although regulators are grappling with the challenges posed by fintech and international regulatory responses are still in their inception, there have been some encouraging signs of regulatory cooperation. Probably two of the most important initiatives aimed at supporting fintech businesses are regulatory cooperative fintech communities and regulatory sandboxes.[35]

Within a country, cooperative fintech communities provide direct support for businesses in their efforts to meet regulatory requirements. By engaging constructively with the fintech industry through such communities, national regulators can learn about new financial technologies and create more flexible regulatory processes. This community model could expand to the regional level to improve cooperation among national regulators.

A simple approach to building a collaborative regional fintech community is through memorandums of understanding (MOUs). This is a recent phenomenon—the first was signed by the Australian Securities and Investments Commission and the United Kingdom (UK) Financial Conduct Authority in March 2016.[36] The primary purpose of fintech MOUs is to provide a framework for cooperation and referrals and to set out how authorities plan to share and use information on innovations in their respective markets. The agreements also set out how regulators support businesses. Assistance is provided prior to a business's submission of an application for authorization, during the authorization process, and after the business is authorized (Bromberg, Godwin, and Ramsay 2018).

If fintech MOUs evolve from bilateral into regional agreements or even global multilateral agreements, cooperative fintech communities can reap much larger and enhanced benefits from innovation. In CAREC, a regional or multilateral agreement would be the best way to handle challenges posed by emerging fintech innovations. A regional agreement would set up mechanisms for fintech businesses seeking common or consistent standards in CAREC countries with different rules and regulations, and it could significantly cut the costs of doing business across the region. For example, the European Commission suggested introducing "basic principles for firm support at EU level, which could 'eventually lead to an automatic referral system between [innovation] hubs'" (Bromberg, Godwin, and Ramsay 2018).

Regulatory sandboxes, at the domestic level, involve licensing exemptions and conditional relief from regulatory requirements, so that fintech businesses may test concepts in a controlled environment established by the regulator in consultation with the business. The concept can be used to promote cross-border regulatory harmonization and to enable fintech innovators to expand rapidly, whether regionally or globally.

[35] ESMA and EBA (2018, p. 5) distinguish these two as follows: "Innovation hubs ... provide a dedicated point of contact for firms to raise enquiries with competent authorities on FinTech-related issues and to seek non-binding guidance on the conformity of innovative financial products, financial services or business models with licensing or registration requirements and regulatory and supervisory expectations. Regulatory sandboxes .. provide a scheme to enable firms to test, pursuant to a specific testing plan agreed and monitored by a dedicated function of the competent authority, innovative financial products, financial services or business models. Sandboxes may also imply the use of legally provided discretions by the relevant supervisor (with use depending on the relevant applicable EU and national law) but sandboxes do not entail the disapplication of regulatory requirements that must be applied as a result of EU law."

[36] For a detailed explanation of bilateral and multilateral fintech MOUs, refer to Bromberg, Godwin, and Ramsay (2018).

The Global Financial Innovation Network (GFIN) is an example of a global sandbox. GFIN is an international alliance of government regulators led by the UK's regulatory body to provide financial firms with an environment for testing cross-border solutions. Since trials can be conducted in multiple jurisdictions, this is likely to substantially increase the amount of data available to both regulators and fintech firms about market dynamics and regulatory environments in participating countries (World Bank 2020). Another example is an idea for an industry sandbox offered by the Association of Southeast Asian Nations (ASEAN) Financial Innovation Network (AFIN): a cloud-based marketplace for the distribution of fintech solutions to financial institutions located in multiple jurisdictions.

Passporting Arrangements

The introduction of a special passport for fintech firms to ease their entry into other jurisdictions is another idea for regional regulatory cooperation in CAREC. The passporting arrangement would be somewhat rigid, and would require that countries agree on a common set of rules and a single process for registration.

One such passporting arrangement is the Asia Region Funds Passport (ARFP) Memorandum of Cooperation, signed by Australia, Japan, the Republic of Korea, and New Zealand. The ARFP aims to provide a multilaterally agreed framework to facilitate the cross-border offering of high-quality managed funds. This idea could be developed into a regional fintech passport. Greg Medcraft, as chair of the Australian Securities and Investments Commission, raised the possibility of introducing a fintech passport in Asia, and suggested the development of equivalent processes around regulation at a forum in Singapore (Bulling and Chasser 2016).

The EU suggested the same idea in 2018. The European passport gives those firms that are duly authorized and supervised by their home member states the possibility to provide their services in all other member states and to scale up in the entire EU single market (European Commission 2018).

CAREC countries may select a few exemplary cases and introduce rules for selected fintech firms to follow when testing innovations in other countries in the region. Once a pilot case has achieved success, the scope of harmonized regulatory and supervisory requirements for fintech activities, including a passporting arrangement within the region, could be gradually expanded.

TARGETS AND ACTION PLANS FOR A CAREC CAPITAL MARKET CATCH-UP

CAREC countries have starkly different abilities to employ fintech in the development of their capital markets. Significant gaps in the basic structure of their fintech markets and the level of sophistication of their capital markets will determine when the advantages of fintech innovations will be available to all. The speed of catch-up is a central question in the development of a functional regional road map. The IMF's index system for financial market development can capture present and target levels of capital market development in the region; for this reason, it is a useful starting point for mapping out the stages of the journey (IMF Data n.d.).

In 2021, the IMF index for advanced capital markets was 0.53. The target level of 70% of the advanced markets' position would be a score of 0.37. The same indexes for CAREC countries were much lower than 0.37, except for the PRC. This makes the target level an ambitious, yet reasonable one for the CAREC countries. The index for Kazakhstan in 2021 was 0.24, while those for the Kyrgyz Republic, Tajikistan, and Turkmenistan were all near zero.

On the other hand, the level of fintech development in the CAREC countries can be captured by referring to the index system developed by Peter Lovelock in Chapter 1 of this volume, or to Umar (2021).
To see the fintech development level of CAREC countries according to Lovelock, the aggregate index incorporating the four pillars (finance, technology, capability, and regional cooperation) or, alternatively, a focus on technology and capability, can be used. However, the gap in progress within the CAREC region is significant, no matter what the index. It, therefore, seems reasonable to view the timespans required to achieve the 70% goal as likely to be significantly different among the CAREC member countries.

Road Map Outline and the Stages for Policy Implementation

Basic structure

A three-stage approach (Figure 4.3) for

- institutional and technological improvement,
- fintech promotion, and
- fintech expansion.

Development target

- 70% level of the advanced capital market development.

Time required to achieve the target

- 10 to 20 years, depending on the present level of fintech and capital market development.

Figure 4.3: Outline of CAREC Capital Markets Road Map

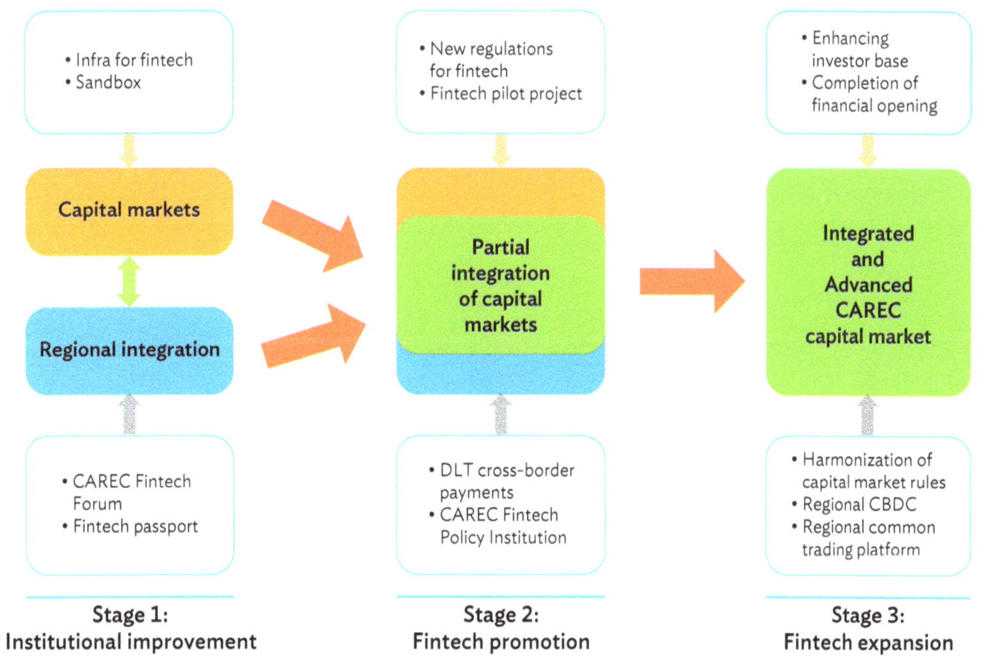

CAREC = Central Asia Regional Economic Cooperation, CBDC = central bank digital currency, DLT = distributed ledger technology, fintech = financial technology, infra = infrastructure.
Source: Authors.

Stage 1: Institutional Improvement

First, what is needed most at the beginning of the road map is to set up a basic institutional framework and technological infrastructure to support the fintech applications for capital market development. A strong priority would be an overhaul of traditional capital markets through the introduction of best practices and deregulation. In the absence of an underlying financial market infrastructure, such as an exchange or central securities depository (CSD), an institutional framework should be established early on.

Second, all the CAREC countries need to agree on the basic direction of fintech use for capital market development and on the regulatory principles as soon as possible, if they have not already done so. Third, a regulatory sandbox could be introduced early on. New legislation would not necessarily be a prerequisite for that, as an administrative order might suffice. Fourth, the introduction of a fintech center or a collaborative regional fintech community could be accomplished at this stage because it would require neither complex legislation nor significant monetary backup. Fifth, it will be necessary to improve the basic technological infrastructures such as broadband access and fast mobile internet networks. Finally, the regulators in each country will need to encourage private actors to adopt fintech applications for basic financial services as much as possible.

Regarding regional integration, it would be desirable for CAREC member countries to expand their cross-border financial transactions even before fintech has been fully applied to them. Member countries need to start a dialogue on the liberalization of capital flows in the first stage of the road map. Also, basic fintech cooperation could begin among the member countries that have already introduced a regulatory sandbox and innovation hub. Technological cooperation can be expected, especially among countries whose fintech progress index is above the average under Pillar 2 (Chapter 2) of technology and infrastructure development.

Stage 2: Fintech Promotion

During the second stage, fintech applications should be adopted proactively to encourage capital market development. Some fintech applications may not be readily available at this stage due to the lack of technological capability. So, efforts to promote the development of fintech-relevant technologies such as artificial intelligence (AI) and machine learning (ML), blockchain, biometric authentication, big data, and cloud computing would be required. In addition, enacting or revising existing regulations will be needed in tandem with newly introduced products, services, and technologies. Many measures will admittedly be difficult to introduce because of the legislative complexity and the need for significant monetary support. For example, setting data-protection standards, introducing crypto asset regulations, and proposing rules on cross-cutting technologies will require a complex legislative process. Questions such as "what to regulate," "whom to regulate," and "who will regulate" should be answered following the basic regulatory principle made public during the first stage, but its concrete application would require much more expertise, coordinating aptitude, and effort from the regulators. If some fintech applications are not immediately available because of technological or institutional problems, but are considered helpful for capital market development later on, then a pilot project to improve applicability can be tried. One of the pilot projects worth deploying is the introduction of a central bank digital currency (CBDC). Experience accumulated at this stage with CBDCs will be useful later for domestic market development and regional cooperation.

To encourage regional integration, it would be desirable to start regional fintech cooperation by implementing policies over which there is little conflict, and for which it will be easier to arrive at a regional consensus.

It would also be strategically better to promote financial- and fintech-cooperation projects together with economic-cooperation projects to further deepen regional integration. In this sense, a project to create a regional free trade agreement (FTA) would be a viable option. Regardless of whether an FTA is pursued at this stage, regional fintech cooperation will need to expand to most member countries. For that, the fintech policy forum established during the first stage would have to become a formal regional institution.

Stage 3: Fintech Expansion

The adoption of fintech applications will presumably expand to encompass the entire capital market and all financial services, developing the capital market to the target level (70% of the benchmark countries). To reach that target, continuous effort will be required to overhaul not only the capital market, but also the entire financial system. For example, it will be important to broaden the institutional investor base. Institutional investors such as insurance companies, pension funds, asset management firms, and banks are important because they are major sources of demand in government bond and private capital markets, and they are facilitators of financial innovations that drive market development. Also, financial opening will need to be completed at this stage to increase the demand for domestic financial products and reinforce competition in that market.

A harmonization of rules for the stock and bond markets will help integrate regional capital markets. For the integration of bond markets, a regional credit guarantee arrangement could be introduced to facilitate cross-border investment. A regional CBDC, especially a wholesale CBDC, can be introduced among some members to facilitate cross-border remittance and securities settlements. Fintech applications should be expanded to the regional level so that the regional capital market can be further developed through fintech cooperation. To support regional fintech cooperation, it would be desirable to establish concrete and specific regional arrangements such as a CAREC fintech policy institution, infrastructure fund, or free trade area. Table 4.2 summarizes the basic directions and policies needed in each stage.

Table 4.2: Basic Directions and Policy Implementation, by Stage

Stage	Basic Direction	Policies
Stage 1: Institutional improvement	• Set up regulatory principles for fintech applications. • Develop basic technological infrastructure for fintech applications. • Adopt fintech applications for basic financial services. • Start dialogue on the liberalization of capital flows. • Start fintech and technological cooperation among countries with above-average fintech development levels regarding Pillar 2.[a]	*For the domestic market:* • Stock and bond markets (deregulation and introduction of best practices) • Regulatory sandbox • Fintech center or innovation hub • Enhanced broadband access and fast mobile internet networks *For regional integration:* • Fintech passport • Connections between regulatory fintech communities and regulatory sandboxes • CAREC fintech policy forum

continued on next page

Table 4.2 *continued*

Stage	Basic Direction	Policies
Stage 2: Fintech promotion	• Adopt fintech applications aggressively to encourage capital market development. • Start regional fintech cooperation with policies that are easy to implement. • Expand regional fintech cooperation to most member countries. • Start discussions on harmonization of the rules on capital markets.	*For the domestic market:* • Development plan for fintech-relevant technologies • Implementation of new regulations or revision of existing regulations • Launching of pilot projects *For regional integration:* • DLT cross-border payments • Digital ID • Coordination of fintech regulations • CAREC fintech policy institution • CAREC free trade agreement
Stage 3: Fintech expansion	• Expand fintech adoption to the entire capital market and to all financial services. • Develop the capital market so it reaches the target level (70% of the benchmark countries). • Establish concrete regional arrangements that will help to promote regional fintech cooperation.	*For the domestic market:* • Enhanced institutional investor base • Completed financial opening *For regional integration:* • Harmonization of rules for capital markets and introduction of a regional credit-guarantee arrangement. • Regional CBDC • Digital financial profile • Regional common trading platform • CAREC infrastructure fund

CAREC = Central Asia Regional Economic Cooperation, CBDC = central bank digital currency, DLT = distributed ledger technology, fintech = financial technology, ID = identification.

[a] Pillar 2 refers to technology (the others are, in order: finance, capability, and regional cooperation). See this volume, Chapter 1: Measuring Fintech Progress in Central Asia, by P. Lovelock.

Source: Authors.

Promotion Strategy: Policy Priorities

Although various policies are often promoted together, it is very difficult to successfully complete them all. Some may conflict with each other, and some programs may have to be abandoned. Therefore, it is necessary to set the intensity and duration of the policies according to priority. High-priority policies should be pursued intensively for a long time.

Several factors guide the identification of high-priority policies. These include the following:

- The feasibility at each stage, considering the conditions evaluated during the first stage of the ADB project (Appendix): for example, a fintech sandbox is relatively easy to implement in many CAREC countries, even under current conditions; for those countries, its implementation would be recommended in the first stage.

- The ripple effect to induce further reforms: even when conditions are not yet ripe, a policy with a long-run ripple effect should be introduced as soon as possible. For example, in some CAREC countries, basic infrastructure may be hard to build at an early stage. Since basic infrastructure is much needed for inducing further reforms, however, its installation should be completed early on, and it should be maintained for a long time.
- Easy agreement on implementation: for regional implementation, the possibility of reaching an agreement on actions must be considered, in addition to the question of feasibility. For example, the central banks of some CAREC countries may be capable of and interested in introducing a regional CBDC in the second stage, much earlier than the other members would prefer. The introduction of a regional CBDC in Stage 2 would thus be a divisive issue, so the recommendation would be to have all the CAREC countries introduce the regional CBDC in the last stage.

Table 4.3 summarizes the intensity and duration of the promotion of various policies at each stage, based on each policy's level of priority.

Table 4.3: Strength of Policy Promotion, by Stage

Policy	Stage 1	Stage 2	Stage 3
Color range for policy-promotion intensity	strong	middling	weak
The direction of fintech development			
Basic technological infrastructures			
Regulatory principles			
Fintech passport			
Innovation hub			
CAREC fintech policy forum (institution)			
Fintech sandbox			
Enacting or revising existing regulations			
Coordination of fintech-enabling regulation			
CAREC free trade agreement			
Fintech-relevant technologies			
DLT cross-border payments			
CBDCs			
Digital ID			
Digital financial profile			
Platform for regional trading system			
Regional CBDC			
CAREC infrastructure fund			

CAREC = Central Asia Regional Economic Cooperation, CBDC = central bank digital currency, DLT = distributed ledger technology, fintech = financial technology, ID = identification.

Source: Authors.

It would be better and more desirable to promote several ideas for strengthening regional integration simultaneously, rather than separately in CAREC. For example, the regional payment and settlement system, fintech sandboxes and passports, and the harmonization of rules on capital markets could be included in a CAREC FTA (CAREC Institute and ADB 2019).

Country Differences and the Policy Implementation Strategy

Discussion of the policy implementation by stage can sometimes give the impression that CAREC is composed of homogeneous members. However, what is emphasized throughout this volume—including this chapter—is that the levels of capital market and fintech development across the region are remarkably diverse. To view these differences more precisely, the authors developed a composite index based on four criteria: (i) the IMF financial market (FM) index; and (ii) Pillar 2 (technology), (iii) Pillar 3 (capability), and (iv) Pillar 4 (regional cooperation) of the fintech progress index introduced in Chapter 1 of this volume. Pillar 1 in the fintech progress index is finance, but here the authors have substituted the IMF index because they were interested specifically in the development of capital markets, rather than that of the broader financial system.

Standard scores for each of the four criteria are summed into a kind of composite index from which country ranking of capital market and fintech development can be derived. Table 4.4 summarizes the results of this exercise. The table shows that the composite index scores for the PRC exceed those of the other CAREC countries by a large margin. This shows why the PRC is considered an outlier in this sample.

Table 4.4: CAREC Country Rankings for Capital Market and Fintech Development, 2021

	Financial Market		Technology		Capability		Regional Cooperation			
Country	CI	ST	CI	ST	CI	ST	CI	ST	Sum	Rank
Azerbaijan	0.21	0.35	55.9	0.40	81.8	1.70	33.3	(0.65)	1.81	3
PRC	0.64	2.70	68.8	0.72	78.5	1.41	100.0	1.94	6.77	1
Georgia	0.03	(0.63)	39.2	(0.01)	59.5	(0.31)	44.4	(0.22)	(1.16)	7
Kazakhstan	0.24	0.52	50.6	0.27	71.2	0.75	66.7	0.65	2.18	2
Kyrgyz Republic	0.01	(0.74)	24.9	(0.37)	54.9	(0.72)	66.7	0.65	(1.18)	8
Mongolia	0.11	(0.19)	54.3	0.36	54.5	(0.76)	44.4	(0.22)	(0.80)	5
Pakistan	0.14	(0.03)	36.2	(0.09)	58.5	(0.40)	44.4	(0.22)	(0.73)	4
Tajikistan	0.00	(0.79)	21.5	(0.46)	53.4	(0.86)	66.7	0.65	(1.46)	9
Turkmenistan	0.02	(0.68)	0.04	(0.99)	50.0	(1.16)	11.1	(1.51)	(4.34)	10
Uzbekistan	0.05	(0.52)	46.3	0.16	66.7	0.34	22.2	(1.08)	(1.09)	6

( ) = negative value, CAREC = Central Asia Regional Economic Cooperation, CI = composite index, fintech = financial technology, PRC = People's Republic of China, ST = standard score.

Notes:

1. The values in the "Sum" column are the sums of the standard scores of the four criteria for each CAREC country.
2. The "Rank" column shows the CAREC country rankings based on the values shown in the "Sum" column.

Source: Authors.

Country Groups

Based on Table 4.4, we can regroup the CAREC member countries (except for the PRC) into three subgroups:

(1) *Leading*: Kazakhstan, Azerbaijan, and Pakistan.

(2) *Middle*: Mongolia, Uzbekistan, and Georgia.

(3) *Lagging*: Kyrgyz Republic, Tajikistan, and Turkmenistan.

Broadly speaking, the leading group has already implemented most of the domestic policies of the first stage, and are ready to start on the second stage. Also, these countries may initiate proposals for regional cooperation on fintech and capital market development.

The middle group has relatively weak traditional capital markets, so at the beginning it will need to focus more on improving the structure of its stock and bond markets. The lagging group is weak on all criteria, except regional cooperation. Thus, these countries should focus on strengthening the basic infrastructure of their fintech and capital markets in both the first and second stages, before expanding fintech adoption.

It should be stressed again, however, that the situations of member countries even within each group are quite diverse. In the leading group, **Kazakhstan** already has somewhat-developed capital markets and financial market infrastructure in place, comparatively high digital technology, and a favorable regulatory and business environment. Kazakhstan would not find it difficult to reach the target level in 10 years.

Azerbaijan ranks highest in the capability pillar, and second behind the PRC in the technology pillar. These facts imply that Azerbaijan could rapidly boost capital market development using its potential in fintech technology and its regulatory and business capabilities. Fintech could be leveraged to improve traditional capital markets and introduce alternative financing platforms.

Even though Azerbaijan has little experience in regional cooperation, it is expected to show leadership by making full use of its potential, as shown in the technology and capability pillars, for capital market development. Areas of leadership could include the regional fintech passport, regional regulatory sandbox and collaborative regional fintech community, regional harmonization of digital ID regulations, and cross-border payments using distributed ledger technology (DLT) and similar systems.

By contrast, **Pakistan** is classified as a leading group member even though its scores for the technology and capability pillars are lower than average. Pakistan merits inclusion in the leading group because it has longtime and relatively mature traditional capital markets. However, it is important for Pakistan to improve its regulatory and business environment to attract foreign investors and fintech start-ups, and to accelerate innovation among domestic players (Chapter 8).

Countries in the middle and lagging groups will need more time in the first stage than will the leading-group countries. In the middle group, stock and bond markets do not play important roles in the financial landscape of each country. The scores for the technology and capability pillars are roughly in the middle of all CAREC countries. The step-by-step approach through the policy implementation strategy shown in Table 4.2 would be the most suitable for the middle-group countries. The success of the road map for CAREC's emerging fintech markets will depend largely on whether these countries accomplish the implementation strategy. If they show enthusiasm for regional cooperation, many regional arrangements, including an FTA, would be feasible.

Mongolia has a higher score in the technology pillar than in the others, which implies that the country needs to focus on improving its legal framework and on supporting more fintech innovation initiatives.

Georgia scores better in the capability pillar than several other countries, but needs to improve the basic infrastructure of its fintech and capital markets. Although Georgia has a not-so-high score in the regional cooperation pillar, it has had the experience of setting up and running institutional public–private dialogue platforms—including in Georgia, Uzbekistan, and Kazakhstan—and it could lead a suggested CAREC fintech forum.

Uzbekistan is somewhat similar to Georgia, but should exert more effort to improve its basic infrastructure. Uzbekistan has had the least regional-cooperation experience so far, and needs to be more proactive in fintech and financial cooperation.

The countries in the lagging group have very poor scores in all the categories, except regional cooperation, which implies that they will need to spend more time in the first stage than both the middle and leading groups. Their deeply negative scores in the financial market pillar suggest that, above all, they must exert a great deal of effort to revive their dormant stock and bond markets. They also score very low in the technology and capability pillars, and so need to improve their technological, regulatory, and business environments by making huge investments in basic infrastructure, setting up an appropriate legal system, and increasing digital skills (including digital financial knowledge). For **Turkmenistan**, the scores in the technology and regional cooperation pillars are particularly low, almost outliers. Thus, the country needs to work harder and for a longer time to establish its basic infrastructure and simultaneously expand its cross-border transactions with neighboring countries.

CONCLUSION

Regional cooperation is needed to accelerate capital market development in the CAREC region. It is an optimal strategy for speeding up regional financial integration, as it would create wide and deep capital markets in which firms could choose the most efficient sources of funding and investors could simultaneously choose the most productive investment opportunities. Regional cooperation is also needed to cope with the potential risks of financial globalization and regional financial integration. Regarding regional fintech-cooperation strategies, this chapter has focused on regional cooperation for payments and remittances, capital market integration, and cross-border fintech regulation and supervision.

It should be recognized that capital market development is a difficult goal that can only be achieved through continuous policy efforts across various areas. Although the goal can indeed be better approached through fintech and regional cooperation, changes are likely to occur more slowly than would be ideal, due to structural and immutable constraints. Therefore, policy authorities need to take a step-by-step and strategic approach guided by a comprehensive, well-structured plan that may take a decade to complete for some countries and as much as 2 decades for others.

Considering the low levels of development of the fintech and capital markets in the CAREC region, the significant fintech gaps among the region's countries, and the ripening state of intraregional cooperation, a specific road map is needed along which policies can be better implemented and the intended results attained. It will also be necessary to maintain a balanced view of the costs, risks, and benefits that could be obtained by facilitating the use of fintech and promoting capital market integration. If government policies are conceived and implemented based on these basic perspectives, and the strategies adopted induce proactive action by private economic agents, the CAREC countries will enjoy the economic development, financial stability, and financial inclusion that strong capital markets can bring.

REFERENCES

Asian Development Bank (ADB). 2021. *Technical Assistance for Financial Technology for Regional Cooperation in Central Asia Regional Economic Cooperation Countries*. https://www.adb.org/projects/55122-001/main.

———. 2022. *Recent Technological Advances in Financial Market Infrastructure in ASEAN+3: Cross-Border Settlement Infrastructure Forum*.

Bank for International Settlements (BIS). 2024. Project Aperta: Enabling Cross-Border Data Portability Through Open Finance Interoperability. https://www.bis.org/about/bisih/topics/open_finance/aperta.htm.

Bromberg, L., A. Godwin, and I. Ramsay. 2018. Cross-Border Cooperation in Financial Regulation: Crossing the Fintech Bridge. *Capital Markets Law Journal*. 13 (1). pp. 59–84. https://papers.ssrn.com/sol3/papers.cfm?abstract_id=3105141.

Bulling, J. and M. Chasser. 2016. Will There Be an Asia Pacific “FinTech Passport” in the Future? *K&L Gates, FinTech and Blockchain Law Watch*. 14 December. https://www.fintechlawblog.com/2016/12/14/will-there-be-an-asia-pacific-fintech-passport-in-the-future/.

Central Asia Regional Economic Cooperation (CAREC) Institute. 2021. *CAREC Regional Integration Index: Some Progress, but New Push Required*. https://www.carecinstitute.org/wp-content/uploads/2021/02/CRII-edited-10-Feb-2021_HK3.pdf.

CAREC Institute and ADB. 2019. CAREC Integrated Trade Agenda 2030. *Issues Papers*. February. https://www.carecprogram.org/uploads/CAREC-Integrated-Trade-Agenda-2030-Issues-Papers.pdf.

Davidovic, S. et al. 2019. Strategy for Fintech Applications in the Pacific Island Countries. *IMF Departmental Papers*. No. 19/14. International Monetary Fund, Asia and Pacific Department. https://www.imf.org/en/Publications/Departmental-Papers-Policy-Papers/Issues/2019/08/21/Strategy-for-Fintech-Applications-in-the-Pacific-Island-Countries-46862.

Eichengreen, B. and R. Hausmann. 1999. Exchange Rates and Financial Fragility. *NBER Working Papers Series*. No. 7418. National Bureau of Economic Research. https://www.nber.org/papers/w7418.

European Commission. 2018. *FinTech Action Plan: For a More Competitive and Innovative European Financial Sector*. Communication from the Commission. https://eur-lex.europa.eu/legal-content/EN/TXT/HTML/?uri=CELEX:52018DC0109&rid=15.

European Securities Markets Authority (ESMA) and European Banking Authority (EBA). 2018. *FinTech: Regulatory Sandboxes and Innovation Hubs*. Joint Report. European Supervisory Authorities (ESAs). https://www.esma.europa.eu/document/joint-esa-report-regulatory-sandboxes-and-innovation-hubs.

He, D. et al. 2017. Fintech and Financial Services: Initial Considerations. *IMF Staff Discussion Notes*. No. 2017/005. International Monetary Fund. https://www.imf.org/en/Publications/Staff-Discussion-Notes/Issues/2017/06/16/Fintech-and-Financial-Services-Initial-Considerations-44985.

Hendershott, T. et al. 2021. FinTech as a Game Changer: Overview of Research Frontiers. *Information Systems Research*. 32 (1). pp. 1–17. https://pubsonline.informs.org/doi/10.1287/isre.2021.0997.

International Monetary Fund (IMF) and the World Bank. 2018. The Bali Fintech Agenda. *IMF Policy Papers*. No. 2018 (050). IMF. https://www.elibrary.imf.org/view/journals/007/2018/050/007.2018.issue-050-en.xml.

———. 2019. Fintech: The Experience So Far. *IMF Policy Papers*. No. 2019/024. IMF. https://www.imf.org/en/Publications/Policy-Papers/Issues/2019/06/27/Fintech-The-Experience-So-Far-47056.

IMF Data. n.d. Financial Development Index (accessed 23 November 2022).

Kagan, J. 2024. Financial Technology (Fintech): Its Uses and Impact on Our Lives. *Investopedia*. 25 March. https://www.investopedia.com/terms/f/fintech.asp.

Kim, I. J. and Y. Rhee. 2010. Global Financial Crisis and East Asian Monetary Cooperation Revisited. *Frontiers of Modern Economics*. 2010. pp. 311–333.

Kose, M. et al. 2006. Financial Globalization: A Reappraisal. *NBER Working Paper Series*. No. 12484. National Bureau of Economic Research. https://www.nber.org/system/files/working_papers/w12484/w12484.pdf.

Moon, W. and Y. Rhee. 2012. *Asian Monetary Integration: Coping with a New Monetary Order After the Global Financial Crisis*. Edward Elgar Publishing Ltd.

Negre, A. and W. Cook. 2021. *Interoperability in Digital Financial Services: Emerging Guidance for Funders*. Technical Note. Consultative Group to Assist the Poor (CGAP). https://www.cgap.org/sites/default/files/publications/2021_01_Technical_Note_Interoperability_Digital_Financial_Services.pdf.

Ratha, D. et al. 2023. *Leveraging Diaspora Finances for Private Capital Mobilization*. Migration and Development Brief 39. World Bank and KNOMAD. https://documents1.worldbank.org/curated/en/099740408142422676/pdf/IDU-84dfd61b-e135-4242-a202-3728b2e8fa86.pdf.

Restoy, F. 2019. *Market Integration: The Role of Regulation*. Speech prepared for the Institute of International Finance (IIF) Market Fragmentation Roundtable. 10 April. https://www.bis.org/speeches/sp190415.htm.

Rhee, Y. and H. Chai. 2006. Comparison of Financial Integration Process Between East Asia and Europe. *Asia-Pacific Journal of EU Studies*. 4 (2). pp. 105–124.

Rhee, Y. and P. Messerlin. 2021. *[Democratic People's Republic of Korea] and Economic Integration in East Asia*. Routledge.

The Economist. 2021. The Race to Redefine Cross-Border Finance. 21 October. https://www.economist.com/finance-and-economics/the-race-to-redefine-cross-border-finance/21805736.

Tumpel-Gugerell, G. 2010. *Financial Integration and Stability: Efficiency Gains vs. Pitfalls*. Keynote address prepared for the conference titled, Heterogeneous Nations and Globalized Financial Markets: New Challenges for Central Banks, organized by the National Bank of Poland. 10–11 June.

Umar, K. 2021. *Financial Inclusion and Fintech in CAREC: Constraints and Prospects*. Working Paper. CAREC Institute. https://www.carecinstitute.org/wp-content/uploads/2021/01/CI-working-paper-fintech-in-CAREC-11-Jan-2021.pdf.

World Bank. 2014. *Guidelines for the Successful Regional Integration of Financial Infrastructures*. http://documents.worldbank.org/curated/en/553331468182345838/Guidelines-for-the-successful-regional-integration-of-financial-infrastructures.

———. 2020. *Fintech in Europe and Central Asia: Maximizing Benefits and Managing Risks*. Fintech Note No. 4. https://openknowledge.worldbank.org/server/api/core/bitstreams/3cf7bb28-19b1-542c-bcb7-6d7835812af8/content.

5

Using Fintech to Drive Capital Markets in CAREC

Hee-Yul Chai and Yeongseop Rhee

INTRODUCTION

When capital markets are well developed, savings can be mobilized efficiently, risk management is more effective, and foreign direct and portfolio investments are encouraged. Together, these lead to better industry performance and economic growth. Developed capital markets also contribute to macroeconomic stability, which is a prerequisite for building a market-friendly investment climate. However, as in most of the Central Asia Regional Economic Cooperation (CAREC) region, the majority of developing countries lack developed capital markets. Banks dominate their finance sectors; and their markets for bonds, equities, and derivatives are small and often dormant.

The People's Republic of China (PRC) is the only CAREC member with advanced capital markets, despite their relatively poor accessibility, according to financial market development indexes compiled by the International Monetary Fund (IMF) (IMF Data n.d.). The IMF data show that, besides the PRC, financial market development in CAREC exceeded the emerging market average for 2021 only in Azerbaijan and Kazakhstan.

Capital markets in developing countries are mainly underdeveloped because of the difficulty in meeting the macroeconomic, financial, institutional, and technological conditions needed to make progress. Macroeconomic conditions include the size of the economy, fiscal balance, and price stability. Necessary financial market conditions include a robust banking sector, a strong institutional investor base, and opportunities for financial opening. The institutional and technological conditions revolve around investor protection, sound corporate governance, efficient financial market infrastructures, and information and communication technology (ICT) that is fit for purpose.

The development of capital markets should be regarded as critical for achieving economic prosperity in CAREC. Adequate policies are required to achieve the macroeconomic, financial, and institutional conditions necessary for capital market development. However, policy implementation will not reap rewards easily or immediately. Under these circumstances, innovations in financial technology (fintech) can be important for accelerating capital market development. Fintech innovation can significantly enhance the efficiency of securities trade and post-trade activities in traditional capital markets, and it can be pivotal in redesigning or replacing traditional capital markets.

The private sector should drive efforts to leverage fintech to provide such services as peer-to-peer (P2P) lending, equity crowdfunding, mobile trading, digitized security token offerings (STOs), compliance automation, and customer relationship management (CRM). However, policymakers play an important part in maximizing benefits and minimizing risks brought about by fintech disruption.

Government authorities need to set the direction for fintech utilization in capital markets, regulate newly introduced goods and services, introduce regulatory sandboxes to encourage engagement, set standards on data and cross-cutting technologies, and reconcile conflicts of interest over policies.

The importance of regional cooperation in supporting efforts to accelerate capital market development in CAREC was stressed in Chapter 4, and bears repeating here.

ISSUES AND PERSPECTIVES REGARDING CAREC

Why Capital Markets Are Important

Funding Growth

As a country's economy grows, it cannot rely solely on public funds or bank loans for corporate investment or infrastructure development. Capital markets that can connect private savings with businesses or regions that need funds become all the more important. Banks, as so-called delegated monitors, or delegated risk managers, tend to be reluctant to provide mid- to long-term finance and reluctant to provide loans unless borrowers can demonstrate their financial performance or provide collateral (Diamond 1984; Hakenes 2004).[37]

By contrast, capital markets may gather investors willing to make long-term investments in companies that demonstrate outstanding technological prowess or adaptability, despite not having much of a financial history. Such investors are attracted to well-developed venture capital markets, and these markets will flourish when venture capitalists can easily exit through the sale of shares to retail investors through initial public offerings (IPOs), which require a developed stock market (Black and Gilson 1999). For this reason, capital markets can be important for the supply of financing for venture firms and mid- to long-term corporate facilities.

Extensive empirical research has confirmed that capital market development contributes to growth through investment promotion.[38] Most empirical analyses report that the size of the stock and corporate bond markets, measured by market capitalization or transaction volume, has a positive effect on economic growth. Besides that quantitative element, the development of the capital market must be considered from a qualitative perspective. In a "qualitatively" developed capital market, economic agents can freely buy and sell products at regular and transparent prices.[39] Since market size and liquidity are the basis for qualitative development, the quantitative and qualitative aspects of capital market development are closely connected. However, they do not necessarily coincide. Even a big and liquid market may have problems with price opacity and autonomy of trading. Nevertheless, most empirical analyses of the drivers or effects of capital market development focus on the quantitative aspects because the qualitative dimension is not easy to evaluate.[40]

37 Diamond (1984) explains why a bank is delegated the costly task of monitoring loans written with firms. Hakenes (2004) presents a model with banks acting as agents that manage risk for the principals.

38 See World Bank (2019) for a comprehensive survey on the causes and effects of capital market development.

39 The meaning of "qualitative" in the context of capital markets comes from Demekas and Nerlich (2020).

40 The IMF defined financial development in terms of depth (size and liquidity of markets), access (ability of individuals to obtain financial services), and efficiency (ability of institutions to provide financial services at low costs and with sustainable revenues, and the level of activity of capital markets) (Sahay et al. 2015). Here, access and efficiency correspond to quality. The IMF articulated a financial development index system based on this comprehensive concept of financial development, which is an important research innovation. Details of the index system are discussed later in this chapter.

Financial Stability

Capital market development is important not only for promoting economic growth, but also for achieving financial stability. In a banking crisis, capital markets provide funds in the place of banks, and so stem the spread of a crisis to the real sector. Capital markets function as a kind of "spare tire" that complements the banking system.[41] Of course, amid international financial turmoil, foreign investors may withdraw their investments from an emerging economy with more developed capital markets than other emerging economies, possibly causing that economy to receive a relatively greater shock. However, developed and liquid capital markets generally respond more stably to external shocks. Indeed, if a capital market is attractive, it will be possible for that market to maintain stability by means of inflows of foreign funds, despite capital outflows in times of international financial turmoil. For example, during the taper tantrum following the changes in United States (US) monetary policy in 2013, since more capital flowed into the Republic of Korea than flowed out, stability in both the capital and foreign-exchange markets was maintained.

Why Most Capital Markets in Emerging Economies Are Not Developed

Although capital market development is good for economic growth and financial stability, the financial systems in most developing economies are bank-based, with underdeveloped capital markets. The main reason is that it is not easy to create the macroeconomic, financial, and institutional conditions necessary for capital market development. A tour through each of these dimensions is illuminating.

Macroeconomic Conditions

First, macroeconomic conditions comprise economic size, fiscal balance, and price stability. Economic size is a basic precondition for capital market development. Small and medium-sized enterprises (SMEs) prefer bank lending over financing through capital markets because they do not want to pay the fixed costs or fulfill the transparency requirements for bond or equity issuance. A country with a small economy will find it difficult to build advanced capital markets because there are few companies large enough to raise funds through them. The limited size of the government bond markets in smaller countries is another reason why these countries find it difficult to build developed bond markets. A small government bond market makes it difficult to form a risk-free yield curve, which is the basis for the development of a corporate bond market. The size of the economy per capita is important, as well as the size of the economy overall. As people become wealthier due to an increase in per capita gross domestic product (GDP), it becomes easier to meet the institutional requirements necessary for capital market development—such as the protection of property rights, regulatory competence, and corporate governance. In addition, as incomes and savings increase, the demand base for tradable financial products such as stocks and bonds will expand.

Fiscal soundness can contribute to the development of a capital market by increasing macroeconomic stability. If public finance is weak and requires a lot of government debt issuance, it will crowd out funds for private investment, possibly hindering the development of the capital market. Furthermore, the risk premium of the government debt in a country with the possibility of default or foreign exchange crisis is inevitably high. In that case, private firms will find it extremely difficult to raise funds through capital markets. However, fiscal deficits are not necessarily detrimental to capital market development.

41 This analogy came from Alan Greenspan, who as chairman of the United States (US) Federal Reserve in 1999 argued that the banking crisis in East Asia would not have been so severe if the stock market had the legal means to supply funds to companies. Levine, Lin, and Xie (2015) tested Greenspan's hypothesis using data from more than 3,600 companies in 36 countries that had experienced at least one banking crisis between 1990 and 2011. They reported that the more well-established the legal system for shareholder protection was, the easier it was for companies to raise funds in the stock market, and the more resilient they were to banking shocks.

An appropriate level of deficit and an issuance of government bonds of various maturities will enable the formation of a risk-free yield curve—the cornerstone of a corporate bond market. The government fiscal deficit would thus have a two-way effect on capital market development. Empirical analyses have noted the crowding-in effect when a fiscal deficit has a positive effect on the corporate bond market (World Bank 2019). This suggests that a bond market can be developed with a fiscal deficit of an appropriate size, though excessive fiscal deficits impair macroeconomic stability, and so are undesirable.

Price stability has an important meaning in the development of the capital markets. In an economy with a high inflation rate, the government bond yield itself is high, hindering the development of the corporate bond market. Furthermore, in an economy with a high inflation rate, financial repression that favors real assets such as real estate over financial assets will occur, weakening the demand base in the capital market.[42]

Financial Market Conditions

The financial market conditions that must be fulfilled to enable the development of a capital market include a robust banking sector, institutional investor base, and financial opening.

Capital market development usually occurs after the banking industry reaches a certain level of development. Banks are the primary dealers of government bonds and are important institutional investors. Banks also act as windows for foreign investors who want to enter the domestic market. Many studies report that private domestic credit as a percentage of GDP has a significant effect on capital market development (Claessens, Klingebiel, and Schmukler 2007; Kowalewski and Pisany 2017).

For the development of a capital market, the existence of institutional investors, such as insurance companies, pension funds, and asset management firms, as well as banks, is important. Institutional investors are not only major sources of demand in government bond and private capital markets, they are also facilitators of financial innovation, which drives market development.

Financial opening contributes to the development of a capital market by expanding the demand base for financial products. In addition, the presence of foreign investors has a positive effect on the development of the capital market by triggering improvements in related aspects, such as corporate governance and financial infrastructure. However, the financial opening may harm the development of the capital market by exacerbating macroeconomic instability. Therefore, the ability to properly absorb the negative effects of financial opening on macroeconomic stability is a prerequisite to maximizing the positive effects of financial opening. Such capacity is closely related to the effectiveness of regulatory and supervisory systems.

Institutional Conditions

This third category covers the protection of investors, sound corporate governance, efficient financial market infrastructures, and a certain level of information and communication technology—all of which can be considered the institutional (and technological) conditions for capital market development.

The most basic institutional condition for capital market development is the establishment of institutional bases for investor protection. Whether an investor can safely protect their investment is the most basic consideration in making an investment decision.

[42] "Financial repression" is a term that was introduced by Shaw (1973) and McKinnon (1973) to designate policies that cause the returns from savings to be lower than the inflation rate. A cap on the interest rate is necessary when financial repression occurs in conjunction with a high inflation rate.

From the initial stage of market development, it is important to have clear legislation on property rights for capital market products and collateral, as well as a judicial system that enables the prompt resolution of disputes. On the other hand, whether regulatory and supervisory authorities effectively monitor capital markets is also important for investor protection. Political stability is another essential factor in the development of capital markets, as it would be difficult to attract long-term investments in jurisdictions where political authorities could easily confiscate private property.

The establishment of transparent corporate governance is important for the development of a bond market, but it is especially important for the development of a stock market. One of the most important reasons for the underutilization of stock markets as a source of financing for companies is the agency problem.[43] Therefore, reducing the agency problem that exists between executive officers and shareholders, or between controlling shareholders and other shareholders, will contribute to the development of the stock market while making stock investments more attractive. To alleviate the agency problem, it is important to improve corporate governance, as well as disclosure and accounting systems. Stocks will become more attractive investment instruments when corporate governance makes it difficult for executives or controlling shareholders to pursue their own interests. Corporate governance can be improved by government policy or at the request of investors, including institutional investors. Although there is no clear empirical evidence on the impact of foreign investors on corporate governance, the higher the proportion of foreign investors in emerging markets, the stronger the voices for institutional improvement, a tendency that favors environments where improvements in corporate governance can be expected.

It is also necessary for the development of a capital market to have well-equipped financial market infrastructures, such as a stock exchange, central securities depository (CSD), and credit rating agency. In addition, it is important to possess and utilize a certain level of ICT that will enable digitalization to improve the efficiency of securities issuance, trading, post-trade activities, and back-office processes.

Some of the factors that are important for capital market development listed above must be provided from the initial stage of market formation. Other factors are more important as the capital markets become mature. On the other hand, some conditions are related to the overall economic and social system, while others are limited to the finance sector. Finally, some changes can be driven by political will and effort alone, while others are not easy to achieve through government policy without support from private initiatives and/or other factors. Table 5.1 classifies these three criteria.

How to Develop Capital Markets in CAREC

The answer to this question is clear: It is necessary to implement policies that will provide the necessary factors for capital market development as summarized in Table 5.1. Progress will improve the size, access, and/or efficiency of the capital market, and thereby increase the IMF's indicators for CAREC countries.

There is no one-size-fits-all approach for all CAREC member states. For countries in the initial stage of capital market development, with indicators below the average for emerging market economies, policymaking must start by addressing the most basic institutional framework. In the absence of basic institutions such as a stock exchange or CSD—which, for example, is the case in Turkmenistan—such institutions will have to be established as soon as possible.

43 An agency problem occurs when an agent charged with acting on behalf of another group, the principal, is prevented from doing so by a conflict of interest.

Table 5.1: Factors in Capital Market Development

Factor	Early-Stage?	System-Wide?	Policy-Driven?
Sizable economy	X	○	△
Sizable per-capita economy	△	○	
Fiscal soundness	△	○	○
Price stability	X	○	△
Robust banking sector	△	X	△
Institutional investor base	X	△	△
Financial opening	X	X	○
Property rights	○	○	○
Prompt dispute resolution	○	○	○
Effective regulation and supervision	△	△	△
Sound corporate governance	X	△	△
Stock exchange	○	X	○
CSD	○	X	○
Rating agency	△	X	△
ICT	○	○	△

○ = "very much," △ = "somewhat yes," X = "no," CSD = central securities depository, ICT = information and communication technology.

Note: A blank cell indicates that the column head does not apply.

Source: Authors.

Raise the Demand Base

In countries with the basic institutions already in place, it will be necessary to focus on introducing an incentive system to increase transactions. For example, even though Tajikistan has had its central securities trading platform, the Central Asian Stock Exchange (CASE), since 2015, that market is quite dormant. Not many potential investors in the stock market may be willing to enter, and companies may still hesitate to go public. In the initial stage of the market, only investors with a strong risk appetite may have participated, resulting in low trading volume and high price volatility.

Boosting public demand through policies such as tax incentives for investing in the stocks of privatized former state-owned enterprises may be helpful, but such policies need to be pursued cautiously, as investors who experience capital losses may start to shun stocks and distrust financial policy authorities. Another way to increase the demand base in the stock market is to promote the pension system. For example, the Government of Armenia initiated a pension program that forces every worker to set aside 5% of their salary in private pension plans, starting in January 2014. Since the launch of the program, the Armenian stock exchange witnessed a large inflow of pension fund money. Increasing the demand base for stocks through pension reform is an important strategy that could be emulated by many CAREC countries suffering chronic shortages of demand for stocks.

Increase the Number of Listed Companies

Many companies will hesitate to go public because the nonmonetary costs involved in an IPO are very high. Furthermore, since family businesses—which have a strong tendency to avoid outsider participation—comprise the majority of companies in developing countries, policymakers may consider introducing policies to reduce that tendency. For example, the Government of the Republic of Korea introduced the Public Corporation Inducement Act in 1972, limiting the shareholdings of outside investors. This measure helped to significantly increase the number of listed companies. Another possibility would be to encourage family businesses to issue preferred stocks that included no voting rights, but explicitly paid dividends (Chami, Fullenkamp, and Sharma 2009). These changes would also help the bond market development because companies that have gained a market reputation will be able to issue corporate bonds.

Focus on Developing the Government Bond Market

The development of a corporate bond market presupposes a well-functioning market for government bonds of various maturities. There is a wide variation among the CAREC countries when it comes to government bonds. Whereas the Government of Kazakhstan issues bonds of various maturities, for example, the bonds issued by the Government of Tajikistan are limited to shorter maturities. To increase the diversity of issuance, governments should make an effort to improve credibility, increase demand, and expand infrastructure and related markets. These efforts will gradually provide the foundation for the emergence of government bonds with longer maturities, and they will be needed to build a yield curve that will attract investors.

Incentivize Banks

Since banks dominate the financial system throughout most of the CAREC region, their cooperation is very important for capital markets to function. However, since banks may regard the capital market as a competitor for loan customers, it is difficult to expect them to actively engage in developing the capital market. Appropriate incentives will, therefore, be necessary to induce banks to accept measures to promote capital market development. For example, policymakers could facilitate the participation of banks in the capital market as liquidity providers. In addition, banks should be allowed to sell collective investment products and provide asset management advisory services, adding new sources of revenue to their traditional interest income.

Develop the Judicial System

For capital market development, it is also essential to establish a judicial system that will ensure the protection of property rights and reliable dispute resolution. All countries have legislative clauses protecting property rights. However, the actual practice of the judicial systems in CAREC countries is generally not very reliable. According to the World Justice Project's 2024 "WJP Rule of Law Index," covering 142 countries and other jurisdictions, the highest-ranked CAREC country included in the survey was Georgia (ranked 49), followed by Kazakhstan (65), Mongolia (66), and Uzbekistan (83). The PRC was ranked 95 (World Justice Project 2024). Improving the functioning of the judicial system in the CAREC countries will require multidimensional efforts, such as limiting government power, reducing corruption, and strengthening regulatory enforcement.

Catalyze Fintech

All these policy areas are important. However, they will not produce the desired effects easily or immediately. That is why fintech innovation can be an important catalyst of capital market development. It can significantly enhance the efficiency of securities trade and post-trade activities. Furthermore, fintech innovations could redesign or replace traditional capital markets; it is to this possibility that this discussion now turns.

THE ROLE OF FINTECH IN CAPITAL MARKET DEVELOPMENT

Initially, fintech focused on payment and settlement services, where entry barriers were low and public demand high. It has gradually expanded into lending, financial investment services, and insurance. This section examines fintech's impact on financial investment services and capital markets.

Fintech promotes efficiency in financial products and service delivery, offering cost reductions, saving time, and increasing convenience for financial institutions, customers, and regulators. Beyond efficiency, fintech solutions fundamentally change how financial products and services are offered, creating a new financial industry ecosystem that challenges customer loyalty to traditional financial institutions. Increased competition improves financial efficiency, transparency, and access, addressing long-standing barriers to inclusion. New business models facilitated by fintech can make it possible for firms and individuals to get access to financial services that would not have been possible without them, therefore mitigating financial exclusion and narrowing the financial gap. Fintech models enable access to services previously unavailable, especially in developing countries.

Despite its potential, fintech presents challenges to consumer protection, fair competition, financial integrity, and stability. A balanced view of risks and opportunities is required to assess its role in capital market development.[44] Two methods can be used to examine fintech's impacts: (i) analysis based on technologies such as artificial intelligence (AI), distributed ledger technology (DLT), blockchain,[45] and big data; or (ii) a categorization based on user needs and financial services, such as capital raising, trading, and investment. This chapter will follow the second method.

The effects of fintech on capital markets and financial investment services vary between the developed and developing countries due to their differing financial and institutional environments. Thus, after addressing general impacts, this chapter will focus on considerations relevant to developing countries, and on areas particularly important in CAREC.

IMPACTS OF FINTECH ON FINANCIAL INVESTMENT SERVICES

Raising Capital

Online or mobile alternative financing platforms are usurping the role of banks and brokers in linking investors with individuals and firms looking for capital. These new platforms include such opportunities as peer-to-peer (P2P) lending, equity crowdfunding, initial coin offerings (ICOs), and security token offerings (STOs).

P2P lending connects individuals willing to lend money directly to those seeking loans, without a financial intermediary. Unlike traditional banks, P2P platforms allow lenders to choose borrowers, provide credit analysis, set interest rates, manage collateral, and facilitate transfers without transforming assets.

---

[44] See, for example, IMF (2018). The IMF and World Bank Group jointly proposed a framework called the "Bali Fintech Agenda" to help member counties harness the opportunities for advances in financial technologies, while managing their risks. The agenda is organized around a set of 12 elements balancing opportunities and risks.

[45] Strictly speaking, blockchain is a kind of DLT. However, the two are used interchangeably in this chapter.

Lenders know who is receiving their money, and borrowers understand where their loans originated. P2P lenders resemble securities brokers more than traditional banks. Data sources, such as tax payments and utility bills, can be used to assess a borrower's ability to make repayments, which is especially useful in developing countries with limited financial records. For instance, Optimal NMax LLC launched Mongolia's first P2P lending service in 2018, using psychological tests to evaluate decision-making capacity and maturity.

Equity crowdfunding refers to fundraising by issuing shares to a large number of small investors through online or mobile platforms. It can be reward-based or involve equity.[46] Individuals or groups participating in reward-based (non-equity) crowdfunding offer funds in exchange for tangible (e.g., goods) or intangible (e.g., service, reputation, identity) returns. By contrast, investors in equity crowdfunding receive shares that can produce profits through dividends or corporate mergers and acquisitions, or by selling the shares if the firm goes public. This method has the potential to solve the financing gaps of start-ups. A company that succeeds in equity crowdfunding will be able to attract angel investors.

ICOs sell encrypted digital tokens to investors on the blockchain in exchange for currency or mainstream cryptocurrencies such as Bitcoin or Ethereum. Tokens issued through ICOs are called "utility tokens," as they give users the right to purchase goods or services from the token issuer, though they cannot claim a share of the token issuer's profit or net assets. ICOs are often referred to as "digital security" crowdfunding. Indeed, when the tokens are used as a means of exchange for the future use of a product or service, the ICO is similar to reward-based crowdfunding (OECD 2019).[47]

STOs sell subscriptions to newly issued security tokens, digitalized representations of assets in the form of encrypted tokens based on DLT. These tokens can either exist only within the blockchain or be backed by an off-chain asset; and they are considered a proxy for asset-backed securities on the blockchain (OECD 2020). Unlike utility tokens, security tokens purchased with STOs confer ownership of the assets underlying the token issuance. If the underlying asset is stock, its holder may receive a portion of profits generated by the token issuer as a dividend or take part in its management.

Banks tend to be reluctant to provide loans unless the borrower's financial performance is demonstrated, or collateral can be provided. However, investors participating in alternative financing platforms may be willing to provide funds at their own risk if they consider the prospects bright, even if the borrowers have insufficient past financial performance. In this respect, alternative financing platforms share similar characteristics with traditional capital markets or venture capital markets.[48] This has special significance for financing start-ups and small and medium-sized enterprises (SMEs) in developing countries, where traditional capital markets are not developed.

From an investor's view, such platforms can be attractive investment alternatives. Individual investors can participate directly in large-scale investment projects, such as movies or public development projects through P2P lending or equity crowdfunding. Alternative financing platforms may fit with investors who prefer a high-risk and high-return profile and with those who can voluntarily publicize a project to increase its likelihood of success.

[46] Although the expression "loan-type crowdfunding" or "debt-based crowdfunding" can sometimes be seen in the literature, it is the same as the P2P lending mentioned above.

[47] The difference is that ICOs are based on blockchain technology, whereas reward-based crowdfunding is not.

[48] As most companies that raise funds from alternative financing platforms are seed or early-stage firms, they are closer to the angel or venture capital markets than to the stock or bond markets in which mature companies participate.

These alternative financing platforms also carry risks and challenges, not least being less regulated. The "wisdom of the crowd" could mitigate asymmetric information problems, but investments could also be tainted by herd behavior, while problems such as borrower fraud cannot be underestimated.

Among the above platforms, the most recently introduced STOs are noteworthy, as they preserve the advantages of existing platforms, but offer a better chance of addressing risks and challenges, thanks to better-conceived regulations on information disclosure and unfair trade; and token owners are reviewed through a Know Your Customer (KYC) process to ensure adherence to anti-money laundering/combating the financing of terrorism (AML/CFT) regulations. On the other hand, various types of assets can be divided and tokenized, making it possible for firms to raise funds based on the low-liquid assets that they hold, such as real estate, machinery, and copyrights.

Unlike traditional securities, which require traditional market intermediaries and market infrastructures, tokenized assets require a mature token issuance ecosystem. For STOs to become a reality, security token issuers, security token issuance platforms, and security token trading platforms must be in place. Not many countries have such an ecosystem. The legal status of tokenized assets for equities is an acute problem because most countries do not legally recognize them as true equity, but only as a right to equity. For these reasons, STO volumes are not yet large, even in advanced economies. Nevertheless, these hurdles are expected to be overcome eventually.[49] Then, tokenized securities will help SMEs to raise funds through an automated process based on DLT, reducing the time and cost of issuance.[50]

Trading and Investment

The impacts of fintech on trading and investment include pre-trade analytics, investment advisory, and trade execution. Advances in computing power and predictive modeling, as well as improved accessibility to big data, make it possible to make predictions. Artificial intelligence (AI) and machine learning (ML) leveraging vast amounts of structured and unstructured data, including through social media, can be useful in that regard. Investment banks are increasingly using those technologies in their research, with Dataminr and Visible Alpha as examples of providers of real-time information and predictions based on AI and ML technology.[51]

Fintech solutions are changing traditional asset- and wealth-management businesses. Investment technology solutions help fund managers and clients make better investment decisions based on solid data analytics. Robot advisers provide automated portfolio management advice and strategies for general investors, which will naturally result in less human intervention in asset management (Kwon and Cho 2018).

[49] Quinlan & Associates, a strategy consultancy specializing in the financial services industry, anticipated that the global listed trading volume of security tokens would reach $162.7 trillion by 2030, representing 42.9% of the share of global market-traded products, and that more than $4 trillion worth of security tokens will be issued in 2030, representing 27.4% of market share (Quinlan, Chung, and Trehan 2021).

[50] OECD (2020) enumerates several experimental cases, such as bond issuance on public blockchains in the UK, bond issuance on private and permissioned blockchains by the World Bank, tokenized convertible bonds issuance by the French bank Société Générale, and tokenized equity issuance on the London Stock Exchange.

[51] Dataminr is a company providing real-time information based on AI technology. It was founded in 2009 in New York. Visible Alpha is an investment research company founded in 2012 by some of the world's leading investment banks, such as Bank of America, Merrill Lynch, Citigroup, Jefferies, Morgan Stanley, and UBS.

The most notable change brought about by technological development in the retail trading space is the advent of online and mobile trading platforms. By assisting individual investors, these platforms have significantly increased the trading volume in securities, while demanding low brokerage fees and minimum deposits. Other solutions provided by fintech firms for retail trading include financial website comparison platforms, financial aggregator platforms, and social trading and investment platforms.[52] The financial aggregator platform lets customers check and transact accounts of financial companies in one place. More recently, financial institutions have become increasingly interested in the metaverse as a next-generation virtual interface with clients. It will likely become a common space for people to make investments and receive advice without having to visit branch offices of financial companies.

Trading platforms aimed at institutional investors are also noteworthy. Through ICT-based trading-platform innovation, integrated banking systems have introduced not only listed stocks and exchange-traded derivatives, but also unlisted stocks, corporate bonds, nonperforming loans (NPLs), and structured product brokerage platforms to expand the range of targeted trading products and reduce transaction costs. In addition, they are adopting an open-platform strategy that discloses the information necessary for transaction execution and risk management, and discloses related application programming interfaces (APIs) to all departments and major customers.

These fintech innovations are helping to broaden the investor base and enhance efficiency in trading and investment. The application of AI in asset price prediction and portfolio formation, the emergence of low-cost online and mobile investment platforms, and the use of website comparison platforms help novices invest in securities more easily, with reduced time and costs. The development of trading platforms for institutional investors has reduced transaction costs and improved price discovery.

That said, the new models also pose significant risks and challenges. Trading platforms must be controlled effectively for AML/KYC compliance. The risk of bad investment advice is higher for non-face-to-face platforms than for offline interactions. While social trading and investment platforms can harness the "wisdom of the crowd," they can also encourage herd behavior, and make recommendations that are unsuitable for investors who have different risk appetites and are at risk of manipulation.

According to Statista, digital investments were expected to have a transaction value of $3.22 trillion in 2023,[53] and total $5.27 trillion in 2027. Robo-advisors, the market's largest category, were expected to transact $2.76 trillion in 2023. The United States has the largest cumulative digital transaction value.

In CAREC countries where capital markets are not sufficiently developed, it is difficult to expect that fintech solutions will have a similar effect on capital markets as in advanced economies. Nevertheless, online, mobile, and metaverse trading platforms, as well as robot investment advisories, will contribute to a broadening of the investor base by attracting a younger generation familiar with ICT technology.

Post-Trade

Fintech technologies are creating new solutions that are addressing pain points in clearing, settlement, collateral, margin management, and other post-trade processing. DLT has the potential to improve securities clearing and settlement. The calculation of counterparties' obligations may be done on a

52 Refer to IOSCO (2017, pp. 23–29) for a more detailed explanation of these platforms.

53 See Statista (n.d.). The market for digital investment includes online brokerages, robo-advisors, and mobile trading apps. It also includes the use of AI and ML algorithms to assist with investment and portfolio management.

transaction-by-transaction basis or on a net basis. For clearing and settlement arrangements to operate in traditional capital markets, financial intermediaries entrusted by market participants (e.g., banks and broker-dealers) and financial market infrastructures that connect banks and broker-dealers (e.g., clearing houses and CSDs) will be required to intervene.[54]

With DLT, the history and current ownership of a transaction are recorded in a distributed ledger, and asset transfers can be implemented with a smart contract based on prior agreement. The use of DLT-based solutions for the digital representation of securities can automate many functions of financial intermediaries and financial market infrastructures, improving the speed and efficiency of clearing and settlement. The US Depository Trust & Clearing Corporation (DTCC) and the Australian Securities Exchange (ASX) are exploring blockchain for this purpose. DLT can be used for trading and settlement of financial derivatives, in addition to securities. DLT could improve efficiency through automated margin and collateral management and settlement through smart contracts.

Improved transparency and immutability in record keeping, along with automation in clearing and settlement through DLT, could significantly reduce time and costs compared with those of manual processes. While blockchain could theoretically eliminate the current delays of up to 3 days in security and bond settlements, the delays often reflect market needs, which vary by asset type, transaction volume, liquidity requirements, and market maker impact (FINRA 2017). Thus, DLT adoption may not guarantee real-time savings.

The use of blockchain for the delivery and payment legs of a settlement does not imply the demise of financial intermediaries, insofar as the arrangement is based on net clearing and a permissioned blockchain. However, a securities trade and post-trade arrangement that bypasses them may emerge, and may look like today's decentralized exchanges for the direct sale of crypto assets between traders, using stablecoins for settlement. In the future, security tokens representing stocks or bonds could be traded and settled against crypto assets such as stablecoins without any intermediaries.

In advanced economies where traditional markets and financial intermediaries are influential, it is difficult to imagine capital markets being replaced by decentralized exchanges. However, in the CAREC countries where traditional capital markets are not yet developed, the possibility that STOs will be activated and a decentralized exchange will perform the same functions as a traditional stock market cannot be ruled out.

Attention must be paid to the risks of involving decentralized finance (DeFi) in securities trading and settlement. A decentralized exchange is limited to trading crypto assets because DeFi is not yet trusted. If DeFi using stablecoins becomes a well-established practice for securities trading and settlement, and is linked with the existing financial system, its impact on the economy could be significant. While stablecoins offer convenience in the blockchain and metaverse space, they contain significant risk in the real economy, including potential the mismanagement of assets by operators, which could jeopardize their value stability.

[54] In general, a clearing house acts as a buyer to the seller of a concluded contract and as a seller to the buyer. In this case, the clearing house is called the "central counterparty clearing house" (CCP). By contrast, a CSD is an institution that holds securities deposited by customers and effectuates ownership transfer according to the clients' request through a book entry, rather than by a transfer of physical securities.

A "coin run" may occur if trust in the coin operators falters.[55] In addition, monopolistic stablecoin operators could abuse their economic power.[56] For these reasons, stricter regulations on stablecoins are anticipated.[57]

Other Back-Office Activities

Increased competition and strengthened regulation have put pressure on incumbent capital market participants in advanced economies to reduce costs of back-office activities by turning to advanced technologies. Activities that fintech solutions are likely to replace or complement include compliance, internal control, client onboarding, client relationship management, and corporate actions.

Compliance is complex and burdensome because financial institutions must respond to a raft of regulatory requirements in a timely and evidence-based manner. With Ernst & Young (2015) estimating the costs of compliance at 40% of financial companies' costs, increased compliance efficiency through the automation of manual tasks will be key. Compliance efficiency could be reached more easily if regulatory bodies cooperate with the establishment of fintech-driven solutions for compliance and reporting. For example, when regulatory bodies participate as nodes in a permissioned blockchain to access real-time and direct-trade data of regulated companies, regulatory reporting becomes more efficient.

Financial companies can prevent staff errors through AI-based anomaly detection technology that flags deviations from consumers' past transaction patterns. Anomaly-detection technology can be also used for the supervisory purpose of detecting unfair trades in exchanges. In addition to AI, blockchain may help facilitate effective controls by recording transactions with minimal human intervention, promoting accountability, maintaining record integrity, and providing an irrefutable record (Burns et al. 2020). That blockchain allows more frequent, more detailed monitoring of more tasks will greatly increase the effectiveness of a firm's internal controls.

Client onboarding and client relationship management are other areas where fintech solutions can reduce costs. Non-face-to-face client onboarding can be promoted, using encryption and biometric authentication technology, and can be useful when financial institutions are geographically dispersed across a large territory. In addition, the inconvenience of duplicate authentication can be reduced through cooperation between financial firms. Brokers and dealers in the Republic of Korea introduced a blockchain-based system in 2017 that updates details of clients across the entire blockchain consortium whenever a member receives client authentication. Therefore, the client does not need to go through separate authentication again when transacting with other institutions.

Corporate action when firms initiate an event that affects their investors, such as a distribution of dividends or a stock split, is a promising area for fintech solutions. Technology that improves the accuracy and transparency of shareholder votes through blockchain technology, and that prevents voting manipulation, is drawing attention because it could have an important impact on corporate governance. Heightened trust in non-face-to-face voting would increase the participation of minority shareholders in corporate decisions.

[55] The collapse of Terra USD (UST) and its sister cryptocurrency, LUNA, in 2022 clearly show how stablecoins are vulnerable to coin runs.

[56] Since network externality works for currency circulation, it is highly likely that only a small number of stablecoins will be used.

[57] In September 2020, the European Commission announced that it would implement stricter liquidity management policies and capital regulations for stablecoin operators of a certain size or larger.

By using AI or blockchain for back-office activities, financial companies could increase productivity and respond more quickly and appropriately to new demands from customers and regulators. The global customer relationship management (CRM) market was estimated to be worth between $58 billion and $64 billion in 2021. It is expected to increase as a result of factors such as rising demand for AI-powered global CRM systems, the growing use of social media platforms for customer engagement, and the desire to improve customer satisfaction and loyalty.

The adoption of new technologies in the back office can lead to problems, however, including idle staff and branches. Imperfect automated algorithms may introduce new operational risks, and the increased use of new technologies implies more volatile customer needs. These problems are not new, but rather a deepening of the challenges posed by the ongoing digital transformation of finance.

Fintech may also produce new problems. Today's AI is mostly implemented through ML, creating its own algorithms from data. Thus, algorithms can create ethical controversies. For example, an AI chatbot can deliver hate speech based on improper learning data. To prevent this, transparency and fairness of AI algorithms need to be improved, and AI governance within a firm must work properly.[58] It must be backed by a legal framework such as the European Union's (EU's) pioneering Artificial Intelligence Act, 2021,[59] which regulates AI systems based on four categories of risk.

FINANCIAL INVESTMENT SERVICES AND FINTECH DISRUPTIONS

Feasibility and Necessity

In developed economies, fintech is impacting financial investment services such as alternative financing platforms, trading and investment, post-trade activities, and back-office functions. Which services are most relevant to fintech disruption in the CAREC region? And how can they be improved? Relevance can be assessed based on two factors: (i) institutional and technological feasibility, considering the development stages of CAREC's fintech and capital markets; and (ii) the need to address the financial gaps in the region. Since the PRC is at a far more advanced stage than the other CAREC members, this section will focus on the average levels of capital market and fintech development in CAREC, excluding the PRC. Discussion that is specific to a particular emerging fintech market in the region will be noted as such.

The analysis addresses the relevance of financial investment services to fintech disruption in the CAREC region. The relevance can be ranked by combining two criteria: feasibility and necessity. In terms of feasibility, the service area is marked High (H) if the underlying technology is widely used in advanced economies, and the institutional conditions needed to provide the service are not complicated.

58 AI governance refers to the decision-making structure within a company related to the establishment of AI-related ethical principles and standards, and to the preparation of AI-related risk management policies. For a more detailed description of this, see IOSCO (2021).

59 The European Commission's proposal, presented in April 2021, is a key element of the EU's policy on the regulation of AI (EU 2021). On 6 December 2022, the Council reached an agreement on a general approach (negotiating mandate) to this regulation, and entered interinstitutional talks with the European Parliament ("trilogues") in June 2023.

It is indicated as Low (L) for technology still in the proof-of-concept stage and for which the needed institutional conditions are complicated. It is indicated as Medium (M), if the technology is not widely used and the needed institutional conditions are not complicated, or if the technology is widely used and the needed institutional conditions are complicated.

In terms of necessity, a High (H) rating indicates that the investment service is contributing directly to capital market revitalization or is filling the financing gap for SMEs; Middle (M) when it indirectly contributes to the development of the capital market by improving market infrastructure, investor access, or financial literacy; and Low (L) when it has minimal or no measurable impact on capital market development or SME financing. Based on these two criteria, P2P lending (and equity crowdfunding), mobile trading, STOs, compliance automation, CRM, robo-advisories, and securities settlements were selected as service areas that CAREC should focus on in applying fintech solutions for the development of capital markets (Table 5.2). The relative significance of those services for capital market development may differ slightly among countries, according to the availability of technology, the regulatory environment, and the nature of their financing gaps.

Table 5.2: Relevance of Financial Investment Services for Fintech Disruption in CAREC

Criteria	P2P Lending/Equity Crowdfunding	Mobile Trading	STO	Automation of Compliance	CRM	Robot Advisory	Securities Settlement
Feasibility	H	M	L	M	M	M	L
Necessity	H	H	H	M	M	L	M

CAREC = Central Asia Regional Economic Cooperation, CRM = customer relationship management, fintech = financial technology, H = High, L = Low, M = Medium, P2P = peer-to-peer, STO = security token offering.

Source: Authors.

Peer-to-Peer Lending and Equity Crowdfunding

P2P lending and equity crowdfunding are the priority areas to be promoted,[60] considering that they do not require high-level technology,[61] and the need to respond to firms' financing gaps is high (Table 5.3). Although banks dominate the domestic financial landscape in all countries in the region, the proportion of firms or small firms using banks to finance investment or production is not high, which implies a high financing gap facing the firms. Although Mongolia and Georgia have relatively well-functioning banking systems, fewer than half their firms use banks to finance investment or working capital. Thus, the need to activate alternative financing platforms is important in almost all the CAREC countries.

The regulatory environment for P2P lending and equity crowdfunding varies from country to country. A 2019 survey conducted by the World Bank and the Cambridge Centre for Alternative Finance (CCAF) found that about one-third of the included jurisdictions allowed alternative finance sectors to grow without regulation (World Bank and CCAF 2019). Among the CAREC countries, the PRC, Kazakhstan, and Pakistan regulated P2P lending or equity crowdfunding. Many CAREC countries, including Mongolia and Uzbekistan, neither regulated nor prohibited alternative finance platforms.

60 Whereas P2P lending involves direct loans paid back with interest, crowdfunding offers shares in the company for which the capital is being raised.

61 If such a business is developed in the form of a blockchain-based DeFi, institutional and technological feasibility will have to be evaluated much lower. However, it is assumed here that an administrator at the center of the platform proactively provides related services.

Table 5.3: Financing Gap Indicators for CAREC Countries

(%)

Country	Firms with a Bank Loan or Line of Credit	Small Firms with a Bank Loan or Line of Credit	Firms Using Banks to Finance Investment	Firms Using Banks to Finance Working Capital
Azerbaijan (2019)	16.8	9.1	24.4 (2013)	19.4
PRC (2012)	25.3	13.9	14.7	22.1
Georgia (2019)	43.3	38.0	34.5	31.5
Kazakhstan (2019)	17.2	12.0	14.0	13.2
Kyrgyz Republic (2019)	25.8	17.4	16.7	18.8
Mongolia (2019)	39.3	26.8	47.9	37.5
Pakistan (2013)	6.7	3.4	8.1	8.6
Tajikistan (2019)	18.0	13.1	8.3	12.8
Uzbekistan (2019)	22.2	18.6	26.2	23.7

CAREC = Central Asia Regional Economic Cooperation, PRC = People's Republic of China.

Notes:

1. The years in the parentheses are the years of observation.
2. There are no data for Afghanistan or Turkmenistan.

Source: World Bank Global Financial Development Database (accessed 8 December 2022).

In many CAREC countries, there are fintech companies that participate in P2P lending, even without a defined legal framework; and some of them have a sizable share of their country's loan industry. In Tajikistan, for example, zypl.ai has used AI technology to offer a quick credit-rating solution for microlending. The digital loan segment, with more than 30% of the fintech market in Kazakhstan, is one of the most developed parts of the country's loan industry. And lending to fintech companies accounted for 20.2% of loans in Mongolia in 2021.[62]

However, the lack of a clear legal foundation may hinder the sector's growth and weaken financial regulatory goals such as consumer protection. CAREC member governments need to create an alternative financing regulatory framework that enables businesses to obtain capital while safeguarding investors and borrowers. For platforms to effectively help start-ups and SMEs in the CAREC region, platform moderators must provide valuable information to investors, supported by technology that utilizes unstructured data and a solid data-related legal framework.

Another important way to activate the P2P lending market is to allow institutional investors to participate. This may result in a chronic shortage of funding, as has been the experience in many countries, but it may open a secondary market for the shares issued through equity crowdfunding. For example, the Korea Exchange opened KRX Startup Market (KSM) in 2016 to facilitate the trading of shares of start-ups and SMEs that had raised capital through equity crowdfunding.[63]

62 The information here is from the technical assistance reports of national consultants.

63 The number of companies registered in this market increased from 37 at the beginning to 131 as of February 2023. However, the number of companies that actually trade, and the scale of their transactions, remain limited.

Mobile Trading Platforms

To promote the development of a capital market, it is necessary to expand the demand base for financial investment products. The experience of many countries shows that mobile trading has contributed significantly to the expansion of retail demand. In the CAREC region, internet and mobile phones are widely used, but not commonly for financial services. For example, the proportion of people in the region who use the internet or mobile phones to access an account is below the world average, except in the PRC and Mongolia (Table 5.4). The CAREC countries need to expand their internet and, especially, mobile financial services in line with the already widespread penetration of mobile phones.

Table 5.4: Internet and Mobile Phone Penetration in CAREC Countries

Country	Individuals Using the Internet[a]	Mobile-Cellular Subscriptions[b]	Used a Mobile Phone or the Internet to Pay Bills[c]	Used a Mobile Phone or the Internet to Send Money[c]	Used a Mobile Phone or the Internet to Access an Account[d]
Azerbaijan	85	102	7		2
PRC	70	119	60	69	38
Georgia	73	128	25	19	9
Kazakhstan	86	129	51	47	18
Kyrgyz Republic	51	130	9	12	6
Mongolia	63	133	43	66	38
Pakistan	25	80	6	6	8
Tajikistan	22	121	4	3	8
Turkmenistan	21	155	0		2
Uzbekistan	71	100	16	10	7
World	63		34	35	25

CAREC = Central Asia Regional Economic Cooperation, PRC = People's Republic of China.

Note: An empty cell indicates that the column head does not apply.

[a] The values in this column are per 100 habitants in 2020, except in the Kyrgyz Republic (in 2019), Tajikistan (2017), and Turkmenistan (2017).

[b] The values in this column are per 100 habitants in 2020.

[c] The values in this column are per 100 habitants over 15 years of age in 2021, except Azerbaijan (2017) and Turkmenistan (2017).

[d] The values in this column are per 100 habitants over 15 years of age in 2017.

Sources: International Telecommunication Union. https://www.itu.int; and World Bank. n.d. The Global Findex Database 2021 (accessed 12 January 2023).

The first step in developing mobile capital market services is the provision of a mobile trading platform by existing broker-dealers. Most CAREC countries, except the PRC, have not even reached this stage. Given their small transaction volumes, it may be considered premature to introduce a mobile trading system. As the next step, brokers specialized in mobile trading can be expected to open for business; and related services such as trading platform comparison websites and social trading platforms will likely emerge. If the stock-investing population increases following these changes, then stock prices will rise and a virtuous cycle will be formed by corporate interest in raising funds through the stock market.

It is also necessary for attractive companies to be listed on the stock market to trigger a broadening of the investor base. To this end, the government may consider introducing incentives to promote the listing of companies. If there are regulations that prevent the emergence of new businesses, however, they will need to be relaxed. The introduction of a regulatory sandbox where new businesses can be challenged without being affected by existing laws and regulations can be a practical way to promote financial innovations.

Security Token Offerings

STOs are not yet widely used even in developed countries. However, as we saw earlier, given the successful cases of tokenized security issuance, STOs can still make headway globally sooner or later. In CAREC, many technological and legal hurdles need to be overcome for this method to spread, and it is not expected to be active in the short term. However, given that STOs are very likely to play a very important role in filling the financial gap, countries in the region need to build a token ecosystem by improving technological aptitude and overhauling related legal frameworks.

One might question whether these efforts are worth it. However, traditional capital markets in most CAREC countries are not working nicely either. The incremental benefits of establishing a token ecosystem can be quite large in CAREC, compared with the countries where traditional financial markets are well established. Therefore, it seems a good direction for CAREC countries to establish a token ecosystem along with efforts to establish traditional financial market infrastructures as a strategy for promoting capital market development.

Compliance and Customer Relationship Management

Digitalizing and automating the back-office activities of financial investment firms will be important for the development of the capital market. In advanced economies, fintech firms that provide business-to-business (B2B) services occupy an important proportion of the fintech landscape. It would be desirable for them to play an active role in CAREC (Chapter 6). In the initial stage, fintech firms need to support the digitalization of the back-office activities of financial firms. However, this alone will not be sufficient to achieve cost-reduction targets if they remain simply digitalized. The efficiency of back-office activities could be improved significantly through a shift from the digitalization stage to the automation stage, and the use of AI and blockchain technologies could be very useful. Therefore, it will be necessary to develop compliance and internal control using those technologies in the mid to long term.

Since the global financial crisis did not destroy the profitability of financial institutions in developing-economy capital markets, unlike in developed countries, the need to cut costs by embracing new technologies may not have been so urgent. However, financial firms in the region should pay attention to how back-office activities leverage new technologies, as it is just as necessary for them to respond appropriately to strengthening regulations applied globally, to reduce costs, and to provide their clients with better services.

POLICYMAKING FOR FINTECH IN CAPITAL MARKET DEVELOPMENT

Although promoting fintech in the capital market is the job of private economic agents such as fintech firms, investment banks, and brokers and dealers, the role of policymakers is important for maximizing the benefits and minimizing the risks of fintech disruption. Furthermore, policymakers have a distinct leveraging role because fintech products and services associated with capital markets and financial investment services are still rare in most CAREC countries.

The role of policy authorities can be broadly divided into (i) the overhaul of the policy and regulatory framework related to the use of fintech in the capital market, and (ii) the formation of an environment that facilitates the use of fintech in the capital market.[64]

Overhauling the Fintech-Related Policy and Regulatory Framework

About half the countries in Central Asia, responding to the 2019 IMF-World Bank Global Fintech Survey, answered that they had established a national fintech-development strategy, while the rest said they planned to do so (World Bank 2020). This suggests that most countries include fintech in their national development agenda. The basic direction of fintech utilization for the capital market should be consistent with this development strategy. The future policy direction should be set based on the country's technological level, the status of its financial market infrastructure, and the significance of the finance sector and capital market for national economic development.

Setting the Basic Direction

The basic direction of fintech use in capital market development should be to help secure policy coherence by aligning with policy goals in various fields and clarifying the principles of regulation. Since establishing a fintech firm or utilizing technology requires significant private investment, policy uncertainty will hinder the sector's development. Therefore, the government needs to set policy priorities for private fintech-related investment and promote its utilization. It will also be necessary to help financial companies prepare for fintech-related risks from the beginning by proposing the basic principles of regulation.

Proposing policy goals and regulatory principles suitable for each CAREC country's circumstances will be an important basis for guiding the actions of private economic actors in the direction desired by the policy authorities. Take, for example, the Azerbaijan 2030 agenda. The country's five national priorities for socioeconomic development include a steadily growing economy and areas of modern innovations and competitive human capital. According to the agenda, the capital and insurance markets need to be developed more quickly as key channels for the economy's long-term investment resources. It also emphasizes how crucial technology will be to advancing the economy. The potential contribution of fintech to economic growth in general, and to the expansion of capital markets in particular, is not mentioned. Considering this, the Government of Azerbaijan must create a separate document outlining its plans to advance fintech by creating a more favorable business environment and upgrading the country's underdeveloped ICT sector.

Enacting or Revising Regulations on New Products and Services

When the private sector introduces services or products, regulators will have to make sure that they can be regulated through existing laws and enforcement decrees. If the applicability of the existing regulations is ambiguous, authoritative interpretation will be necessary. In many cases, regulating new products or services may require laws to be revised or new laws to be enacted. Crypto assets, including stablecoins, P2P lending, equity crowdfunding, initial coin offerings (ICOs), and security tokens, are examples of products and services that should be given clear legal interpretations. The necessity of establishing clear legislation on the use of fintech is more pronounced in countries with civil law traditions.

64 Although these are discussed separately for convenience, the two issues strongly overlap. This is because a significant number of government policies and regulations concern the establishment of an environment that will facilitate the use of fintech; and the major means of establishing such an environment are policies or regulations related to fintech innovation.

In principle, businesses that are not explicitly allowed can be understood to be prohibited under civil law. So, it is more important to have a clear legal basis for the introduction and use of fintech in civil law countries, compared with common law countries, where legal ambiguity provides a space for innovative activities. According to JuriGlobe, most jurisdictions in CAREC are based on civil law, although Kazakhstan's Astana International Financial Centre (AIFC) has a separate legal framework based on English common law (University of Ottawa n.d.).

Regulators need to balance the costs and risks with benefits and opportunities when enacting or revising laws related to new services or products. It would be helpful for regulators to observe how a new business can be harmonized with existing laws and institutions by allowing it to spend time in a regulatory sandbox. The regulatory sandbox is expected to promote financial innovation and help improve financial inclusion. Regulators are more likely to move away from a passive position, and instead actively seek out technology companies, while buying time to observe any problems that the application of new technologies may cause. From the company's point of view, the launching will be more promising because of reduced regulatory uncertainty. Thanks to these changes, investment in fintech firms is also expected to increase.

Wherever new capital market services leveraging fintech are allowed, a new competitive landscape will be deployed. Alternative financing platforms, for example, will compete with traditional financial markets. In principle, new products and services leveraging fintech should be promoted to maximize consumer benefits. However, in some cases, the maximum benefit to consumers may favor fintech firms and disadvantage incumbents such as banks and investment companies. If, under this principle, a new fintech business is allowed, with a lighter regulatory burden for new entrants than for incumbents, unequal market treatment will not be warranted. The application of consumer benefit maximization should be balanced with consumer protection, market integrity, and financial system stability.

A widely known principle governing the power game between fintech firms and incumbents is probably the principle of "same function, same risk, same regulation."[65] Firms performing the same function should have to abide by the same regulations because they incur the same risks. However, this principle may protect incumbents to the detriment of new entrants when the same strict regulations are imposed despite clear functional differences. On the other hand, if the licensing units for capital market services are not sufficiently subdivided, fintech firms providing limited services would be obligated to satisfy the same licensing requirements for capital, staffing, and facilities, which may discourage them from applying for a license. Therefore, regulators will have to be very careful not to overly burden fintech firms.

Creating Standards for Data Protection and Cross-Cutting Technologies

To promote the use of fintech for capital markets, standards will be necessary for regulations on elements commonly used or applied across various financial services. These include data used in various services and the underlying technologies used for those services.

Today, data are the most important raw material in fintech-related technologies such as AI, machine learning (ML), and data analytics. The development of fintech needs to establish an environment in which financial companies can easily access structured and unstructured data, while appropriately protecting personal information. Therefore, policy authorities need to review existing data-related legislation and revise if necessary.

[65] Agustín Carstens, general manager of the BIS, described a level playing field in a speech in January 2018 as follows: "When banks and fintech firms vie for the same customers with similar services and by taking similar risks, they should be similarly regulated: same risk, same regulation" (Carstens 2018).

The most advanced jurisdiction in this regard is the EU. Through the General Data Protection Regulation (GDPR), which came into effect in May 2018, the EU protects customers' rights to access, transfer, request corrections in, and delete their data; it also strengthens corporate responsibility with regard to data use. This regulation is now a global standard for data protection.

A similar legal framework for data protection has been introduced in several CAREC jurisdictions. For example, access to and the use or processing of personal data are governed in Uzbekistan by the Law on Personal Data, which was adopted in July 2019. Only after receiving the consent of the subject of personal information can anybody, whether an individual or a legal entity, use personal data. In September 2021, referring to the GDPR, the Government if Uzbekistan enacted the Personal Information Protection Act to lay the legal foundation for institutional guarantees for cybersecurity, data security, and personal information protection.

The National Bank of Georgia began offering interested individuals the chance to register with the Credit Information Bureau from September 2022. Fintech firms will thus gain access to the data they need and be able to offer brand-new, cutting-edge goods and services. CAREC countries that have not yet revised personal data-related legislation need to update it to reinforce personal data protection rights.

Policy authorities should also decide whether the screen scraping of personal data should be allowed; this a technique whereby one company can automatically extract information from the sites of other companies, public institutions, and governments based on prior customer consent. While this technology can be convenient for customers transacting with a financial company—for example, to receive an asset management service—personal information leakage and excessive traffic can be problematic. For this reason, the EU allows only the transfer of personal information through the application-programming-interface (API) method, which unifies communication protocols; and the EU has prohibited screen scraping. On the other hand, the API method is generally known to be more expensive.

CAREC's emerging fintech markets will nonetheless have to rely on the API method for personal data transfer, as it is better at protecting privacy and contributes to secure interoperability between fintech platforms. Interoperability is the ability of a single application to communicate with many different applications. It means that consumers will not be locked into a particular application or platform, but will instead be free to change between different platforms. So, interoperability enhances competition in the fintech industry.[66]

As non-face-to-face financial services gradually expand, the need to verify the identity of the other party and to authenticate certain facts is growing. Electronic identification and authentication technologies used for onboarding, identification related to anti-money laundering/combating the financing of terrorism (AML/CFT), and other electronic document-forgery-prevention processes are changing. As the communication environment shifts from desktop computers to mobile devices, the use of electronic identification and authentication methods such as biometric technology and the identity protection personal identification number (IP-PIN) is expanding, along with electronic signature technology based on public key infrastructure (PKI). Therefore, the policy authority's legal framework must line up with technological changes regarding the permissible scope of electronic identification and authentication methods, the responsibilities of the certification body, and the supervision of the certification body.

66 Interoperability also increases financial inclusion because it allows customers to transact outside the network created by their own service provider. Negre and Cook (2021) discuss the interoperability of payment services.

The EU again provides a good example. It enacted the Regulation on Electronic Identification, Authentication and Trust Services (eIDAS) in 2014 (EU 2014), to replace electronic signature guidelines that had been in force since 2000 (EU 1999). This regulation conformed to the new technological environment, and as the only regulation on electronic identification and authentication used by countries throughout the EU, it formed the basis of a single digital market that will promote the development of fintech and the integration of capital markets.

As a fintech-based technology, AI can be used for market analysis, financial product recommendation, credit evaluation, fraudulent transaction detection, and monitoring compliance. To address the ethical challenges that may occur when AI replaces human decision-making, financial institutions must be able to effectively supervise and control AI systems and maintain "responsibility." Policy authorities need to provide guidelines for self-regulation.

Coordinating Fintech Policy Authorities

Fintech policies are related to the work of government authorities such as those dealing with policies on finance, information and telecommunications, competition, and science and technology. This means that inefficiencies may arise due to conflicts of jurisdiction concerning policy proposals and execution. To minimize this problem, an effective coordination of interests will be required regarding fintech development and regulation.

The Monetary Authority of Singapore (MAS) provides a good example of an initiative in this context. The MAS is in charge of monetary policy, financial regulation, and financial supervision, and thus plays a central role in coordinating government-wide fintech policies. The MAS established a Fintech and Innovation Group (FTIG) within its organizational structure in 2015 to coordinate the fintech-development policies initiated by each ministry and uphold its regulatory responsibility in the industry. FTIG has now four divisions, governing payment development and data connectivity, fintech infrastructure, the fintech ecosystem, and AI development.

Forming an Environment That Facilitates Fintech Use

Increasing Fintech Awareness

A very basic condition for capital market development is to increase financial literacy. This is especially the case in the CAREC region, where financial literacy is gaining increasing importance as a policy objective in many countries. Even though fintech products are widely provided, if people do not fully understand what they are, the products are less likely to promote capital market development through fintech. Thus, for fintech to enhance capital market development, it is essential to increase awareness and adoption through training and capacity-building initiatives.[67]

Upgrading the Technological Infrastructure

Basic technological infrastructures, such as broadband and fast mobile internet networks, are prerequisites for maximizing the benefits of fintech. Unlike advanced economies whose technological infrastructures are mature, most CAREC countries must consider the improvement of their technological infrastructures to be an important ingredient of their fintech strategies. If the basic ICT infrastructures are still lacking, policy capabilities will have to be focused on the improvement of those technologies.

[67] OECD (2018) published a guidance that offers actionable steps for the design and implementation of financial education initiatives on digital financial services, to strengthen the digital financial literacy of consumers and entrepreneurs.

The next step will require efforts to promote the development of fintech-relevant technologies such as AI and ML, blockchain, biometric authentication, big data, and cloud computing. The focus should be on the development of services that policymakers want to strategically foster. For example, AI and ML, data and analytics, and cloud computing are needed for the deployment of P2P lending. Distributed ledger technology (DLT) can be useful for post-trade processing, compliance, and reporting. Of course, it would be preferable to establish a development strategy promoting services that already use technologies with a secure foundation in the country, rather than technologies with no foundation. Policy authorities in CAREC countries would do well to select the capital market service areas and technologies for intensive nurturing based on their country's circumstances and strategic framework of financial development. This will create the basis for a virtuous cycle between financial services and underlying technologies.

Encouraging Industry Engagement

To establish a dynamic fintech ecosystem in which fintech firms and existing financial companies cooperate and compete, many countries have already been operating organizations that support exchanges between existing financial companies and fintech start-ups. For example, the Committee of Sydney, the city's think tank, launched a Financial Services Knowledge Hub in 2015 to promote networking by financial and related industries with their peers. The hub established Stone & Chalk, the largest cooperative fintech community in Asia, which provides start-ups with space, information, mentoring, and opportunities for fundraising. The Republic of Korea's Financial Services Commission was instrumental in launching Fintech Center Korea in 2015 to support the emergence of innovative financial services and the growth of the local fintech industry.

In CAREC, Georgia can be cited as an example of public–private cooperation to promote fintech (Chapter 3). Two public–private dialogue platforms in Georgia are used to address government regulations pertaining to fintech, and there are private sector initiatives to remove barriers to fintech development. For example, Georgia's Investors Council is a forum established with the European Bank for Reconstruction and Development (EBRD) to enable representatives from the Government of Georgia and its regulatory agencies to meet periodically with the leaders of significant business associations and with the local directors of international financial institutions to examine issues raised by various stakeholders. There is also the Georgian Public–Private Partnership Platform on Cyber Security—organized by the Digital Governance Agency. A joint initiative of the EU ("Strengthening Cyber Security Capacities in Georgia") and the United Kingdom ("United Kingdom–Georgia Cyber Cooperation") is responsible for carrying out the project.

CONCLUSION

Capital market development should be considered an important part of the strategy to build economic prosperity in the CAREC countries. It is important not only for promoting economic growth, but also for achieving financial stability. It can be achieved if the policy efforts required to satisfy the necessary macroeconomic, financial, and institutional conditions are adequate. The truth is that policy efforts cannot produce desired results easily or immediately, yet fintech innovation will be an important catalyst that will accelerate capital market development. Fintech innovation could significantly improve the efficiency of securities trading and post-trade activities in traditional capital markets. It could also redesign or replace traditional capital markets.

Based on the criteria of feasibility and necessity, this chapter has recognized that P2P lending and equity crowdfunding, mobile trading, STOs, compliance automation, and AI applications for CRM are the service areas that CAREC should focus on when using fintech solutions to develop capital markets.

The use of fintech solutions to provide these services, in the interest of developing capital markets, should be driven by the private sector. However, policymakers need to take responsibility for maximizing the benefits and minimizing the risks brought about by fintech disruption. Their role can be broadly divided into two functions: (i) overhauling the policy and regulatory framework related to the use of fintech in the capital market, and (ii) creating an environment that will facilitate it.

REFERENCES

Black, B. and R. J. Gilson. 1999. Does Venture Capital Require an Active Stock Market? *Journal of Applied Corporate Finance.* 11 (4). pp. 36–48. https://econpapers.repec.org/article/blajacrfn/v_3a11_3ay_3a1999_3ai_3a4_3ap_3a36-48.htm.

Burns, J. et al. 2020. *Blockchain and Internal Control: The COSO Perspective*. Committee of Sponsoring Organizations of the Treadway Commission (COSO) / Deloitte. https://www2.deloitte.com/us/en/pages/audit/articles/blockchain-and-internal-control-coso-perspective-risk.html.

Carstens, A. 2018. *A Level Playing Field in Banking*. Keynote address prepared for the Institute of International Finance Board of Directors dinner. 21 January. https://www.bis.org/speeches/sp180130.htm.

Chami, R., C. Fullenkamp, and S. Sharma. 2009. A Framework for Financial Market Development. *IMF Working Papers*. No. 9/156. International Monetary Fund. https://www.imf.org/en/Publications/WP/Issues/2016/12/31/A-Framework-for-Financial-Market-Development-23128.

Claessens, S., D. Klingebiel, and S. Schmukler. 2007. Government Bonds in Domestic and Foreign Currency: The Role of Institutional and Macroeconomic Factors. *Review of International Economics.* 15 (2). pp. 370–413. https://onlinelibrary.wiley.com/doi/10.1111/j.1467-9396.2007.00682.x.

DeLisle, B. 2018. SATIS Group Report: 78% of ICOs Are Scams. *CryptoSlate*. 17 July. https://cryptoslate.com/satis-group-report-78-of-icos-are-scams/.

Demekas, D. G. and A. Nerlich. 2020. *Creating Domestic Capital Markets in Developing Countries: Perspectives from Market Participants*. EM Compass Note 77. https://www.ifc.org/content/dam/ifc/doc/mgrt-pub/emcompass-note-77-creating-domestic-cap-markets-dev-countries.pdf.

Diamond, D. W. 1984. Financial Intermediation and Delegated Monitoring. *The Review of Economic Studies.* 51 (3). pp. 393–414. https://www.jstor.org/stable/2297430.

Ernst & Young (EY). 2015. *EY's Global Governance, Risk and Compliance Survey 2015*. http://www.ey.com/GRCsurvey2015.

European Union (EU). 1999. Directive 1999/93/EC of the European Parliament and of the Council of 13 December 1999 on a Community Framework for Electronic Signatures. https://eur-lex.europa.eu/eli/dir/1999/93/oj/eng.

———. 2014. Regulation (EU) No. 910/2014 of the European Parliament and of the Council of 23 July 2014 on Electronic Identification and Trust Services for Electronic Transactions in the Internal Market and Repealing Directive 1999/93/EC. https://eur-lex.europa.eu/legal-content/EN/TXT/?uri=CELEX%3A02014R0910-20241018.

———. 2021. Proposal for a Regulation of the European Parliament and of the Council Laying Down Harmonised Rules on Artificial Intelligence (Artificial Intelligence Act) and Amending Certain Union Legislative Acts {SEC(2021) 167 final}—{SWD(2021) 84 final}—{SWD(2021) 85 final}. https://eur-lex.europa.eu/resource.html?uri=cellar:e0649735-a372-11eb-9585-01aa75ed71a1.0001.02/DOC_1&format=PDF.

Financial Industry Regulatory Authority (FINRA). 2017. *Report on Distributed Ledger Technology: Implications of Blockchain for the Securities Industry*. http://www.finra.org/industry/report-distributed-ledger-technology-implications-blockchain-securities-industry.

Hakenes, H. 2004. Banks as Delegated Risk Managers. *Journal of Banking and Finance*. 28 (10). pp. 2399–2426. https://www.sciencedirect.com/science/article/abs/pii/S0378426603002401.

International Monetary Fund (IMF) Data. n.d. Financial Development Index. https://data.imf.org/?sk=f8032e80-b36c-43b1-ac26-493c5b1cd33b (accessed 15 January 2023).

IMF and the World Bank. 2018. The Bali Fintech Agenda. *IMF Policy Papers*. No. 2018 (050). IMF. https://www.elibrary.imf.org/view/journals/007/2018/050/007.2018.issue-050-en.xml.

International Organization of Securities Commissions (IOSCO). 2017. *IOSCO Research Report on Financial Technologies (Fintech)*. https://www.iosco.org/library/pubdocs/pdf/IOSCOPD554.pdf.

———. 2021. *The Use of Artificial Intelligence and Machine Learning by Market Intermediaries and Asset Managers*. Final Report. https://www.iosco.org/library/pubdocs/pdf/IOSCOPD684.pdf.

Kowalewski, O. and P. Pisany. 2017. What Is Driving the Corporate Bond Market Development in Asia? *IÉSEG School of Management Working Papers*. No. 2017-ACF-03. Lille Catholic University. https://ideas.repec.org/p/ies/wpaper/f201703.html.

Kwon, M. K. and S. H. Cho. 2018. *Fourth Industrial Revolution and Capital Markets—Artificial Intelligence and Blockchain*. Research Report 18-04 (in Korean). Korea Capital Market Institute.

Levine, R., C. Lin, and W. Xie. 2016. Spare Tire? Stock Markets, Banking Crises, and Economic Recoveries. *Journal of Financial Economics.* 120 (1). pp. 81–101. https://papers.ssrn.com/sol3/papers.cfm?abstract_id=2548282.

McKinnon, R. I. 1973. *Money and Capital in Economic Development.* The Brookings Institution.

Negre, A. and W. Cook. 2021. *Interoperability in Digital Financial Services: Emerging Guidance for Funders*. Technical Note. Consultative Group to Assist the Poor (CGAP). https://www.cgap.org/sites/default/files/publications/2021_01_Technical_Note_Interoperability_Digital_Financial_Services.pdf.

Organisation for Economic Co-operation and Development (OECD). 2018. *G20/OECD INFE Policy Guidance on Digitalisation and Financial Literacy*. https://www.gpfi.org/publications/g20oecd-infe-policy-guidance-digitalisation-and-financial-literacy.

———. 2019. *Initial Coin Offerings (ICOs) for SME Financing*. https://www.oecd.org/en/publications/initial-coin-offerings-icos-for-sme-financing_ee35cc9a-en.html.

———. 2020. *The Tokenisation of Assets and Potential Implications for Financial Markets.* OECD Blockchain Policy Series. https://www.oecd.org/en/publications/the-tokenisation-of-assets-and-potential-implications-for-financial-markets_83493d34-en.html.

Quinlan, B., J. Chung, and E. Trehan. 2021. *Cracking the Code: The Evolution of Digital Assets to the Mainstream*. Quinlan & Associates. https://www.quinlanandassociates.com/wp-content/uploads/2021/09/Quinlan-Associates-Cracking-the-Code.pdf.

Sahay, R. et al. 2015. Rethinking Financial Deepening: Stability and Growth in Emerging Markets. *IMF Staff Discussion Notes*. No. 2015/008. International Monetary Fund. https://www.imf.org/en/Publications/Staff-Discussion-Notes/Issues/2016/12/31/Rethinking-Financial-Deepening-Stability-and-Growth-in-Emerging-Markets-42868.

Shaw, E. S. 1973. *Financial Deepening in Economic Development*. Oxford University Press.

Statista. n.d. Digital Investment – Worldwide (database). https://www.statista.com/outlook/dmo/fintech/digital-investment/worldwide (accessed 23 November 2022).

University of Ottawa, JuriGlobe – World Legal Systems Research Group. n.d. About JuriGlobe. http://www.juriglobe.ca/eng/apropos/index.php.

World Bank. 2019. Capital Market Development and the FinTech Revolution: Opportunities and Challenges. https://live.worldbank.org/capital-market-development-fin-tech-revolution.

———. 2020. *Fintech in Europe and Central Asia: Maximizing Benefits and Managing Risks*. Fintech Note No. 4. https://documents1.worldbank.org/curated/en/640021585934004225/pdf/Fintech-in-Europe-and-Central-Asia-Maximizing-Benefits-and-Managing-Risks.pdf.

World Bank and CCAF (Cambridge Centre for Alternative Finance). 2019. Regulating Alternative Finance: Results from a Global Regulator Survey.

World Justice Project. 2024. WJP Rule of Law Index. https://worldjusticeproject.org/rule-of-law-index/ (accessed 15 January 2023).

PART III

FINTECH ECOSYSTEMS IN PRACTICE

6

Fintech, E-Commerce, and Trade Finance: Lessons for CAREC

Leah Castro and Minsoo Lee

INTRODUCTION

Experience over many decades has proven the tenets of Jacob Viner's pioneering work, *Theory of Customs Union*. In 1950, Viner emphasized that consumer welfare would increase with freer trade within a customs union, leading to lower costs of goods. He foresaw two possible outcomes: (i) the positive outcome of trade creation; and (ii) the negative outcome of trade diversion, in which a customs union switches trade from a more efficient exporter toward a less efficient one (Viner 1950).

The technological advancements that are revolutionizing global trade in both goods and services accentuate the positive of trade creation, and have pushed the concept of trade diversion into obsolescence. The internet has given rise to electronic-commerce (e-commerce) and financial technology (fintech), expanding the possibilities of international trade. E-commerce has facilitated retail trade and expanded consumer choices, while fintech has transformed the global payments system. Furthermore, new fintech payment modes are challenging traditional methods, such as bank letters of credit.

Technology has not only benefited bulk export and import businesses, but has also produced a new category of trade known as "cross-border online retail trade." This involves buying and selling goods in smaller volumes, known as "business-to-consumer" (B2C) transactions. Amazon, founded by Jeff Bezos in 1994, is the largest global online retail firm and a key player.

Cross-border online retail trade relies on the shipment of goods in small parcels by logistics firms like DHL, FedEx, TNT, UPS, Aramex, and Ninja Van. Previously, major shipping lines dominated global trade logistics, but with the demand for speedy delivery, new players have emerged, emphasizing air freight.

Viner's "customs union" concept has expanded into regional cooperation and integration (RCI). Some Central Asia Regional Economic Cooperation (CAREC) member countries have bilateral or multilateral agreements that involve aspects of customs cooperation and trade facilitation. For instance, several are members of the Eurasian Economic Union (EAEU), a customs union comprising Armenia, Belarus, Kazakhstan, the Kyrgyz Republic, and Russia. The People's Republic of China (PRC) and Pakistan have a free trade agreement known as the China–Pakistan Free Trade Agreement (CPFTA), which facilitates trade between the two countries.

RCI goes beyond harmonized tariffs and customs regulations to include the establishment of a customs union. It includes collaboration among neighboring countries to strengthen trade linkages and promote cross-border infrastructure, financial linkages, and regional trade in public goods. In this changing online-retail landscape, the traditional distinction between trade creation and trade diversion is no longer relevant.

“Trade diversion” now refers to consumers searching online for the best quality and lowest price. This raises the question of how RCI should address trade and financial linkages in a virtual global retail marketplace created by e-commerce and fintech.

Trade finance plays a crucial role in the growth of cross-border online retail trade. E-commerce sellers require operating capital and revolving credit for goods production and inventory. Several fintech firms provide business credit to e-commerce retail companies at lower costs. E-wallets and virtual credit cards from fintech firms such as PayPal, Alipay, WeChat, Klarna, and Affirm are challenging the dominance of such firms as Visa and Mastercard. Fintech firms provide consumers with a safe payment system and lower-cost credit access.

While trade facilitation has been extensively researched, with a view to reducing export and import costs, limited research has been done on trade creation resulting from new technologies such as fintech. Cross-border online retail trade is still a small proportion of total global trade, but its growth is having a significant impact on consumers and micro, small, and medium-sized enterprises (MSMEs). E-commerce empowers consumers by providing a wider range of product choices and prices, while offering lower start-up costs for digital entrepreneurs and opportunities for MSMEs to integrate into the global retail business.

CAREC member countries with relatively small domestic markets stand to benefit from expanding cross-border online retail trade, which would lead to more viable business opportunities for e-commerce and fintech firms, and for investors. This book aims to provide an initial examination of both the domestic and cross-border online retail trade.

Data Challenges

There has been growing interest in the impact of e-commerce, particularly the cross-border online retail trade, on economic development. Notably, B2C e-commerce is believed to enhance consumer welfare and promote the inclusion of MSMEs (ADB and UNESCAP 2018; Jo, Matsumura, and Weinstein 2019; Huang 2021; Telma 2015).[68] However, severe constraints on publicly available data limit the empirical evidence, and consensus is lacking on terminology and methodologies.

A 2019 World Bank study highlighted several data challenges, including the fact that most countries do not collect official data on e-commerce (Ferrantino and Koten 2019). Much of the available data resides with private institutions, including e-commerce platform operators and analytical services aimed at marketers, making them either confidential or expensive to access. This hampers efforts to utilize cross-country data to provide relevant policy advice on promoting e-commerce. Also, absent standardized terminology, terms such as “digital trade,” “e-commerce,” and “e-trade” are used interchangeably.

The most widely used definition of B2C e-commerce comes from the Organisation for Economic Co-operation and Development (OECD). The definition states that B2C e-commerce involves the sale or purchase of goods or services conducted over computer networks through methods specifically designed for order placement (UNCTAD 2016). The payment and ultimate delivery of goods or services do not necessarily have to be conducted online. An e-commerce transaction can involve enterprises, households, individuals, governments, and other public or private organizations. Orders made through the web, extranet, or electronic data interchange are included, while orders made by phone, facsimile, or a manually typed email are excluded. This definition is also adopted by the World Bank, the United Nations Conference on Trade and Development (UNCTAD), and by private market data and research firms such as Statista.

[68] Jo, Matsumura, and Weinstein (2019) explicitly state that e-commerce improves consumer welfare and promotes the inclusion of MSMEs, while the other references imply the same.

Even as B2C e-commerce is driving a rapid transformation in the retail sector, there is limited consensus on the percentage of retail sales occurring online, and retailers have different approaches to counting sales. Consumers do not explicitly differentiate between online and in-store purchases. Estimates of online shopping are often derived from consumer surveys, while more accurate data can be obtained from the sales revenues of e-commerce firms (e.g., Amazon) and retailers. Private data sources, such as Euromonitor, EMARKETER, and Statista,[69] provide e-commerce data based on consumer and e-commerce firm surveys.

In this chapter, the focus is on B2C e-commerce, specifically on global online retail trade, and the term "e-commerce" refers exclusively to the B2C type. Global online retail trade is divided into two types: domestic and cross-border.

ECONOMIC DEVELOPMENT IMPACT OF ONLINE RETAIL TRADE

In the mid-1990s, prominent retailers expanded their operations internationally by establishing physical stores in emerging markets. Through these brick-and-mortar outlets, they connected consumers outside their home countries—such as the United States and countries in the European Union (EU)—to retail and wholesale stores selling a wide range of goods, including food, clothing, and other products, at more competitive prices.

However, amid this trend of expanding physical stores, a significant shift was taking place. In 1994, Jeff Bezos founded Amazon.com, Inc. in the United States. Although Bezos may not have foreseen it, his venture would have a profound impact on retail business. What began as an online bookstore soon evolved into the largest e-commerce firm in the world.

Alibaba, founded in 1999 by Jack Ma in the PRC, is challenging Amazon's dominance, particularly in Asia. Such competition fosters greater value for consumers and compels firms to enhance their efficiency.

The emergence of new technologies has empowered retailers to achieve economies of scale and cost reductions, leading to lower prices for consumers. The advent of e-commerce and fintech has facilitated retail market expansion beyond what was imaginable in the 1990s. Consequently, the economic development impact of online retail trade should not be underestimated.

While there is a wealth of studies, reports, and news on the rapid growth of global e-commerce retail sales, these resources are primarily focused on commercial users of e-commerce for strategic market positioning. These commercial users include sellers, fintech firms, and other financial institutions, as well as online advertising firms. However, few studies provide in-depth analysis of the economic development impact of e-commerce, particularly in relation to consumer welfare, the inclusion of MSMEs, and gender equity.[70]

The Growth of Global E-Commerce

Global e-commerce retail sales revenue grew significantly in almost a decade—quadrupling in value from $1.3 trillion in 2014 to $5.7 trillion in 2022. It is projected to reach $8.1 trillion in 2026 (Figure 6.1).

69 For instance, see Statista n.d.

70 Two studies worth noting are IFC et al. (2021) and Jo, Matsumura, and Weinstein (2019).

Figure 6.1: Global E-Commerce Retail Sales, Data and Forecasts, 2014–2026
($ billion)

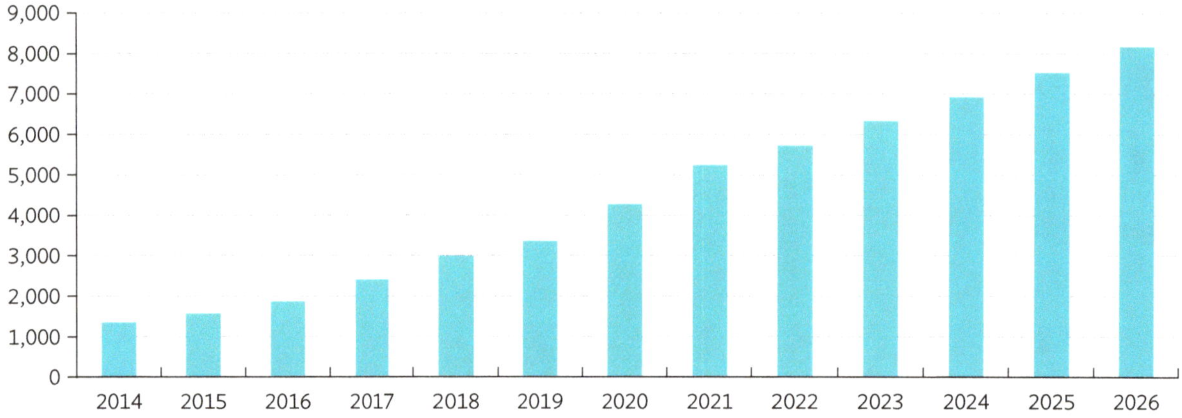

e-commerce = electronic commerce.
Note: The values for 2025 and 2026 are projections.
Sources: EMARKETER. *Worldwide Ecommerce Retail Forecast* (2014–2022); and Statista.

The rate of growth averaged 23% during 2017–2021. Global e-commerce retail sales revenue is projected to grow at a slower average rate of 9% during 2022–2026 (Figure 6.2). However, the e-commerce share of total global retail sales almost tripled to 20% in 2022 from 7% in 2015 (Table 6.1). That is projected to increase to 26% by 2026.

Figure 6.2: Global E-Commerce Retail Sales Growth, Data and Forecasts, 2017–2026
(%)

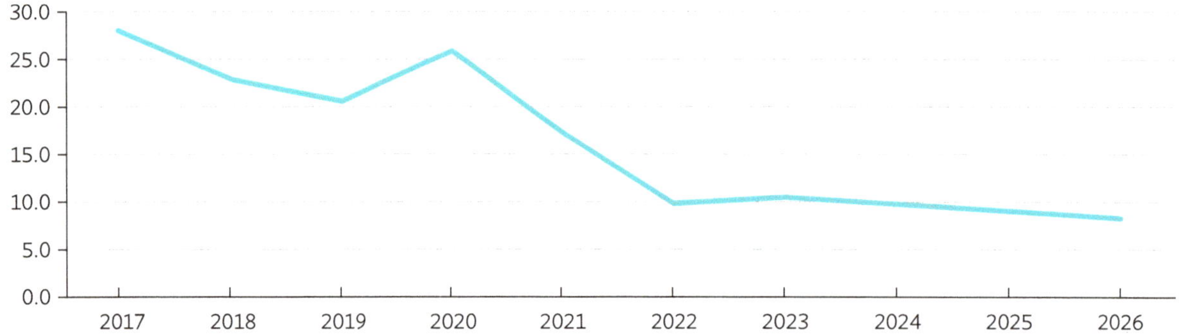

e-commerce = electronic commerce.
Note: The values for 2025 and 2026 are projections.
Sources: EMARKETR. *Worldwide Survey* (2017–2022); and Statista.

Table 6.1: E-Commerce Share of Total Global Retail Sales, Data and Forecasts, 2015–2026
(%)

Year	Shares
2015	7.4
2016	8.6
2017	10.4
2018	12.2
2019	13.8
2020	17.8
2021	18.8
2022	19.7
2023	20.8
2024	21.9
2025	23.0
2026	24.0

e-commerce = electronic commerce.
Note: The values for 2022–2026 are projections.
Sources: EMARKETER. *Worldwide Survey* (2015–2022); and Statista.

Table 6.2: Fastest-Growing E-Commerce Retail Sales, by Country, 2022
(%)

Rank	Country	Growth
1	Singapore	36.0
2	Indonesia	34.0
3	Philippines	25.9
4	India	25.5
5	Argentina	25.3
6	Australia	20.0
7	Malaysia	18.3
8	Thailand	18.0
9	Mexico	18.0
10	Brazil	17.2
	World	**9.7**

e-commerce = electronic commerce.
Sources: EMARKETER. 2022. *Worldwide Survey*; and Statista.

In 2022, Asia was the largest e-commerce market in the world, accounting for half of global e-commerce retail sales revenue. The Americas (27%) and Europe (20%) trailed behind Asia. Global e-commerce retail sales revenue in Asia amounted to $2 trillion in 2022 (Figure 6.3). The top Asian countries, where e-commerce retail sales revenue posted the highest growth rates, were as follows: Singapore (36%), Indonesia (34%), the Philippines (26%), and India (25%), as shown in Table 6.2. The growth rates posted by these countries were way higher than the global average of 10%.

Figure 6.3: Global E-Commerce Retail Sales Revenue, Regional Shares, 2022
(%)

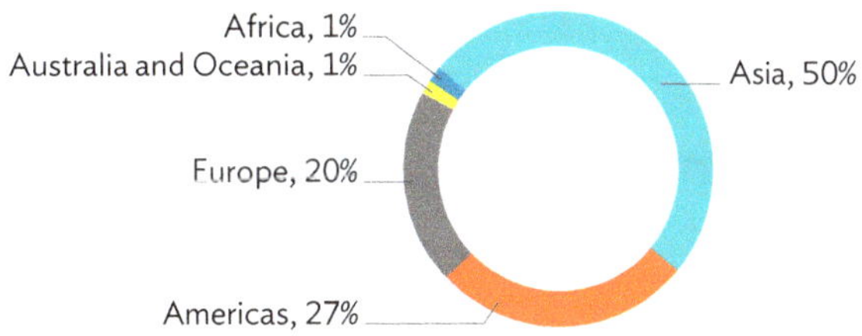

e-commerce = electronic commerce.
Sources: EMARKETER. *Worldwide Survey* (2015–2022); and Statista.

Online Shopping: Perceived Benefits and Drawbacks

Despite the lack of strong empirical evidence, it has been suggested that B2C e-commerce increases consumer welfare.

What are the perceived benefits (or incentives) of global e-commerce?

The top benefits, as summarized in Table 6.3, and based on consumer surveys conducted in 2019 and 2022, are convenience, a wide range of product choices beyond what domestic markets offered, and better prices. Convenience can be translated into time savings for consumers. Better prices imply lower prices, resulting in consumer savings and improved real incomes.

Table 6.3: Main Benefits and Incentives of E-Commerce Cited by Global Consumers, 2019 and 2022

(% of respondents)

Main Benefits Cited	Consumer Respondents in 2019	Consumer Respondents in 2022
It's flexible, you can shop at any time	...	45
Better prices, you can compare shop	63	37
Don't have to go to the store	...	36
More variety of products; wider range of categories	34	34
Free and discounted shipping	47	...
No crowds, it's COVID-19-safe	...	32
Easy to find what I need	...	26
Ability to research products; read product reviews	32	25
Can shop beyond your geographic area	...	22
Speed of delivery	32	...

... = data not available, COVID-19 = coronavirus disease, e-commerce = electronic commerce.

Sources: Dynata. 2022. *Global Consumer Trends: The New Experience Economy*. https://www.dynata.com/content/GCT_The-New-Experience-Economy.pdf; Statista; and UPS.

A 2019 study by the National Bureau of Economic Research (NBER) examined the impact of e-commerce on pricing behavior and welfare using a unique set of Japanese data for 1991–2016 (Jo, Matsumura, and Weinstein 2019). The data set contains household expenditure shares by retail channel—catalogs, e-commerce, and physical stores—for the set of goods that make up the Japanese consumer price index (CPI). The study findings are as follows:

- The entry of e-commerce firms significantly raised the rate of intercity price convergence for goods sold intensively online, but not for other goods.
- E-commerce also lowered the relative inflation rates for goods sold intensively online.
- Reductions in price dispersion raised welfare by 0.3%.
- E-commerce also lowered the variety-adjusted prices on average by 0.9%, and more in cities with highly educated populations.

What are the perceived drawbacks to online shopping?

Almost half of consumers in a 2022 survey noted missing the shopping experience (46%) and lack of quality assurance (45%). About a third pointed to delayed shipping and fraud as major drawbacks (Table 6.4). For cross-border online shopping, the main drawbacks were delivery fees, delayed shipments, and nondelivery of purchases (Table 6.5).

Table 6.4: Main Drawbacks of E-Commerce Cited by Global Consumers, 2022

Main Drawbacks Cited	% of Consumer Respondents
No opportunity to touch or feel products	46
Can't be sure of the quality	45
Returns can be complicated	34
Shipping problems or delays	32
Risk of fraud	31
Does not support local retailers	23
Bad for the environment	16
No sales assistance, the shopping experience isn't as good	13

e-commerce = electronic commerce.

Sources: Dynata. 2022. *Global Consumer Trends: The New Experience Economy*. https://www.dynata.com/content/GCT_The-New-Experience-Economy.pdf; and Statista.

Table 6.5: Main Drawbacks of Cross-Border Online Shopping Cited by Global Consumers, 2018

Main Drawbacks Cited	% of Consumer Respondents
Delivery shipping costs	25
Delivery time not fast enough	24
Concern that I may not receive the item	24
Customs/duty fees/taxes	24
Difficult process for returning products	22

Sources: Ipsos. 2018. *Online Survey Worldwide*. https://www.ipsos.com/en-sg/ipsos-predictions-2018; PayPal; and Statista.

Most of the drawbacks to online shopping have been addressed by e-commerce firms. Regarding quality assurance, returns and refunds are available options for online shoppers, while the likes of Amazon and Alibaba have implemented "free shipping" for a minimum amount purchased. Shipping delays resulting from customs processes have also been addressed through small parcelized shipments and the "de minimis" rule, which is discussed later in this chapter in the context of lessons from the Association of Southeast Asian Nations (ASEAN).

More than half (57%) of consumers polled in 2021 felt confident enough to have made at least one cross-border online purchase in the previous year. Restrictions on movement during the coronavirus disease (COVID-19) pandemic (2020 and 2021) increased their willingness to make cross-border online purchases (Table 6.6).

Table 6.6: Attitude Toward Cross-Border Online Shopping Among Global Consumers, 2021

Attitude Cited	% of Consumer Respondents
Had made at least one online purchase from another country in the prior 12 months	57
Considering making an online purchase from abroad	22
Agree that shopping more online during the pandemic increased their willingness to consider cross-border e-commerce purchases	43

e-commerce = electronic commerce.

Sources: Censuswide; Logistyx Technologies. 2021. *Online Survey Worldwide*. https://retailtechinnovationhub.com/home/2021/10/27/logistyx-technologies-flags-cross-border-e-commerce-concerns; and PR Newswire.

On a global scale, about 75% of consumers surveyed said that they were willing to spend anywhere between $260 to $520 monthly on cross-border online purchases (Table 6.7).

Table 6.7: Global Consumer Confidence in Cross-Border Online Shopping, by Monthly Expenditure, 2021

	Level of Confidence (% of respondents)		
Monthly Expenditure	Quite/Very Confident	Quite/Very Unconfident	Neither Confident Nor Unconfident
Up to $65	37	41	21
$65–$259	53	31	16
$260–$520	71	22	7
$521 and over	69	20	11

Note: Percentages may not total 100% due to rounding.

Sources: ClearSale; Sapio Research. 2021. *Online Survey Worldwide*. https://offer.clear.sale/global-ecommerce-consumer-behavior; and Statista.

Fraud, although mentioned, does not seem to be a very important concern for online shoppers. Perhaps, they believe that the cost of fraud will be borne by the e-commerce firms, banks, credit card firms, and fintech firms. However, consumer awareness is still important, even if fraud does not seem to be a major concern. Most cross-border online retailers have set up safeguards, including against payment fraud.

Product safeguards are as important as payment risk in the global online retail trade. Policies that promote trade in safe consumer products will raise consumer confidence in cross-border online shopping. In 2020, the United Nations Conference on Trade and Development (UNCTAD) adopted recommendations for preventing cross-border distribution of known unsafe consumer products (UNCTAD 2022). They include strengthened data, information sharing, and the coordination of policies among governments. Likewise, for firms and consumers, the 2021 *Guidelines for Online Product Safety*, from Consumers International, includes global recommendations for action to protect consumer welfare (Consumers International 2021).

What are the preferred ways to shop online?

In a 2021 global consumer survey, about one-third of the respondents (32%–33%) preferred the "buy online, ship to home" option for apparel, footwear, and appliances. The same preference was stated by about one-fourth of the respondents (26% to 27%) for home furnishings and health-and-beauty products (Table 6.8). In 2022, online marketplaces were the preferred channel for 35% of consumers (Table 6.9). To date, the biggest of these marketplaces are Alibaba and Amazon.

Table 6.8: Preferred Ways to Shop Online by Consumers Globally, by Selected Product Category, 2021
(% of respondents)

Product Category	Buy Online, Ship to Home	Buy Online, Pick Up at Store	Buy Online, Pick Up Curbside	Buy Online, Pick Up at a Collection Point
Apparel and footwear	33	6	4	3
Appliances	32	6	4	2
Home furnishings	27	7	4	2
Health and beauty	26	7	4	3
Back-to-school supplies	17	6	4	2
Brand-name food product	15	7	4	2
Groceries	13	6	5	1
Alcohol	12	6	4	2

Sources: Salesforce. 2021. *Worldwide Survey*. https://www.salesforce.com/news/stories/state-of-marketing-in-2021/; and Statista.

Table 6.9: Global Online Purchases, by Channel, 2022

Channel	% of Consumer Respondents
Online marketplaces (e.g., Alibaba, eBay, JD.com, Mercato)	35
Supermarkets and grocers	17
Social on-app purchasing (includes gaming and metaverse)	14
Retailer sites (e.g., ASOS, Boohoo, John Lewis, JD Sports, Argos)	12
Via an aggregator or delivery app (e.g., Uber Eats, Deliveroo)	11
Direct-to-consumer, branded sites, and apps (e.g., Nike, Apple, Dyson)	7
Others	4

Note: The data are from a global survey conducted in March and April 2022.
Sources: Statista; and Wunderman Thompson. 2022. *Online Survey Worldwide*.

Small Enterprise Inclusion, Gender Equity, and Logistics Business Expansion

The share of micro, small, and medium-sized enterprises (MSMEs) in direct international trade is disproportionately low compared with their share in overall economic activity. This discrepancy is observed across all countries, and the gap tends to widen as firm size decreases (OECD 2021).

The inclusion of MSMEs in international trade has been made possible through cross-border online retail platforms. Online marketplaces, such as Amazon, offer retail outlets for MSMEs, with the investment cost of selling online falling within their capital and operating budgets. The cost advantages of selling online include the following (Retail Dogma n.d.):

- lower initial setup costs and faster start-up,
- reduced operating costs,
- access to customers beyond the seller's geographic location,
- ability to reach specific demographics that prefer online purchases, and
- the need for less inventory.

According to Amazon's 2022 *Small Business Empowerment Report*, the company had approximately 2 million third-party selling partners, the majority of which were small and medium-sized enterprises (SMEs) (Amazon 2022). The report noted that in 2021, Amazon and its third-party lending partners provided $1.4 billion to support the business expansion of SMEs in the United States. Furthermore, Amazon invested $100 million to encourage customers to buy from small business sellers on "Prime Day" and throughout 2021.

Statista data indicated that in 2019, there were approximately 2.9 million active sellers in the Amazon marketplace, about 69% of them SMEs. Many of these sellers, around 38% (1.1 million), were based in the United States, constituting a significant portion of the global Amazon marketplace sellers (Statista 2025a).

In Southeast Asia, Lazada serves as an online marketplace that enables MSMEs to grow their businesses. As a pioneer in B2C e-commerce in the region, Lazada, majority-owned by Alibaba Group Holding Limited, boasts 400,000 sellers and 3,000 brands, catering to 560 million consumers (Lazada n.d.). It offers tailored marketing, data, and service solutions to its sellers, and in 2018, made a commitment to support 8 million e-commerce entrepreneurs and SMEs in Southeast Asia by 2030 (*Digital News Asia* 2018).

The Lazada Philippines marketplace alone had approximately 20,000 MSMEs selling their products in 2018 (*BusinessWorld* 2018). In 2021, the International Finance Corporation (IFC) partnered with the European Commission, Kantar Public, and Lazada to explore the potential of e-commerce in closing gender gaps and opening more markets to women-owned businesses in Southeast Asia (IFC et al. 2021).

As noted above, the rise of online retail trade, particularly small parcelized cross-border shipments, has also fueled the growth of logistics firms such as DHL, FedEx, TNT, UPS, Aramex (established in 1982), and Ninja Van (established in 2014), which specialize in express delivery services.

In 2018, Amazon launched its Delivery Service Partner (DSP) program, providing entrepreneurs with an opportunity to set up and operate their own delivery businesses. Amazon reports that the program has now expanded to include over 3,000 DSPs across 14 countries, creating at least 275,000 jobs and facilitating the delivery of over a billion parcels worldwide.

The CAREC region B2C e-commerce market size in 2022 was 1.1 billion users. Setting aside the PRC's developed market, the combined size of the region's nine emerging fintech markets, although reduced to 84 million users during the COVID-19 pandemic, still represented a huge jump from the 63 million users in 2019. In 2019, online shoppers in the emerging fintech markets accounted for an average of 13% of internet users in the region (Table 6.28). This measure rose significantly in 2020, when about 59% of internet users went online to shop.[71] This increase, however, did not translate into higher B2C e-commerce revenues. In contrast to the ASEAN region, many online shoppers in CAREC browse through the online marketplaces without actually making purchases. The COVID-19 pandemic lockdowns may have contributed to the rise in online shopping, but the upward trend is expected to continue as consumers recognize the convenience of online shopping and gain confidence in the digital payment systems. The B2C e-commerce revenue share remained at 1% of the total, and the PRC share of B2C e-commerce revenue remained dominant at 99%.

The benefits from expanding B2C e-commerce, both domestic and cross-border, include increased consumer welfare, inclusion of MSMEs, and gender equity. To promote cross-border retail trade expansion, CAREC's emerging fintech markets need to take advantage of the increased opportunities for cooperation through free trade agreements (ADB and CAREC Institute 2022).

ONLINE RETAIL TRADE: DOMESTIC AND CROSS BORDER

A Market Overview

This study examines the B2C type of e-commerce known as "global online retail trade," focusing on domestic and cross-border transactions ("online shopping").

As discussed in the previous section, global e-commerce retail sales revenue has grown substantially since 2015. E-commerce sales nearly tripled as a proportion of global retail sales, from 7% in 2015 to 20% in 2022—and it is expected to reach 26% by 2026. However, determining the breakdown between domestic and cross-border e-commerce sales revenues remains a challenge.

Data from Statista reveals that the share of e-commerce retail sales revenue generated by cross-border e-commerce in several Asian countries—such as the PRC, India, and Japan—averaged just 6% in 2022. In a 2018 consumer survey amalgamating data from Statista, PayPal, and Ipsos, 40% of respondents reported shopping both domestically and cross border, while 8% reported shopping exclusively through cross-border channels. Thus, the value of the cross-border online retail trade is still insignificant. The key challenge lies in finding ways to stimulate growth in cross-border online retail trade.

UNCTAD (2021) observed that while most online shoppers primarily make purchases from domestic suppliers, about 360 million (one in four) online shoppers engaged in cross-border transactions in 2019, and interest in cross-border online shopping has continued to grow. According to UNCTAD's estimates, the portion of cross-border online shoppers among all online shoppers increased from 20% in 2017 to 25% in 2019.[72]

In 2022, more than a third (36%) of consumers globally engaged in online shopping through the leading marketplaces in their regions. Just under a third utilized search engines to look for products (Table 6.10).

71 This percentage was calculated based on the B2C e-commerce market size (Statista) and the most recent data for CAREC internet penetration, which were for 2020 (Lovelock 2023, Table 4).

72 The UNCTAD 2021 report only included countries that regularly compiled data on online retail sales. These countries included Australia, Canada, the PRC, the Republic of Korea, Singapore, the United Kingdom, and the United States, which collectively represented 65% of global B2C e-commerce in 2019.

Table 6.10: Leading Online Shopping Search Sites for Products, 2022

Search Sites Cited	% of Consumer Respondents
Leading marketplace in the region	36
Search engines	30
Social media sites	23
Other marketplaces	21
Retailer sites	18

Sources: Censuswide; Statista; and Wunderman Thompson online interviews, 25 March–7 April 2022.

Globally, Amazon emerged as the top retail website based on the number of visits, which was a staggering 3.2 trillion. Alibaba's Aliexpress had 486 million visits (Tables 6.11 and 6.12). It is important to note, however, that "visits" does not directly translate into actual purchases and revenues.

Table 6.11: Leading Global Retail Websites, by Traffic, 2022

Retail Website	Monthly Traffic (million visits)
amazon.com	3,162
ebay.com	589
walmart.com	581
aliexpress.com	486
etsy.com	468
amazon.de	340
rakuten.co.jp	279
homedepot.com	201
target.com	195

Sources: Semrush. 2022. *Survey Worldwide*; and Statista.

Table 6.12: Leading Global E-Commerce and Shopping Websites, by Visit Share, 2022

E-Commerce/Shopping Website	Share of Visits (%)
amazon.com	13
ebay.com	3
amazon.co.jp	3
amazon.de	2
aliexpress.com	2

e-commerce = electronic commerce.

Sources: Similarweb. 2022. *Survey Worldwide*; and Statista.

According to sales revenue data from 2022 and projected figures for 2027, Alibaba demonstrates superior performance compared with Amazon (Table 6.13). In 2022, Alibaba's share of global e-commerce retail sales stood at 14%. However, projections suggest that Amazon will slightly surpass Alibaba, by 1%, in 2027. As the major players in the global online retail market, Alibaba and Amazon also have the biggest market capitalization of all e-commerce firms. In 2021, the gross merchandise value (GMV) of Alibaba outperformed Amazon.[73]

[73] Gross merchandise value (GMV) refers to the value of total goods sold before relevant expenses are deducted. In e-commerce, GMV is the total sales value for merchandise sold through a marketplace over a specific time frame.

Table 6.13: Leading Global E-Commerce Retailers, by Sales Revenue, 2022 and 2027

	E-Commerce Retail Sales Revenue ($ billion)		Share of Global E-Commerce Retail Sales Revenue (%)	
E-Commerce Retailer	2022	2027 (projected)	2022	2027 (projected)
Alibaba	781	1,138	14	14
Amazon	691	1,201	12	15
Pinduoduo	445	806	8	10
JD.com	363	632	6	8
eBay	78	91	1	1
All Retailers Globally	**5,717**	**8,148**[a]	**100**	**100**

e-commerce = electronic commerce.

[a] This figure is a projection for 2026, serving as a proxy for 2027. The data are taken from Table 6.1, which included projections up to 2026 only.

Sources: Edge by Ascential; JD.com. 2022. *Survey Worldwide*; and Statista.

Alibaba's platforms, Taobao and Tmall, achieved a remarkable GMV of $1.4 trillion,[74] while Amazon's GMV was less than one-third of that, at $390 billion.

The dominance of Amazon and Alibaba could have adverse effects on both MSMEs and consumers. Examples include Amazon's practice of selling its own brand, Amazon Essentials, which directly competes with third-party sellers, and both Amazon's and Alibaba's shifting the cost of "free shipping" to the sellers (who then may feel compelled to pass on the full shipping cost to consumers).

During 2020–2022, large, capitalized e-commerce firms like Alibaba and Amazon experienced a revenue compound annual growth rate (CAGR) of 22%,[75] whereas online travel firms such as Booking.com, Expedia, and Airbnb witnessed a CAGR of 73% (Table 6.14), thanks to the significant increase in travel as countries began opening up to tourists in 2021. In 2022, international tourism growth exceeded expectations due to pent-up demand and the relaxation of pandemic travel restrictions (UNWTO n.d.).

What is the size of the global consumer class? According to Kharas and Fengler (2021), the global consumer class is defined as individuals living in households that spend at least $11 per day per person (Kharas and Fengler 2021). In 2021, the estimated size of the global consumer class was 4 billion people, with Asia accounting for 55% of this population. In terms of consumer class spending, Asia contributed 41%, equivalent to approximately $26 trillion (Table 6.15; Figure 6.4). Furthermore, projections suggest that by 2032, Asia will account for half of the world's consumer spending. As of 2020, the PRC dominates the Asian market, and is expected to account for the largest consumer class by 2030. Among the ASEAN countries, notable growth is anticipated in Indonesia, the Philippines, and Viet Nam.

74 Taobao and Tmall are online shopping platforms owned by the Alibaba Group. Taobao was launched in 2003. It was the largest digital retail platform in the PRC in terms of GMV from February 2021 to March 2022 (Analysys Mason). Tmall was launched in 2008. It is the largest third-party online and e-commerce platform for global brands and retailers in terms of GMV from February 2021 to March 2022 (Analysys Mason).

75 The compound annual growth rate, or CAGR, is the mean annual growth rate of an investment over a specified period longer than 1 year.

Table 6.14: Revenue Growth of Selected Online Service-Company Verticals, 2020–2022

Types of Online Service Company Verticals	CAGR (%)
Online travel (e.g., Booking.com, Expedia, Airbnb)	73
Marketplaces (e.g., Allegro, Delivery Hero, Uber)	45
Classifieds (e.g., Autohome.com.cn, Scout24, Zillow)	44
Large cap e-commerce (e.g., Alibaba, Amazon, eBay)	22
E-commerce (e.g., Ocado, Zalando, HelloFresh)	19

CAGR = compound annual growth rate, e-commerce = electronic commerce.

Notes:

1. A vertical market refers to companies that share a commonality, typically a specific niche market. Companies that operate in vertical markets may sell just one or multiple products and/or services. Vertical markets are specific and targeted, typically appealing to a certain customer group.
2. CAGR is the mean annual growth rate of an investment over a specified period longer than 1 year.

Sources: GP Bullhound; S&P. 2022. *Capital Survey Worldwide*; and Statista.

Table 6.15: Global Consumer-Class Market Size and Spending, by Region, 2021

	Asia	Rest of the World	Total	Asia's Share (%)
Consumer class (in billion people)[a]	2.2	1.8	4.0	55.0
Consumer class spending ($ trillion)	26.0	37.0	63.0	41.3

[a] This is defined as individuals living in a household that spends at least $11 per day per person. In 2021, the global middle class ($11–$110 per day per person) represented the biggest share, with 3.75 billion people.

Source: H. Kharas and W. Fengler. 2021. Which Will Be the Top 30 Consumer Markets of This Decade? 5 Asian Markets Below the Radar. Commentary. *Brookings*. 31 August. https://www.brookings.edu/articles/which-will-be-the-top-30-consumer-markets-of-this-decade-5-asian-markets-below-the-radar/.

Figure 6.4: Global Online Retail Consumer Market, Shares and Spending, 2021

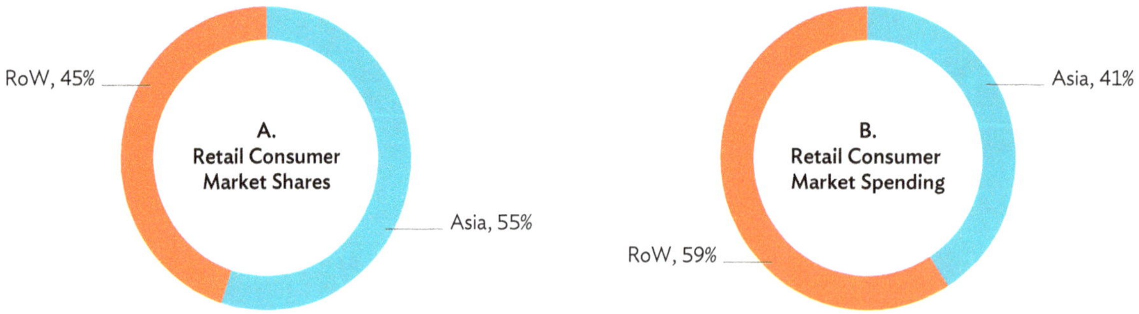

RoW = rest of the world.

Source: H. Kharas and W. Fengler. 2021. Which Will Be the Top 30 Consumer Markets of This Decade? 5 Asian Markets Below the Radar. Commentary. *Brookings*. 31 August. https://www.brookings.edu/articles/which-will-be-the-top-30-consumer-markets-of-this-decade-5-asian-markets-below-the-radar/.

Smartphones are the preferred device for a large majority of consumers—accounting for 71% of online traffic, and 61% of orders and purchases (Table 6.16). In 2022, the countries with the most smartphone users were the PRC, with 974 million; and India, with 659 million. Among the ASEAN countries, Indonesia ranked first, with 188 million; the Philippines ranked second, with 70 million users; and Viet Nam, third, with 65 million users (Statista 2025b).

Table 6.16: Global Online Retail Website Visits and Purchases, by Device, 2022

	Device Type, % of Respondents		
Activity	**Smartphone**	**Desktop**	**Tablet**
Traffic	71	26	3
Orders and purchases	61	36	3

Sources: Salesforce. 2022. *Research Survey Worldwide*; and Statista.

In 2021, the most popular products purchased through cross-border online shopping marketplaces were clothing and footwear—cited by 56% of consumer respondents in a survey conducted that year (Table 6.17).

Table 6.17: Leading Cross-Border Online Shopping Product Categories, 2021

Product Category	% of Consumer Respondents
Clothing and footwear	56
Sport, hobbies, and leisure	44
Health and beauty	42
Consumer electronics, computers, and smartphones	41

Sources: Censuswide; DC Velocity; Logistyx Technologies. 2021. *Online Survey Worldwide*; and Statista.

Online Retail Trade: The Market in the People's Republic of China

The PRC has the largest global consumer class and dominates the Asian market, with 899 million people, nearly twice that of India, which stands at 473 million (Calballero and Fengler 2023; Kharas and Fengler 2021). Projections suggest that the PRC will continue to hold its position as the biggest consumer class at least until 2030. Although PRC cross-border online shoppers made up only a fraction of the consumer class, their number increased nearly sixfold, from 23 million in 2015 to 155 million in 2021 (Table 6.18). Cross-border online retail sales continue to grow in the PRC, even though the rate of increase in the number of cross-border online shoppers has slowed down.

In 2022, the PRC overwhelmingly dominated B2C e-commerce revenues in the CAREC region, accounting for 99% (Table 6.19). The total B2C e-commerce revenue for the CAREC region in that year amounted to $1.32 billion, with the PRC alone contributing a staggering $1.30 billion. Without that contribution, the B2C e-commerce market in CAREC would be negligible. It is evident that the PRC holds immense significance as an e-commerce market within the region, and cannot be overlooked.

Table 6.18: People's Republic of China: Cross-Border Online Shopping Market Size and Retail Sales, 2015–2021

Year	Number of Cross-Border Online Shoppers (million)	Year-On-Year Change (%)
2015	23	...
2016	42	83
2017	66	57
2018	89	34
2019	125	41
2020	140	12
2021	155	11

... = data not available.
Source: Statista.

Table 6.19: E-Commerce Revenue—People's Republic of China vs. the Other CAREC Countries, 2017, 2022, and 2027

Country or Region	2017	2022	2027[a]
PRC ($ million)	422,700	1,306,000	2,375,000
PRC share (%)	99	99	99
Other CAREC countries ($ million)	3,333	13,942	23,772
Other CAREC countries share (%)	1	1	1
Total CAREC ($ million)	**426,033**	**1,319,942**	**2,398,772**

CAREC = Central Asia Regional Economic Cooperation, e-commerce = electronic commerce, PRC = People's Republic of China.
Note: The figures refer to business-to-consumer (B2C) revenues.
[a] The values for 2027 are projections.
Source: Statista. 2022. *Digital Market Outlook*.

FINTECH: A DRIVER OF ONLINE RETAIL TRADE

Fintech has emerged as a major driver of online retail trade (both domestic and cross border) and of trade finance. E-commerce sellers rely on operating capital and revolving credit for their production and inventory needs, and fintech firms have stepped in to provide business credit to e-commerce retail companies at lower costs. They offer innovative solutions such as electronic wallets (e-wallets) and virtual credit cards, challenging the dominance of traditional credit card firms such as Visa and Mastercard. Examples of such fintech firms include PayPal, Alipay, WeChat, Klarna, and Affirm. By providing consumers with a secure payment system and access to lower-cost credit, fintech firms have significantly contributed to the growth of online retail trade. Furthermore, e-commerce platforms such as Lazada, owned by the Alibaba Group, offer additional features such as "buy now, pay later" and cashback options, enabling consumers to access credit and receive rebates on purchases.

The exponential growth of B2C e-commerce can largely be attributed to fintech innovations. An ADB study in 2021 outlined several notable facts about fintech and retail e-commerce. One was that "fintech payments have revolutionized retail transactions by accommodating even smaller payment values" (Huang 2021). Convenient payment options are a key benefit to both online shoppers and sellers. Moreover, fintech allows online sellers to efficiently track sales and operating expenses, and make budget adjustments in real time. Fintech is also known to reduce cybersecurity concerns and prevent fraud more effectively. In Mongolia, for instance, whereas point-of-sale (POS) losses from credit card fraud rose by 156% in 2021, fraudulent payments for online purchases declined by 4% (ADB 2023, Table 5).

In 2021, nearly half (49%) of global e-commerce payments were made using digital or mobile wallets, while credit cards and charge cards accounted for 21% of payments by transaction volume (Figure 6.5). Worldpay forecasts that the share of digital and mobile wallets will increase to 53% by 2025 (Statista n.d.; Worldpay 2021), while credit and charge card usage will decline to 19%. In Asia and the Pacific, digital and mobile wallets dominate the e-commerce payments volume, accounting for 69% (Table 6.20). However, in North America (at 31%) and Latin America (39%), credit and charge cards remain the preferred modes of payment.

Figure 6.5: Global E-Commerce Payment Methods, Transaction Volume Shares, 2021

(%)

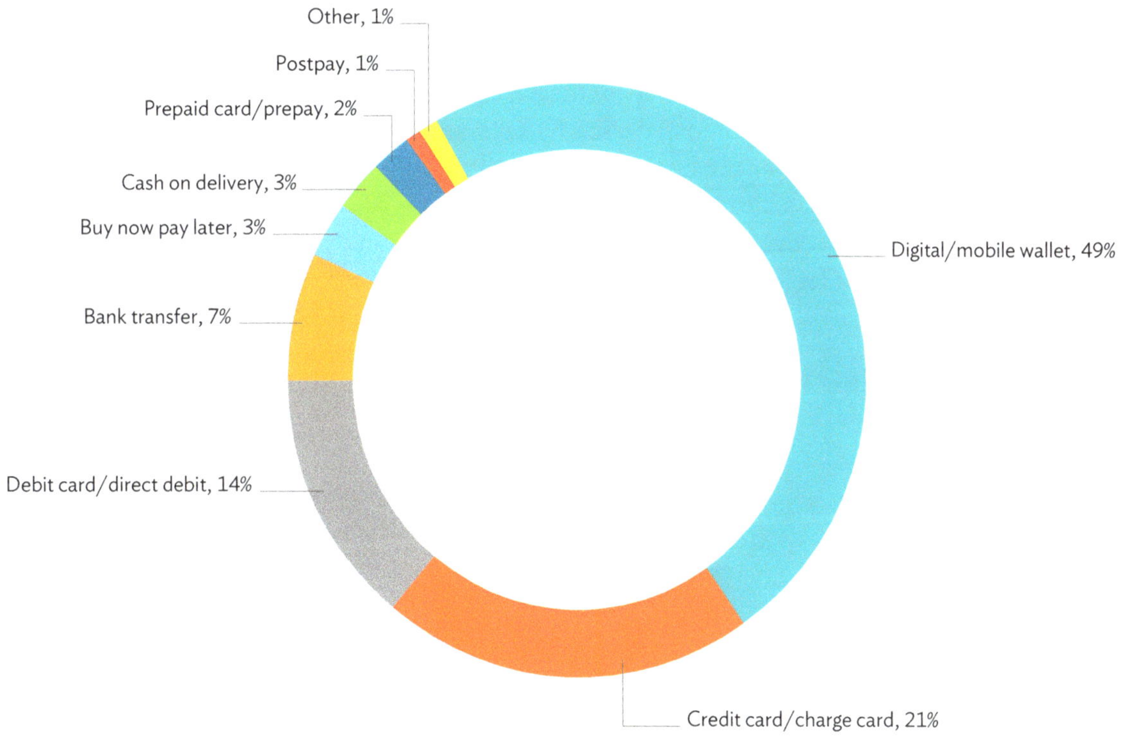

e-commerce = electronic commerce.

Sources: Statista; Worldpay. 2021. *Survey Worldwide*; and various secondary data sources (all accessed 8 December 2022).

Table 6.20: Global E-Commerce Payment Methods, Transactions Volume Shares, by Region, 2021
(%)

Selected Payment Method	World[a]	North America	Latin America	Europe	Asia and the Pacific	Middle East and Africa
Digital or mobile wallet	49	29	19	27	69	17
Credit card or charge card	21	31	39	25	13	31
Debit card	13	21	18	17	8	13
Bank transfer	7	8	10	14	5	16
Buy now, pay later	3	4	0	8	1	1
Cash on delivery	3	2	4	2	3	14
Direct debit	1	1	1	4	...	2
Prepay	1	2	...	1		2
Prepaid card	1	1	1	1	...	3
Postpay	1	...	7	...	1	...
Other	1	1	1	1	1	2

... = data not available, e-commerce = electronic commerce.

Note: An empty cell indicates that the column head does not apply.

[a] The percentages in this column does not total 100% due to rounding.

Sources: Statista; and Worldpay. 2021. *Survey Worldwide* (accessed 8 December 2022).

The case of PayPal provides compelling evidence for the widespread use of digital or mobile wallets in online payments. As of 2017, it ranked among the top four players in the global digital payments industry, alongside Visa, Mastercard, and American Express, though stands out, as it is not a credit card firm. According to the company's data, active PayPal accounts surged from 94 million in 2010 to 432 million by the third quarter of 2022, before leveling off. PayPal dominates the Asian digital-payment platform market for cross border e-commerce (Table 6.21).

Table 6.21: Leading Digital-Payment Platforms for Cross-Border E-Commerce in Selected Asian Countries, 2021
(%)

Country	PayPal	WorldFirst	Alipay	Airwallex	Payoneer	LianLian Global	PingPong	Other
Philippines	74	...	10	...	5	...	...	11
Indonesia	69	...	5	...	5	...	...	21
Malaysia	62	1	19	...	4	...	...	14
Thailand	58	5	22	5	...	3	...	7
Viet Nam	56	11	9	...	6	3	3	12
Singapore	55	26	7	4	4	...	...	4
Japan	28	41	3	...	28	...	...	...
ROK	16	56	2	...	24	...	...	2
PRC	4	43	3	...	22	16	12	...

... = data not available, e-commerce = electronic commerce, PRC = People's Republic of China, ROK = Republic of Korea.

Sources: Deloitte. 2021; and Statista.

Available data in 2018 indicate that the acceptance by global online merchants of e-wallets was not as widespread as perceived. A little under a third (29%) of global online merchants preferred payments by e-wallets (Table 6.22). The data, however, are no longer current, and the picture as of 2025 should be significantly different.

Consumers have increasingly used e-wallets for online shopping, as indicated in Figure 6.6. During 2014–2021, the impressive growth in global B2C e-commerce coincided with the rise in the number of active PayPal users. This is also evidence that e-wallets are widely accepted by global online merchants.

Table 6.22: Mobile Wallet Payment Acceptance by Global Online Merchants, 2015–2018

Year	% of Global Online Merchant Respondents
2015	24
2016	34
2017	22
2018	29

Sources: Kount survey worldwide, 2015–2018; and Statista.

Figure 6.6: Active PayPal Users and Global E-Commerce Retail Sales Revenue, 2014–2022

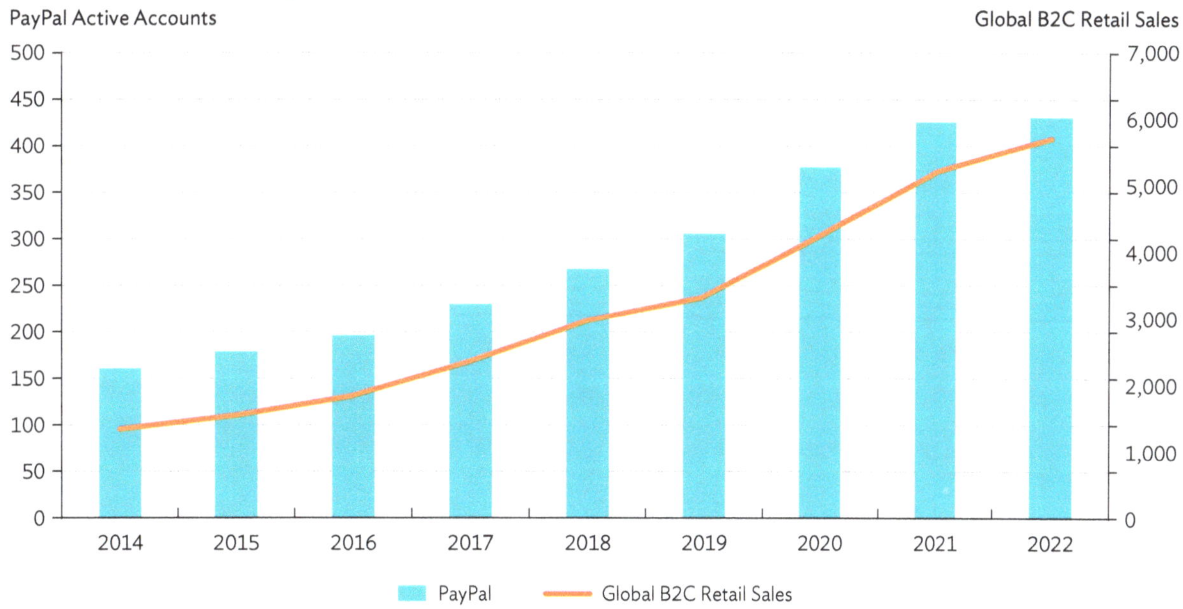

B2C = business-to-consumer, e-commerce = electronic commerce.
Sources: EMARKETER. *Worldwide Survey* (2014–2022); PayPal (2010–2022); and Statista.

Along with global players such as PayPal, Alipay, WeChat, and Google Pay, there are several popular e-wallets in the Asian markets. Popular e-wallets in selected Asian markets are listed in Table 6.23.

In addition to e-wallets, fintech firms also provide virtual credit cards to consumers engaged in cross-border online retail trade. Examples of virtual credit cards issued in the United States and EU markets include Afterpay, Affirm, and Klarna (Table 6.24). Together with e-wallets, virtual credit cards are challenging the dominance of traditional credit cards such as Mastercard and Visa.

Table 6.23: Popular E-Wallets for E-Commerce, Selected Asian Markets, 2023

Country	E-Wallet	Corporate Ownership
Bangladesh	bKash	Banglatec (fintech firm)
India	Paytm	Paytm (fintech firm)
Indonesia	OVO	Lippo Group (conglomerate)
Malaysia	GrabPay	Grab (technology firm)
Philippines	GCash	Globe Fintech Innovations Inc., aka Mynt (fintech firm)
Thailand	TrueMoney	Ascend Money (fintech firm)
Viet Nam	Moca	Moca Technology and Service Corporation (technology firm)

e-commerce = electronic commerce, e-wallet = electronic wallet.

Sources: *Epay*. 2023. Do You Know the Most Popular E-Wallets in Different Southeast Asian Countries? 29 March. https://www.epay.com/en-US/news/most-popular-E-wallets-in-different-Southeast-Asian-Countries; and *sumHR*. 2022. Top 20 Digital Wallets In India for Online Transactions: Go Cashless. 19 December. https://www.sumhr.com/blog/digital-wallets-india-list-online-payment-gateway/.

Table 6.24: Selected Fintech Firms in E-Commerce, United States and European Union Markets, 2022

Fintech Firm	Basic Details	Source
Payability	Accelerated daily payouts and capital advances for inventory and marketing for e-commerce sellers in the following marketplaces: Amazon, Walmart, Newegg, and Shopify; at least $10,000 in monthly sales	https://www.payability.com/
Afterpay	BNPL for consumers; digital Afterpay Card to add Apple Wallet or Google Wallet; 19 million active Afterpay customers globally	https://www.afterpay.com/en-US
Affirm	Virtual credit card; BNPL for consumers; marketplaces: Amazon, Walmart, and Delta Vacations, among others; for sellers, access to over 12.7 million high-lifetime-value customers	https://www.affirm.com/how-it-works
Klarna	Virtual credit card; BNPL for consumers; partner stores: Versace, Pomellato, Nike, Moschino, and Fenty Beauty, among others	https://www.klarna.com/us/
Rho Technologies	Builds tech-forward cash and spend management solutions for clients, integrating all the financial tools businesses need on one easy, centralized platform	https://www.rho.co/
OFX	Money transfers; global payment solutions, including tax payments, goods purchases, staff salaries, and payments to suppliers; over 1 million customers; transfers in 50+ currencies to 170+ countries; has moved $140 billion+ globally	https://www.ofx.com/en-us/
Xero	Accounting software for small businesses, accountants, and bookkeepers; over 3.5 million subscribers	https://www.xero.com/us/

continued on next page

Table 6.24 *continued*

Fintech Firm	Basic Details	Source
Sage 50	Accounting, finance, and payroll software designed for small businesses; covering cash flow and invoicing, payments and banking, and advanced inventory management	https://www.sage.com/en-us/products/sage-50cloud/
Zoho Books	Online accounting software; covering end-to-end accounting, financial management, inventory management, and business workflow automation	https://www.zoho.com/us/books/
Bill Spend & Expense	Business credit provider of up to $15 million; includes corporate credit cards for e-commerce and retail companies, small and medium-sized businesses	https://www.bill.com/product/spend-and-expense

BNPL = buy now, pay later, e-commerce = electronic commerce, fintech = financial technology.

Source: J. Hufford. 2024. 13 Top Fintech Companies for Ecommerce Businesses. *ecommerceCEO*. 20 November. https://www.ecommerceceo.com/top-fintech-companies/.

Promoting the participation of micro, small, and medium-sized enterprises (MSMEs) in international trade, particularly cross-border online retail trade, fosters inclusive growth. However, MSMEs face various constraints in accessing trade finance loans from traditional banks, due to their limited resources and collateral. In addition, they often lack the capacity to navigate the complex and fragmented trade finance system. According to an ADB study conducted in 2022, the trade finance gap is estimated at around 10% of global merchandise trade, representing significant missed economic and development opportunities (ADB 2022b). Fintech firms have emerged with a range of solutions (Table 6.24), but it is not clear whether their contributions are significant when it comes to closing the trade finance gap for MSMEs. The 2022 ADB study highlights the need for a global effort to enhance trade finance resources, digitalization, and implementation of common standards to close trade finance gaps.

LESSONS FROM ASEAN FOR THE EMERGING FINTECH MARKETS OF CAREC

Several factors have been identified as crucial contributors to the remarkable expansion of B2C e-commerce in Asia and the Pacific. These include internet accessibility and speed, online security, and financial inclusiveness driven by fintech innovation (Kang, Wang, and Ramizo 2021). In addition, changes to trade facilitation and tax collection have supported the e-commerce ecosystem.

Notable progress in fintech innovations led the ASEAN B2C e-commerce market to expand to 351 million users in 2022 from 156 million in 2017, a 126% increase. Moreover, 33% growth is projected during 2022–2027, reaching 466 million users. During the same period, the B2C e-commerce markets in 6 of the 10 ASEAN countries more than doubled in size (Table 6.25).[76]

[76] Online population data from Statista are available only for six ASEAN member countries: Indonesia, Malaysia, the Philippines, Singapore, Thailand, and Viet Nam.

Table 6.25: ASEAN E-Commerce Market Sizes, by Number of Users, 2017–2027

ASEAN Member Country	Number of Users (millions)										
	2017	2018	2019	2020	2021	2022	2023	2024	2025	2026	2027
Brunei Darussalam	0.1	0.1	0.2	0.2	0.2	0.2	0.2	0.2	0.2	0.2	0.2
Cambodia	2.3	3.0	4.0	4.8	5.6	6.3	7.0	7.4	7.8	8.3	8.8
Indonesia	70.0	93.0	119.0	138.0	159.0	179.0	196.0	209.0	221.0	234.0	245.0
Lao PDR	0.9	1.1	1.4	1.7	2.0	2.3	2.5	2.7	2.9	3.2	3.4
Malaysia	8.4	9.9	11.9	13.1	14.4	15.6	16.7	17.5	18.3	19.0	19.6
Myanmar	5.3	7.2	9.6	11.5	13.4	15.0	16.3	17.1	18.0	18.9	19.7
Philippines	23.5	27.9	34.6	38.9	43.3	47.3	51.5	53.6	55.8	58.3	60.4
Singapore	2.1	2.4	3.0	3.1	3.3	3.5	3.7	3.9	4.1	4.2	4.3
Thailand	22.8	25.7	30.7	33.7	36.6	39.2	41.2	42.3	43.5	44.7	45.8
Viet Nam	26.3	34.2	39.6	45.6	51.8	57.6	63.0	66.9	70.9	74.8	78.4
Total ASEAN	**161.7**	**204.5**	**254.0**	**290.6**	**329.6**	**366.0**	**398.1**	**420.6**	**442.5**	**465.6**	**485.6**

ASEAN = Association of Southeast Asian Nations, e-commerce = electronic commerce, Lao PDR = Lao People's Democratic Republic.

Notes:

1. The data presented here are for the business-to-consumer e-commerce market—specifically, the use of e-commerce marketplaces for the purchase of goods.
2. The values represent estimates for 2022, and projections for 2023–2027.

Source: Statista. n.d. Digital Market Outlook (accessed 24 November 2022).

Cross-border online retail trade remains a relatively small proportion of total global online retail trade, impeded by constraints posed by complex border-crossing procedures such as customs duty and tax collection and customs clearance (ADB and UNESCAP 2018). Issues such as the misdeclaration of goods and over- and under-invoicing add to the challenges.

To overcome these constraints and promote regional trade cooperation among the ASEAN countries, the World Customs Organization (WCO) has established cross-border e-commerce standards (Jacildo 2021).[77] The "de minimis" rule reduces costly customs revenue collection for small parcelized shipments by granting customs tax and duty exemptions and minimal clearance procedures to items valued below a certain threshold. The objective is to ensure that customs administrations do not spend more on tax collection than the actual tax collected. The de minimis rule is jointly supported by the International Chamber of Commerce (ICC) and the WCO (ICC 2016; WCO n.d.-b).

[77] The World Customs Organization (WCO), established in 1952 as the Customs Co-operation Council (CCC), is an independent intergovernmental body whose mission is to enhance the effectiveness and efficiency of Customs administration. It represents 185 customs administrations across the globe that collectively process approximately 98% of world trade (WCO n.d.-a).

Cross-border online retail trade stands to benefit significantly from ASEAN's regional cooperation initiatives, which have been established over the course of several decades. Key initiatives include the e-ASEAN Framework Agreement from 2000 and the 2005 agreement on the ASEAN Single Window for trade facilitation (ASEAN 2000; ASEAN n.d.). Among the e-ASEAN initiative's important provisions are national laws and policies for cross-border e-commerce transactions based on international norms, while the ASEAN Single Window and its iterations have significantly expedited cargo and promoted ASEAN economic integration (ASEAN n.d.).

The remarkable growth of e-commerce revenues in the ASEAN region can be attributed to fintech innovations that have enabled government policies and regional cooperation. In 2022, total B2C e-commerce revenue in the region quadrupled to $117 billion from $26 billion in 2017. It is projected to reach $219 billion in 2027, with the highest increase in Indonesia (Table 6.26). All ASEAN countries are expected to more than double their B2C e-commerce revenues by 2027.

Table 6.26: ASEAN and CAREC E-Commerce Revenues, 2017, 2022, and 2027
($ million)

	E-Commerce Revenue		
Region/Country	2017	2022	2027
ASEAN Member Countries			
Brunei Darussalam	86	154	258
Cambodia	317	1,015	2,102
Indonesia	9,009	55,970	104,100
Lao People's Democratic Republic	218	637	1,270
Malaysia	2,212	8,613	16,980
Myanmar	1,052	2,968	5,800
Philippines	5,729	15,620	29,540
Singapore	1,451	5,628	10,450
Thailand	3,746	18,280	32,810
Viet Nam	3,219	11,350	21,590
Total ASEAN	**25,987**	**117,267**	**219,100**
CAREC Member Countries			
Azerbaijan	742	1,762	3,448
PRC	422,700	1,306,000	2,375,000
Georgia	192	561	1,146
Kazakhstan	1,046	2,878	5,909
Kyrgyz Republic	168	415	799
Mongolia	92	374	716
Pakistan	458	6,066	8,101

continued on next page

Table 6.26 *continued*

Region/Country	E-Commerce Revenue 2017	2022	2027
Tajikistan	98	255	472
Turkmenistan	105	297	543
Uzbekistan	433	1,335	2,640
Total CAREC	**426,034**	**1,319,943**	**2,398,774**
Total CAREC Without PRC	**3,334**	**13,943**	**23,774**

ASEAN = Association of Southeast Asian Nations, CAREC = Central Asia Regional Economic Cooperation, e-commerce = electronic commerce, PRC = People's Republic of China.

Notes:

1. The data presented here are for the business-to-consumer e-commerce market.
2. The data for 2027 are projections.
3. No data were available for Afghanistan.

Source: Statista. *Digital Market Outlook* (2017, 2022, and 2027).

By contrast, a comparison between the B2C e-commerce revenue of the CAREC region without the PRC and that of the ASEAN region reveals a significant disparity (Table 6.26; Figure 6.7). In 2022, the total B2C e-commerce revenue in the CAREC region was just 12% of the ASEAN total, and this is projected to remain unchanged through 2027. It is important to note that the PRC stands as an outlier, and that online marketplace browsing does not necessarily translate into e-commerce revenues in the rest of the CAREC region.

Figure 6.7: E-Commerce Revenues in ASEAN and CAREC (Without the People's Republic of China), 2017, 2022, and 2027
($ million)

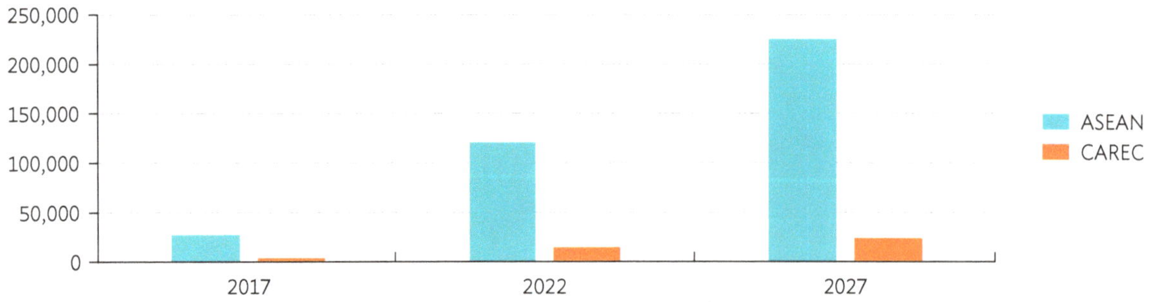

ASEAN = Association of Southeast Asian Nations, CAREC = Central Asia Regional Economic Cooperation, e-commerce = electronic commerce.

Notes:

1. This figure focuses on business-to-consumer e-commerce.
2. The data for 2027 are projections.

Source: Statista Digital Market Outlook.

CAREC FINTECH AND TRADE CREATION

Preliminary Findings

Fintech innovations alone have shown limited impact on economic growth and consumer welfare in the CAREC region, especially when compared with the thriving B2C e-commerce market in the ASEAN countries (as discussed in the previous section). Valuable lessons can be learned from ASEAN's experience with B2C e-commerce, particularly with regard to regional cooperation.

Considering the findings from the report on CAREC fintech progress indicators described in Chapter 1, it is not surprising that B2C e-commerce revenue in CAREC lags behind that in ASEAN. In 2019, online shoppers in Georgia, Kazakhstan, and Tajikistan did not even number one-third of internet users (ADB 2022), even though they have the highest percentage of online shoppers among internet users in CAREC (Table 6.27).

Table 6.27: Shoppers on CAREC Online Platforms, 2019

Country	Shop Online (% of population)	Shop Online (% of internet users)
Azerbaijan	5	6
People's Republic of China	62	79
Georgia	14	21
Kazakhstan	24	28
Kyrgyz Republic	6	8
Mongolia	7	9
Pakistan	1	7
Tajikistan	10	27
Turkmenistan	3	6
Uzbekistan	2	5

CAREC = Central Asia Regional Economic Cooperation.

Note: Data for Afghanistan were not available.

Source: Asian Development Bank. 2022. *E-Commerce in CAREC Countries: Infrastructure Development*. pp. 64–65 (Table 5.2). https://www.adb.org/sites/default/files/publication/781526/e-commerce-carec-countries-infrastructure-development.pdf.

In 2022, the B2C e-commerce market in CAREC included 1.1 billion users, or 84 million users when excluding the PRC (Table 6.28); by contrast, there were 366 million users in ASEAN. B2C e-commerce in the CAREC's nine emerging fintech markets expanded by 80% from 2017 (47 million users) to 2022, whereas in ASEAN, it grew by 126% in the same 5 years. If CAREC realizes its expected growth of 28% during 2022–2027, the number of users in the B2C e-commerce market in those nine economies will reach 108 million. Pakistan, Uzbekistan, and Kazakhstan accounted for 85% of the total in 2022.

Table 6.28: CAREC E-Commerce Market Size, by Users, 2017–2027

CAREC Member Country	Number of Users (millions)										
	2017	2018	2019	2020	2021	2022	2023	2024	2025	2026	2027
Azerbaijan	2.3	2.6	3.1	3.3	3.5	3.6	3.7	3.8	3.9	3.9	4.0
PRC	710.0	770.0	860.0	930.0	990.0	1,050.0	1,100.0	1,170	1,230.0	1,280.0	1,340.0
Georgia	0.9	1.1	1.3	1.5	1.6	1.8	1.9	2.0	2.1	2.2	2.2
Kazakhstan	3.0	3.4	4.2	4.4	4.5	4.7	4.9	5.1	5.2	5.3	5.4
Kyrgyz Republic	0.9	1.2	1.5	1.7	2.0	2.2	2.4	2.6	2.7	2.8	3.0
Mongolia	0.5	0.6	0.8	0.9	1.1	1.2	1.3	1.5	1.6	1.7	1.8
Pakistan	32.3	37.9	41.0	47.7	51.4	54.8	58.2	61.6	65.1	68.0	70.8
Tajikistan	0.8	1.1	1.4	1.7	2.0	2.2	2.5	2.7	2.9	3.1	3.2
Turkmenistan	0.5	0.7	0.9	1.0	1.2	1.4	1.6	1.7	1.8	2.0	2.1
Uzbekistan	5.5	6.7	8.5	9.9	11.2	12.4	13.4	14.0	14.6	15.3	15.9
Total CAREC	**756.7**	**825.3**	**922.7**	**1,002.1**	**1,068.5**	**1,134.3**	**1,189.9**	**1,265.0**	**1,329.9**	**1,384.3**	**1,448.4**
Total CAREC Without PRC	**46.7**	**55.3**	**62.7**	**72.1**	**78.5**	**84.3**	**89.9**	**95.0**	**99.9**	**104.3**	**108.4**

CAREC = Central Asia Regional Economic Cooperation, e-commerce = electronic commerce, PRC = People's Republic of China.

Notes:

1. The data presented here are for the business-to-consumer e-commerce market—specifically, the use of e-commerce marketplaces for the purchase of goods.
2. The values represent estimates for 2022, and projections for 2023–2027.
3. Data for Afghanistan were unavailable.

Source: Statista. n.d. Market Insights (accessed 24 November 2022).

In 2019, online shoppers in CAREC's emerging fintech markets accounted for an average of 13% of internet users (Table 6.28). This percentage rose significantly in 2020, to 59% of their combined online population.[78] The increase, however, did not translate into higher B2C e-commerce revenues (Figure 6.7). The 2022 ADB and CAREC Institute study noted that cybersecurity and delivery (the reliability of B2C e-commerce logistics) remained major concerns for consumers in the region. Added to these constraints on the growth of B2C e-commerce were inadequate knowledge and working capital for MSMEs, limiting their ability to participate in B2C e-commerce; a lack of national fintech and e-commerce strategies; and the absence of regional cooperation agreements to deal with both.

A World Economic Forum white paper reiterated the need for regional and global cooperation to address cross-border payment regulatory barriers (WEF 2023), as they restrict cross-border online retail trade.

[78] These percentages were calculated based on B2C e-commerce market sizes (data from Statista) and the most recent data for CAREC internet penetration, which is from 2020 (Lovelock 2023, Table 4).

POLICY RECOMMENDATIONS FOR CAREC

Fintech innovations, enabling government policies, and regional cooperation are pivotal in expanding domestic markets through cross-border online retail trade. However, opportunities for regional trade agreements to foster cross-border e-commerce growth in CAREC are limited. ADB and the CAREC Institute have emphasized that regional cooperation can facilitate e-commerce growth in Central Asia and improve consumer welfare there (ADB and CAREC Institute 2022). To unlock the potential of cross-border online retail trade, the study recommended four actions:

- Improve internet infrastructure to expand access and lower costs.
- Enhance cybersecurity and promote digital and financial literacy.
- Upgrade payment systems to enable smoother online transactions.
- Enhance the reliability of delivery services, while reducing costs.

The CAREC Institute, through Samad, Masood, and Ahmed (2023), further highlights the point that the absence of pragmatic trade agreements impedes trade generation and facilitation at border-crossing points. This impact is more pronounced in cross-border online retail trade, particularly with small parcel shipments. Drawing on lessons from ASEAN's regional cooperation initiatives, CAREC could develop mechanisms to facilitate cross-border e-commerce growth (Chapter 9).

This volume's road-map approach to developing a cooperative fintech community in CAREC notes that disparate regulations on market entry, and a lack of standardized protocols, limit the expansion of B2C e-commerce (Chapter 2). To mitigate these effects, it recommends the following actions:

- Create one CAREC fintech market that would benefit from economies of scale, become more efficient and less costly, and so provide more affordable access for consumers.
- Collaborate on policies to promote connectivity and financial integration, leveraging each existing financial infrastructure.

B2C e-commerce in the region could also be boosted by two specific actions that are part of the road map and featured in Chapter 1:

- Develop cross-border digital payment infrastructure and fast-payment systems (FPS) to support good governance and ensure safety and reliability: from Pillar 1 (finance).
- Develop cross-border trade finance to provide working capital to international trade entities: from Pillar 4 (regional cooperation).

Fintech is a crucial driver of B2C e-commerce, which, in turn, elevates consumer welfare. Expanding markets beyond domestic borders through fintech will be vital for the CAREC economies, given their limited domestic markets. To achieve interoperability and cross-border e-commerce facilitation, regional cooperation and commitment similar to that experienced in ASEAN will be necessary. Regional cooperation in the digital future must include both a fintech and an e-commerce strategy. Stakeholders must recognize the substantial contribution that fintech could make to CAREC's economic growth and development.

REFERENCES

Amazon. 2022. *Small Business Empowerment Report*. https://assets.aboutamazon.com/56/ff/42fe2d294620b21432c7bbb59d1e/amzn-small-business-empowerment-2022-final.pdf.

Asian Development Bank (ADB). 2022a. *E-Commerce in CAREC Countries: Infrastructure Development*. https://www.adb.org/sites/default/files/publication/781526/e-commerce-carec-countries-infrastructure-development.pdf.

———. 2022b. *Toward Inclusive Access to Trade Finance: Lessons from the Trade Finance Gaps, Growth, and Jobs Survey*. https://www.adb.org/publications/inclusive-access-trade-finance.

———. 2023. *Financial Technology for Regional Cooperation in Central Asia Regional Economic Cooperation Countries*. https://ewsdata.rightsindevelopment.org/files/documents/01/ADB-55122-001_TdYynoL.pdf.

———. n.d. ADB's Work in Regional Cooperation and Integration. https://www.adb.org/what-we-do/topics/regional-cooperation/overview.

ADB and Central Asia Regional Economic Cooperation (CAREC) Institute. 2022. *E-Commerce in CAREC Countries: Infrastructure Development*. Asian Development Bank. https://www.adb.org/sites/default/files/publication/781526/e-commerce-carec-countries-infrastructure-development.pdf.

ADB and United Nations Economic and Social Commission for Asia and the Pacific (UNESCAP). 2018. *Embracing the E-Commerce Revolution in Asia and the Pacific*. https://www.adb.org/sites/default/files/publication/430401/embracing-e-commerce-revolution.pdf.

Association of Southeast Asian Nations (ASEAN). 2000. E-ASEAN Framework Agreement. https://agreement.asean.org/media/download/20140119121135.pdf.

———. n.d. ASEAN Single Window: Overview of the Sector. https://asean.org/our-communities/economic-community/asean-single-window/.

BusinessWorld. 2018. Lazada Philippines to Expand Partnerships with Brands, MSMEs. 7 December. https://www.bworldonline.com/editors-picks/2018/12/07/203256/lazada-philippines-to-expand-partnerships-with-brands-msmes/#:~:text=At%20present%2C%20there%20are%20around,enter%20the%20e%2Dcommerce%20market.

Caballero, J. and M. Fengler. 2023. China and India: The Future of the Global Consumer Market. Commentary. *Brookings*. 14 April. https://www.brookings.edu/blog/future-development/2023/04/14/china-and-india-the-future-of-the-global-consumer-market/#:~:text=Size%3A%20At%20899%20million%20people,half%20that%20at%20473%20million.

Consumers International. 2021. *Guidelines for Online Product Safety*. https://www.consumersinternational.org/news-resources/news/releases/new-guidelines-building-consumer-confidence-and-trust-in-the-digital-economy/.

Digital News Asia. 2018. Lazada to Cultivate 8mil e-Commerce Entrepreneurs, SMEs by 2030. 15 November. https://www.digitalnewsasia.com/digital-economy/lazada-cultivate-8mil-e-commerce-entrepreneurs-smes-2030.

Ferrantino, M. J. and E. E. Koten. 2019. *The Measurement and Analysis of E-Commerce: Frameworks for Improving Data Availability*. World Bank. https://documents.worldbank.org/en/publication/documents-reports/documentdetail/927771578286460819/the-measurement-and-analysis-of-e-commerce-frameworks-for-improving-data-availability.

Huang, Y. 2021. Retail Fintech Payments: Facts, Benefits, Challenges, and Policies. In C.-Y. Park, J. Villafuerte, and J. T. Yap, eds. *Managing the Development of Digital Marketplaces in Asia*. Asian Development Bank. pp. 131–173. https://www.adb.org/sites/default/files/publication/761016/managing-development-digital-marketplaces-asia.pdf.

Hufford, J. 2024. 13 Top Fintech Companies for Ecommerce Businesses. *ecommerceCEO*. 20 November. https://www.ecommerceceo.com/top-fintech-companies/.

International Chamber of Commerce (ICC). 2016. ICC Policy Statement on Global Baseline De Minimis Value Thresholds (2015). News release. 11 November. https://iccwbo.org/news-publications/policies-reports/icc-policy-statement-on-global baseline-de-minimis-value-thresholds-2015/.

International Finance Corporation (IFC) et al. 2021. *Women and E-Commerce in Southeast Asia*. International Finance Commission. https://www.ifc.org/en/insights-reports/2021/women-and-ecommerce-sea.

Jacildo, R. 2021. Trade and E-Commerce in Asia: Policy Considerations. In C. Y. Park, J. Villafuerte, and J. T. Yap, eds. *Managing the Development of Digital Marketplaces in Asia*. Asian Development Bank. pp. 99–130. https://aric.adb.org/pubs/digitalmarket/managing-development-digital-marketplaces-asia_CH4.pdf.

Jo, Y. J., M. Matsumura, and D. E. Weinstein. 2019. The Impact of E-Commerce on Relative Prices and Consumer Welfare. *NBER Working Paper Series*. No. 26506. National Bureau of Economic Research. https://www.nber.org/system/files/working_papers/w26506/w26506.pdf.

Kang, J. W., T. Wang, and D. Ramizo. 2021. The Role of Technology in Business-to-Consumer E-Commerce: Evidence from Asia. *ADB Economics Working Paper Series*. No. 632. Asian Development Bank. https://www.adb.org/sites/default/files/publication/675186/ewp-632-technology-adoption-b2c-e-commerce-asia.pdf.

Kharas, H. and W. Fengler. 2021. Which Will Be the Top 30 Consumer Markets of This Decade? 5 Asian Markets Below the Radar. Commentary. *Brookings*. 31 August. https://www.brookings.edu/articles/which-will-be-the-top-30-consumer-markets-of-this-decade-5-asian-markets-below-the-radar/.

Lazada Group. n.d. About Lazada. https://www.lazada.sg/about/#:~:text=ABOUT%20LAZADA&text=As%20the%20pioneer%20of%20the,%2C%20data%2C%20and%20service%20solutions.

Organisation for Economic Co-operation and Development (OECD). 2021. Trade Finance for SMEs in the Digital Era. *OECD SME and Entrepreneurship Paper 24*. http://web-archive.oecd.org/2021-05-03/587090-Trade%20finance%20for%20SMEs%20in%20the%20digital%20era.pdf.

Retail Dogma. n.d. Brick & Mortar Retail vs. Online Retail: Cost Comparison. https://www.retaildogma.com/brick-and-mortar-retail-vs-online-retail/.

Samad, G., A. Masood, and J. Ahmed. 2023. Geographical Proximity and Trade Impacts in the Central Asia Regional Economic Cooperation Program Region. *ADB East Asia Working Paper Series*. No. 60. Asian Development Bank. https://www.adb.org/sites/default/files/publication/870111/eawp-060-geographical-proximity-trade-impacts-carec.pdf.

Statista. 2025a. Number of Active Amazon Marketplace Sellers in 2019, by Country; https://www.statista.com/statistics/1086664/amazon-3p-seller-by-country/.

———. 2025b. Ranking of the Number of Smartphone Users by Country 2024. https://www.statista.com/forecasts/1146962/smartphone-user-by-country.

———. n.d. Who We Are: The Company Behind the Success. https://www.statista.com/aboutus/.

Telma, T. 2015. The Power of Retail: Delivering Development Impact in Emerging Markets. *Devex*. 17 August. https://www.devex.com/news/the-power-of-retail-delivering-development-impact-in-emerging-markets-86722.

United Nations Conference on Trade and Development (UNCTAD). 2016. In Search of Cross-Border E-Commerce Trade Data. *UNCTAD Technical Notes on ICT for Development*. No. 6 (Unedited). United Nations Conference on Trade and Development. https://unctad.org/system/files/official-document/tn_unctad_ict4d06_en.pdf.

———. 2021. Estimates of Global E-Commerce 2019 and Preliminary Assessment of COVID-19 Impact on Online Retail 2020. *UNCTAD Technical Notes on ICT for Development.* No. 18. United Nations Conference on Trade and Development. https://unctad.org/system/files/official-document/tn_unctad_ict4d18_en.pdf.

———. 2022. Trust in Cross-Border e-Commerce: The Case for Consumer Product Safety. https://unctad.org/meeting/trust-cross-border-e-commerce-case-consumer-product-safety.

United Nations World Tourism Organization, or UN Tourism (UNWTO). n.d. Impact Assessment of the Covid-19 Outbreak on International Tourism. https://www.unwto.org/impact-assessment-of-the-covid-19-outbreak-on-international-tourism.

Viner, J. 1950. *The Customs Union Issue*. Carnegie Endowment for International Peace. https://archive.org/details/customsunionissu0000vine.

WEF (World Economic Forum). 2023. *Unlocking Interoperability: Overcoming Regulatory Frictions in Cross-Border Payments*. White paper. https://www.weforum.org/publications/unlocking-interoperability-overcoming-regulatory-frictions-in-cross-border-payments/.

7

The Political Economy of Fintech in Pakistan

Mujtaba Zaidi

INTRODUCTION

The disruptive impact of technology in Pakistan's financial market is mounting at an unprecedented rate and set to continue with the inclusion of a largely unbanked population. However, for financial technology (fintech) to take root, it is imperative that policymakers and stakeholders collaborate on a mutually agreed-on regulatory framework for the presentation of user-friendly interfaces.

The political economy analysis in this chapter provides a snapshot of the Pakistan fintech industry as of 2024, and discusses the influence of key players, as well as the regulatory, technological, and cross-sector landscape of initiatives likely to spur its growth. The chapter also offers recommendations for regional-cooperation initiatives for fintech development in Pakistan. An overview of the major players with the power and interest to influence the growth and direction of the industry sets the scene (Table 7.1).

Table 7.1: The Fintech Ecosystem in Pakistan

Regulators	Three key regulators have prominent roles in the development of fintech: the State Bank of Pakistan (SBP), which oversees the financial aspects; the Pakistan Telecommunication Authority, which manages technology infrastructure; and the Securities and Exchange Commission of Pakistan, which oversees corporate governance and regulatory sandbox initiatives. The SBP is the most influential regulator, yet the absence of a unified governance framework poses compliance challenges and contributes to overregulation.
Facilitators	Several policy institutions support cross-cutting areas essential for fintech. For example, the National Database and Registration Authority manages digital identity and citizen information. The Special Technology Zones Authority regulates technology zones established to foster innovation. The Federal Investigation Agency focuses on cybersecurity, while the Banking Ombudsman provides consumer protection. The Ministry of Information Technology and Telecommunication develops the legal and policy frameworks for technology and infrastructure.
Enablers	The stakeholders, who provide reach and resources for fintech, include mobile network operators, investors, and business and technology incubators.
Innovators	Fintech in Pakistan has grown rapidly since 2020, with many different types of start-ups offering diverse financial services. A broad range of fintech firms are key licensed players in the ecosystem.
Collaborators	National and international civil society organizations have a vital role in building networks for cross-learning, social impact, and communities of practice.

continued on next page

Table 7.1 *continued*

Users	Karandaaz, a not-for-profit fintech incubator, reported the following in a Financial Inclusion Insights survey (where each 1% increase in financial inclusion brings in 2.3 million more consumers): • Between 2016 and 2022, financial inclusion in Pakistan increased from 9% to 30%, representing the proportion of individuals aged 15 and above with accounts at government-regulated institutions providing comprehensive financial services.[a] • Digital financial inclusion rose from 7% in 2014 to 13% by 2017; and, as per a Global Findex survey, it was 14.9% in 2021. • The level of financial literacy was static, at 19%, during 2020–2022. • Formal borrowers, defined as individuals aged 15+ with active loans from financial service providers, increased from 2.64% in 2017 to 3.51% in 2022.[b] • Access to banking services increased from 9% in 2016 to 15% in 2020. • There is a growing awareness of the concept of mobile money. • The percentage of the population holding mobile money accounts increased from 4% in 2017 to 9% in 2022.[c] • Monthly lending by NBFIs increased from $119 billion in October 2019 to $186 billion in September 2023.[d]

fintech = financial technology, NBFI = nonbank financial institution.

[a] As per a survey by Financial Inclusion Insights (FII), financial inclusion is defined as the proportion of individuals (aged 15+) who hold an account with an institution that provides a full suite of financial services and comes under some form of government regulation.

[b] The FII survey defines borrowing as the percentage of respondents (aged 15+) who currently have a loan with one of the following: (i) a bank, (ii) a mobile money account, (iii) a microfinance institution, (iv) a savings or lending group, or (v) any other institution or financial service provider.

[c] This refers to the proportion of individuals aged 15+ who have a registered mobile money account. FII defines registered users as individuals who have a financial account registered in their name or registered jointly in their own and someone else's name.

[d] This term is defined as the month-end position of loans and advances issued by lending NBFIs. Data are disaggregated according to the types of lending NBFIs—i.e., *modarabas*, leasing companies, investment banks, and nonbank microfinance companies (NBMFCs). A surge in values from October 2019 reflects the fact that NBMFCs were introduced into the data.

Source: Author.

Important challenges for the fintech industry in Pakistan include limited digital literacy, distrust in digital services, and cultural barriers. In terms of legislation and regulations, the State Bank of Pakistan (SBP) and the Securities and Exchange Commission of Pakistan (SECP) have introduced policies, but the "one-size-fits-all" approach has proven less effective for small and medium-sized enterprises (SMEs) and fintech start-ups. Moreover, a lack of fintech-specific primary and secondary legislation is hindering the sector's growth. On the other hand, policymakers lack the knowledge and resources required for formulating and implementing relevant laws. Finally, the lack of regional collaboration, the foreign investment challenges, the absence of national or regional mentoring opportunities, and the lack of infrastructure for reaching remote areas are among the issues that require solutions through collaborative and integrated approaches.

Background of the Political Economy

Pakistan's unmet financial needs are well recognized. According to the World Bank's *Global Findex Database 2021*, Pakistan is ranked as the world's fourth-least banked country (Demirgüç-Kunt et al. 2018). Only 21% of adults in Pakistan have a formal financial account, while about half of the bankable population is not included in either formal or informal finance. About 36% of the people served rely on informal financial services. The SBP's 2019 *Pakistan Financial Inclusion and Infrastructure Report* noted that about 100 million adults remained excluded from formal financial services (SBP 2020b).

Microfinance covers about 35% of urban and peri-urban areas, but is scarce in rural areas. Smallholder farmers are especially underserved, with 29% entirely excluded, and most of the others relying on traders and moneylenders for credit, often linked to input purchases and future produce sales (Pakistan Microfinance Network 2021). A key barrier to financial service provision is the high cost of banking operations and infrastructure, especially for reaching remote, unbanked populations.

Women in Pakistan face significant barriers when trying to access finance, with only 7% holding a bank account. The *Financial Inclusion and Infrastructure Report* highlighted this gender gap, noting that in 2019 women received just 3% of SME loans and 19% of microfinance loans (Market Development Facility 2020). While limited mobility, security concerns, and restricted decision-making widen the financial inclusion gap for women, the revised National Financial Inclusion Strategy aimed to generate 20 million women's transaction accounts by 2023. Unlike traditional institutions, fintechs are increasingly seizing this opportunity by developing products to address this gap (Karandaaz Pakistan 2021).

Until 2015, fintech growth in Pakistan lagged behind the needs of potential beneficiaries. Barriers included data security threats, intellectual property risks, difficulty attracting talent and customers, and regulatory uncertainty. These challenges discourage entrepreneurs from entering, innovating, and investing.

This chapter aims to build an empirical foundation for policy and regional cooperation. It explores policy dynamics and informs fintech decisions by analyzing critical factors and key actors in Pakistan.

The Asian Development Bank (ADB 2013) recommended analyzing the political economy, as this would improve the diagnosis of development issues, risk assessments, and support design, leading to improved results and policy change opportunities (Moncrieffe and Luttrell 2005). This chapter uses a sector analysis approach to diagnose policy and institutional constraints, stalled reforms, and incentives in the fintech sector, and to explore how actors could drive policy change. It draws on national and international policy documents, legislative frameworks, institutional reports, and research on fintech development. It also includes interviews with personnel in government, technology and finance sectors, the SBP, major fintechs, and fintech networks and incubators.

Study Objectives and Framework

Key objectives include mapping the roles and responsibilities of fintech stakeholders; identifying influence and interest-based relationships within the ecosystem; exploring the sector's evolution by assessing the core factors affecting its growth in Pakistan; and informing interventions, particularly for regional collaboration.

The study aims to navigate complex policy dynamics and guide fintech-related decisions in Pakistan by identifying key factors, influential actors, and potential reforms.

Figure 7.1 highlights the theoretical framework for assessing opportunities. Significant limits include the fact that political and economic challenges made data from 2022 obsolete; the methodologies came from different sources and so were not aligned (even as preference was given to government sources); and political polarization continued to hinder the development of a consensus for advancing fintech, and this affected the selection of study participants.

Figure 7.1: Framework for Advancing Fintech in Pakistan

Fintech in Pakistan

What is changing and how?	What factors are influencing change?	What change is required?	How can change be achieved?

In Terms of

Finance

F1. FI account holders
F2. Mobile money accounts
F3. Digital payment experience
F4. FI account wages received
F5. Debit or credit card
F6. Utility payments made

Capability

C1. Foundational frameworks (Data governance, customer base, privacy, customer data sharing, and others)
C2. Fintech laws and regulations
C3. Digital literacy
C4. Initiatives supporting fintech

Regional Cooperation

R1. International commitments
R2. Cross-border initiatives
R3. Policy alignments
R4. Participation in regional and international platforms

Technology

T1. Internet users
T2. Mobile broadband subscriptions
T3. Fixed broadband speed
T4. Fast retail payment system
T5. National digital identity
T6. Tech adoption and investment
T7. API specifications
T8. Data models
T8. Identity protocols
T9. Cybersecurity

Opportunities

O1. Partnership acceleration
O2. Financial inclusion program
O3. Economic relief efforts
O4. Empowering gig workers
O5. Harnessing the IoT

API = application programming interface, FI = financial institution (licensed by the State Bank of Pakistan), fintech = financial technology, IoT = Internet of Things.
Source: Author.

Recommendations

Pakistan can position itself as a front-runner in the dynamic world of fintech. The approach to leveraging fintech's potential to expand financial inclusion and economic growth will have to encompass regulations, capacity building, and regional collaboration. In sum, it should do the following:

- **Adopt a tailored approach to regulating fintech firms.** Include specific licensing categories, proportional fees for smaller players, and collaborative oversight to boost innovation, competition, and growth while protecting consumers.
- **Promote financial inclusion through fintech innovation.** Streamline licensing processes and regulatory assistance for innovative financial products. Provide comprehensive financial and technical support to fintech firms. Grants, funding opportunities, and capacity-building programs would accelerate the development of innovative fintech solutions, contributing to economic growth and competitiveness in the finance sector.

- **Reform the tax system to promote fintech.** Making tax laws clearer, implementing tax rate reductions, and streamlining tax procedures would create a more financially feasible environment. By promoting tax awareness and facilitating compliance, the Government of Pakistan can foster a culture of tax adherence in the fintech industry.
- **Build capacity.** Individual, institutional, and environmental capacity-building initiatives are essential for advancing fintech growth in Pakistan. Establish academic partnerships to offer relevant courses, enhance digital literacy, and provide specialized orientations for legislators and policymakers. This would empower the fintech ecosystem, while research and development collaborations, open data governance, and institutional strengthening would ensure systematic growth and accountability.
- **Deepen regional collaboration.** Collaborating with other countries and learning from their innovative approaches will offer valuable insights for fintech development in Pakistan. Regional investor meetings, conferences, and conventions can foster shared understanding and enable cross-border investments and initiatives. A focus on underserved and unserved areas and on the facilitation of digital financial services for remote populations would promote financial and digital inclusion.

Fintech's power for disruption lies in its ability to recognize and respond to unmet financial-service needs among targeted users. Achieving digital financial inclusion will require building strong stakeholder collaboration. The identification of key stakeholders—their roles, interests, and coordination methods—is essential for creating a unified vision and cohesive ecosystem for effective fintech development.

THE FINTECH ECOSYSTEM IN PAKISTAN

Pakistan is a highly legislated country with a significant public sector and policy infrastructure, as well as a wide range of current and potential stakeholders. One of the key purposes of this book is to determine the key actors responsible for fintech growth, those who are either influencing or who could potentially influence the fintech indicators identified in Chapter 1. Pakistan's major fintech ecosystem stakeholders are divided into seven categories (Figure 7.2), each of which can be examined in turn.

Figure 7.2: Fintech Ecosystem Players

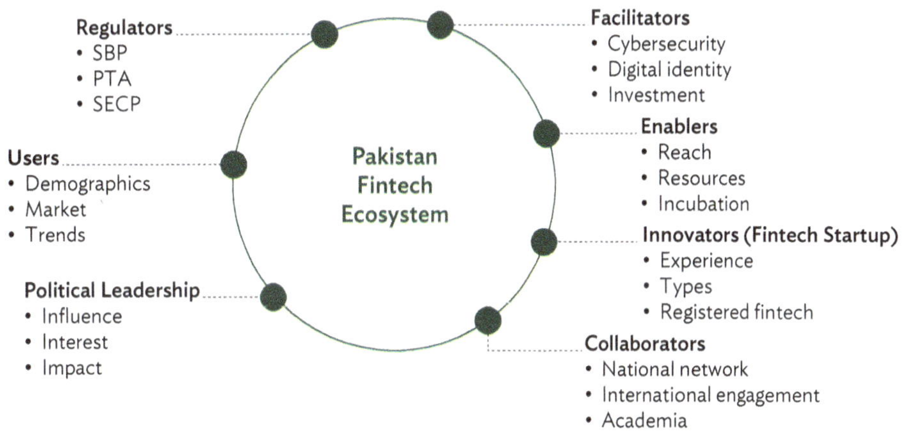

fintech = financial technology, PTA = Pakistan Telecommunication Authority, SBP = State Bank of Pakistan, SECP = Securities and Exchange Commission of Pakistan.

Source: Author.

Fintech Regulators

The four pillars identified within the ADB project to assess fintech growth requirements are finance, technology, capability, and regional cooperation (Chapter 1). The regulation and promotion of activities under all four is the purview of three distinct institutions: the State Bank of Pakistan (SBP), the Pakistan Telecommunication Authority (PTA), and the Securities and Exchange Commission of Pakistan (SECP). Though sharing similarities, these primary regulatory bodies have different scopes and functions that determine how they influence fintech development in Pakistan.

State Bank of Pakistan

A significant number of indicators under the finance, capability, and regional cooperation pillars are directly relevant to the scope of the central bank. The SBP promotes and regulates fintech by fostering innovation while ensuring financial stability, consumer protection, and regulatory compliance. The SBP aims to create a balanced ecosystem that supports growth and maintains integrity and trust in Pakistan's financial system. Added to these key functions are cross-border engagement and regional cooperation.

The SBP has expressed significant commitment to establishing the fintech sector in Pakistan, with policy frameworks and social-engagement campaigns and initiatives articulating its interest. As the authority and decision-maker power in matters related to monetary policy, financial regulations, and payment systems, it exercises control over financial institutions, including fintech firms.

Within the perspective of regional collaboration, the SBP has a mandate to foster initiatives such as the National Payment Systems Strategy (NPSS), and to collaborate with international organizations such as international banks. External factors, including global trends in digital finance and the need for Pakistan's financial system to adopt international standards, influence these initiatives.

Especially since 2020, the SBP has taken an active role in fintech, including consultations with a broad range of stakeholders over regulations. To align its functions with fast-changing technologies and regulate electronic financial services, the central bank has introduced several initiatives, including the ones shown in Figure 7.3.

Pakistan Telecommunication Authority

The Pakistan Telecommunication Authority (PTA), as the state regulator, is tasked with ensuring that a well-regulated, competitive, and efficient telecommunications industry benefits both consumers and industry stakeholders.

The second and third pillars mentioned in Chapter 1 highlight the importance of technology (including infrastructure) and capabilities—aspects addressed by the PTA. With 11 broad divisions, the PTA is engaged in a variety of functions for promoting and regulating telecommunication technologies and initiatives (PTA 2023). It provides an enabling environment for mobile banking, electronic commerce (e-commerce), digital payments, and innovation; as well as a regulatory framework in collaboration with the SBP and SECP. Its operations leverage internet users, mobile broadband subscriptions, broadband access and quality, and a range of other indicators in the technology and capability pillars. The PTA licenses these services, and its other responsibilities include cybersecurity, data protection, and consumer protection.

Figure 7.3: Timeline of the State Bank of Pakistan's Digital Financial Services

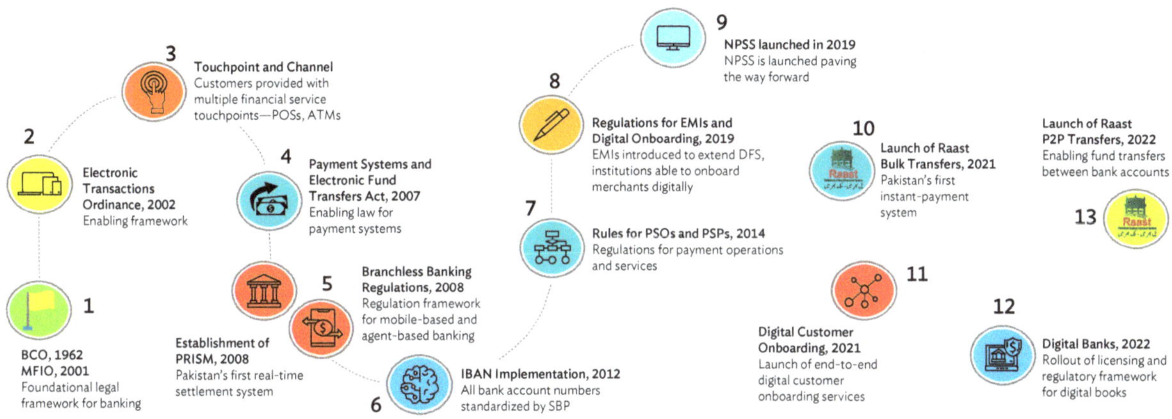

BCO = Branchless Banking Customer Onboarding, DFS = digital financial services, EMI = electronic money (e-money) institution, IBAN = International Bank Account Number, MFIO = Microfinance Institutions Ordinance, NPSS = National Payment Systems Strategy, P2P = peer-to-peer, POS = point of sale, PRISM = Pakistan Real-time Interbank Settlement Mechanism, PSO = payment system operator, PSP = payment service provider, SBP = State Bank of Pakistan.

Note: Raast is Pakistan's instant-payment system.

Source: State Bank of Pakistan. Digital Financial Index. https://www.sbp.org.pk/dfs/index.html.

The PTA's support for fintech growth balances innovation and market expansion with the telecom operators' goals of efficient connectivity and equitable access. It also encourages digital literacy and consumer protection through civil society organizations. The PTA's performance review shows a strong commitment to developing Pakistan's fintech sector, with policy frameworks and social engagement campaigns highlighting this interest.

The PTA has a significant influence in promoting fintech collaborations with telecom operators to leverage existing infrastructure with specialized services and to drive innovation. Regulatory policies may affect the affordability and accessibility of fintech services, affecting different socioeconomic groups. The PTA could offer a platform for aligning fintech with civil society to improve digital literacy and protect consumers, which is also an area of interest for PTA. Furthermore, concerning regional cooperation, the PTA is the gateway for governance and implementation of international agreements such as digital trade agreements. The PTA may also serve as the focal point of the Government of Pakistan for indigenizing global trends in technology and financial services, to influence the domestic fintech market.

Securities and Exchange Commission of Pakistan

The SECP is mandated to regulate and develop the corporate sector and nonbank financial markets under the Securities and Exchange Commission of Pakistan Act, 1997. These include, but are not limited to, capital markets, mutual funds, nonbank financial institutions, *modarabas* (partnerships between an investor and financial manager), insurance companies, and private pensions.

The main SECP objectives are to (i) maintain fair, orderly, and efficient markets; (ii) promote robust corporate and insurance sectors; (iii) protect the rights of investors; (iv) facilitate capital formation; and (v) develop an efficient and dynamic regulatory framework. The SECP functions relevant to fintech development include supervising and regulating all firms, issuing licenses for digital banks in collaboration with the SBP, and overseeing the role of fintech start-ups in corporate affairs. Besides raising awareness about the benefits and risks of fintech and digital assets, the SECP promotes innovation and competition, serving as the lead regulator for the Sandbox Framework (SECP 2019) and supporting fintech incubation.

SECP goals regarding fintech are fourfold: (i) maintaining a balanced and cohesive ecosystem through the regulation of key stakeholders; (ii) fostering innovation; (iii) protecting fintech users through regulation, compliance, and licensing; and (iv) providing a framework to protect and promote fintech investment.

The SECP sets the regulatory agenda, along with the SBP and PTA, through its emphasis on corporate governance, influence on policy outcomes, and utilization of different financial and capital market instruments. The SECP may also play a role in neutralizing the disruptive effects of fintech with a broader view of utility, innovation, and market growth. Global standards, international agreements, and technological advancements influence its regulatory approach.

Fintech Service Facilitators

Besides regulators, several state agencies engage in the fintech ecosystem, particularly in alignment with the capability pillar of fintech indicators. Government entities serve as facilitators in various areas of fintech development and operations across Pakistan, and although wielding less power, influence, and interest than the primary regulators, they are integral to the national capability framework for fintech development. These institutions collaborate with each other, as well as with regulators, the private sector, and civil society organizations. The key facilitators are listed just below, by area of operations.

Digital Identity

The **National Database and Registration Authority (NADRA)** oversees digital identity operations in Pakistan by maintaining the security and integrity of the Computerized National Identity Card (CNIC). Featuring a unique ID number for every citizen, CNIC is used for e-banking and cellular network authentication. NADRA also maintains the electoral rolls, taxation, and driver's licenses. NADRA has formed partnerships with public and private sector organizations to advance digital-identity initiatives and to develop new applications and services that utilize digital-identity data. Among these initiatives are the following:

- **e-Sahulat.** In 2008, NADRA launched Pakistan's first e-commerce platform, e-Sahulat, starting with KIOSK machines and expanding to digital integrations. The platform, which provides low-cost, secure payment and collection services, is supported by over 17,000 franchisees, and processes about 12.5 million transactions monthly. It integrates with most national utility providers and telecom operators, and has recently added services from government departments, such as the Punjab Land Record Authority, Punjab Arms License Authority, Islamabad Excise and Taxation Department, Excise and Taxation Department Punjab, the Ministry of Housing and Works, and the Federal Board of Revenue.
- **E-commerce verification.** NADRA has partnered with e-commerce firms to provide identity-verification services for online transactions.
- **Mobile network identity verification.** NADRA has collaborated with mobile network operators to provide identity-verification services for SIM card registration.
- **Fintech partnerships.** NADRA has established partnerships with several fintech firms in Pakistan to provide identity-verification services for various financial transactions, such as opening bank accounts, applying for loans, and investing in mutual funds.

- **Application programming interfaces (APIs).** NADRA permits APIs to enable third-party organizations to access its digital-identity data. These APIs include the CNIC verification API, which allows organizations to verify the identity of citizens and improves the security of their services. Access to NADRA's API is strictly regulated.

Investment Promotion

The **Special Technology Zones Authority (STZA)** was established in 2021 to create opportunities for technology start-ups, and investors. It develops technology zones to help build a scientific and technological ecosystem, and supports it with institutional and legislative backing. The STZA facilitates investment in technology firms, including fintech, by providing operational benefits in designated zones and helping access the Fintech Sandbox by the SECP. Its role is crucial to the third and fourth pillars of the fintech indicators framework (capability and regional cooperation).

Consumer Protection

The **Banking Ombudsman**, supervised by the Ministry of Law and Justice, is the authority in charge of arbitration between consumers and banks. It promotes informal conflict resolution, but also offers formal complaint channels. Although the ombudsman does not have a direct role in fintech, its consumer protection and grievance roles could enable it to extend support.

Legal and Policy Frameworks

The **Ministry of Information Technology and Telecommunication (MoITT)** formulates legislation and policies to advance Pakistan's information technology (IT) and telecom sectors. It coordinates interprovincial efforts, addresses electronic crimes, and supports digitization. Notably, the ministry collaborated with the China Academy of Information and Communication Technology (CAICT) on the *Pakistan National ICT Industry Development White Paper*, which outlines the Pakistan Vision 2025 and a policy framework for digitization and telecom growth. This framework emphasizes integrated technologies, digital infrastructure development, and workforce capacity strengthening (MoITT 2022).

The **Ministry of Planning and Development** has a mandate to support initiatives for equitable economic growth. Two initiatives remain relevant to the scope of opportunities for fintech: (i) the Pakistan Innovation Fund, established in 2023, which supports start-ups and welcomes international and local fintech initiatives; and (ii) an initiative to foster physical, power, and digital connectivity targeted at the 20 poorest districts in the country, which provides access to new markets and innovations.

Safeguarding the Digital Financial Landscape

The **Federal Investigation Agency (FIA)** has a crucial role in developing fintech by safeguarding the digital financial landscape, ensuring regulatory compliance, and investigating cybercrimes. As fintech transforms the finance sector, the agency is responsible for ensuring a secure environment for innovation and financial inclusion.

Key functions in support of fintech development include the following: cybersecurity and digital fraud prevention, including investigations of cyberattacks on fintech platforms and programs to educate the public about scams and fraud; enforcing anti-money laundering/combating the financing of terrorism (AML/CFT) and Know-Your-Customer (KYC) regulations; investigating financial crimes; enhancing transparency and trust in the ecosystem; providing regulatory oversight in coordination with the SBP, PTA, and SECP, including the establishment of a comprehensive fintech regulatory framework to help ensure fairness and promote responsible innovation; and intellectual property protection that encourages entrepreneurs to invest in research and development. The FIA also investigates disputes involving online transactions, and engages in capacity building with partners in civil society and the private sector to help create a skilled workforce that can tackle emerging challenges.

Financial Security

The **Financial Monitoring Unit (FMU)** has the primary mandate of combating money laundering and terrorist financing. It plays a crucial role in shaping the landscape of fintech development. Under the Anti-Money Laundering Act, 2010, the FMU is authorized to collect, analyze, and disseminate information in suspicious-transaction reports or currency-transaction reports. Banks, nonbank financial institutions, and professionals may file such reports. The FMU's responsibilities are of paramount importance in ensuring the integrity, security, and regulatory compliance of digital financial services. Its functions include the following:

- **AML/CFT compliance.** The FMU monitors and analyzes fintech transactions for unusual or suspicious activities that could potentially involve money laundering or terrorist financing. By enforcing stringent regulations, the FMU helps create a secure environment for fintech operations.
- **Transaction monitoring and reporting.** The FMU is responsible for receiving, analyzing, and disseminating suspicious-transaction reports and currency-transaction reports from financial institutions, including fintech firms. This ensures that illicit financial activities are promptly identified, reported, and investigated.
- **Enhancing regulatory compliance.** FMU oversight encourages fintech entities to adopt robust AML/CFT frameworks aligned with national and international regulatory standards. Its vigilance reduces the risk of financial crimes and fosters better conditions for fintech growth.
- **Intelligence sharing and collaboration.** The FMU collaborates with domestic and international counterparts to exchange financial intelligence. This remains crucial for building confidence in regional or cross-border transactions, as the intention is to address cross-border financial crimes and cyber threats, to safeguard the global fintech ecosystem.

Private Sector Fintech Enablers

Private sector enablers play a vital role in driving fintech development. They include mobile network operators (MNOs) that expand financial services, investors driving research and innovation, business-to-business (B2B) service providers offering technology infrastructure, incubators supporting start-ups to foster growth and innovation, and civil society collaborators enhancing social impact. They all utilize their unique strengths to help create a thriving fintech environment.

Regulators and government-based facilitators understand that these enablers offer expertise, resources, and infrastructure that are essential for fintech development, and welcome their input into policymaking. Market conditions, the regulatory landscape, and user feedback shape enabler approaches; and these enablers contribute valuable insights for improving regulatory frameworks and market practices.
Each group of private sector enablers plays a crucial role in advancing fintech, as detailed in the next section.

Mobile Network Operators

The National Financial Inclusion Strategy, 2015 recognized MNOs as key stakeholders in the strategy. MNOs have improved access to mobile banking services in remote areas and played a crucial role in developing a digital payments ecosystem by partnering with businesses, utility providers, and government agencies. Also, MNOs collaborate with fintech firms, microfinance institutions, and microfinance banks to create and deliver innovative financial products, such as microloans, savings accounts, and insurance policies to underserved populations. Through these partnerships, MNOs leverage their technological infrastructure and extensive agent networks to extend financial services to rural and underbanked areas, bridging gaps left by traditional banking services. Pakistan has four major MNO players (Table 7.2).

Table 7.2: Mobile Network Operators in Pakistan, 2022

Mobile Network Operator[a]	Active Subscribers (millions)	Market Share (%)	Services Offered
Jazz (Mobilink and Warid)	74.31	38.6	2G, 3G, 4G LTE, prepaid and postpaid, mobile banking, internet
Telenor Pakistan	48.70	25.3	2G, 3G, 4G LTE, prepaid and postpaid, easypaisa (mobile banking), internet
Zong (China Mobile Pakistan)	44.47	23.1	2G, 3G, 4G LTE, prepaid and postpaid, mobile banking, internet
Ufone (Pakistan Telecommunication Mobile Limited)	23.29	12.1	2G, 3G, limited 4G LTE, prepaid and postpaid, mobile banking, internet
Total[a]	**190.77**	**99.1**	

G = generation, LTE = long-term evolution.

[a] The list of mobile network operators and the data shown here do not include mobile service providers operated by the Special Communications Organization (SCO), a government entity.

Source: Pakistan Telecommunication Authority. 2022. *Pakistan Telecommunication Authority Annual Report 2022*. https://www.pta.gov.pk/category/pta-annual-report-2022-906566043-2023-06-01.

MNO contributions and initiatives for promoting financial inclusion include the following:

- **Mobile banking services.** MNOs have launched mobile banking platforms that let users open and manage mobile wallet accounts for saving, paying bills, and transferring funds. Notable examples include JazzCash, by Jazz; easypaisa, by Telenor Pakistan; and UPaisa, by Ufone.
- **Branchless banking.** MNOs and banks collaborate to offer branchless banking services, such as JazzCash (a partnership between Jazz and Mobilink Microfinance Bank) and easypaisa (between Telenor and Telenor Microfinance Bank). HBL Konnect also partners with MNOs, allowing access to services through Unstructured Supplementary Service Data (USSD) codes and SMS banking. These collaborations enable users to bank through their mobile phones. By sharing infrastructure, these partnerships reduce costs and extend banking services to areas lacking traditional bank branches.
- **Mobile-based lending and insurance.** Mobile-based lending in Pakistan simplifies access to credit and extends services to rural and underbanked areas. Platforms such as JazzCash and easypaisa offer quick microloans based on mobile wallet activity. Tez Financial Services provides short-term loans using mobile and social data, while Finja offers digital credit to small and medium-sized enterprises (SMEs) and individuals. Similarly, mobile-based partnerships such as easypaisa and MicroEnsure, and JazzCash and BIMA Pakistan provide affordable life, health, and accident insurance with minimal paperwork.
- **Financial literacy and awareness.** MNOs often publicize their financial services and promote financial literacy. They provide information and training to customers on how to use mobile banking platforms and other financial services, helping build trust in digital financial solutions.

- **Partnerships with government and international organizations.** MNOs have forged significant partnerships to advance their services and infrastructure. Jazz collaborates with NADRA to enhance digital-identity services, and partners with Ericsson and the World Bank internationally. Zong works with the Federal Board of Revenue of Pakistan to improve e-tax services, and has teamed up with China Mobile International to advance technology solutions. Telenor collaborates with Mastercard to facilitate digital payments. Ufone has joined with Pakistan Post and Mastercard to broaden its service offerings. HBL Konnect partners with Visa and Western Union to enhance digital payments and international money transfers, while Finja works with FINCA Microfinance Bank to provide digital credit services.

Table 7.3 highlights key initiatives and contribution of MNOs.

Table 7.3: Mobile Network Operator Contributions to Financial Inclusion in Pakistan

Initiative (Year When Initiated)	Beneficiaries/Consumer Segment	Modality of Service	Role of Mobile Network Operators
Benazir Income Support Programme (2008)	Poorest families, with a focus on women	Unconditional cash transfers	Distribution of funds via mobile banking and agent networks
Asaan Mobile Account Scheme (2020)	The general public, particularly in remote and rural areas	Simplified mobile-account-opening process using USSD codes	Collaboration with the SBP to facilitate account opening
Raast Instant Payment System (2021)	Individuals, businesses, government entities	Digital payment platform for P2P, P2B, B2B, G2P transactions	Infrastructure and support for digital payment transactions
Ehsaas Emergency Cash Program (2020)	Low-income families affected by political and economic crises	Financial assistance through cash transfers	Disbursement of funds via JazzCash, easypaisa, and agent networks
Ehsaas Kafaalat Programme (2020)	Most vulnerable women	Monthly cash stipend through digital payment systems	Distribution of stipends through JazzCash, easypaisa, and agent networks
Ehsaas Amdan (Income) program (2020)	Vulnerable households in rural areas	Income-generating assets such as livestock or small-scale businesses	Support for transactions and access to funds via mobile banking services and agent networks
G. Cross-border payments (2020)	Pakistanis living abroad and their families	Inbound remittances through partnerships with international remittance-service providers, such as MoneyGram, Western Union, and Xpress Money	Facilitated remittances via mobile wallets and agent networks, ensured compliance with SBP regulations and policies

B2B = business-to-business, G2P = government-to-person, P2B = person-to-business, P2P = peer-to-peer, SBP = State Bank of Pakistan, USSD = Unstructured Supplementary Service Data.

Source: Author.

Investors

Several who were interviewed for this book identified limited investment in fintech as an issue. With data on the volume of investment not publicly available, it remains hard to put a dollar figure on flows. However, Karandaaz reports a mix of investors, highlighting the contribution of angel investors, accelerators, corporate investors, and donors (Table 7.4).

Table 7.4: Prominent Investors and Their Fintech Portfolios in Pakistan

Investment Company	Country of Origin	Portfolio of Fintech Firms
Sarmayacar[a]	Pakistan	CreditBook, PayPro, Retailo
Karandaaz Pakistan[b]	Pakistan	Finja, Tez Financial Services, CreditFix, Invoice Wakalah
IFC	United States	Telenor Microfinance Bank (easypaisa), MCB Islamic Bank, JS Bank
Quona Capital	United States	Finja, Tez Financial Services
Antler Global	Singapore	CreditBook
47 Ventures	United States	Finja
Innov8 Limited	Dubai	PayPro
Wavemaker Partners	Singapore	Retailo
Fatima Gobi Ventures[c]	Pakistan and the PRC	Airlift Express, Tez Financial Services
Kingsway Capital	United Kingdom	SadaPay

fintech = financial technology, IFC = International Finance Corporation, PRC = People's Republic of China.

[a] Sarmayacar. n.d. Portfolio: Backing Ground-Breaking Ideas. https://www.sarmayacar.com/portfolio.

[b] Karandaaz Pakistan. 2025. https://www.karandaaz.com.pk/.

[c] Fatima Gobi Ventures. n.d. Portfolio. https://fatimagobi.vc/portfolio/.

Source: Author.

These investors often enabled Pakistani start-ups to benefit from their experience in developing and commercializing fintech products, with their initiatives providing a significant boost to the local fintech market.

Incubators

Federal and provincial government departments steering information technology, and allied agencies such as IT boards, have invited the private sector to help develop business-incubation centers, and implemented policies supporting fintech start-ups. These business incubators are pivotal in developing an entrepreneurial fintech ecosystem. Their key objectives include accelerating fintech innovation, facilitating growth of early-stage fintech firms, and helping these firms to bring transformative financial technologies to market while adhering to regulations. Incubators offer a range of support services, resources, mentorship, funding, and networking opportunities to help start-ups refine their ideas and business models and link up with investors.

Prominent examples of incubators demonstrate how these centers have brought innovative fintech to market (Table 7.5).

Table 7.5: Selected Incubators for Fintech Start-Ups in Pakistan

Incubators	Supported Fintech Firms
National Incubation Center The NIC is a public–private partnership involving the Ministry of Information Technology and Telecommunication, Ignite (formerly known as National ICT R&D Fund Company), and Teamup. It has centers in Islamabad, Lahore, Karachi, Peshawar, and Quetta. The NIC offers mentorship, office space, funding opportunities, and networking for technology and fintech start-ups.	CreditFix (credit scoring and financial inclusion) Qayaam (online property rental platform) Unikrew Solutions (digital employment platform)
Plan9—PITB's Tech Incubator Plan9 is an initiative of the PITB that focuses on incubating technology-based start-ups. It provides office space, mentorship, networking, and access to investors for early-stage tech and fintech start-ups.	Paysys Labs (mobile payments and digital wallet) Ricult (agricultural finance platform) Finja (digital lending and financial services)
The Nest I/O The Nest I/O is a technology incubator and community hub launched by P@SHA (also known as Pakistan Software Houses Association for IT and ITES), with support from Google for Startups, Samsung, and the United States Department of State. It offers coworking spaces, mentorship, networking opportunities, and access to resources for tech and fintech start-ups.	Tez Financial Services (digital lending and financial services) PublishEX (blockchain-based platform for digital assets) Savyour (cashback and rewards app)
National Incubation Center Lahore NICL, formerly known as the LUMS Center for Entrepreneurship, is an initiative of Lahore University of Management Sciences. It offers a comprehensive incubation program, providing start-ups with mentorship, funding opportunities, office space, and networking to help them grow in the technology and fintech sectors.	Finovators (AI-based financial advisory platform) AgriMart (agricultural finance and supply-chain platform) Minerva (digital education financing)
Invest2Innovate The "ecosystem" called "i2i" is an accelerator and seed fund that supports early-stage social enterprises, including technology and fintech start-ups, in Pakistan. It offers a 16-week accelerator program, mentorship, funding, and networking opportunities to help start-ups scale their businesses.	KarloCompare (financial product–comparison platform) Invoice Wakalah (invoice discounting platform) CreditBook (digital bookkeeping app for small businesses)

AI = artificial intelligence, fintech = financial technology, i2i = Invest2Innovate, LUMS = Lahore University of Management Sciences, NIC = National Incubation Center, NICL = National Incubation Center Lahore, PITB = Punjab Information Technology Board.

Source: Author's compilation from interviews.

Business-to-Business Service Vendors

In the rapidly evolving landscape of the fintech sector, constructive collaborations among various players are essential for driving innovation and growth. A diverse array of B2B service providers is pivotal for enabling fintech firms to expand their capabilities, enhance customer experiences, and navigate the intricate landscape of financial services. Outsourcing and allied services make a critical contribution to the fintech ecosystem's vitality. Table 7.6 features key providers.

Table 7.6: Key Fintech Support Services and Providers in Pakistan

Service	Provider
Cloud infrastructure	AWS, Microsoft Azure, DigitalOcean, CloudFusion, and StormFiber
Cybersecurity solutions	Cybernet, Secureworks, Comodo, LMKR, CyberSec, and Jazz Solutions
Legal and compliance services	RIAA Barker Gillette, Haidermota BNR, KPMG Pakistan, EY Pakistan, and SMA Law Associates
Marketing and PR services	GroupM Pakistan, Ogilvy Pakistan, JWT Pakistan, Adcom Zenith, Optimedia, and MBLM
Payment gateway and processing services	JazzCash, easypaisa, Keenu, NetConnect, Avanza Premier Payment Services, and Nayatel
Data analytics and business intelligence	Teradata Pakistan, IBM Pakistan, SAP Pakistan, SAS Pakistan, and Anthro Insights
Financial partnerships	UBL, HBL, MCB Bank Limited, Bank Alfalah, and Allied Bank Limited
APIs and integration solutions	Abacus Consulting, TPS, 10Pearls, Systems Limited, and Viftech Solutions
Consulting and advisory services	Deloitte Pakistan, Grant Thornton Anjum Rahman, BDO Ebrahim & Co., and A.F. Ferguson & Co. (PwC Pakistan)

API = application programming interface; AWS = Amazon Web Services; fintech = financial technology; HBL = Habib Bank Limited; PR = public relations; PwC = PricewaterhouseCoopers; SAP = Systems, Applications, and Products; UBL = United Bank Limited.
Source: Author.

FINTECH INNOVATIONS

Fintech is transforming Pakistan's financial markets by driving innovation and pushing traditional institutions to adapt. Emerging start-ups are providing new digital financial services that cater to underserved communities. This disruption is encouraging existing players to innovate to reach a wider audience. Significant growth in the since 2020 has been supported by key regulators such as the SBP and by collaborative efforts involving state and nonstate actors (Figure 7.4). Fintech start-ups are optimistic about growth and the potential for new products tailored to local needs if regulators and stakeholders can help sustain momentum.

Among notable digital payments achievements, easypaisa almost doubled its money transfers in a year, to Pakistan rupees (PRs)859 billion ($3 billion) in the first half of 2022. Over 10% of the telecommunication industry's airtime sales are now processed through the app, which supports over 250 payment use cases. In another success, NayaPay raised $13 million in a seed round in February 2022, led by Zayn Capital, MSA Novo, and Graph Ventures. Initially targeting students and freelancers, NayaPay received its license from the SBP in August 2021.

Figure 7.4: Fintech Applications in Pakistan

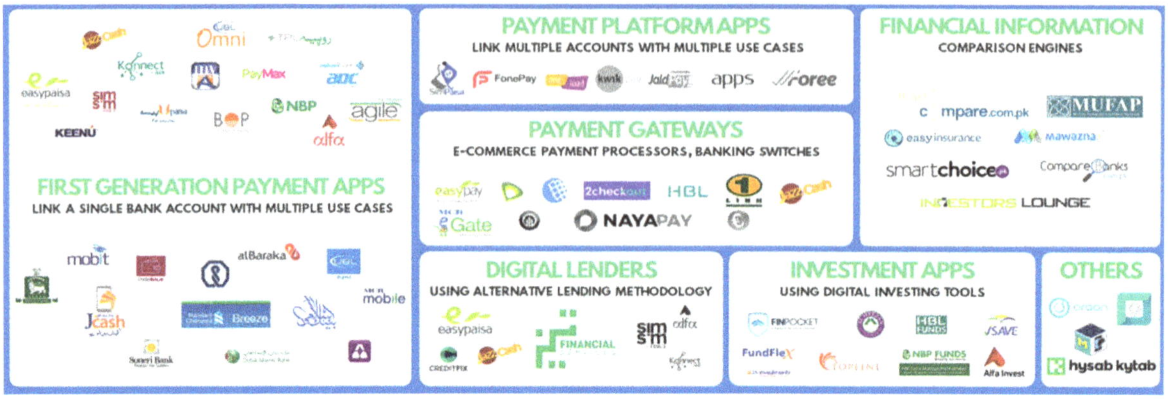

e-commerce = electronic commerce, fintech = financial technology.
Source: Author.

In fiscal year (FY) 2024 (ended 30 June 2024), retail payment volumes rose from 4.7 billion to 6.4 billion transactions, a 36% annual increase. The value of these transactions grew from PRs403.5 trillion ($1.4 trillion) to PRs546.6 trillion ($1.9 trillion). This surge underscores the rising confidence in and convenience of digital transactions among consumers (SBP 2024). Various fintechs have started providing digital finance services. Most are related to the B2B and payment categories. B2B encompasses a range of services and opportunities and, like business-to-consumer (B2C), includes both local and international service providers (Table 7.7).

- **Payment processing services.** Fintech firms such as JazzCash, easypaisa, Keenu NetConnect, Avanza Premier Payment Services, and NayaPay offer payment gateway solutions for businesses seeking to accept digital payments.
- **API integration.** Finja, Khushhali Microfinance Bank, Viftech Solutions, TPS, and Systems Limited provide APIs for businesses to integrate fintech services into their platforms.
- **Regulatory compliance solutions.** Companies such as Symmetry Group, nCino (formerly DocFox), Femisys, and Secured KYC offer AML and KYC solutions to help businesses meet regulatory requirements. Karandaaz platforms also provide AML and customer due-diligence checks.
- **Fraud prevention solutions.** SecureMetric, Cypherglass, Innov8 Limited, and Interactive Intelligence provide tools to detect and prevent fraudulent activities in transactions.
- **Digital identity verification.** Providers such as NADRA (BVS), Karandaaz, SimSim, and Mobilink Microfinance Bank offer digital identity-verification services for secure customer onboarding.
- **Lending as a Service (LaaS).** Finja, Khushhali Microfinance Bank, NayaPay, Meezan Bank, and U Microfinance Bank Ltd. offer lending platforms that enable businesses to provide financing to customers.
- **Accounting and financial management.** International firms such as Abacus Consulting, SAP Pakistan, QuickBooks Pakistan, and Oracle Pakistan offer software solutions for accounting and financial management.

Table 7.7: Business-to-Business Service Providers and Areas in Pakistan

Service Providers	Number of B2B Service Areas
E-wallet	15
Payments and billing	26
Loans	14
Insurtech[a]	4
Money transfer and remittance	2
Blockchain	5
Capital market	6
Wealth management	9
Mortgage and real estate	1
Regtech[b]	1
Banking apps	21

B2B = business-to-business, e-wallet = electronic wallet.

[a] Insurtech is insurance technology.

[b] Regtech is the application of IT to regulatory monitoring, reporting, and compliance.

Source: Author.

Collaborating Networks and Civil Service Organizations

Multiple stakeholders involved in this book highlighted the lack of platforms and relevant networks as a challenge for fintech growth and knowledge sharing. However, major fintech networks focus on supporting existing and emerging firms in Pakistan and on broadening the network of stakeholders.

The **Universal Services Fund**, a government-owned organization funded by the telecom industry, manages and implements telecom and broadband projects nationwide. Its key priorities include gender inclusion, digital literacy, and broadened access to digital services and finance through fintech. **Karandaaz Pakistan** provides credit facilities and investment linkages to SMEs, and works to improve digital financial inclusion, for instance, through data-sharing initiatives (Karandaaz Pakistan 2023 n.d.). The not-for-profit organization also supports innovative solutions for empowering women's enterprises and for raising agricultural productivity and e-commerce through digital-payment training for farmers (Karandaaz Pakistan 2022).

The **Pakistan Fintech Network (PFN)** promotes the fintech industry and works to improve service quality through collaboration among regulators, corporations, consumers, vendors, academics, and investors. The key priorities are addressing emerging issues through the engagement of its 52 members and fostering an open space for start-ups. The PFN and Karandaaz have agreed to jointly support the fintech ecosystem in Pakistan, with Karandaaz providing a grant to the PFN for developing a fintech program. The **Pakistan Microfinance Network (PMN)** represents 46 bank and nonbank microfinance institutions, with a mandate to expand inclusive financial services. In late 2020, the PMN launched Munsalik, a digital platform connecting microfinance providers, digital service providers, and customers that enables mobile wallet accounts for microfinance loans. The PMN's key functions include knowledge management, business analytics, promotion of fintech benchmarks, consultations with policymakers, the building of partnerships, and the provision of training and academic linkages.

Fintech Users

Fintech's user-centric structure often bypasses traditional barriers, focusing on user needs. Thus, understanding both current and potential users is vital for growth. With the significant and growing interest in technology-enabled financial services in Pakistan, user input is a key factor in shaping policies and ensuring the success of specific apps. Fintech is expected to catch on further, with improvements in user experience and trust, access, financial literacy, and service diversity.

The key to boosting demand is the value proposition, which emphasizes the benefits and relevance of fintech solutions. Innovation, user-friendly interfaces, and the convenience and low cost of mobile and online platforms enhance the appeal of fintech solutions, compared with that of traditional finance. Security and privacy are fundamental, as the level of trust in fintech data protection and transaction security will significantly impact demand.

Effective marketing strategies and awareness campaigns will amplify the allure of fintech by highlighting its benefits, while word-of-mouth recommendations will enhance this effect. Regulatory compliance boosts credibility and legitimacy, while partnerships with established financial entities, customizable experiences, and personalized services further attract users. In addition, fintech solutions that make a positive societal impact will reinforce the industry's appeal.

User Trends in Digital Financial Services

This section examines the growing consumer base for digital financial tools among Pakistan's population of 224.78 million people (NIPS 2022). During FY2024, the digital payment ecosystem showed strong growth, continuing a trend from previous years. The SBP's *Annual Payment Systems Review – FY24* (2024) highlighted the increases that occurred in mobile and internet banking and in online transactions. Key trends in financial services during FY2024 included the following:

E-wallets. The introduction of electronic wallets (e-wallets) issued by electronic money institutions (EMIs) is a recent development in the payment system, even though payment cards have been used for decades. By the end of the second quarter of FY2024, EMIs had successfully opened 2.7 million e-wallets, more than doubling the number in just four quarters (Figure 7.5). Use of e-wallets is growing at an average pace of 23%. During the second quarter, digital wallets offered by branchless banking service providers increased 3.9%, to 67.2 million mobile wallets.

Figure 7.5: Growth in the Number of E-Wallets, Pakistan, FY2023/24
(million)

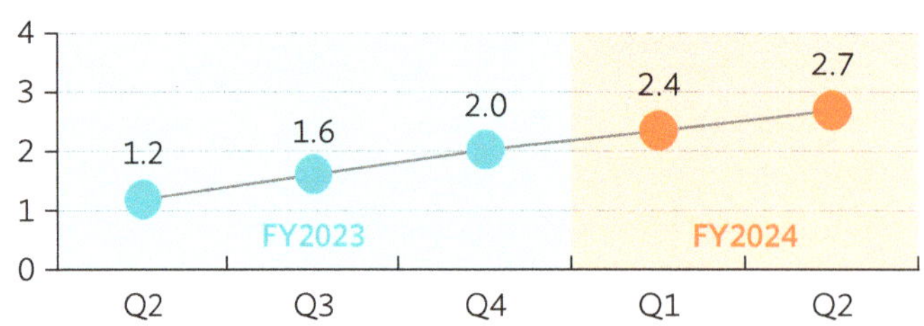

e-wallet = electronic wallet, FY = fiscal year, Q = quarter.
Note: The fiscal year ends on 30 June of the indicated year (i.e., FY2024 ended on 30 June 2024).
Source: State Bank of Pakistan. 2024. *Annual Payment Systems Review – FY24*. https://www.sbp.org.pk/PS/PDF/FiscalYear-2023-24.pdf.

Mobile and internet banking. Acceptance of mobile phone banking for e-banking transactions has grown with the increased availability of smartphones and internet access. During the second quarter of FY2024, the number of registered internet users grew 5.4%, while the number of registered mobile banking customers grew 8.0% (Figure 7.6).

Figure 7.6: Growth in Internet and Mobile Phone Banking Combined, Pakistan, FY2024

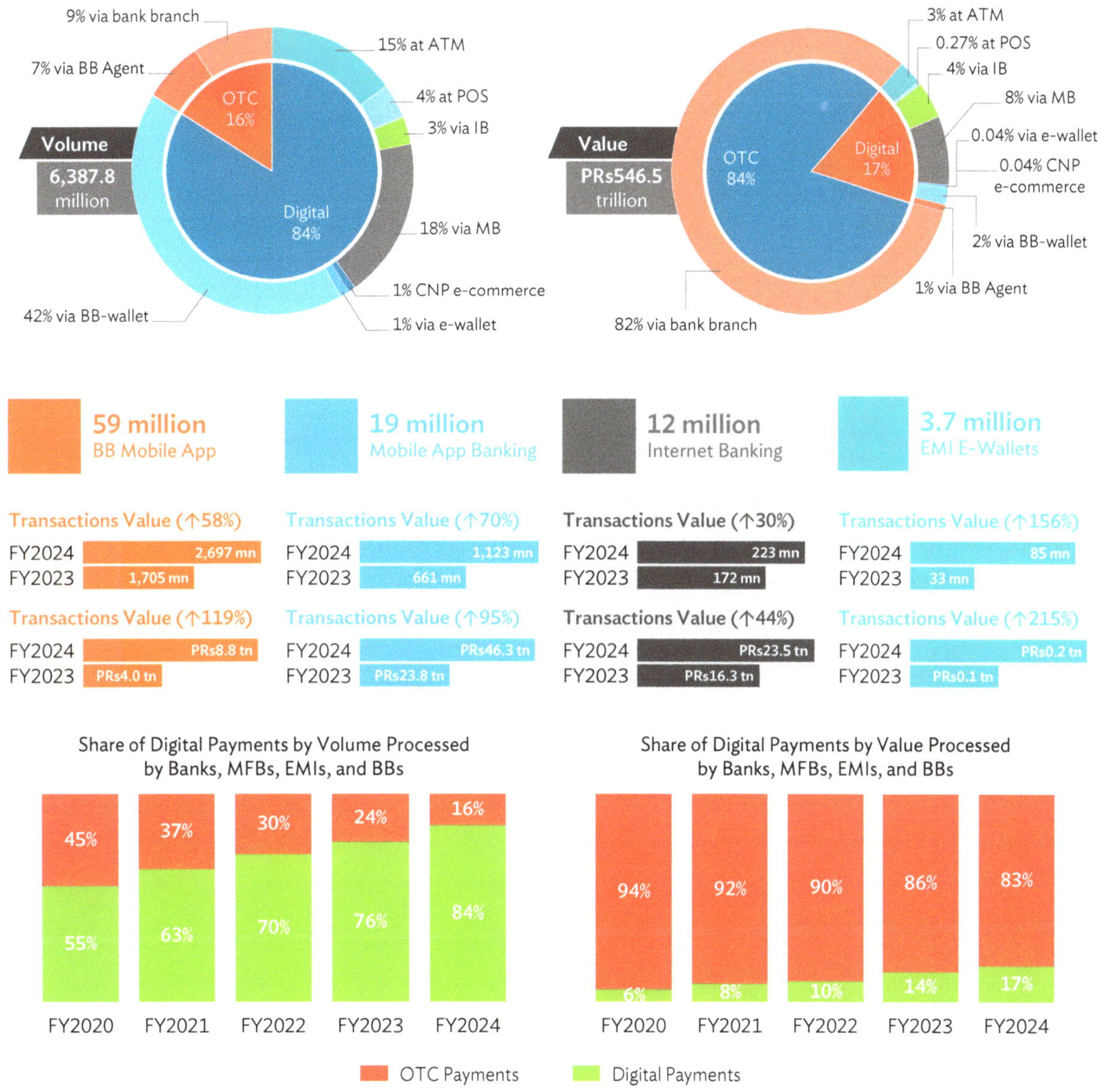

BB = branchless bank, CNP = Card-Not-Present, e-wallet = electronic wallet, EMI = electronic money institution, FY = fiscal year, IB = internet banking, MB = mobile banking, MFB = microfinance bank, mn = million, OTC = over the counter, POS = point of sale (machines), PRs = Pakistani rupees, Q = quarter, tn = trillion.

Note: The fiscal year ends on 30 June of the indicated year (i.e., FY2024 ended on 30 June 2024).

Source: State Bank of Pakistan. 2024. *Annual Payment Systems Review – FY24*. https://www.sbp.org.pk/PS/PDF/FiscalYear-2023-24.pdf.

The volume of bill payments through digital channels surpassed paper-based methods in 2024. The value of online mobile banking transactions reached PRs16.3 million that year, and internet banking reached 10.8 million users.

The SBP's Raast payment system for P2P transfers allows citizens to send payments using mobile phone numbers. By the end of June 2022, the system registered 15 million Raast users, and processed over 8 million transactions, amounting to PRs102 billion in value. Following the implementation of Raast bulk payments and P2P transactions, the SBP introduced the Raast person-to-merchant (P2M) model, enabling users to make direct payments to merchants through the Raast system.

EVOLUTION OF FINTECH GOVERNANCE IN PAKISTAN

With the rapid growth of fintech players, the regulating authorities in Pakistan have explored ways to support and regulate this emerging industry. Since 2005, lead regulators such as the SBP, Securities and Exchange Commission of Pakistan (SECP), Pakistan Telecommunication Authority (PTA), and the Ministry of Information Technology and Telecommunication (MoITT) have developed frameworks, rules, and policies that, although not specifically designed for fintech, are used to protect the interests of customers and investors, and to promote the use of new technologies for financial inclusion.

This section explains how Pakistan's fintech governance has had different phases of development, and how each phase was shaped by the evolving technological, economic, and social landscape. This phased approach highlights how regulators have responded strategically to the market's maturing, scaling digital finance to meet emerging demands. As technology advanced and financial needs shifted, priorities were adapted to these changes, fostering growth in areas such as financial inclusion, consumer protection, and innovation. This phased approach demonstrates a clear journey from building the basic infrastructure to achieving a sophisticated digital ecosystem. The progression not only underscores Pakistan's approach, but also provides an understanding of the route taken for other developing economies looking to align their fintech policies with dynamic market needs. The evolution of fintech is presented here in four distinctive phases.

Phase I: Foundation-Building Through Technology and Legal Infrastructure (2001–2007)

In the early 2000s, Pakistan began with a vision of making services delivered through digital finance accessible, secure, and relevant for its growing population. Among the key first steps was the Electronic Transactions Ordinance, 2002, which recognized digital contracts and transactions and set the stage for trust in digital financial services, thereby laying the groundwork for reliance on digital safety and secure financial transactions. Building on this, in 2003, the SBP introduced KYC guidelines to ensure that banks verified customer identities rigorously, contributing to the transparency and accountability crucial for consumer confidence. Around the same time, Pakistan's technological infrastructure set the conditions under which digital finance could be realized. Broadband and mobile networks began to bring connectivity to areas previously isolated from modern financial services through digital transactions. The Payment Systems and Electronic Funds Transfer Act, 2007 responded to this shift by providing a structured framework for digital payments. This act was instrumental in creating a secure, standardized system that allowed banks, businesses, and consumers to move money electronically with ease and trust.

Government agencies such as the SBP, PTA, and MoITT worked closely together during this phase, aligning their policies to support both technology and finance. Each agency offered its expertise to ensure that regulatory frameworks were robust enough to support digital finance, while remaining adaptable. This collaboration was essential for creating the conditions in which fintech could take root.

Phase II: Promotion of Financial Inclusion and Capacity Building (2008–2014)

In the second phase, the focus shifted to bringing financial services to rural and underserved areas to boost communities and strengthen economic resilience. In 2008, Pakistan introduced branchless banking regulations, which allowed banks to partner with networks of local agents who could provide financial services outside bank branches. These agents became the face of financial access in remote areas, helping people deposit, withdraw, and transfer money using their mobile phones. For the first time, many people in rural communities could access basic banking without traveling long distances to the nearest bank branch. The introduction of the National Financial Inclusion Strategy in 2015 underscored the importance of human capital, as local communities gained digital literacy and financial services.

Telecom firms played a critical role here. With their widespread networks, they partnered with banks to create a web of mobile banking services that could reach virtually every corner of the country. These partnerships allowed banks to tap into telecom infrastructure and mobile technology, making financial services accessible and affordable even in the most remote areas. This collaboration was key to building trust, as people were often more familiar with local telecom providers than with formal banks. To support these initiatives, the SBP and the government launched public awareness campaigns to build financial literacy. Training programs equipped agents with the skills to assist users, while outreach efforts taught communities about the benefits and safety of mobile banking. Gradually, people became more comfortable with using digital wallets and branchless banking for everyday needs.

The results were transformative. Millions of people gained access to financial services, often for the first time in their lives. But challenges remained. Some communities were hesitant to embrace digital finance and agents faced operational hurdles such managing cash flows and meeting demand. Despite these obstacles, Pakistan's push for financial inclusion laid the groundwork for future fintech innovations. The Pakistani regulatory landscape grew in sophistication as authorities shaped regulations to meet the specific needs of underserved populations, underscoring the role of policy in enhancing human capital utilization.

Phase III: Strengthened Digital Payments and Expanded Regulatory Expertise (2015–2020)

The third phase reflected an ambition to meet the rising demand for digital payments and to align Pakistan's regulatory environment with global fintech standards. One of the most significant initiatives during this phase was the National Payment Systems Strategy (NPSS), which set out to build an efficient, dependable, and user-friendly payment ecosystem capable of handling the needs of a digitally savvy public on a large scale. The strategy aimed to reduce reliance on cash transactions by encouraging electronic payments, ensuring that every transaction could be processed quickly and securely. Raast, the country's first instant-payment system, was an essential component of this strategy. Launched by the SBP, Raast introduced features such as real-time payments, bulk transfers, and advanced security measures. It represented a vision of what a national digital payment system could be.

By providing interoperability across financial institutions, Raast facilitated smoother connections within Pakistan's financial system, making digital transactions simpler and more accessible for a broader base of clients. Another key achievement during this phase was the introduction of regulations for EMIs, which were given the green light to offer cost-effective and user-friendly digital wallets, payment solutions, and electronic money (e-money) services. EMI regulations not only opened the door to new fintech players, but also set important consumer protection standards, requiring EMIs to implement secure systems, follow customer due diligence protocols, and comply with transaction limits. The regulations were crafted with consumer security and trust in mind, and aimed to ensure that new fintech solutions met high standards of transparency and reliability.

The SECP introduced the Fintech Regulatory Sandbox in 2019. This allowed start-ups to test their fintech solutions in a controlled environment, where they could experiment without immediate regulatory constraints. This initiative was a nod to international best practices, as regulatory sandboxes worldwide have been known to foster innovation by providing a safe space for trial and error. By offering this framework, the SECP empowered fintech innovators to push boundaries, knowing that if their solutions proved viable and safe, a route would be open for them to operate on a larger scale.

Throughout this period, Pakistan's regulatory bodies also focused on ensuring that these new technologies could integrate with global standards. Partnerships with international organizations helped align Pakistan's fintech policies with global practices. The Digital Pakistan Policy, 2018 further emphasized the need for a secure, efficient digital payment infrastructure, and encouraged private investment in technology-driven financial solutions. These collaborations and strategies made it possible for Pakistan to implement standards that mirrored global expectations.

Phase IV: Enhanced Consumer Experience and Protection (2021–present)

Pakistan's fourth phase of fintech evolution has been marked by a forward-looking approach under which regulators anticipate and adapt to increasingly complex needs in a rapidly digitizing world. One of the most significant initiatives has been the SBP's Digital Banking Licensing Framework. This was designed to allow fully digital banks to operate entirely online, providing financial solutions through mobile apps and websites. The introduction of this licensing regime aimed to create a more competitive, innovative banking environment with wider reach. This has created a greater need for cybersecurity and data protection, addressed by the National Cyber Security Policy, 2021 and the Cyber Security Framework. These policies aim to establish robust data-security protocols and to enforce regulatory standards for all entities handling critical financial data—standards that protect not only consumers, but also the infrastructure of the digital-finance ecosystem. Consumer protection and regulatory compliance have received substantial attention. Updated KYC requirements and stronger AML measures ensure that digital transactions are transparent and secure. These requirements force fintech firms to maintain high standards of accountability, protecting users from fraud and misuse of their financial data.

From a technological perspective, the fourth phase has seen improvements in key digital payment systems and innovations aimed at streamlining the user experience. The Raast system has been upgraded to expand its functionality, enabling features such as instant P2P transfers and alias-based payments. The platform's ease of use and speed makes digital payments accessible for everyday transactions. International collaborations have played a significant role during this phase, as Pakistan seeks to align its governance with global standards. Figure 7.7 summarizes the evolution of fintech in Pakistan, with key milestones identified.

Figure 7.7: Evolution of Fintech Regulation in Pakistan

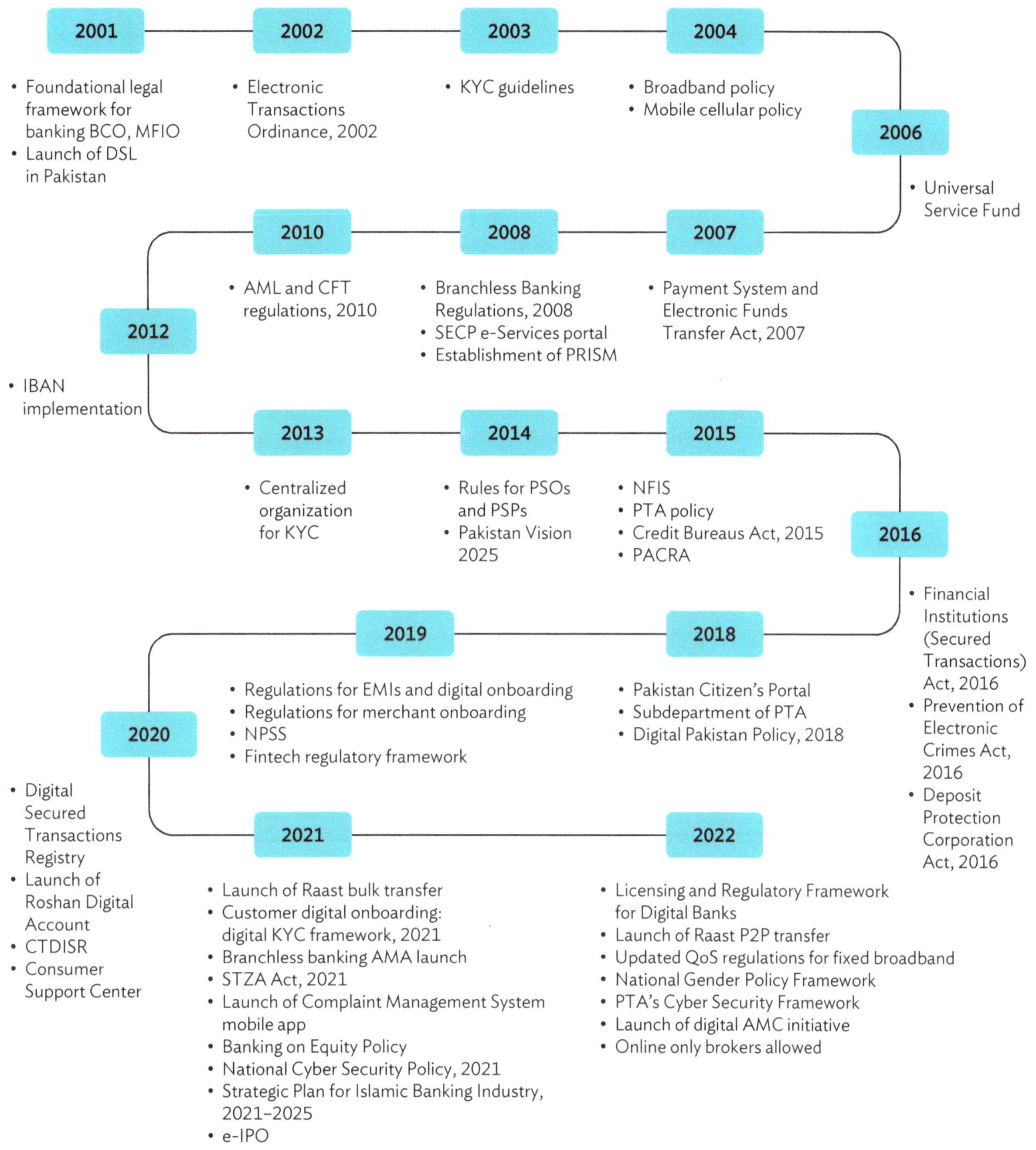

AMA = Asaan Mobile Account, AMC = asset management company, AML = anti-money laundering, BCO = Banking Companies Ordinance (1962), CFT = combating the financing of terrorism, CTDISR = Critical Telecom Data and Infrastructure Security Regulation (2020), DSL = digital subscriber line, e-IPO = electronic initial public offering, EMI = electronic money institution, fintech = financial technology, IBAN = International Bank Account Number, KYC = Know Your Customer, MFIO = Microfinance Institutions Ordinance (2001), NFIS = National Financial Inclusion Strategy (2015), NPSS = National Payment Systems Strategy (2019), P2P = peer-to-peer, PACRA = Pakistan Credit Rating Agency, PRISM = Pakistan Real-time Interbank Settlement Mechanism, PSO = payment system operator, PSP = payment service provider, PTA = Pakistan Telecommunication Authority, QoS = quality of service, SECP = Securities and Exchange Commission of Pakistan, STZA = Special Technology Zones Authority.

Source: Author.

Despite these advancements, challenges persist. Interoperability between digital payment platforms remains a work in progress, as does the task of enhancing cybersecurity against increasingly sophisticated threats. In addition, while digital banking has made strides in reaching rural populations, there is still room for improvement in financial literacy and accessibility. These challenges underscore the importance of an adaptive regulatory approach as Pakistan continues its journey toward a fully digital economy.

Influence of Economic Conditions

The nexus between economic conditions and fintech growth is complex. The most common view identifies fintech as an independent variable that propels economic growth by providing access to capital for businesses, increasing efficiency, and improving transparency. A second view holds that fintech has short-term disruptive impacts that may hurt the job market and some industries.

An alternative view depicts fintech growth as a derivative of increased economic activity. As economies grow, the availability of more money to spend and invest creates a demand for new financial products and services, such as mobile banking, P2P lending, and investment platforms. More financial transactions mean more users and higher volumes, leading to more profitability. Greater surpluses and opportunities generated by economic growth can lead to more investments in fintech. A further possibility is that increased demand will lead to a more favorable regulatory environment. While it remains important to account for prominent economic indicators, this is a topic for future exploration.

OPPORTUNITIES TO EXPAND REGIONAL COOPERATION

Pakistan has recently taken measures to support digital economic growth and the fintech industry. Even though progress has been slower than in other comparable countries, Pakistan's digital financial service market has the potential to reach $36 billion by 2025. Both national and international collaboration are required to exploit this growing opportunity. One example of regional cooperation took place in 2019, when Pakistan became a member of the Financial Stability Oversight Council and the Islamic Financial Services Board (IFSB). The IFSB is an international organization that promotes financial stability and oversight of the Islamic finance industry. Below are other examples of regional collaborations for promoting fintech in Pakistan.

Pakistan–PRC. The Shenyang Economic and Technological Development Area (SEDA) of the People's Republic of China and the Special Technology Zones Authority (STZA) of Pakistan recently signed a letter of intent to boost cooperation in the technology sector between the two organizations (*Express Tribune* 2022).

Pakistan–United Arab Emirates (UAE). Pakistan is collaborating with the UAE on several ongoing initiatives.

- Euronet Pakistan, a banking and payments technology firm, and the Dubai-based fintech company YAP have partnered together to operate as an EMI in Pakistan (ProPakistani 2022).
- The UAE has the second-largest Pakistani expatriate community in the world, and is the second-largest source of remittances to Pakistan. Bank AL Habib, in Pakistan, and the UAE's Mashreq bank have signed a strategic partnership agreement that offers free remittance transfers from the UAE to Pakistan. It will also support QuickRemit without any remittance fees (Bleach 2022).

Pakistan–Switzerland. Pakistan-based National Data Consultants and Temenos of Switzerland have signed a partnership to expand market reach in several countries, including Bahrain, Kuwait, Oman, Pakistan, Qatar, Saudi Arabia, and the UAE (*Fintech Finance News* 2022).

Pakistan–Malaysia. Telenor Microfinance Bank, in partnership with Valyou of Malaysia, has introduced a blockchain-based cross-border remittance service that focuses primarily on underbanked communities in Pakistan. The plan was unveiled in 2019 by the SBP governor as a major fintech milestone; however, the plan has not yet been implemented.

The Bali Fintech Agenda, established during the 2018 International Monetary Fund (IMF) and World Bank Group annual meetings in Bali, consists of 12 principles that guide policymakers and regulators in fostering a safe, inclusive, and innovative fintech environment. The agenda has been serving as a guiding framework that enables Pakistan to harness the benefits of fintech. Table 7.8 maps out Pakistan's progress concerning relevant Bali principles.

Table 7.8: The Bali Fintech Agenda in Pakistan's Context

Bali Fintech Agenda's 12 Policy Elements	Possible Translation into Pakistan's Context	Current Status
Embrace the promise of fintech.	Use of a regulatory sandbox, innovation hubs.	Regulatory sandbox established innovation hubs and technology parts.
Enable new technologies to enhance the provision of financial services.	Technologies to be tested in a sandbox.	The SBP has launched three cohorts under the fintech regulatory sandbox to allow the testing of new business models and financial products.
Reinforce competition and the commitment to open, free, and contestable markets.	Different pricing for different utility-type services.	Improvements are under consideration.
Foster fintech to promote financial inclusion and develop financial markets.	Relaxed capital requirements for fintech licensing.	Improvements are under consideration.
Monitor development closely to deepen understanding of evolving financial systems.	Frequent meetings, and forums with stakeholders.	So far, fintech networks are limited in Pakistan. The main networks are PFN and PMN.
Prepare the regulatory framework and supervisory practices for the orderly development and stability of the financial systems.	A fintech-supportive approach based on principles and functional regulations.	At present, there are no fintech-specific regulations. However, the SBP and SECP are developing frameworks and policies to support Pakistan's digital economy.
Safeguard the integrity of the financial system.	Use of a KYC utility.	Improvements are under consideration.
Modernize legal frameworks to provide an enabling legal landscape.	A fintech-supportive approach based on principles and functional regulations.	At present, there is no single law with regulations addressing all fintech-related areas. However, the SBP and SECP are developing frameworks and policies to support Pakistan's digital economy.

continued on next page

Table 7.8 *continued*

Bali Fintech Agenda's 12 Policy Elements	Possible Translation into Pakistan's Context	Current Status
Ensure the stability of the domestic monetary and financial systems.	Compliance with FATF and AML recommendations.	Improvements are under consideration.
Develop a robust financial and data infrastructure to sustain fintech benefits.	Cloud computing and a shift away from data restrictions.	Further efforts are required to enable fintech industry growth.
Encourage international cooperation and information sharing.	Shift away from data restrictions.	Improvements are under consideration.
Enhance collective surveillance of the international monetary and financial systems.	Compliance with FATF and AML recommendations.	Improvements are under consideration.

AML = anti-money laundering, FATF = Financial Action Task Force, fintech = financial technology, KYC = Know Your Customer, PFN = Pakistan Fintech Network, PMN = Pakistan Microfinance Network, SBP = State Bank of Pakistan, SECP = Securities and Exchange Commission of Pakistan.

Sources: Author; and International Monetary Fund (IMF) and World Bank. 2018. *The Bali Fintech Agenda: A Blueprint for Successfully Harnessing Fintech's Opportunities*. https://www.imf.org/-/media/Files/Publications/PP/2018/pp101118-bali-fintech-agenda.ashx.

RECOMMENDATIONS

Adopt Regulatory Approaches

Bespoke framework for fintech firms. A bespoke and adaptive regulatory framework will be needed to cater to the ever-evolving fintech landscape. This includes the establishment of specific licensing categories tailored to the unique requirements and risks of fintech operations, proportional licensing fees to enable the entry of smaller players, and a collaborative regulatory approach among the relevant authorities.

Fintech-specific licensing categories. Regulators must devise distinct licensing categories that cater explicitly to the diverse requirements and risks of fintech firms. With a nuanced approach, these regulations would help fintech start-ups navigate the regulatory landscape more efficiently. They would also encourage fintech innovation, competition, and growth, while ensuring consumer protection.

Proportional licensing fees. It will be essential to adopt a proportional licensing fee structure to create an inclusive environment that encourages smaller fintech firms to participate in the market. By tailoring fees based on their size and nature of operations, regulators can level the playing field, empower start-ups, and foster a dynamic fintech ecosystem that will contribute to the finance sector's growth. This would also be a key welcoming factor for regional fintech.

Collaborative efforts. Acknowledging the dynamic nature of fintech, a collaborative regulatory approach among relevant authorities will be crucial. Close coordination and information sharing will lead to a unified regulatory framework, free from gaps or duplicative measures, that will enable fintech firms to operate efficiently and encourage innovation and adaptability to emerging trends. Such a framework would also encourage and lay the groundwork for regional cooperation.

Accounting for global transaction systems. To enhance Pakistan's digital payment landscape and attract global players such as PayPal, the government should prioritize financial-inclusion initiatives, collaborate with financial institutions to increase credit card penetration, and establish a favorable regulatory framework to ensure compliance with local laws and consumer-protection objectives.

Promote Financial Inclusion Through Fintech

This recommendation highlights the importance of incentivizing fintech firms to target the unbanked and underserved segments of the population. Regulators can achieve this by offering streamlined licensing processes, targeted funding programs, and regulatory support for innovative financial products and services tailored to these segments' unique needs.

Targeting unbanked and underserved people. To foster financial inclusion and improve the economic well-being of underserved populations, regulators must incentivize fintech firms to actively address their needs. Streamlined licensing processes, targeted funding programs, and regulatory backing will motivate fintech firms to bridge the financial divide and extend vital services to historically excluded individuals.

Incentivizing products and services for the unbanked and underserved. Regulatory authorities should introduce incentives for fintech firms that prioritize inclusivity in their operations. By offering tax benefits, grants, or funding opportunities, regulators can encourage the development of innovative solutions that address the financial requirements of unbanked and underserved segments of the population. Establishing clear evaluation criteria for inclusivity will further foster a culture of innovation centered around the provision of financial services for all members of society.

Support Innovation

This recommendation emphasizes the need to provide comprehensive financial and technical support to fintech firms. Grants, funding opportunities, and capacity-building programs will accelerate the development of innovative products and services, bolstering economic growth and competitiveness in the finance sector.

Financial and technical assistance. A robust support framework comprising grants, low-interest loans, and investment funding will empower fintech start-ups to overcome financial barriers and explore groundbreaking solutions. Additionally, technical assistance, mentorship programs, and access to advanced infrastructure will stimulate innovation and enhance the implementation capabilities of fintech firms, fostering economic progress at both national and global levels.

Funding opportunities and capacity building for fintech firms. To nurture a culture of innovation and growth, regulators must establish a well-structured support system. Grants and other funding opportunities, as well as capacity-building programs, will provide vital support, enabling fintech start-ups to access resources, experiment with new ideas, and scale successful ventures. With these initiatives in place, regulators can drive the growth of the fintech ecosystem and establish Pakistan as a hub for innovative fintech developments.

Enact Tax Reforms That Will Promote Fintech

Clearer tax laws. The formulation of explicit and succinct guidelines or regulations will elucidate the tax implications for fintech firms. As a result, enterprises would gain a comprehensive understanding of their tax obligations, thus facilitating their adherence to the tax laws.

Tax reductions. Lowering the prevailing tax rates for fintech firms or introducing targeted tax breaks for specific fintech activities would render the operating environment more financially feasible for these firms, thereby stimulating innovation.

Streamlined tax procedures. The simplification of the tax-filing process or the provision of online filing options tailored to the needs of fintech firms could significantly enhance the ability of these firms to comply with tax regulations, thereby reducing the administrative burden on the government. In addition to the Federal Board of Revenue, active involvement from regulatory bodies such as the SECP and SBP would be crucial in streamlining tax procedures for fintech enterprises.

Greater tax awareness. The government could disseminate educational materials, provide resources to incubators and universities, and/or organize training sessions to raise awareness among fintech firms regarding the intricacies of tax laws. By promoting tax literacy, fintech enterprises would gain better insight into their tax responsibilities, mitigating the risk of noncompliance and promoting a culture of tax adherence in the fintech industry.

Final Word: On Technical Assistance

Despite the efforts of state institutions, investors, and local fintech networks, Pakistan significantly lags behind its regional peers in fintech development, as the discussion on indicators in Chapter 1 has shown. Stakeholder feedback indicates that, without addressing internal capacity challenges, Pakistan may continue to struggle to match regional standards and participate in broader initiatives. Key capacity-development areas identified include individual, institutional, and environmental aspects. As a fitting note on which to end this chapter, the following section outlines technical assistance areas where collaboration could be enhanced between Pakistan and other CAREC countries for fintech growth.

Individual Capacity

While there are some profoundly qualified individuals in Pakistan's fintech ecosystem, the number remains fairly limited in comparison with the skills, technology, and digital financial services that the country needs. With this in mind, several potential initiatives have been identified for increasing individual capacity.

Academic partnerships with local institutions. Offering relevant courses would help nurture local innovators.

Digital literacy. Despite 64% of Pakistan's population being young, digital literacy remains low, with significant gaps based on gender, location (rural vs. urban), and employment status, and among people with disabilities. Improving digital literacy regarding technology use (as well as service reliability, benefits, and cultural acceptance) will be essential for gaining individual support for fintech solutions.

Specialized orientations. This entails assisting legislators and policymakers in navigating the different dimensions of their respective roles. **Conferences and seminars** could serve as a gateway for knowledge transfer, enhancing individual capacities for targeted roles and areas of contribution—specifically, legislative and policy frameworks, facilitation of cross-border transactions, interpretability, data protection, and a comprehensive ecosystem. **Compliance and audit capacity** will be needed to enable fintech firms to evolve rapidly and in significantly different ways. Local industry and incubation facilities will have to provide better support to emerging start-ups. While regulators and industry leaders are supportive, a joint action plan and guidance could further assist smaller players and initiatives.

Institutional Capacity

Key institutional capacity areas for fintech development may be supported through technical assistance. Regulators and market players emphasize the need for harmonized growth, rather than isolated efforts. A structured road map with integrated objectives, landmarks, and milestones—agreed upon by all fintech stakeholders in Pakistan—is recommended. Learning from innovative emerging fintech markets in other CAREC members or similarly developed nations will be crucial, and may require further research and collaboration.

Research and development. One of the highest-priority areas for collaboration is research. It has been noted that comparative analysis between legislative and governance frameworks, followed by evidence-based advocacy, may yield significant transformative effects within the targeted institutions.

Open data governance. Effective research and evidence for fintech depend on open data governance. Pakistan, a signatory of the open government partnership since 2016, has initiated a central data portal and open government policy, among other efforts. Aligning fintech approaches with these initiatives and learning from experienced countries such as Georgia could provide valuable insights and quick wins.

Legislative frameworks. Systematic fintech growth will require specific legislation at the federal and provincial levels, along with capacity development for policymakers. The current "one-size-fits-all" approach by the SECP and SBP may not support start-ups and small and medium-sized enterprises (SMEs) effectively. There is a strong interest in adapting and learning from best practices in this evolving sector.

Institutional Strengthening

Strengthening infrastructure is crucial for fintech development in Pakistan. Many government departments use outdated technologies due to insufficient infrastructure, skills, and adaptability. The government is working to attract international investments to improve the industry's infrastructure and skills.

Integrated governance. The fintech ecosystem needs an integrated governance system with centralized facilitation. Current processes are less effective and require better coordination. A one-stop shop for compliance, registration, licensing, and operations could be established to streamline support from regulators and government departments.

Cross-border initiatives. These are considered sensitive issues, given the privacy and protection concerns involved. The policy areas may need to be more clearly developed for cross-border engagements. The Ministry of Foreign Affairs, Economic Affairs Division, and the Board of Investment may need to become more actively involved in developing the appropriate frameworks for facilitating such initiatives.

A participatory approach and inclusive platforms. These will be essential for developing new fintech strategies and reviewing existing ones, such as the government's National Financial Inclusion Strategy, 2015. Regularly bringing together stakeholders on these platforms will be crucial for effective policy adaptation and fintech growth.

Reporting and oversight. The involvement of federal and provincial institutions will be needed to ensure periodic progress sharing and an agile response mechanism.

Environmental Capacity

Investor meetings and conferences. Regional investor meetings and experience-sharing conferences will be crucial for learning about reforms, adaptations, and cross-border investment opportunities.

Regional coordination. There will be a need for regional collaboration to develop industry-specific expertise and solutions that meet international standards and commitments, especially for start-ups.

Regional conventions. Conventions that protect the interests of citizens, investors, and countries can foster shared understanding, prompt necessary adaptations, and improve debate within the country and with regional investors.

Focus on underserved areas. Most fintech services in Pakistan target developed cities, leaving remote areas underserved. Creating mechanisms and environments for digital financial services to reach these populations will be essential for financial and digital inclusion.

Cross-learning. Cross-learning among investors and fintech firms in Pakistan and throughout the region could enhance information exchange, foster partnerships, and leverage local market expertise.

REFERENCES

Asian Development Bank (ADB). 2013. *Guidance Note: Use of Political Economy Analysis for ADB Operations.* https://www.adb.org/documents/guidance-note-use-political-economy-analysis-adb-operations.

Bleach, T. 2022. Mashreq Offer Free Remittance Transfers from the UAE to Pakistan. *Fintech Times*. 25 November. https://theFinTechtimes.com/mashreq-free-remittance-transfers-uae-pakistan.

Demirgüç-Kunt, A. et al. 2018. *The Global Findex Database 2017: Measuring Financial Inclusion and the Fintech Revolution*. World Bank Group. https://documents.worldbank.org/en/publication/documents-reports/documentdetail/332881525873182837/the-global-findex-database-2017-measuring-financial-inclusion-and-the-fintech-revolution.

Express Tribune. 2022. Pakistan, China Aim to Boost Tech Cooperation. 2 August. https://tribune.com.pk/story/2369046/pakistan-china-aim-to-boost-tech-cooperation.

Fintech Finance News. 2022. Temenos and NdcTech Sign Partnership to Expand Market Reach in Bahrain, Kuwait, Oman, Pakistan, Qatar, Saudi Arabia, and UAE. 15 December. https://ffnews.com/newsarticle/FinTech/temenos-and-ndctech-sign-partnership-to-expand-market-reach-in-bahrain-kuwait-oman-pakistan-qatar-saudi-arabia-and-uae.

International Monetary Fund and World Bank. 2018. *The Bali Fintech Agenda: A Blueprint for Successfully Harnessing Fintech's Opportunities*. https://www.imf.org/-/media/Files/Publications/PP/2018/pp101118-bali-fintech-agenda.ashx.

Karandaaz Pakistan. 2021. *FinTech Ecosystem of Pakistan*. https://karandaaz.com.pk/wp-content/uploads/2021/06/FinTech-Ecosystem-of-Pakistan.pdf.

———. 2022. Karandaaz Partners with GrowTech to Digitize Agricultural Value Chain. News release. 20 December. https://karandaaz.com.pk/media-center/news-events/karandaaz-partners-growtech-digitize-agricultural-value-chain/.

———. 2023. Karandaaz Pakistan Signs Data Sharing Agreement with TASDEEQ Credit Bureau. Press release. 6 March. https://karandaaz.com.pk/media-center/news-events/karandaaz-pakistan-signs-data-sharing-agreement-tasdeeq-credit-bureau/.

———. n.d. Innovation Investments: Facilitating Transformational Change Within the Ecosystem. https://karandaaz.com.pk/our-programs/karandaaz-innovation/.

Lovelock, P. 2022. FinTech Indicators System. ADB Technical Assistance for Financial Technology for Regional Cooperation in CAREC Countries. Unpublished.

Market Development Facility. 2020. *Financial Inclusion in Pakistan: The Business Case for the Financial Inclusion of Rural Women*. https://marketdevelopmentfacility.org/wp-content/uploads/2022/02/Financial-Inclusion-in-Pakistan-FINAL-.pdf.

Ministry of Information Technology and Telecommunication (MoITT). 2022. *Pakistan National ICT Industry Development White Paper*. https://moitt.gov.pk/SiteImage/Misc/files/Pakistan%20National%20ICT%20Industry%20Whitepaper.pdf.

Moncrieffe, J. and C. Luttrell. 2005. *An Analytical Framework for Understanding the Political Economy of Sectors and Policy Arenas*. Overseas Development Institute. https://gsdrc.org/document-library/an-analytical-framework-for-understanding-the-political-economy-of-sectors-and-policy-arenas/.

National Institute of Population Studies (NIPS). 2022. Population, Labour Force and Employment. In *Pakistan Economic Survey 2021–22*. Government of Pakistan, Finance Division. pp. 225–239. https://www.finance.gov.pk/survey_2022.html.

Pakistan Microfinance Network. 2021. *Microfinance Sector: An Overview*.

Pakistan Telecommunication Authority (PTA). 2023. Strategy and Development. https://www.pta.gov.pk/en/strategy-and-development--171221.

ProPakistani. 2022. YAP Selects Euronet Pakistan as Their Technology Partner to Operate as an EMI in Pakistan. Press release. 30 May. https://propakistani.pk/2022/05/30/yap-selects-euronet-pakistan-as-their-technology-partner-to-operate-as-an-emi-in-pakistan/.

Securities and Exchange Commission of Pakistan (SECP). 2019. *The Securities and Exchange Commission of Pakistan Regulatory Sandbox Guidelines, 2019*. https://www.nccpl.com.pk/files/market_information/secp_regulatory_sandbox_guidelines/secp_regulatory_sandbox_guidelines_2019.pdf.

State Bank of Pakistan (SBP). 2020a. *Annual Performance Review 2019–20*. https://www.sbp.org.pk/reports/annual/arFY20/Vol-1/annual-index-eng.htm.

———. 2020b. *Pakistan Financial Inclusion and Infrastructure Report 2019*.

———. 2022. *Payment Systems Review for the Fiscal Year Ended June 30, 2022*. https://www.sbp.org.pk/PS/PDF/FiscalYear-2021-22.pdf.

———. 2024. *Annual Payment Systems Review – FY24*. https://www.sbp.org.pk/PS/PDF/FiscalYear-2023-24.pdf.

Vaghjiani, K. 2022. Global FinTech Landscape. ADB Technical Assistance for Financial Technology for Regional Cooperation in CAREC Countries. Unpublished.

8

Driving Fintech Innovation: A Regional Stocktake

Khimji Vaghjiani, Yerlan Khassenbekov, Etibar Shirinov, Enkhbayar Batmunkh, and Aibek Kadyraliev

INTRODUCTION

Any exploration of the possibilities for cooperation on transforming the delivery of financial services throughout the nations of Central Asia can best start by establishing a clear understanding of the current state of fintech development across the region and how it began to take root—enabling firms such as GoldenPay in Azerbaijan, Kaspi Bank in Kazakhstan, and Click in Uzbekistan to provide new types of customer service and experience and to optimize efficiency when delivering financial products to ordinary citizens across a range of incomes.

The history of financial technology (fintech) innovation in the Central Asia Regional Economic Cooperation (CAREC) countries is a short one. A range of fintech firms now aim to apply fintech to deliver value—both to stakeholders and customers—and to gain a competitive edge in a growing market. In many cases, organizations have leveraged fintech to access new market segments and geographic regions that would have otherwise been inaccessible. Ensuring that fintech is integrated and developed on par with global standards is crucial for connecting the region's economies to the global financial ecosystem and wealth.

Figure 8.1: Key Fintech Drivers in Selected CAREC Countries

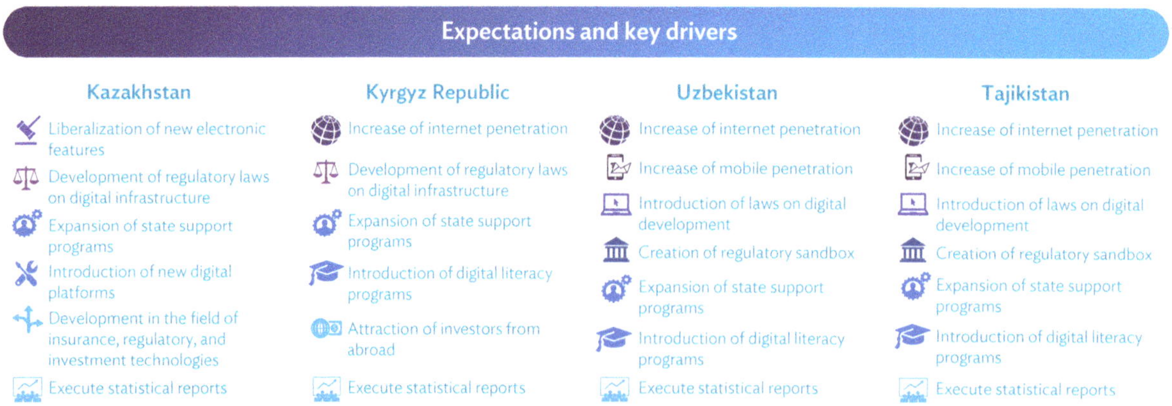

CAREC = Central Asia Regional Economic Cooperation, fintech = financial technology.

Source: KPMG. 2020. Overview of Fintech Development in Central Asia. https://assets.kpmg/content/dam/kpmg/kz/pdf/2020/12/Overview-of-Fintech-Development-in-Central-Asia.pdf.

Adoption is happening so fast that a description of conditions in any one of CAREC's nine emerging fintech markets will be outdated almost as soon as it is compiled. However, as Figure 8.1 highlights—using Kazakhstan, the Kyrgyz Republic, Tajikistan, and Uzbekistan as examples—governments in those CAREC countries have the potential for fintech growth and financial inclusion, if they take a giant leap forward by identifying and supporting common market drivers to achieve fintech goals. These drivers apply equally to other countries that make up the CAREC fintech road map countries: Azerbaijan, Georgia, Mongolia, Pakistan, and Turkmenistan. It is important that national policymakers create an enabling environment for investment in fintech innovations and for conditions that support creative solutions to real-world problems, whether delivered through public or private sector agents of change.

Given the dynamic evolution of fintech and the road map's aim to foster regional collaboration, this chapter presents a snapshot as of 2024, and concentrates on use cases and innovation successes generated by private sector providers, government authorities, and regulatory environments that have encouraged or directly supported these innovations.

Fintech markets are growing at different rates across the emerging fintech markets in CAREC, amid an increasing embrace of technological advances (including high subscription rates for mobile phones) and a realization of the challenges (such as whether regulatory environments foster or block innovation) that together shape the capacity for market growth. Figure 8.2 serves as a reminder to all stakeholders of the challenges and risks among which opportunities for rapid growth are set—again with conditions in Kazakhstan, the Kyrgyz Republic, Tajikistan, and Uzbekistan as typical examples of the impediments to the expansion of fintech markets and products.

Figure 8.2: Common Challenges and Major Risks in Fintech Development in CAREC

Each country lacks accurate statistics on digitalization and online transactions

Challenges for fintech development
- Unfavorable government policy
- Lack of foreign investments

Major risks arising from fintech
- Financial consumer protection risks arising from new products and business models
- Cybersecurity risks
- Currency risks
- Data protection risks

Challenges for fintech development
- Low internet penetration
- Small market with low maturity and low competition
- Unstructured government and regulatory strategy on digital financial services
- Lack of targeted and effective promotion of digital channels by financial institutions

Major risks arising from fintech
- Same as in Kazakhstan

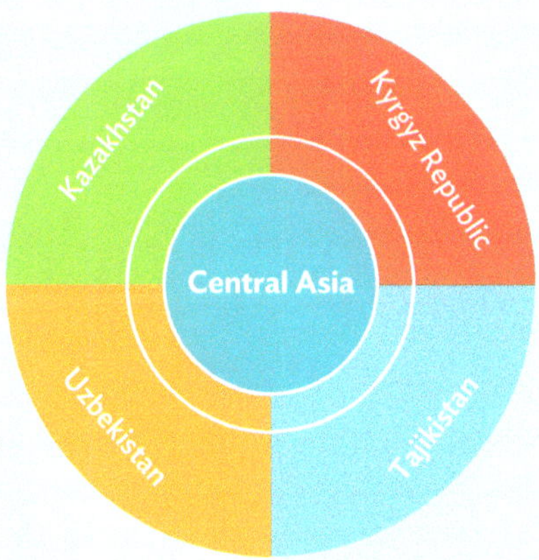

Challenges for fintech development
- Low mobile phone and internet penetration
- Lack of a clear fintech development strategy and broader institutional support for fintech
- Limited access to finance and investments

Major risks arising from fintech
- Cybersecurity risks
- Currency risks

Challenges for fintech development
- Poor infrastructure, monopoly of state-owned telecom providers
- Uncertain business environment for new players in the fintech space
- Small market with low maturity
- Limited access to finance and investments

Major risks arising from fintech
- Cybersecurity risks
- Currency risks

CAREC = Central Asia Regional Economic Cooperation, fintech = financial technology.

Note: All four countries lack complete and accurate statistics on digitalization and online transactions.

Source: KPMG. 2020. Overview of Fintech Development in Central Asia. https://assets.kpmg/content/dam/kpmg/kz/pdf/2020/12/Overview-of-Fintech-Development-in-Central-Asia.pdf.

With these opportunities and obstacles in mind, governments need to pursue integrated, liberal, and, at times, difficult policies to catalyze progress across the whole fintech ecosystem and align them with real consumer needs. That means working in tandem with private firms to develop fintech products, and with development partners who can provide technical assistance and funding. The desire to democratize financial inclusion through transformative technologies is among the reasons why the fintech road map advocates for a regional forum for sharing knowledge and innovation (Chapter 9).

PRIVATE SECTOR FINTECH ROLES

Emerging fintech markets in CAREC need to engage with the private sector right from the beginning—from the conceptualization of a financial-inclusion strategy to the development of a legal and regulatory framework, to the implementation of digital-adoption policies. In addition to the development partners' technical support, their financial assistance will be critical for embedding financial and technological infrastructure vital for improving financial inclusion. They need to extend generous financing in the form of loans, technical assistance, equity investment, and grants to the governments and private sector. Some national regulators have opted, not only to work with in-country private sector representatives, but also with global private firms, to draw from the broadest range of global ecosystem experiences. An example is the National Bank of Georgia's invitation to the software company Ripple to help create the ecosystem for its central bank digital currency (CBDC) and to pilot several use cases.

Investments in Supporting Successful Innovation

During 2001–2023, $51 billion worth of investments were made in the CAREC region by the Asian Development Bank (ADB), development partners, and CAREC governments (CAREC n.d.). While these figures do not represent direct investments specifically in innovation ecosystems, they have contributed to the region's overall economic stability and infrastructure development. Investment—alongside digital literacy, access to talent, and accelerators—is a key element for developing solid fintech firms that offer innovative solutions to customers.

Among the notable initiatives in the CAREC innovation ecosystem are successful brownfield ventures, in which established institutions partner with fintech firms or come up with new gadget-based platforms to reach a wide customer base or improve the experiences of existing customers.

The establishment of tech parks has boosted competitiveness, stimulated the private sector, and increased the number of high-tech firms doing business. Notable ones are Astana Hub in Kazakhstan, High-Tech Park in Azerbaijan, and the National Information Technology Park in Mongolia.

There has been a revival of activities focused on encouraging innovation, with many countries hosting start-up weekends (e.g., Georgia, Mongolia, Tajikistan, Turkmenistan, and Uzbekistan). A special focus has been placed on tech events and digital development in the region. The main players in organizing events in the CAREC region are the Founder Institute, 500 Global, and Startup Grind.

Considering that a cooperative fintech community can help make markets more efficient and spur financial inclusion, this chapter's stocktake shares innovative use cases from emerging fintech markets in CAREC to highlight developments that—given continued support—could be transferable; they are certainly ripe for scaling up through collaboration among countries across the region. For this reason, this stocktake extends the descriptions of successful innovations in Georgia (Chapter 3) and Pakistan (Chapter 7) to seven other countries.

CASE STUDIES OF INNOVATION IN CAREC FINTECH MARKETS

The seven emerging fintech markets in this chapter's survey of successful support for innovation present a diverse landscape. Geography and demographics (population size and age) drive many of the differences (including those regarding market potential), while government policies and attitudes toward the fintech industry in general, and toward innovation in particular, are also significant. Mongolia, with a relatively small population, and half its people concentrated in the capital city, stands out as a fintech-aware society strongly influenced by the booming digital finance market of the People's Republic of China (PRC), while Kazakhstan is notable for rapid fintech growth that has been spurred by substantial investments in digital infrastructure and innovation and by a proactive regulatory approach to areas such as digital banking, online lending, and blockchain.

Azerbaijan

New entrants into the financial services market in Azerbaijan are introducing disruptive technologies to transform traditional business models, giving them a tech-based edge with the potential to reach most of the country's 10.5 million people. Projects in the innovation ecosystem are on the verge of finding momentum with the help of financial and technical support from the state, given that local investors are rare and the venture capital market is not developed enough to back financial technologies.

For a long time, innovative fintech was not perceived as a serious business in Azerbaijan, despite supportive government interventions. Only a few start-ups gained enough momentum to become sustainable businesses. GoldenPay, one of the country's first fintech firms, is an example of a well-established business. Its Hesab.az portal has expanded the firm's online consumer services to include utility, internet, bank-loan, and other type of payments. In addition, Hesab.az offers cinema tickets, insurance sales, and airline ticket sales.

New players are gaining ground in the payments market (Table 8.1). Payonix, for example, allows QR-code-enabled online payment of utility and mobile-phone bills, insurance premiums, and loan repayments, using cashback earned via contactless-card spending on everyday items such as groceries.

Since few routes are available to those seeking funding for innovations, state incentives are an important for taking innovation from the development stage to the point where it meets the real needs of consumers.

The central bank established a regulatory sandbox to accelerate market adoption, enhance competitiveness, and address the challenges involved in supporting sustainable financial innovation. The adoption of this mechanism for testing innovative services could increase the number of payment services, including those issuing payment cards and electronic money (e-money), and facilitate the formation of an agent network to expand financial inclusion. Providing new payment services (e.g., remittances, e-money, and payment cards) and expanding open application programming interface (API) technology would create new spheres for competition.

Table 8.1: Fintech Innovators in Azerbaijan

Payriff A payment gateway for online stores. Founded in 2021.	**Payonix** Neobanking through the "Payonix" application, downloaded to a smartphone, allows secure and contactless payments using Quick Response codes, P2P transfers, and coupons. Founded in 2018.	**Perkskit** Perkskit is an employee-benefit-management platform based on Sales as a Service. Founded in 2022.
$90,000 raised from the Startup Wise Guys accelerator		
Epoint.az Epoint.az makes online payments and e-commerce accessible to small businesses. Founded in 2021.	KidFi KidFi is a gamified financial-literacy app that teaches children about earning money. Founded in 2022.	**Clopos** Clopos is a next-generation cloud-based point-of-sale solution for restaurant businesses. Founded in 2018.

e-commerce = electronic commerce, fintech = financial technology, P2P = peer-to-peer.

Source: F6S. 2025. 5 Top FinTech Companies and Startups in Baku in June 2025. https://www.f6s.com/companies/fintech/azerbaijan/baku/co.

Incentives for Fintech

▶ Government Assistance

The main funding sources for fintech innovation in Azerbaijan are the Innovation Agency and the Azerbaijan National Academy of Sciences. The Innovation Agency was established to support the development of the IT sector's infrastructure, which led it to support fintech firms directly, alongside the Small and Medium Enterprises Development Agency (SMEDA).

The Innovation Agency, formed in 2018, helps local businesses access modern technologies; supports scientific research; and encourages innovative projects through venture capital, concessional loans, and grants. It has built an incubation and acceleration center to support ideas from the younger generation and bring high-quality intellectual products into the economy. The agency and the National Academy of Sciences each allocates about $70 million–$80 million per year to acceleration program grants.

In addition, the Innovation Agency is involved in a joint consortium with AzIn Telecom LLC and with firms such as Lenovo, Nutanix, and iQRex to provide a platform for fintech firms to access finance for innovation. Baku, Azerbaijan's capital, has hosted international investment and business forums to inform foreign investors about successful innovations. Many measures through presidential decrees offer incentives to entrepreneurs for the development of fintech. The establishment of the Credit Guarantee Fund of Azerbaijan (OJSC), which provides guarantees and interest rate subsidies for entrepreneurs, is one such measure.

▶ Private Funding

Large private corporations have recently started funding innovative ideas, often through incubator competitions offering \$1,000–\$2,000 for development costs. However, gaps in the legislation on venture capital in Azerbaijan push local fintech firms to register abroad. The Turkish venture capital firm Boğaziçi Ventures has opened a branch office in Azerbaijan, planning to invest \$5 million in local fintech innovators, and this move is attracting other foreign venture capital firms to the market.

As mentioned above, venture funding is scarce. Only about 10–15 private individuals in Azerbaijan can be identified as investors in various local and international innovators, and few have their own investment strategies or long-term objectives. Regulations and other legal impediments make it impossible to build venture capital funds. However, three government-led initiatives are being discussed to match private sector funding with state funding.

Peer-to-peer (P2P) lending, an increasingly popular form of funding among small and medium-sized enterprises (SMEs) worldwide, is not yet widely available, although the business-oriented platform EnterpriseAzerbaijan.com, launched by the Center for Analysis of Economic Reforms and Communication, enables local SMEs to fund business ideas through bankable investment projects with the help of crowdfunding.

Besides these sources, other fintech incubations and acceleration programs provide financial support, assistance, training, and other services to those with innovative ideas, nurturing them and helping to bring their products or services to market.

▶ Bank Partnerships and Competition

The intersection of the banking and fintech sectors provides another area of support for innovation. Some financial institutions have initiated partnerships with fintech firms to head off competition and stay relevant.

Activity is mainly focused on the formulation of payment gateways, the issuing of e-money, QR-code payments, Masterpass technology, the issuing of virtual payment cards, and so on. In many cases, Azeri banks and fintech firms are increasingly becoming interdependent. Some fintech firms function as payment aggregators and provide the necessary gateways to commercial banks, enabling them to accept digital payments for mass services. They provide a wide network of payment terminals that collect cash payments on behalf of the commercial banks. By contrast, commercial banks serve fintech firms by providing them with the necessary platforms for executing digital payments.

Collaboration supports progress in the market for digital financial services. One example is Bank Respublika's teaming up with GoldenPay to offer open banking services for customers, which allow them to track their personal accounts and transaction history. Other participants in the digital payment ecosystem are included in Table 8.2.

Table 8.2: Biggest Fintech Firms in Azerbaijan

GoldenPay • Largest online payment company in Azerbaijan (700,000 users in 2022) • Net profit in 2023: AZN2.1 million ($1.2 million) • Founded in 2007	**eManat** • Nearly 5 million users across Azerbaijan • Over 3,000 payment terminals nationwide • Offers 1,000+ payment-related services • Founded in 2022
PashaPay • Operates "m10 e-wallet" and "Milliön" terminals • Over 5 million users • 55 million annual transactions via m10 e-wallet terminals • Founded in 2022	**Portmanat** • Electronic wallet for daily payments • Mobile number that serves as a wallet account number • Founded in 2010
Expresspay • Nearly 2 million users across Azerbaijan • Over 600 payment terminals nationwide • Offers 1,000+ services for payments • Founded in 2013	

AZN = Azerbaijan manat, e-wallet = electronic wallet, fintech = financial technology.

Note: According to the Azerbaijan Fintech Association (Azfina), as of 2023, there were 25 fintech companies operating in Azerbaijan's financial market.

Source: Azfina.

Fintech for Financial Inclusion

Azerbaijan has set the goal of creating an affordable payment ecosystem that, at the same time, is innovative and competitive. Digital financial services are expanding financial inclusion by providing access to underserved populations. The coronavirus disease (COVID-19) pandemic accelerated the adoption of contactless payments, emphasizing the importance of technology in the financial ecosystem. Moreover, the Government of Azerbaijan has introduced programs for financial education that make use of the advantages of digital payment ecosystems for financial inclusion, and will ultimately help grow the fintech ecosystem. Financial literacy is an essential element, and is supported by the Financial Literacy Council, established by the Azerbaijan Banks Association in 2017.

Financial inclusion has become a prominent aspect of economic growth in Azerbaijan, and it has been accompanied by a boom in the development of financial technology, with services that expand financial inclusion primarily provided by banks, nonbank credit organizations, and insurance firms. It is estimated that by 2025, 3.85 million people, about one-third of the population, will be using digital payments.

Access to bank accounts—a fundamental factor in financial inclusion—has been addressed through a "basic banking services" project, implemented in 2021. The package offered bank services free of charge, including opening a current account, issuing a payment card, giving access to electronic banking services, withdrawing cash, and making cashless payments. The package has brought roughly 1.5 million people into the financial system who had previously been excluded. Bank reforms to develop electronic banking services, including mobile and internet banking, and the introduction of innovative payment solutions, have directly expanded financial inclusion.

The Instant Payment System (IPS) developed under the central bank's digital payment strategy, makes it possible to register customers and their bank accounts remotely, to retrieve balance information, maintain accounts, and close them. These operations are based on open banking principles, to ensure a secure system in which vendors and banks can share account details to facilitate payments. Besides 19 banks, the IPS platform connects to the finance ministry's State Treasury Agency and the national postal service, Azerpost. Continued efforts are extending IPS coverage and expanding the range of digital solutions available to users. Further innovations include the introduction of tap to/on phone technology, and an electronic knowledge management system that improves access to information and ensures remote identification. These are backed by efforts to develop the legal basis and unit standards for open finance.

As of 2021, the value of mobile banking had increased by 14.1 times and the volume by 7.4 times from where they were in 2017. For internet banking, the value had increased by 5.1 times and the volume by 2.1 times. In addition, regarding innovative payment solutions, banks had expanded the application of tokenization technology and the issuance of virtual payment cards, while four banks launched an Apple Pay project in 2021.

In parallel, to increase financial literacy, the central bank and Azerbaijan Banks Association, together with international financial institutions, produced several videos during the COVID-19 pandemic. These were broadcast on local television, websites, and social media, and included instructions on protection against coronavirus infection when shopping and on the efficient use of bank payment cards while in a quarantine mode. During the pandemic, all banks in the country transmitted lump sum payments to 600,000 people, part of an Azerbaijan manat (AZN)3.5 billion (about $2 billion) government countercyclical pandemic response package that helped to maintain economic activity and improve the living standards of the poorest citizens.

Various existing financial-education programs can ultimately help grow the fintech ecosystem. One such program is technical and vocational education and training, although it has historically been underfunded, with the skills mismatch revealing outdated training that cannot meet the needs of business. As such, the implementation of financial-literacy measures will be an ongoing process, as Azerbaijan continues to develop more tools for expanding financial inclusion.

▶ Recommendations

The formation of the fintech ecosystem in Azerbaijan is at an early stage. Fintech firms are beginning to gather under a single umbrella, deepen relations with international financial institutions, and identify areas of cooperation with banks and new fields for marketing services.

The adoption of a law on payment services and systems would open up the sandbox regime for fintech start-ups, enabling them to test products and services on more favorable terms. The application of open API technology should be among the priority projects. With its "Open Banking Roadmap" already in place, the government can ensure that fintechs will be able to participate, directly or indirectly, in digital payment systems. This would reduce transaction costs and increase the efficiency of payment operations. Simultaneously, the Azerbaijan Fintech Association's platform for cooperation and experience sharing between its members and international financial institutions should be expanded to apply best international practices and accelerate the use of innovative solutions.

With regard to infrastructure, the government could think about privatizing state-owned enterprises in the telecommunications sector, which would increase transparency and likely lead to more investment and innovation.

In sum, improving the legal framework, creating a more favorable environment for implementing innovative solutions, and expanding collaboration with local and international financial institutions—as well as attracting commercial banks to the fintech field—could all play critical roles in propelling the fintech ecosystem in Azerbaijan to the next stage of development.

Kazakhstan

Kazakhstan stands out among the emerging fintech markets in CAREC when it comes to innovation and the development of real-world services, with the growth of finance and electronic commerce (e-commerce) firms a natural outgrowth of the focus on digitalization by the Government of Kazakhstan and major financial groups. Some interdependence of e-commerce, financial service technologies, infrastructure, and an increasingly digital-savvy population is evident. During 2019–2023, the number of active online banking users in Kazakhstan increased 4.6 times, driven by technological improvements, regulatory support, and greater cashless payment adoption. Significant support for innovation has helped the country approach the point where fintech can grow more organically.

Besides traditional financing services through fintech, activities such as cloud accounting, collective financing (crowdfunding and investing), and promotion of financial literacy have become widespread. Less regulated than their counterparts in mature financial markets, innovators in Kazakhstan have created disruptions in their respective fields. The integration of digital government services, such as the eGov and Smart Bridge platforms, into fintech apps is a defining characteristic of Kazakhstan's ecosystem; and it has made government services widely accessible and improved citizens' experiences. While no statistics are available covering the whole fintech innovation ecosystem, some information on popular firms is available (Box 8.1).

Kazakhstan's fintech sector is a fast-growing and attractive market, with a clear trend toward creating neobanks and super apps driven by the introduction of new financial instruments by both traditional banks and nonbank firms, such as telecommunications companies. The Open Banking initiative, launched by the government in 2023, further strengthens the ecosystem by enabling financial institutions to share anonymized customer data, thereby fostering innovation and competition.

The following characteristics of the fintech market in Kazakhstan are conducive to the creation of promising innovations that could find financial backers and meet the needs of customers.

- There is a well-developed and digitized infrastructure for banking, payment processing, and electronic public services.
- As of 2024, 86% of the population were using mobile banking services, thus stimulating the growth of ecosystems, super apps, and neobanks.[79]
- An undoubted plus is the ability to pay through built-in contactless payment applications (e.g., Samsung Pay, Apple Pay) in retail outlets.
- The adoption by Digital Tenge of OpenAPI standards has enabled financial institutions and start-ups to create competitive solutions while expanding access to services related to a central bank digital currency (CBDC).

The adoption of "buy now, pay later" services is rapidly rising, accounting for over 50% of consumer lending volume in some sectors, with major players such as Kaspi.kz leading the market.

[79] The total number of active mobile banking users in 2024 (23.1 million) exceeded the country's population (20 million) due to two factors: (i) many users maintain multiple accounts across different banks, and (ii) the system is also accessed by nonresidents who utilize Kazakhstan's digital banking infrastructure for financial transactions and services.

The introduction of open banking will accelerate this trend toward greater fintech innovations by expanding the capability of financial institutions to increase their user base among the country's 19 million people, complemented by national biometric identification systems.

Kaspi.kz

The rise of Kazakhstan's first fintech unicorn, Kaspi.kz, instilled confidence in the country's innovation ecosystem. Kaspi.kz evolved from the traditional Bank Kaspiskiy, rebranding itself in 2009 as a platform offering interconnected financial products and banking services. It aims to help Kazakhstani citizens manage their finances, make payments, and access credit lines. The success of Kaspi.kz has set a benchmark for fintech firms, catalyzing partnerships between banks and start-ups (Box 8.1). The number of fintech start-ups increased from over 50 in 2018 to more than 200 in 2024.

Box 8.1

Fintech Firms Transforming Kazakhstan's Financial Landscape

Prominent examples of financial technology (fintech) firms successfully providing innovative services in Kazakhstan include the following:

GoCrowd. An equity crowdfunding platform that connects investors with innovative entrepreneurs, allowing individuals to invest in start-ups and become shareholders. It fosters a community of investors helping to shape the future of emerging firms.

Lending Star. A financial platform designed for small and medium-sized enterprises (SMEs), to sell their accounts receivable and access microfinancing. With about 300 firms selling receivables to about 1 million investors, Lending Star has established itself as a significant player. The firm was founded by former banking experts in 2019 and has won multiple awards, including the Central Asian Visa Everywhere Initiative and Startupbootcamp Dubai.

Monetika. A user-friendly app for recording income and expenses that helps manage personal finances. The app assists users in budgeting, saving, and planning for financial goals by tracking their spending habits.

Paloma 365. A specialist in software for automating sales and warehouse accounting. After several pivots since its establishment in 2013, the platform provides business owners with remote access to analytics and reports, facilitating comprehensive business management from anywhere.

Re:Kassa. A mobile application that serves as an alternative to traditional cash registers. It focuses on supporting SMEs, particularly individual entrepreneurs, by providing a free service for managing cash transactions. The use case of the application, which has more than 350,000 customers, is that it simplifies tax reporting and transaction documentation.

S1lkPay. A new solution for sharing money without transferring funds. The platform, founded by a former financial executive in 2019, allows commercial bank clients to share their credit card limits or balances with trusted individuals, enhancing card utilization and expanding the bank's client base with minimal marketing costs. The major target segment is immigrants working on a temporary basis outside their home countries.

Tayyab. A digital Islamic bank designed to meet the financing needs of Muslims. Users can obtain a digital bank card compliant with shari'a law, allowing them to engage in interest-free financial transactions. The app includes features for payments, money transfers, and personal finance management, as well as tools for tracking prayer times.

Source: K. Vaghjiani. 2023. Global Fintech Landscape. Unpublished draft report.

Kaspi.kz has transformed how financial transactions in Kazakhstan are conducted. A key innovation was the introduction of a P2P system in 2015, which did away with bank fees for users. By revolutionizing cash payments and online transfers, Kaspi.kz has achieved a 70% share of the digital banking market.

The firm has raised funds to solidify its position, with initial public offerings on the London Stock Exchange (October 2020) and Nasdaq (January 2024). The firm's shares continue to be traded on multiple exchanges, including the Kazakhstan Stock Exchange (KASE).

Freedom Holding Corp. is another example of a financial service firm with a well-developed fintech component. The Freedom SuperApp (on Google Play) provides digital banking services in Kazakhstan and in Uzbekistan, as well as traditional brokerage services through branches in Azerbaijan, the Kyrgyz Republic, and Tajikistan. Services offered online in Kazakhstan include mortgages and loans, insurance products, and tickets for flights and events. The Freedom SuperApp exemplifies the trend toward business super apps, which integrate multiple financial services into a single platform.

iKapitalist, S1lkPay, and other innovative firms have already opened operations outside of Kazakhstan and Central Asia. The same goes for venture capital (access to finance) and broader investment activities (angel investments, corporate investments, syndicates, or mezzanine financing). There have been certain developments in crypto. Not much is known so far, but amendments to laws, based on the experience of the Fintech Hub of the Astana International Financial Centre (AIFC) and market activities, are in place to expedite the introduction of crypto into the economy.

iKapitalist

iKapitalist is Kazakhstan's first licensed investment and loan crowdfunding platform. It allows individuals to invest as little as $750 in promising innovators. The platform connects investors with businesses in need of direct loans, providing an opportunity for both parties to benefit. As a resident of the Fintech Hub, iKapitalist enjoys preferential terms that facilitate its operations. By 2024, the platform had facilitated $40 million in more than 19,000 investments and loans.

The leaders in the following fintech subsectors are already quite visible in the market, and are developing fast:

- **Payments:** 15 entities (*Onay, Innopay, Yurta Pay, Smart Gas, EasyPay, TypiPay, PayBox, ioka, Tayyab, FeebMe, Pyypl, Wooppay, OneClick, SmartPay, WalletOne*)
- **Mobile payments:** 13 entities (*Rahmet, Typi, TUVIS, Sagi, Senim, AituPay, Tolem, Partners Pay, OxyPay, OneVision, Collect&Pay, S1lkPay, CardB*)
- **Insurance technology:** 2 entities (*BoolloSafe, ODEN*)
- **Financial markets:** 4 entities (*1Banker, E-Squad, MoiBankir, Finance.kz*)
- **Earned wage access:** 3 entities (Prosper Pay, Alga Pay, Buhta)
- **Financial literacy:** 9 entities (*Finmentor.kz, EZ Finance, CORNER, Cashflow Islamic, Monetika, Aksham, Finpark, Antidolg, SmartGrades*)
- **Point-of-sale (POS) terminal:** 10 entities (*Webkassa, Paloma 365, re:KASSA, To'le KKM, Payda, LightKassa, WiponKassa, NurKassa, PartnersPay, Asistent*)
- **Digital identification (ID):** 4 entities (*Biometric, Digital ID, Verigram, Alaqan*)
- **Investments:** 8 entities (*iKapitalist, Tabys, QuantDART, Cake, GoCrowd, Nurzher, Baysai, Cooper.man*)
- **Online loans:** 11 entities (*AYA Credit, Otbasy 365, Lending Star, ne.BANK, Kredit24, Proportunity, Dossym, OGO Bank, Mycar Finance, Klaram, Solva*)

- **Cloud accounting:** 8 entities (*Maxinum, iFirm, Asistent, Salyq, Moy uchet.kz, Aspex, Buhta, Quarta*)
- **Licensed crypto exchanges:** 7 entities (*ATAIX Eurasia, Intebix, Swiftex, CaspianEx, BigONE, Bybit, Upbit*)
- **Artificial intelligence (AI) in fintech:** 1 entity (*NeuronStore*).[80]

The Innovation Ecosystem and Infrastructure

Kazakhstan's innovation ecosystem began its development in the private sector, while the main state drivers of the development of a fintech industry are the Astana Hub and the Astana International Financial Centre (AIFC), described in Box 8.2. Financial services delivered through fintech are still at the nascent stage, with most players being micro or small businesses.

The landscape for bringing innovation to market revolves around the country's largest urban areas, Astana and Almaty, while other regions are creating enabling environments in which innovation could develop. Almaty is represented by several private incubators, accelerators, coworking places, and private venture investors (not all of whom can be considered business angels) that individually and through syndicates or venture clubs are investing in fintechs (Figure 8.3).

Figure 8.3: Private Entities in Kazakhstan Venture Financing

Places for growth

Incubators, Accelerators

1. MOST (Almaty)
2. SmArt.Point (Almaty)
3. Alatau Creative hub
4. EBRD Star Venture
5. nFactorial (Almaty)
6. Almaty Management University
7. KBTU Startup incubator (Almaty)
8. Technology park Kazakh State University (Almaty)
9. De Montfort University
10. Turan University
11. Google for startups
12. Startup Academy
13. Visa Everywhere Initiative
14. Spark Lab
15. KASE incubator
16. TechGarden accelerator (SKA)

Technoparks

1. Altay (Ust-Kamenogorsk)
2. Algoritm (Uralsk)
3. Technopark KazNTU named after Satpayev (Almaty)

Validation

Coworking Spaces

1. MOST (Almaty)
2. SmArt.Point (Almaty)
3. Level 8 (Almaty)
4. The Hub Co-working (Shymkent)
5. IQ
6. Pixel Co-working (Almaty)
7. Sail (Almaty)
8. D&C Lab (Almaty)
9. Fifty Four (Almaty)
10. Multispace (Astana)
11. IHub

Laboratories

1. UNICEF Innovations Lab (Almaty)
2. International University of Information Technologies Lab (Almaty)
3. Beeline Startup Lab (Almaty)
4. Centras Alpha Lab (Almaty)
5. IntelSense.io (Almaty)
6. BIM+ Lab
7. Smart Data Ukimet
8. Blockchain & Big Data
9. UNDP accelerator labs
10. Zemte Studio

Association and Events

Key Tech and Innovation Communities

1. TechnoWomen
2. Almaty IT community Lab (Almaty)
3. Creative Kazakhstan
4. Central Eurasian Forum (Almaty)
5. Digital Almaty Forum (Almaty)
6. Digital Bridge (Astana)
7. Venture financing and equity investment association

Programming Schools

1. Alem (Astana)
2. Halyk Academy
3. Kolesa Academy
4. Intellection
5. nFactorial
6. Qwant
7. Decode
8. Kaspi Lab

Financing

Venture Funds

1. Centras Venture Fund
2. MOST Ventures
3. White Hill Capital
4. Almaty Venture Lab
5. Activat
6. MyVentures
7. Catapult Ventures
8. Shanyraq VC
9. Jas Ventures
10. Falconry Ventures
11. Tesla Capital
12. Sturgeon Capital
13. Business angels
14. Umay Ventures Lab

Alternative Financing

1. Starttime.kz (crowdfunding)
2. Qazinnovations (grants)
3. Astana Hub (grants)
4. Fund of Science (grants)

EBRD = European Bank for Reconstruction and Development, KASE = Kazakhstan Stock Exchange, KazNTU = Kazakh National Technical University, KBTU = Kazakh-British Technical University, SKA = Samruk-Kazyna Accelerator, UNDP = United Nations Development Programme, UNICEF = United Nations Children's Fund.

Source: Authors.

80 The AI fintech sector is populated for the most part by digital subsidiaries of major Kazakhstani commercial banks.

Box 8.2

Astana as a Center for Digital Innovation and Finance

The establishment of a digital financial center, designed to drive regional development and innovation, is a key component of the work of the Astana International Financial Centre (AIFC). The AIFC adopted a development strategy in 2020 to create a regional concentration of interconnected businesses, suppliers, and institutions for sharing resources, infrastructure, knowledge, and professional connections.

By the end of 2024, 3,515 firms were registered with the AIFC; as many as 1,000 of them were from 85 foreign countries, while more than 2,500 firms were Kazakhstani. The People's Republic of China had the biggest foreign representation in the AIFC community, with 110 participants, followed the European Union (66 participants), Russia (64), the United Kingdom (33), and the United States (31).

The AIFC's FinTech Lab regulatory sandbox, consisting of 68 registered firms, provides a platform for testing innovative solutions without legal risks. The sandbox aims to reduce traditional service costs, benefiting promising new financial technology (fintech) firms and financial service users. It allows AIFC residents to exchange experiences with 50 financial regulators and organizations and to test new products and services with real customers globally.

The AIFC platform offers firms access to the capital market through its own exchange, where firms can raise funds through public offerings of shares or bonds. Key incentives for potential residents include business protection, tax optimization, free movement of labor, the application of English common law, and investment access. The AIFC also established its own court and International Arbitration Center, independent of the Kazakhstani judiciary system. Participants are regulated by the Astana Financial Services Authority (AFSA) and, as of 1 July 2024, the total assets of the finance-sector firms at the AIFC had reached over $1.8 billion.

The AIFC's Tech Hub established its own venture capital support division, aiming to create a healthy venture capital environment and increase investment opportunities in Central Asia. The division's investor network includes international venture capital funds, angel investors, corporate investors, accelerators, and family offices. The Tech Hub also has the in-house VentureRocket Eurasia platform to attract regional and global capital. This platform aims to educate potential investors on assessing innovative firms, understanding investment risks, and concluding investment deals.

The AIFC's legal regime for the financial sector facilitates venture investor transactions in line with international standards. It requires investors and venture funds to incorporate firms into the AIFC ecosystem. Since August 2020, venture investment transactions exceeding $5 million had been structured at the AIFC, including the use of convertible loans as investment instruments. The 30 finalists of the Kazakhstan Digital Accelerator structured deals valued at $50,000 each, leveraging AIFC regulations. In addition, a memorandum of cooperation signed in 2020 between the AIFC and Quest Ventures had facilitated $3 million in investment deals through the AIFC platform by the end of 2024.

Source: Y. Khassenbekov. 2023. Financial Technology for Regional Cooperation in CAREC Countries: Uzbekistan, Tajikistan and Kazakhstan. Unpublished draft report.

Support for Innovation

State Support

Five key state-owned institutions that support innovation development and act as major players in Kazakhstan's fintech sector are listed here, and expanded upon later in the chapter:

- Astana Hub international technopark;
- Tech Garden, an autonomous cluster fund for innovative technologies;
- Nazarbayev University Research and Innovation System (NURIS);
- Fintech Hub of the AIFC; and
- Fund of Science.

Astana Hub International Technopark

The Astana Hub International Technopark has a mission to develop Kazakhstan's innovative ecosystem; support high-tech projects to strengthen the country's economy; and become a development center for IT firms, investors, and other stakeholders. Its operating rules were developed and approved by the Ministry of Digital Development and Aerospace Industry (MDDIAI).

The Astana Hub has supported many start-ups through various acceleration and incubation programs, and offers assistance that, among other forms, includes trips to international events to pitch ideas to potential investors and customers and access to research and development (R&D) centers run by international IT-related firms such as Huawei, Lenovo, IBM, Nokia, and Amazon. Online incubator services are provided to almost 8,000 teams. More than 10,000 resident firms—including firms from the PRC, Estonia, Germany, Singapore, Spain, and the United States (US)—have passed through the incubation and acceleration programs, which now enjoy preferential terms granted to Astana Hub residents (e.g., tax breaks).

Astana Hub aims to position itself as an international center for the development of IT innovations, where large IT firms, venture capitalists (funds, angel investors), and experts from the field (trainers, mentors, trackers, and others) provide full-fledged support to Astana Hub residents. Hence, it aims to create a community that generates, tests, and implements ideas, rather than simply serving as a place for the growth and promotion of innovation.

Tech Garden

Established in 2003 and granted the legal status of a special economic zone (SEZ) in 2014, Tech Garden offers acceleration programs and collaborations with international IT giants such as IBM, ARM Holdings, and Autodesk. Tech Garden operates the Smart Industry Management Platform (SIMP), a marketplace of domestic IT solutions for industry. It also manages technological laboratories, such the Center for Digital Industry IntelliSense-LAB and the BIM+ LAB, which support the development and implementation of Industry 4.0 technologies.

Firms in the acceleration programs are given the opportunity to solve tasks and streamline their goals and strategies with the aid of the program mentors, and to present their projects to investors. Tech Garden's ecosystem for innovation consists of 297 resident and associate participants, of which 175 are from new firms; 70 from large and established firms; 23 from universities; 25 from R&D centers; 2 from technoparks; 1 from a state development institute; 1 from an investment fund; and several from large mining firms, service entities, and laboratories.

Nazarbayev University Research and Innovation System

Nazarbayev University established the Nazarbayev University Research and Innovation System (NURIS) as a private venue for developing an innovation cluster. NURIS must partner with different stakeholders capable of filling the gaps. Facilities include a technopark and a "Fab Lab," where individuals can create prototypes, collaborate with like-minded people, and work with advanced equipment for 3D prototyping. Programs such as the QuickStart Acceleration Program and ABC Incubation help young entrepreneurs develop and scale their start-ups. By 2024, 694 projects had passed through incubation process and 159 teams (30 of which were NURIS residents) had graduated from the acceleration program. The ABC Incubation and QuickStart programs were sponsored by NURIS. In addition, the Akimat of Astana (regional state authority) provided NURIS with three blocks of its SEZ Astana-Technopolis for launching the ABC-I2BF Seed Fund, in partnership with the venture fund I2BF. Training for "business angels" and a bootcamp for technology entrepreneurship are complemented by events for pitching ideas.

Private Sector Support for Innovation

The Kazakhstan ecosystem for innovation is also supplemented by university graduates wishing to show their entrepreneurial acumen and spirit. Once they have developed an idea and created a team, they can turn to a group of firms that provide incubation and investment services. MOST is one such firm.

MOST Holding

MOST Holding founded the first private business incubator in Kazakhstan, supporting technology entrepreneurs at all stages of business development. The incubator started off as a university-sponsored program, established as part of Narxoz University in 2011 (MOST Ventures n.d.). MOST supports young entrepreneurs wishing to establish or grow their micro or small enterprises. The programs MOST offers do not restrict the participants; in fact, they work to empower women and support vulnerable segments of Kazakhstan's population (YBI 2025). MOST acts as a vehicle that innovators can use to work on their projects, exchange experiences, receive mentoring from experienced businesses and facilitators, and attract capital for their business ideas. To strengthen its position, MOST has become an official member of organizations such as Youth Business International and Global Entrepreneurship Week, partnering with the Seedstars World Competition, Startup Weekend, Get in the Ring, and other international initiatives to support promising innovations (Devex n.d.). MOST launched a venture investment branch in 2020, which transformed the MOST Business Incubator into MOST Ventures, a $50 million fund for financing innovation.

Terricon Valley

The Terricon Valley IT hub was established in 2014, the result of a collaboration between Karaganda State University and Abylkas Saginov Karaganda Technical University. Terricon Valley founded Kazakhstan's Association for IT Development, which aims to bring together technology firms from around the Karaganda region. It has an extensive network of partners that includes the Karaganda Technical and Construction College, Karaganda Politechnic College, the Eurasian Foods Group of Firms, and the Supera Business Incubator. Terricon Valley also has a close working relationship with Astana Hub.

Terricon Valley has been known to utilize its venue for hackathons, start-up weekends, knowledge-transfer events featuring renowned guest speakers, and other activities. In 2024, it opened the WOOPPAY fintech lab and the XNET urban development lab.[81]

[81] Wooppay specializes in e-wallets and the management of personal accounts.

In addition to becoming a regional center for innovation, Terricon Valley aims to become an education center for IT specialists in Kazakhstan. To this end, it started a massive online education program in 2020 that caters to students from partner educational organizations and other groups. Terricon Valley aims to train as many as 10,000 software programmers, data scientists, and specialists in other IT spheres.

▶ Incubator at the Kazakh-British Technical University

The Kazakh-British Technical University (KBTU) Startup Incubator was established in 2017 to support the innovative ideas of the university's students, but it is also open to entrepreneurs with innovative IT solutions that have cross-sector application. While not all participants achieve success with their initial ideas, many emerge as successful entrepreneurs who are able to leverage their experience in other innovative technology ventures. The university's incubation programs are designed not only to scale up promising innovations, but also to foster a cross-functional, interdisciplinary exchange of ideas, equipping entrepreneurs with the skills and resilience they will need to thrive.

Firms that graduate from the KBTU Startup Incubator's intensive 4-week program can transfer to Astana Hub (an official partner). The program has developed solutions in sectors such as robotics, energy supply, EdTech, renewables, smart cities, smart home solutions, safety control systems, the Internet of Things (IoT), and production automation.

KBTU holds the title of the best technology university in Kazakhstan, as most software developers entering the workforce are trained there. KBTU cooperates closely with all the major oil and gas, mining, and production companies in Kazakhstan, developing innovative solutions through its incubator programs.

▶ Recommendations

Ecosystems thrive on risk-taking and unconventional activities at the heart of entrepreneurial ventures. While regulations, such as capital adequacy requirements for fintech in Kazakhstan, set boundaries to protect the public, they must be flexible enough to avoid stifling innovation. However, in post-socialist economies such as Kazakhstan and some neighboring countries, regulators often emphasize control over market outcomes, thereby undermining the freedom necessary for entrepreneurship and technological advancement. Fundamental changes in financial sector regulations are necessary, and the government should reconsider its role in entrepreneurship and private sector development.

Kyrgyz Republic

The Government of the Kyrgyz Republic has been working for years to enhance internet connectivity and IT education across the country. This effort culminated in the adoption of the Digital Kyrgyzstan Strategy, 2019–2023, which aimed not only to improve access to IT and internet education, but also to enhance the country's digital infrastructure and literacy while promoting domestic employment opportunities.

The digital strategy also intended to promote e-government services and platforms, and to foster economic growth through digital transformation of the finance and banking sectors. Although internet penetration in the Kyrgyz Republic had always been low, estimates in January 2024 put the number of internet users at 5.41 million, just under 80% of the population.

All statistical data indicate that noncash payments account for an insignificant part of the money turnover and settlements in the Kyrgyz Republic. According to the central bank, despite the tendency toward an increase in the share of noncash funds in the banking system, most financial settlements are still executed outside of it. The lack of transparency in cash flows means that the shadow economy remains entrenched. For this reason, the government is taking steps to integrate all e-money payment systems into the Elcard system and to ensure the acceptance and interoperability of contactless cards. The objective is to create a single ecosystem for e-money throughout the country (Box 8.3).

Box 8.3

Kyrgyz Republic—Taking Cashless Payments to the Next Phase

The Kyrgyz Republic has a relatively small population (about 7 million), insufficient access to international capital markets, high operating costs, and low financial literacy—all of which help reduce noncash payments to an insignificant portion of the money turnover and settlements in the country.

The Government of the Kyrgyz Republic sees digitalization as a way to increase financial inclusion. The government also believes that it will have a positive effect on public administration, the economy, education, health care, and the provision of social services, as well as on law enforcement efforts to curb corruption in the public sector. Without the cash-flow transparency that digitalization would allow, the shadow economy will remain entrenched.

Information and communication technologies (ICTs) are central to the government's efforts to increase transparency and ensure a wider access for citizens to public services. The National Development Strategy, 2018–2040 involves the creation of an effective public-administration system by building interaction with society based on free access to modern digital technologies, which, in turn, will become an effective tool for eradicating corruption.

Financial inclusion has increased because retail outlets (e.g., chain stores, mobile phone stores) serve as agents of banks, while the payment card market has grown significantly. More than 50% of cards belong to the national Elcard system, while the market shares of UnionPay and Mastercard are still negligible. Moreover, electronic money (e-money) is gaining in popularity.

The government is taking steps to integrate all e-money payment systems into the Elcard chip card system through a phased modernization of its operator, Interbank Processing Center (IPC). The point is to ensure the acceptance and interoperability of contactless cards, with a view to creating a single ecosystem for processing e-money throughout the country, including for the transfer of government staff salaries, pensions, and benefits to Elcard users.

The IPC system, which includes commercial banks as minority shareholders, is aimed at performing settlement functions for retail payments for goods and services, thus reducing the need for cash payments; it would also expand the access of low-income citizens to banking services through the Elcard. In 2020, IPC became an operator for payments using two-dimensional Quick Response (QR) codes.

In 2020, the central bank approved a concept for the development of digital payment technologies by 2022. This was meant to build on a three-stage plan whose implementation had begun in 2000, with the aim of increasing the share of noncash payments and settlements and of increasing the amount of turnover executed in noncash funds.

continued on next page

Box 8.3 *continued*

A 2021 presidential decree provided measures for the further development of the financial market. The decree includes the setting of thresholds for cash payments to reduce the size of the shadow economy, as well as initiatives to stimulate cashless payments, including the use (and regulation) of cryptocurrencies. It also stipulates the formation of state- and local-government databases to enable financial and credit organizations to lend through remote service channels, alongside efforts to integrate the settlement systems of e-money operators. The decree also aims to expand the banking and payment infrastructure in all regions of the country and to bring in the unbanked, given that the low level of financial literacy makes part of the population trust cash more than cashless payments.

Ensuring interoperability and creating a single ecosystem for e-money throughout the country will significantly accelerate the development of digital financial services. Today, there are already quite a lot of local payment instruments; furthermore, the rapid introduction of interoperability will contribute to the use of electronic wallets by the population and to the growth of noncash payments.

The Kyrgyz Republic is also implementing integration projects with the Russian national system of payment cards, and is beginning to study the issues surrounding the integration of national card systems, based on the experiences of various countries. These efforts will help ensure the acceptance and maintenance of the Elcard abroad, the card's use for cross-border payments, and the development of electronic trade within the Eurasian Economic Union.

Source: A. Kadyraliev. 2023. FinTech Development in the Kyrgyz Republic and Pakistan. Unpublished draft report.

Retail outlets such as chain stores and mobile phone stores act as agents of banks, thereby increasing financial inclusion, and the payment card market has grown significantly. More than 50% of cards belong to the Elcard system, while the market shares UnionPay and Mastercard remain negligible; moreover, e-money is gaining popularity.

In October 2024, O!Dengi became the first Kyrgyz fintech firm to launch Visa cards linkable to services such as Google Pay and Garmin Pay. O!Dengi offers a wide range of services through its mobile app, making it convenient for users to manage their finances and pay many different charges, including utility and tuition bills, government services, and taxes.

O!Deng is part of the ALGA Group ecosystem, which provides digital services to more than 3.5 million people, including thorough mobile payment solutions, e-commerce platforms, and financial services such as international and national payment cards. Another example is the transformation of Kompanion Bank from a microfinance institution to a provider of fintech services after obtaining its banking license in 2016. Aligned with its stated mission to become the leading community development financial institution in Central Asia, Kompanion Bank provides free training to improve financial literacy among its customers. It uses a full range of fintech, including online and mobile banking, electronic wallets (e-wallets), and digital payments to provide international money transfers, SME loans, payment and cash services, electronic payment cards, and correspondent relationships with foreign banks.

The DCB Green program, operated by the commercial bank Dos Credobank, focuses on promoting environmentally friendly banking practices and on supporting the development of a green economy. Key aspects include loans arranged through digital platforms for purchasing electric vehicles and for the gasification of households (which help reduce emissions and harmful substances emitted from burning wood and charcoal).

Two years after the launch of the Digital Kyrgyzstan Strategy, the government announced plans to promote fintech innovation through a regulatory sandbox (NBKR 2024), which was designed to create favorable conditions for uptake, while reducing the time and cost of implementing innovative banking and payment services.

Three supervised institutions were granted temporary licenses to conduct specific banking operations in the sandbox. These included issuing preapproved credit cards, accepting Elcard cards for cashless loan disbursements, acquiring bank cards, enabling payments via QR codes, issuing and redeeming proprietary e-money, and providing e-wallet access through payment cards. In addition, the central bank is piloting a project with a microfinance institution.

▶ Recommendations

Ensuring interoperability and creating a single e-money ecosystem throughout the Kyrgyz Republic will significantly accelerate the development of digital financial services from an already substantial number of local payment instruments. The rapid introduction of interoperability will contribute to the use of e-wallets, but it will be necessary to accelerate the digitalization of banking services through open banking, given that digitalization matches needs with solutions, and so provides an efficient way of doing business. In addition, the agent network needs to grow, as the number of points that accept e-wallet payments is still limited.

Despite the significant achievements of the IPC, its corporate structure—in which a significant block of shares belongs to the central bank and the other shareholders are commercial banks—does not allow flexibility or the quick acceptance of solutions, especially when those solutions involve the introduction of new services or investments in technologies.

The establishment of an interdepartmental working group to introduce and regulate measures to support digital payment technologies was enshrined in the concept behind the development of digital payment technologies during 2020–2022. The group consisted of representatives of state bodies and the business community, and its purpose was to help identify and eliminate legal obstacles to the development of laws and regulations regarding innovative payment business models and the introduction of digital business processes, products, and services.

Mongolia

Mongolia is in a strong position in terms of financial access, account ownership, number of banking branches, and the scale of online purchases. The digital economy has been developing rapidly, and fintech is an integral part of daily life in a country where 65% of its 3.4 million people are between the ages of 15 and 64, and nearly half live in Ulaanbaatar, the capital city. There are more than 80 fintech firms, most providing services such as payments, remittances, online loans, and currency conversions. Only a few businesses are engaged in cryptocurrency trading, investments, e-wallets, and internet trading. The country's first digital currency license was issued to Mobifinance NBFI LLC, in 2020.

With the number of providers increasing, the Government of Mongolia is working to include programs and measures in its long-term economic strategies. It included technology-sector development among the economic goals in "Vision 2050," its action plan for 2021–2030, and through the government's e-Mongolia integrated service platform. The platform provides over 1,200 services, and has saved a total of togrog (MNT)64.5 billion ($18 million) for the government and customers in terms of time, particularly in the traffic-congested capital. Digitalization and smart technologies can help address Ulaanbaatar's problems, including traffic jams and air pollution.

A striking example of fintech innovation involves ArdCoin, Mongolia's first blockchain-based loyalty-point or bonus cryptocurrency, which was started in 2017 to streamline the process for customers to collect reward points from vendors (Figure 8.4). This form of digital money is issued by Ard Credit NBFI and trades on Uniswap, the world's largest decentralized exchange (which is built on the Ethereum platform). ArdCoin has also been registered on international monitoring platforms such as CoinMarketCap, Blockfolio, and CoinGecko; and it is traded on the Digital Asset Exchange (DAX), STEX, and Bittrex.

Figure 8.4: The ArdCoin Ecosystem

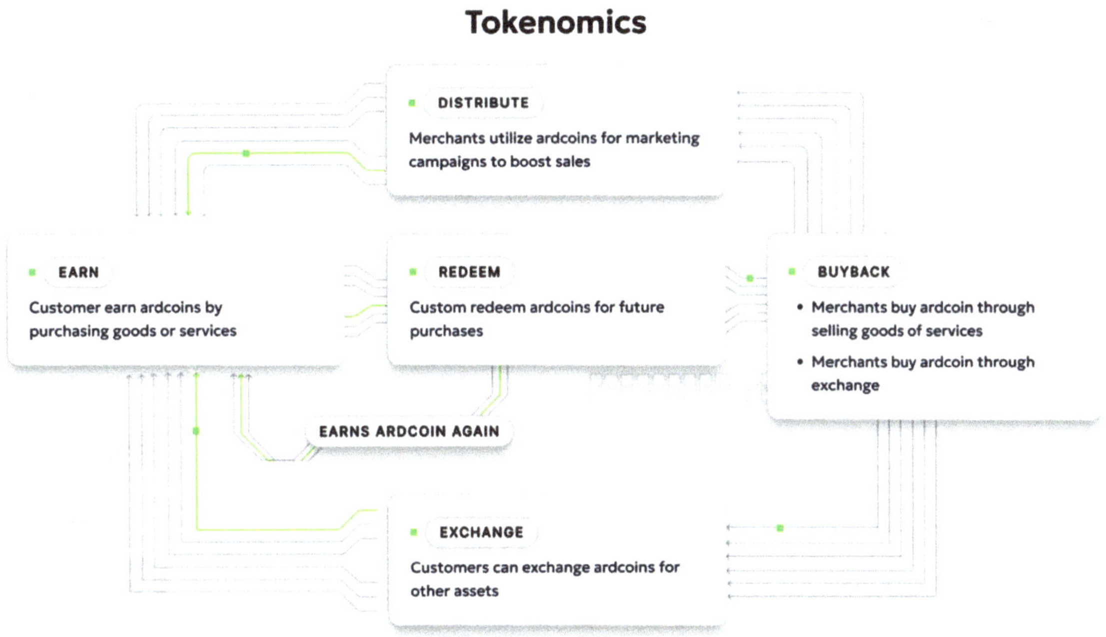

Source: ArdCoin. n.d. Tokenomics. https://www.ardcoin.com/.

Customers can earn ArdCoin cashback awards by making purchases at businesses with loyalty programs that accept ArdCoin as payment, by referring friends, or by participating in community events. One example was The Hu in the Metaverse concert in 2023, which combined a performance by the popular heavy metal Mongolian folk band and with opportunities to earn ArdCoin by engaging in interactive experiences and promotions. Blockchain technology can be used effectively without the need for cryptocurrencies such as Bitcoin. Although it is most often associated with digital currencies, blockchain's core features—decentralization, transparency, and immutability—make it a versatile tool for a wide range of applications beyond just financial transactions.

Even though blockchain technology is not yet fully legalized in Mongolia, the government has stated its intent to support the use of noncash payments, introduce new payment instruments and services, create a legal environment for noncash payments, and develop a payment-system infrastructure that met international standards. The total amount of digital money in Mongolia has increased threefold since 2021. As of the second quarter of 2024, it stood at MNT30.4 billion ($8.5 million) (Mongol Bank n.d.).

Golomt Bank, one of Mongolia's largest banks, has been known for its cutting-edge online offerings since its introduction of open banking in 2020. Many e-commerce platforms, cab services, travel apps, convenience stores, and the e-Mongolia platform are compatible with its system.

Among the many other examples of fintech's delivery of innovative credit and financial products to customers without collateral, or the need to visit a bank branch, is Lend MN NBFI JSC (Nonbank Financial Institution, Joint Stock Company), which in 2018 introduced the fintech business model to the Mongolian market in the form of the Lend MN app, providing micro e-loan services to 1.3 million registered customers by 2024. By the end of 2020, Lend MN had already saved 93,081 customers a total of MNT1.5 billion ($419,288) in indirect borrowing costs (JDF 2022).

Here are some other examples:

- Hipay LLC introduced the first payment gateway service in Mongolia for processing e-commerce transactions. Hipay allows users to make purchases without having to reenter their card information or Personal Identification Number (PIN); the users simply have to register their payment card with any bank in the system. Hipay also includes a "tokenization" service that makes payment transactions quicker.
- Zeel MN Platform NBFI LLC offers peer-to-peer (P2P) financing services through the website Zeel.mn. This new service uses blockchain and AI to score and register credit.
- A platform operated by FinBerry provides mutual fund services focused on loans, rewards, and donations. Although it gives SMEs the chance to swiftly raise the money they need, no legal structure currently governs the service.

Monre Insurance offers products using assessments based on a risk road map; its Laika platform enables users to choose insurance products that suit their needs (without the involvement of intermediaries) and to assess the risks.

Support for Innovation

A significant indicator of the level of fintech development in Mongolia is the fact that the regulatory bodies have been approving legal documents one after another. Important fintech-related regulations that were recently approved include the following: "Regulation on Sandbox Environment" and "Regulation on Digital Currency." That said, new financial sector initiatives and changes are not accurately reflected in the country's legislation. For instance, laws or regulations on privacy and protection of property have not been amended.

A regulatory sandbox is an environment where new businesses can test innovative products and services that are about to be implemented in accordance with the law and regulations. The testing occurs before the licenses are given to the businesses, which hope to bring their products or services to market after developing an effective business model. It is unique in that it empowers the new companies by enabling them to avoid being squeezed out of the competition, and by providing them with full access to industry information.

The "Regulation on Sandbox Environment" came into operation in 2021. According to the regulation, requests to enter the sandbox must be received during the first 10 working days of March or September. Since the regulation was approved and implemented, 12 fintech organizations have submitted requests to enter the sandbox environment. Of these, six requests were rejected, and an on-site inspection of the systems of the four selected organizations was conducted. At present, the financial products and services being tested in the sandbox environment are (i) Mobifinance's open electronic debt tool; (ii) Monpay's digital bond; and (iii) Monimarket Fund's web system, whose services include responding to repo-transaction requests and registering sales and purchases by transaction. If these innovative financial products and services test out well, there will be a need to create a legal environment suitable to the specifics of each one of them. The Financial Regulatory Commission supports giving financial firms the opportunity to test their products and services in the sandbox environment. For this reason, it is developing the necessary legal regulations to enable the successful introduction of these tested products and services to the market.

Recommendations

To make the best possible use of fintech opportunities and increase competitiveness, Mongolia has to recognize the need to regulate firms in a sensible way, instead of ways that end up restraining initiative. The legal ecosystem must become more transparent, and there should be a centralized electronic database of services offered by fintech firms in the social, business, and economic spheres. Overall, the government must manage this rapidly developing world while reducing possible risks by enacting regulations that encourage, rather than stifle, private sector innovation.

It will also be necessary to strengthen the capacity of human resources for fintech in Mongolia, especially by improving financial literacy and education. In addition, the creation of an umbrella organization that would bring together all industry stakeholders would help address the current sticking points and find a way for solutions to be incorporated into government policies.

To support partnerships between banks and fintech firms, regulatory bodies should understand the benefit and purpose of open banking. With high mobile use and financial exposure, Mongolian citizens could access and view their bank accounts through online banking channels and fintech apps. A solid partnership among regulators, the banking sector, and fintech organizations is very feasible, and would boost the finance sector of Mongolia. The creation of a conducive legal environment would have a positive impact on economic stability, in part by attracting international firms and investors.

Tajikistan

Given that almost 93% of Tajikistan's territory is mountainous, internet and digital technologies are still not widespread enough for fintech to spur significant financial inclusion among its 10.6 million citizens. However, the Government of Tajikistan sees regional collaboration among technology firms in CAREC as having the potential to unlock the fintech market. Mobile phone usage exceeds the number of people in the country (a penetration rate of about 102.9%), even though less than half (41.6%) can access the internet (Kemp 2024a).

As of 2023, 18 credit financial institutions were providing payment and e-wallet services; and during that year, 15.1 million noncash transactions worth somoni (TJS)1.7 billion ($172 million) were made through e-wallets. By the end of 2022, online payments had totaled 33.4 million transactions worth TJS8.2 billion ($830 million).

Fintech Innovations (or Services)

The fintech industry has not developed much, in spite of the presence of several commercial banks, credit organizations, and microfinance organizations. There are a few successful innovators in the field, but two stand out: Alif is a neobank, while Zypl.ai provides instant credit scoring of potential borrowers. Both have started to sell their services outside Tajikistan.

Alif

The project began with a basic model for providing interest-free installments for buyers and earning commission from retailers. The main reason for abandoning ready-made banking solutions was the high cost and inflexibility of systems when it came to incorporating local solutions. Alif has an academy for training programmers, and has developed its e-wallet, debit card, and QR payment systems. Alif is the only neobank in Tajikistan that has all components of a modern bank, including

- Alif Pay—online payments system,
- Alif Mobi—mobile e-wallet,
- Alif Shop—the first online shop in Tajikistan, and
- Alif Tech—fintech firm.

Alif Pay and Alif Mobi are popular, as one can pay for mobile communications, utilities, banking services, air tickets and travel, online games, social networks, taxis, deliveries, cable and satellite TV, tuition for schools and child-development centers, and other services. Alif launched operations in Uzbekistan in 2019, offering digital banking, microloans, and installment plans. It also offers digital banking services in Dubai.

Zypl.ai

Zypl.ai is an instant AI-driven credit scoring service, specializing in finance automation and the compilation of synthetic credit scores of consumers and small businesses in 12 emerging markets—including the Czech Republic, Indonesia, the United Arab Emirates, and the US—with 35 enterprise clients (central banks, fintech firms, and microfinance organizations) as software customers; it has also facilitated the underwriting of over $130 million in loans. Zypl.ai initially developed its AI solutions in the Tajikistan market, where it cooperates with leading financial institutions based in the country. Zypl.ai has received significant funding and recognition, including participation in the Silkway Accelerator, a joint program founded by Google for Startups and Astana Hub. Zypl.ai was founded in 2021 by Azizjon Azimi, a graduate of Stanford and Harvard universities, according to its website, and has attracted investors from Luxembourg, Kazakhstan, the United Arab Emirates, and the United States. The firm employs 50 people and is based at the AI & Web3 campus of the Dubai International Financial Center (DIFC), with offices in Tajikistan and Uzbekistan.

The Zypl.ai portfolio of microloans, which are disbursed throughout Asian markets, has exceeded $50 million, and includes direct partnerships with 25 enterprise clients (standard trust banks, fintech firms, and multifamily offices) in 8 countries.

Support for Innovation

Tajikistan's comparatively low innovation activity is directly related to the absence of any mechanism to stimulate the technology sector, so innovative firms may have few chances to develop and succeed. A few initiatives have been implemented and several plans were announced for IT sector development.

Some notable innovative fintech success stories, such as Alif Bank and its linked firms, are boosting morale in the innovation ecosystem and generating investment interest, while business incubators, technoparks, and networking events have started to emerge. The regional authority of Dushanbe, in collaboration with the State Unitary Enterprise "Smart City" announced the opening of an IT park that would aim to develop competitive products and services, support start-ups, and foster innovation through venture financing and partnerships with domestic and foreign investors. Smart City provides essential infrastructure, such as laboratories, and offers financial, marketing, legal, and consulting services to resident start-ups. Residents are expected to benefit from tax exemptions.

In 2018, the government established the State Business Incubator of Tajikistan, with the key function of providing consultations and methodological assistance to entrepreneurs, including tech-based ones. The institution conducts small-scale and limited-time programs focused on incubation, acceleration, consultation, and business financing; however, it is not enough to meet the existing demand for such services. It has branches in five cities—Bokhtar, Kulyab, Khujand, Khorog, and Kanibadam. In 2020, the incubator partnered with the United Nations Development Programme (UNDP) to create a small fund of $63,000 for early-stage entrepreneurs.

With regard to the private sector, tech entrepreneurs are engaged with a few organizations, including the 55 Group (of 55 start-ups), Accelerate Prosperity, and the National Association of Businesswomen. Accelerate Prosperity, an international organization with an office in Tajikistan, pays special attention to IT projects and conducts an incubator program that provides small amounts of financing to new technologies. Graduates of the Dushanbe-based business incubator 55 Group have attracted on average $50,000 in investments.

In March of 2022, Tajikistan's first venture-capital and angel-investor school was opened with the cooperation of the UNDP and the United States Agency for International Development (USAID). It conducts trainings, seminars, and other events dedicated to encouraging innovation. The international organization Startup Weekend has held events in Tajikistan (also Startup Weekend Women events) organized by Techstars and Google for Startups.

Tajikistan does have free economic zones (FEZs), but none of them focus on IT or on innovation-related activities. Besides, to get financial support, a state guarantee, or preferences, a foreign firm must go through a screening process before investing in a project that might be eligible for FEZ residence.

Tajikistan has taken a cautious approach toward cryptocurrency, although the central bank has set up a working group to explore the issue. No explicit prohibitions or regulations on exchange, mining, or circulation exist, but bitcoin miners have been fined for illegal activities by the state Tax Committee.

Recommendations

Establishing robust institutional frameworks is crucial for nurturing an innovation ecosystem that supports fintech, venture capital investments, capital markets, and financial intermediation services.

To formulate effective policy recommendations that promote fintech innovation and enhance regional cooperation and integration in Tajikistan, a comprehensive understanding of its economic, social, regulatory, and business landscapes is essential.

The government first needs to create conditions—through strong and effectively implemented anti-monopoly legislation—that facilitate activities for novice entrepreneurs in the IT sphere through administrative, tax, and other preferences. Finally, the government must ensure extensive education and retraining of young people, who might otherwise continue to leave the country in large numbers.

As for regional collaboration in fintech, Tajikistan could easily adapt to the terms for cooperation and adjust to the current norms, as these are in the nascent stage of development. The first steps should include: (i) strengthening the protection of intellectual property rights, with a focus on assets capable of being sold, rented, pledged, and so on; (ii) removing restrictions on the provision of financial services (i.e., allowing only credit institutions to provide these services); (iii) ending the government monopoly over telecommunications; and (iv) reducing some taxes on small and microbusinesses, including innovation successes, or supporting a special regime for tech entrepreneurs.

Turkmenistan

The fintech ecosystem in Turkmenistan is developing, with several key components contributing to its growth. Financial institutions, particularly state-owned banks such as the State Bank for Foreign Economic Affairs of Turkmenistan, are leading the charge in digital banking initiatives. Private banks are beginning to explore digital transformation to provide enhanced services to customers. A few fintech firms with innovative successes focus on areas such as mobile payments, digital wallets, and online lending. While crucial for innovation, however, they face the challenges of regulatory barriers and limited access to funding. Major telecom firms, such as Turkmentelecom, are investing in digital infrastructure, providing the backbone for mobile banking and digital payments. In addition, organizations such as the UNDP are working with the Government of Turkmenistan to improve the digital infrastructure and promote fintech development through technical assistance and funding.

Key focus areas include mobile banking, digital payments, and online lending platforms. Despite recent improvements, Turkmenistan still has one of the lowest internet penetration rates in Central Asia, at 39.5% (about 2.6 million) of the population in 2024, while 66.2% (4.34 million) have mobile connections, which is low relative to the other emerging fintech markets in CAREC (Kemp 2024b).

Banks in Turkmenistan are increasingly offering mobile banking services, and the adoption of digital payment systems is growing, with more businesses and consumers using electronic payment methods. Halkbank's introduction of the Altyn Asyr payment card has facilitated digital transactions and reduced reliance on cash. The card can be used to pay for telecommunications, TV, internet, and other services. Online lending platforms are emerging, often introduced by foreign fintech firms, providing easier access to credit for individuals and small businesses. Microfinance institutions are leveraging digital platforms to lend to underserved populations, addressing the credit gap in the country.

Government initiatives play a significant role in promoting digital transformation. Policies such as the Concept for the Development of the Digital Economy in Turkmenistan for 2019–2025 and the State Program for the Development of the Digital Economy in Turkmenistan for 2021–2025 aim to improve internet connectivity, promote digital literacy, and support the development of digital services. Increased mobile phone use is driving demand for mobile banking and payment solutions. Efforts to bring more people into the formal financial system are promoting the adoption of fintech solutions. The World Bank estimates that only 40% of adults in Turkmenistan have access to a bank account, indicating a significant scope for enhancing financial inclusion through fintech.

Where to Begin

To accelerate fintech development in Turkmenistan, the following policies are recommended as a way to lay the groundwork for the sector's growth:

- **Develop a comprehensive fintech regulatory framework.** Establish clear and supportive regulations specifically tailored to fintech. They should include guidelines for emerging technologies such as blockchain, cryptocurrency, and digital wallets. A comprehensive regulatory framework will provide clarity and attract more investment into the sector.
- **Establish a regulatory sandbox.** Implement a regulatory sandbox to allow fintech start-ups to test their innovative products and services in a controlled environment. This will encourage experimentation and reduce the risk for start-ups, while providing regulators with insights into new technologies.
- **Enhance data protection laws.** Strengthen data protection and cybersecurity regulations to align with international standards. This will ensure the safe operation of fintech services and build consumer trust.
- **Promote financial inclusion.** Launch targeted initiatives to increase financial inclusion, particularly in rural areas. This could include digital literacy programs and incentives for financial institutions to develop services tailored to underserved populations.
- **Invest in digital infrastructure.** Continue to invest in improvements in digital infrastructure, including the expansion of high-speed internet and mobile network coverage. Public–private partnerships could be effective in funding these projects.
- **Encourage public–private partnerships.** Foster collaboration between the government and private sector to drive innovation. Joint ventures between banks and technology firms could lead to the development of new financial products and services.
- **Facilitate cross-border collaboration.** Work with neighboring countries to harmonize regulations and create a unified framework for fintech. This will facilitate cross-border operations and increase the regional market potential for fintech firms.
- **Simplify foreign investment procedures.** Reform bureaucratic processes and reduce foreign currency controls to attract more foreign direct investment in the local financial sector. This will provide fintech firms with access to much-needed capital.
- **Support the innovation ecosystem.** Provide financial supports, such as grants and tax breaks, to fintech innovators. The creation of incubation centers and innovation hubs could also help nurture new businesses.
- **Monitor and adapt regulations.** Establish a mechanism for the continuous monitoring and adaptation of regulations to keep pace with rapid technological advancements in the fintech sector.

Recommendations

Turkmenistan's fintech sector is at a nascent stage, but it shows promising signs of growth. By addressing regulatory barriers, improving digital literacy, and investing in infrastructure, Turkmenistan could enhance its fintech landscape. Learning from the experiences of neighboring regions in the South Caucasus and Central Asia could help Turkmenistan accelerate its fintech development and enhance financial inclusion. The future of fintech in Turkmenistan looks bright, with many opportunities for innovation and collaboration.

Turkmenistan could collaborate with neighboring countries to create a unified regulatory framework that facilitates cross-border fintech operations. Continued investment in digital infrastructure will be crucial for the growth of fintech in Turkmenistan. Public–private partnerships could be leveraged to fund the expansion of high-speed internet and mobile networks. Collaborations between the government and private sector could drive innovation and expand the reach of fintech services. Finally, joint ventures between banks and technology firms could lead to the development of innovative financial products tailored to local needs.

Uzbekistan

Uzbekistan offers a sizable fintech market and a plethora of firms (Figure 8.5). Given the country's relatively young population—more than half its 37 million people being of working age—growth in digital financial services will only increase, supported by local and international talent.

The trend in Uzbekistan toward the creation of neobanks and super apps is evident. Traditional banks are introducing remote services and transforming into nonbanks, while nonfinancial firms, such as telecom players, are developing their own financial instruments. This trend is turning the local fintech market into a fast-growing sector, attracting firms from abroad and nontraditional banking sectors to a young, growing population and high-tech environment where new products can scale quickly. "Uzbekistan has built a genuinely interoperable open-banking system that is more advanced than in any developed market," said Oliver Hughes, head of international business at the TBC Bank Group, which is based in Georgia and Uzbekistan (Prendergast 2024).

Figure 8.5: Major Players in the Uzbekistan Fintech Sector

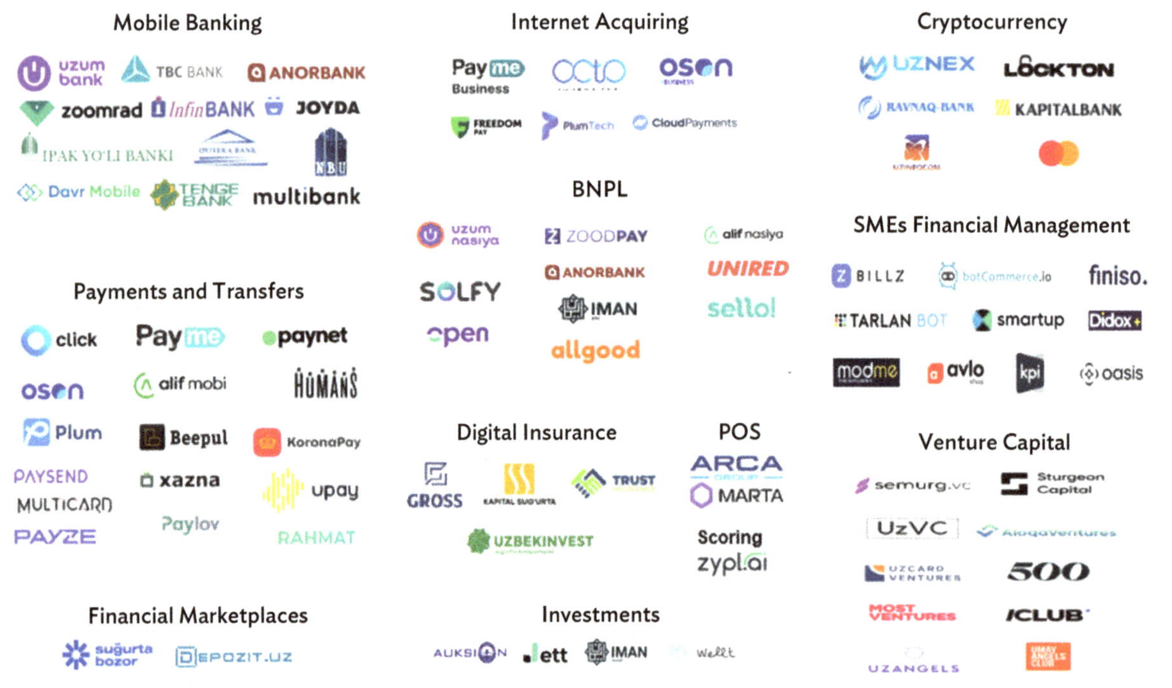

BNPL = buy now, pay later, fintech = financial technology, POS = point of sale, SMEs = small and medium-sized enterprises.
Source: Rise Research. 2023. Fintech Market of Uzbekistan. https://mcfintech.uz/Fintech_in_Uzbekistan.pdf.

Most fintech firms have emerged from companies affiliated with commercial banks or from branded applications that support bank operations. Banks with popular online services include Kapitalbank and Ipak Yuli Bank, while TBC Bank is the driving force among the commercial banks because it is the only modern neobank in Uzbekistan. TBC Uzbekistan has also acquired a full stake in Payme, a widely used digital payment platform serving individuals and SMEs. Universal Bank, through its Unired app, has made a significant transition to online banking.

The introduction of open banking will accelerate the emergence of neobanks and super apps by expanding the capabilities of financial institutions and enhancing customer service. National biometric identification will further support this development by confirming identities during service registration or application.

Super apps stand apart for their holistic offerings. A striking example is Uzum, which recently merged with Click, forming the country's largest ecosystem for digital banking, payments, and e-commerce, catering to over 13 million users. Another example, Humans, provides more than 2 million users with combined financial services, mobile services, and a marketplace for products that offers up to 7% cashback on purchases.

Notable new cases include BILLZ, which offers retail automation solutions; and Sug'urta Bozor, which, with 120,000 active users, is Uzbekistan's first insurance marketplace. In addition, ZoodPay's "Buy Now, Pay Later" services have supported 560,000 loans and connected 30,000 sellers to its marketplace ecosystem.

One of the significant examples of fintech innovation in Uzbekistan is the fully digital banking-service firm Space. Created by Georgia's largest commercial bank, TBC Bank, Space has scaled up regionally. TBC Uzbekistan, built on the Space platform (Chapter 3), is now regarded as the most dynamic and trend-setting neobank in Uzbekistan. TBC Uzbekistan runs Payme, a digital payment app for individuals and small businesses; it also runs Payme Nasiya (Payme Instalments), an installment credit business.

Jett, an investment gateway connecting brokers, fintechs firms, and retail investors, leverages mobile technology to link capital markets and retail investors. By offering services similar to platforms such as Robinhood, Gotrade, and Revolut, Jett has grown quickly. More than 70% of transactions on the Uzbek stock exchange are now conducted through its platform. Jett has also fostered an investment community, with over 4,000 participants in its Investors Club, and provides financial education. Jett wants to expand its services regionally, and is working to find a partner and investor who could help with the expansion.

The fintech firms that are among the most successful innovators, and that have the potential for expansion in Uzbekistan and elsewhere, include the following:

- **Marta.** Provides mobile acquiring services for small businesses. The firm offers a mobile terminal through which one can connect to a smartphone; and it accepts payments via Visa, Mastercard, or UnionPay card. This service is especially interesting because it offers a payment function to residents of remote places in which there is no internet or connectivity is low.
- **Zood.** An ecosystem that unites an e-commerce lending platform (ZoodPay); a marketplace (ZoodMall); a delivery and logistics service (ZoodShip); and a digital bank. As of the end of 2022, Zood boasted 1.1 million active users; 560,000 issued loans; and 30,000 active sellers represented in the marketplace.

- **Oson Pay.** An online wallet application that allows the customer, not only to make payments, but also to view the analytics of the receipts and of the withdrawals made during daily operations.
- **BILLZ.** Provides comprehensive retail-management-automation solutions. The firm offers three types of monthly and annual subscriptions that feature a variety of services. In addition, it has begun to offer online-store construction and financing for its customers. There are 500,000 transactions per month, totaling $25 million per month in transaction turnovers.
- **Sug'urta Bozor.** The first insurance marketplace offering the most user-relevant products of insurance firms in Uzbekistan. The start-up introduced a monthly subscription for auto insurance. Car insurance policies can be purchased without a car inspection. Sales have reached 4,500 insurance policies per month, with 120,000 active users.
- **Unired.** A mobile app from Universal Bank that allows customers to purchase goods in installments without documents. All processes are digitalized, and one can open a bank account or a banking card.
- **Click.** An online wallet that allows users to transfer money to cards from different banks, with low commissions. Click currently possesses 75.7% of Uzbekistan's P2P transaction market, with a customer base of 5.5. million and an average annual turnover of $1.5 billion. In 2023, Click merged with Uzum and became a super app, which is still in use under the name "Click."
- **Factoring.uz.** A full range of factoring services for small businesses. Users can sell their accounts receivables (invoices), thereby obtaining operational financing without collateral and insurance to help them improve cash flow and manage the risks associated with international trade. The services are aimed at small-scale producers of fruits and vegetables, including assistance to micro and small retailers in arranging export factoring.

Support for Innovation

IT Park Uzbekistan (IT Park), established in 2019 as a division of the recently formed Ministry for the Development of Information Technologies and Communications (MDITC), is the focal point for incubation and acceleration programs for fintech innovations, and provides residences to some fintechs. The acceleration and incubation programs last 3 months. In addition, MDITC set up a $10 million venture fund for firms that graduate from the acceleration program at IT Park. By the fourth quarter of 2024, the number of residents reached 2,384, a 44% increase in less than a year.

IT Park conducts acceleration programs that allow innovators from other countries not only to acquire knowledge, but also to obtain grants, including funding for participants in the Acceleration Program at IT Park Uzbekistan. Another program is the CAT Accelerator, organized by the Center for Advanced Technologies (focused on science-based firms), which accepts applications from all Central Asian countries and lasts 5 months. Grants are also given to acceleration program graduates, the winners determined by a brief entrepreneurial contest.

Startups supported by MDITC and other state agencies (e.g., IT Park, Center for Advanced Technologies, Yashnabad Innovative Technopark) have their taxes reduced or waived. In addition to the government-led programs, there are acceleration and incubation programs supported by private organizations. These include IdeaLab, StartupFactory, Ideathon, GameDev, Women in Tech, Technovation, Digital Generation, Tech4Impact, Startup initiatives (UNDP), and Ground Zero.

In the realm of digital training, Uzbekistan has made significant strides. By 2022, the country boasted more than 60 institutions of higher education, including three major universities, and more than 300 IT training centers and schools. More than 1.5 million Uzbek citizens had completed IT training courses by that year, with 1.1 million receiving certificates of completion through the "One Million Uzbek Coders" project by the end of 2023. The key center of IT education is Tashkent University of Information Technologies (TUIT), including its six branches throughout the country. TUIT, together with Inha University of Tashkent and Amity University Tashkent, trains over 29,000 personnel in more than 35 specialties every year, including such fields as AI, data science, information security, and engineering. In addition, branches of foreign universities nurture entrepreneurs in Uzbekistan. The most popular is Westminster International University in Tashkent, which specializes in helping young entrepreneurs realize their ideas and in supporting their business activities outside the university. Several incubation centers in other universities—such as Inha University (Republic of Korea), Management Development Institute of Singapore, and TEAM University—are becoming critical for the acceleration of innovation in Uzbekistan's fintech industry. They are all part of the ecosystem that supports the growth of innovation (Figure 8.6).

Figure 8.6: Elements of the Uzbekistan Innovation Ecosystem

NGO = nongovernment organization.
Source: Startup Indicator. 2020. Uzbekistan Startup Ecosystem Overview.

International players are a clear presence when it comes to promoting innovation in the Uzbekistan fintech industry. Techstars, in collaboration with Ground Zero, has held several start-up weekend events in Tashkent, including one in March 2024. Another notable event in Uzbekistan was Tech4Impact's Central Asia Women in Tech & Science Week, held from 31 May to 4 June 2024. Startup Grind, a global start-up community whose aim is to educate, inspire, and connect entrepreneurs through events, was established in Tashkent in 2021. Also in the capital, IDEMIA, a French firm, launched a fintech lab in 2020.

Central Bank Sandbox

The central bank introduced the country's regulatory sandbox in 1 January 2023. Any legal entity based in Uzbekistan can apply to join, subject to various criteria, among them, (i) if an innovation would improve an existing product or service offered to consumers, (ii) the maximum period would be for the sale of the product or service, and (iii) if the product or service could be made to work within the sandbox's framework of 3 years.

Recommendations

A thriving fintech industry in Uzbekistan will require a comprehensive set of laws, business practices, and expertise, as well as an entrepreneurial culture that can only develop over time. Government of Uzbekistan support for fintech has led to new digital products and solutions that have benefited both consumers and entrepreneurs in both traditional and tech-driven sectors.

Fintech industry players and experts need to be more engaged in building feedback mechanisms about the sector's performance, if they are to take the industry to the next stage. Three critical factors in particular are necessary for rapid fintech development: (i) connectivity infrastructure, including more growth in fixed and mobile internet; (ii) a legal framework with clear rules for fintech activities; and (iii) efforts to deepen the presence of market participants, such as intermediary dealers and brokers.

From a legal regulation standpoint, Uzbekistan has made significant strides, particularly in digital banking and payment systems; improvements are still needed in cybersecurity, however, and they must be achieved without inhibiting private sector development. Moreover, there must be fundamental changes in financial sector regulations and in the state's understanding of its role in entrepreneurship and private sector development. As for regional cooperation, the best start would be to align normative work on regulations in such a way that they become conducive to integration.

Given that the government is leaning toward a separate law on fintech, this should unify the different segments of the industry, with stakeholders paying close attention to market trends. Test runs of legal acts tailored to fintech would be done better in the regulatory sandbox—and only after a technology or a particular amendment has proven that it could have a positive impact on national productivity.

CONCLUSION

The potential for a unified fintech ecosystem is starting to emerge in the CAREC region, one that could be marked by opportunities for the cross-fertilization of innovative ideas and by a welcoming approach to the range of foreign fintech firms that CAREC countries have accepted into their markets and incubation spaces. Yet more direction and cooperation will be needed for this potential to be realized. For the financial institutions, new tech firms, and innovations featured in this chapter to gain traction, government regulators must find ways to end the national and regional fragmentation of fintech ecosystems. Instead, these ecosystems should be assembled into a coherent community that will drive the spread of the best practices, products, and services throughout the region.

Falling behind the frontiers of innovation is a losing proposition. Economies that cannot promote the acceptance and uptake of the benefits of technological advances will fall behind, unable to compete with economies that have found viable ways to increase efficiencies, reduce costs, and raise participation in economic activity through fintech solutions. This book recommends in no uncertain terms that a regional approach is the right way, not only to catch up with global developments, but also to spread solutions now coming to light in the emerging fintech markets of Central Asia, thanks to the entrepreneurial spirit and skills of adept innovators throughout the region. The next and closing chapter of this book takes a pragmatic view of deeper collaborative efforts, observing what fintech has achieved in other regions. And it lays out the necessary steps for strengthening CAREC's emerging fintech markets, noting that the path forward will involve dialogue and deepened ties, with the goal of creating a truly cooperative regional fintech community.

REFERENCES

Central Asia Regional Economic Cooperation (CAREC) Program. n.d. https://www.carecprogram.org.

Devex. n.d. MOST Business Incubator. https://www.devex.com/organizations/most-business-incubator-157890.

Kemp, S. 2024a. Digital 2024: Tajikistan. *DataReportal*. 23 February. https://datareportal.com/reports/digital-2024-tajikistan?form=MG0AV3.

———. 2024b. Digital 2024: Turkmenistan. *DataReportal*. 23 February. https://datareportal.com/reports/digital-2024-turkmenistan?form=MG0AV3.

KPMG. 2020. Overview of Fintech Development in Central Asia. https://assets.kpmg/content/dam/kpmg/kz/pdf/2020/12/Overview-of-Fintech-Development-in-Central-Asia.pdf.

Mongol Bank (Central Bank of Mongolia). n.d. Bank of Mongolia Statistics. https://stat.mongolbank.mn/other (accessed on 23 November 2022).

MOST Ventures. n.d. https://mostfund.vc/.

National Bank of the Kyrgyz Republic (NBKR). 2024. *Annual Report 2023*. Chapter 4. p. 65. https://www.nbkr.kg/DOC/28062024/000000000062630.pdf.

Prendergast, R. 2024. Interview: TBC Bank's Oliver Hughes on What Makes Uzbekistan an Exciting Market. *Retail Banker International*. 20 December. https://finance.yahoo.com/news/interview-tbc-bank-oliver-hughes-163612598.html.

Youth Business International (YBI). 2025. Members: Most Business Incubator. https://youthbusiness.org/blog/members/most-business-incubator/.

PART IV

A FINTECH FUTURE

9

Toward Collaborative Fintech Dialogue

George Kvirikashvili, Khimji Vaghjiani, and Minsoo Lee

INTRODUCTION

Financial technology (fintech) is without a doubt making inroads, and this means that the delivery of financial services could potentially become more inclusive across the member countries of the Central Asia Regional Economic Cooperation (CAREC) Program. Fintech policies in different global regions offer exemplary, but elusive, targets for key stakeholders and decision-makers in the CAREC region to adopt. The challenge in CAREC is to raise fintech in the region from its relatively nascent stage to a level of functionality close to the global benchmark. The global fintech landscape provides an exciting backdrop for exploring strategies regarding the delivery of financial services within the CAREC countries, and regarding trade in financial services among the CAREC countries, and between CAREC and the rest of the world.

This chapter explores practical steps for accelerating fintech development through dialogue and collaboration among regional partners. The previous chapters applied an analytical framework based on the goal of advancing fintech interoperability, and they presented innovative steps for developing CAREC's emerging fintech markets. With increasing opportunities for connection to international trade routes, partnering with existing digital platforms will provide more of an advantage than trying to develop homegrown technologies, at least initially. Successful cases from around the world can be encouraging, yet regulators and enablers need to act fast to seize the same opportunities and to spur the consolidation of national and regional fintech ecosystems.

Given that the range of challenges highlighted in this book are obstacles to fintech adoption, the nine emerging fintech markets in CAREC need to develop tech infrastructure, legislation, regulatory frameworks, and the capacity for cross-border transactions—all of which are key elements for fostering increased activity across the region. An exploration of opportunities in other parts of the world to develop fintech capabilities and spread its use points to a clear path for CAREC government initiatives and private investment. Their embrace has the potential to help economies in the region deliver fintech in leaps and bounds, thereby extending the advantages of innovations developed elsewhere in the world to populations that have had to struggle to access financial services, whether due to the accident of geography or because technology and advances in communications infrastructure have been slow to reach them.

Policymakers would do well to learn about the best practices of other regions, and to tailor those practices to fit their own country contexts, given the diversity of infrastructure and other conditions in CAREC that were examined in Chapter 1. More than technology alone, the development of a fully functional fintech ecosystem can open opportunities to deepen connections with the global economy.

Optimism over the possibilities of a fintech revolution is, however, tinged with realism. After all, Central Asia has barely started on its long journey toward the development of a collaborative regional fintech community; and broad comparisons indicate that, when it comes to innovation and the embrace of digital technology, CAREC is generally years behind many other parts of the world, notably North America, Northern Europe, and Asia. That said, successful models are plentiful and readily available. In most cases, the wheel does not need to be reinvented to create more traction in regional fintech cooperation.

The planned approach advocated in this book would set in motion systematic strategies to accelerate fintech that focus on ecosystem development, government funding, the provision of start-up grants, connectivity to the region's diaspora, and greater intra-CAREC trade—all of which would facilitate the acceptance of innovative fintech-led initiatives.

Global concerns continue to significantly influence the development of the fintech market, both within and across regions. Key issues include the availability of investment capital, regulatory stringency, competitive dynamics, and the efficiency of digital infrastructure. These factors are critical not only for Central Asia, but also for the global fintech landscape.

Fintech investment across all regions of the world dropped from heady heights after the coronavirus disease (COVID-19) pandemic, driven by geopolitical tensions and high interest rates. Total global investment in fintech declined from $62.3 billion in the second half of 2023 to $51.9 billion in the first half of 2024, the lowest 6-month period of fintech funding since the pandemic had struck, in the first half of 2020 (KMPG 2024). However, revenues continued to be robust—growing 14% across the world during the 2 years to June 2024, according to the 2024 Global Fintech Report (BCG and QED Investors 2024). According to the report, an eventual end to the fintech investment chill will leave an environment in which the avoidance of adding risk to the financial system will be as important for fintech development as the ability to generate profitable growth.

Even so, the fundamentals driving the sector point to continued growth. The global fintech sector will reach $1.5 trillion in revenue by 2030, a fivefold increase from 2023, according to estimates from BCG and QED Investors (2024). Growth is expected to be powered by fintechs pressing their well-known strengths to solve customer pain points, offering compelling user experiences and rapid innovations.

The United States (US), Asia, and Europe are now hotbeds of fintech investment. North America and Europe have always been at the leading edge of fintech because of their vast international trade volumes. Investment in fintech shattered records in the years leading up to the pandemic, as surplus funding led investors, particularly in the US, to pour money into fintech start-ups and ecosystems. Record low interest rates before the pandemic created a speculative pool of cash for funding innovation, which was welcomed into CAREC's emerging fintech markets.

Many examples through this book have shown that Asia and the Pacific has experienced drastic improvements in fintech delivery and financial inclusion, with the People's Republic of China (PRC); Hong Kong, China; India; and Singapore standing out for their activity in payments, online e-commerce, shopping, and capital market development.

Cross-border initiatives in other regions can be explored to stimulate discussion about collaborative ways to build an effective marketplace and step more boldly toward a future of fintech-driven innovation in CAREC. The focus of this book is directed at regional-level comparisons, instead of attempting to capture the dynamism of all-too-soon outdated fintech landscapes in national markets elsewhere.

Whereas Chapter 8 presented national contexts as further inputs to the road map for cultivating a collaborative regional fintech community, this chapter offers insights into what can be achieved when countries work together toward shared goals in a phased approach appropriate for disparate levels of economic development and technological readiness. The contrast is offered in the spirit that a little inspiration from outside the region may go a long way.

GLOBAL HARMONIZATION EXPERIENCES

Advantages from key areas of fintech ecosystems can be understood by exploring where they have been harmonized in Asia, along with examples from Europe and the Middle East that demonstrate how the regional integration of payment systems promotes and simplifies cross-border trade, commerce, and people-to-people interactions.

In the dynamic and rapidly evolving landscape of fintech, the call for global harmonization has never been more urgent. The Asian Development Bank (ADB) and other international bodies have consistently advocated for a unified regulatory approach to fintech, emphasizing the myriad benefits of a cohesive framework that transcends national borders (ADB 2016; UNESCAP 2021).

A harmonized regulatory environment provides clear and consistent guidelines for fintech companies operating across multiple jurisdictions. This reduces compliance costs and complexities, allowing firms to focus on innovation and growth. International cooperation in fintech regulation is thus crucial for maintaining financial stability and fostering innovation, as Central Asian governments work to integrate digital services at all levels (FSB 2023a; Muratbekova 2024).

Unified standards ensure that consumers receive consistent levels of protection regardless of their location. This builds trust in fintech solutions and encourages wider adoption. The International Organization of Securities Commissions (IOSCO) highlights the importance of global standards in protecting investors and maintaining fair markets (IOSCO n.d.).

Harmonization facilitates smoother cross-border transactions and interoperability between different financial systems. This leads to more efficient markets and can drive economic growth. The efforts of the European Union (EU) to create a seamless legal environment for fintech through legislative initiatives are a prime example of how harmonization can enhance market efficiency.

A global approach to regulation helps in identifying and mitigating systemic risks. It ensures that regulatory gaps are minimized, and that there is a coordinated response to emerging threats. The role of fintech in global derivatives regulation underscores the potential of fintech to enhance regulatory effectiveness and mitigate systemic risks.

The path to harmonization requires ongoing dialogue among stakeholders, including regulators, industry leaders, and international organizations. Collaborative efforts could help in aligning regulatory frameworks, sharing best practices, and addressing challenges unique to the fintech sector. ADB's initiatives to foster regional cooperation and dialogue among its member countries serve as a model for such collaborative efforts.

Global harmonization in fintech is not just a regulatory necessity, but a strategic imperative. By fostering a collaborative dialogue and building on well-established arguments, one can create a robust and inclusive financial ecosystem that will benefit all stakeholders, enabling them to identify opportunities in the trends shaping the digital future, such as the importance of digital public infrastructure and the transformative emergence of artificial intelligence (AI) (World Bank 2024).

A global assessment of harmonization initiatives for cross-border payments might start with the Asian Payments Network, one of the best multicountry financial-cooperation experiences in the world, given the scale of the network and the sizes of the economies involved.

Asian Payments Network

Established in 2006, with support from the central banks of the members of the Association of Southeast Asian Nations (ASEAN), the Asian Payment Network (APN) is aimed at enhancing payment systems and facilitating cross-border transactions within the ASEAN region. It seeks to accomplish this by streamlining payment processes, reducing transaction costs, and improving the efficiency of financial transactions.

Common standards and guidelines regarding digital financial services, as well as regional collaboration on domestic and regional processing and settlements, will promote interoperability among the various payment systems of the 12 ASEAN member countries.[83] APN is aligned with the ASEAN central banks' Working Committee on Payment and Settlement Systems, an initiative whose primary goal is to establish a more efficient, cost-effective, and secure cross-border retail payment infrastructure within the region. The working committee is closely associated with the development of the ASEAN Integration Card (AIC) as a common platform for retail payments.

APN Hub, operated by the Thailand-based National Interbank Transaction Management and Exchange (ITMX), is the platform for cross-border transactions within the network, which is designed to improve efficiency, lower costs, and enhance collaboration among the 37 member banks. It supports remittances and cross-border ATM services, thereby allowing cardholders to withdraw cash in different countries.

National ITMX offers a range of products and services designed to enhance digital payment infrastructure and facilitate seamless transactions. For retail, a single-payment system and the PromptPay (Thailand) service enable the real-time transfer of funds between different banks—using identifiers such as mobile phone numbers; national, tax, and e-wallet identification (IDs); and bank account numbers—and international money transfers within APN. For business, bulk payments and integrated cash settlements are designed to make transactions more efficient. Trade services include finance for domestic digital supply-chain management, a gateway for international trade transactions and settlements, and an electronic registry for managing and storing trade documents. National ITMX also provides a registry for preventing and monitoring fraud and a platform for ensuring compliance with international trade regulations and standards (National ITMX n.d.).

APN also promotes financial inclusion by providing access to payment services for underserved populations. Overall, it represents a significant step toward modernizing payment systems in Asia, fostering economic growth, and enhancing the ease of doing business across borders.

[83] The 12 member countries of ASEAN are Australia, the PRC, Indonesia, Japan, the Republic of Korea, Malaysia, Myanmar, the Philippines, Singapore, Sri Lanka, Thailand, and Viet Nam.

Automated Quick Payment Transfer

Multinational corporations and regional companies have welcomed opportunities created by the Arabian Gulf System for Financial Automated Quick Payment Transfer (AFAQ) system, which was launched in 2020 as a vehicle for cross-border transactions in the local currencies of the Gulf Cooperation Council (GCC) countries. AFAQ, which means "horizon" in Arabic, provides a safe, secure, and stable ecosystem for real-time, low-cost payments by connecting the six member states' payment systems, also allowing payments in euros and US dollars. It is operated by the Gulf Payments Company, an independent firm owned and funded by the central banks of the GCC (Gulf Payments Company n.d.).

The AFAQ use case is bolstered by the significant increase in trade among the GCC states—Bahrain, Kuwait, Oman, Qatar, Saudi Arabia, and the United Arab Emirates (UAE)—which has more than doubled since 2015. The skyrocketing intraregional trade is partly due to a policy shift away from a reliance in hydrocarbons. This shift has involved structural reforms such as enhancing labor mobility and allowing cross-border access to capital markets, which are strengthening economic cooperation and integration.

AFAQ has ended the reliance on bilateral correspondent-banking frameworks for payments that were made by governments, companies, or individuals in a fragmented payment infrastructure characterized by varying standards and limited integration. For a rapidly integrating regional bloc like the GCC, the use of correspondent banking to process cross-border payments increasingly appeared to be a missed opportunity. In 2016, the GCC Supreme Council, composed of the heads of state of each member country, determined that a robust pan-regional payment system could enhance trade, capital, and remittance flows, potentially unlocking higher economic growth.

The Gulf Payments Company connects member states' real-time gross settlement system payment platforms. The cross-currency AFAQ service went live in December 2021, with Saudi Arabia and Bahrain. Kuwait joined in March 2022, the UAE joined in December 2023, and Oman in May 2024; Qatar is expected to join in future.

AFAQ has the potential to deliver significant benefits for the region's corporate treasurers. As all payments across the GCC will resemble domestic transactions, costs are expected to decrease. Firms can streamline their bank accounts as cross-border payments can now be executed through a single domestic account. Previously, treasury staff had to navigate six different domestic payment systems with varying formats. AFAQ reduces the risk of errors and frees up staff resources. It standardizes payment cut-off and delivery times, harmonizing overseas delivery charges. Treasurers can leverage AFAQ to improve cash management efficiency by establishing a regional hub for payables and collections. By facilitating the easier movement of funds, AFAQ could catalyze broader digitization and automation initiatives.

With five GCC countries now participating in AFAQ, adoption is increasing. About one-third of the region's 200 commercial banks are already connected to the system. Firms will need to update their payment processes, including adjustments in their enterprise resource planning platforms and treasury management, to accommodate the new pan-regional real-time gross settlement system. However, the strong support for AFAQ among corporate treasurers across the region means that payment volumes in the system are expected to grow.

European Union

The EU is a more complicated case. With its long and deep history of harmonization, the EU does not seem to provide a relevant model for CAREC; in some respects, it could even be seen as an indication of the limits of practicability and imagination for Central Asia. Nonetheless, it is still very pertinent to the discussion, as it offers a good example of continual commitment to modernization and regional regulatory cohesion in an evolving financial landscape.

Since 2015, the EU has made significant strides in creating a cross-border payment experience that supports the digital economy. Harmonization initiatives that have contributed to a more efficient, cost-effective, and transparent cross-border payments include the following:

- **Single Euro Payments Area (SEPA).** SEPA has standardized euro payments across Europe, making cross-border transactions as easy as domestic ones. This initiative has significantly reduced costs and increased efficiency. The simplification of euro payments across the EU has made it easier and cheaper for citizens and businesses to make cross-border transactions within the eurozone. SEPA ensures that cross-border payments are subject to the same conditions as domestic payments (ECB 2025b).
- **TARGET Instant Payment Settlement (TIPS).** This European Central Bank (ECB) initiative, launched in 2018 as part of the TARGET2 payment system,[84] facilitates instant cross-border payments in euros, allowing for real-time settlements of transactions 24/7, 365 days a year. This system has been linked with other fast-payment systems globally. Instant payments are delivered through the ECB's cross-currency settlement service, which uses the TIPS platform (ECB 2017).
- **G20 Roadmap for Enhancing Cross-Border Payments.** The EU supports the G20 road map, which aims to make cross-border payments faster, cheaper, more transparent, and more accessible by 2027. Given the broad international focus, successful implementation of the G20 road map could significantly impact EU citizens engaged in cross-border transactions (FSB 2023b).
- **ISO 20022 harmonization.** The adoption of ISO 20022 messaging standards has improved the quality and efficiency of cross-border payments by providing a common language for payment messages. While it is crucial for the backend processes of payment systems, its direct impact on citizens may be less visible compared with the initiatives mentioned above (ISO 20022 Payments n.d.).

These initiatives share a strong coherence in their regulatory frameworks and objectives. They all operate within a rigid rubric established by the EU and the ECB to cultivate a secure, efficient, and integrated payment environment.

The ECB has also supported SEPA by chairing the Euro Retail Payments Board, which brings together industry, government, and consumer representatives involved in the process. The board is responsible for SEPA governance and for fostering the integration, innovation, and competitiveness of euro retail payments.

The European Union regulates SEPA through several regulations and directives, including Regulation (EU) No. 260/2012, for technical requirements for transfers, and the Payment Services Directive, which provides the legal framework for payment services across the EU. In addition, the Cross-Border Payments Regulation ensures that euro-denominated payments involving trade with non-EU countries are as efficient and cost-effective as payments within the EU (EU 2009, 2015, 2021).

84 "TARGET" stands for "Trans-European Automated Real-time Gross Settlement Express Transfer."

Consumer protection and transparency remain at the forefront of each initiative. SEPA ensures that consumers receive clear information regarding fees and transaction times, while TIPS focuses on providing secure, reliable instant payment services. The G20 road map emphasizes transparency in cross-border payments.

Collaboration among stakeholders is another vital aspect of these initiatives. SEPA and TIPS foster cooperation among EU member states, while the G20 road map promotes international collaboration to address cross-border challenges, thereby improving the EU's integration into global standards; and ISO 20022 harmonization paves the way for future technological adaptations.

Other milestones on the way toward seamless cross-border payment experience in the EU are the Instant Payments Regulation (IPR), the EU Digital Identity Wallet, and the European Payment Council's SEPA Payment Account Access (SPAA) scheme.

Instant Payments Regulation

The IPR was adopted by the European Parliament and the Council on 13 March 2024. It aims to accelerate the rollout of instant payments in Europe, covering euro-denominated credit transfers within the EU (ECB 2025a). This regulation amends the Single Euro Payments Area (SEPA) regulation and adds specific provisions for instant credit transfers.

The IPR ensures that payment service providers offering standard credit transfers will also offer instant credit transfers. This regulation aims to make instant payments available 24/7, reducing the time for fund transfers to 10 seconds (European Council 2024). It also mandates equal charges for instant and standard credit transfers, and introduces verification services to reduce fraud. The new regulation will eliminate challenges, such as delayed payment executions and the need to block funds while, by closing gaps in the availability of instant payments across the eurozone, it has the potential to be a game changer in making account-to-account payments a compelling payment method for merchants (Tink 2023).

European Union Digital Identity Wallet

The need for secure digital identification across countries inspired the government-issued EU Digital Identity Wallet (EUDIW). The wallet is regulated by the European Digital Identity Framework, which entered into force in May 2024 to provide a secure and reliable means of digital identification for EU citizens, residents, and businesses (EC and EU Digital Identity Wallet n.d.-a). Several large-scale pilot projects are testing the wallet's functionality and usability in financial services, education, and transportation (EC 2025). Each member state is expected to offer at least one version of the wallet by 2026.

EUDIW users will be able to securely store and share digital documents, such as driving licenses, education certificates, and health records. The wallet also facilitates online transactions, access to government services, and the opening of bank accounts (EC and EU Digital Identity Wallet n.d.-b.). Its use could simplify cross-border interactions and enhance privacy and security for digital transactions.

The wallet promises to eliminate obstacles such as the manual entry of usernames, passwords, and International Bank Account Numbers (IBANs), as well as the unnecessary screenings that users face during customer authentication. This can bring about a revolutionary shift in payments in which both the payer's and merchant's identities seamlessly become part of the transaction process (Tink 2023).

European Payment Council's SEPA Payment Account Access Scheme

The SEPA Payment Account Access (SPAA) scheme was developed to facilitate the exchange of payment account-related data and the initiation of payment transactions. It builds on the EU's revised Payment Services Directive (PSD2) and aims to unlock value-added services while ensuring harmonization and interoperability across Europe (European Payments Council n.d.-b). The scheme was introduced in November 2023 with the publication of a SPAA rulebook.

The SPAA scheme, in particular, enables third-party providers to access payment account information and initiate transactions on behalf of users. It supports services such as payment initiation and account information retrieval, as well as premium features such as payment-certainty mechanisms (European Payments Council n.d.-a). The scheme aims to promote open finance and enhance user experience by providing more flexible and innovative payment solutions. The SPAA scheme establishes a commercial framework for premium APIs that enables enhanced payment functionalities and avoids current account restrictions such as daily payment limits. This initiative offers asset holders, including banks, a chance to achieve a strong return on their PSD2 investments. One approach is to offer premium features that enable asset brokers to deliver specialized payment services.

The project was launched by the European banking and payment industry, represented by the European Payments Council, which designed the SEPA schemes for credit transfers and direct debits, and is developing a scheme for payment cards. It is also working on a new framework for mobile payments.

The EU is laying the groundwork to replace PSD2 with two new pieces of legislation: the Payment Service Regulation (PSR), and a third Payment Service Directive (PSD3). This change is designed to level the competitive field for banks and payment institutions, entities authorized under PSD2 to provide payment services to clients and businesses. This is intended to lead to better open banking services, streamlined authentication, easier access to payment systems and credit institution accounts, and improvements in security by extending IBAN name check requirements.

Project mBridge

Project mBridge serves an international example of an interoperable space used by a collaborative initiative to explore the possibilities for central bank digital currencies (CBDCs) in cross-border payments. The project is managed by key central banks and monetary authorities: the Digital Currency Institute of the Peoples Bank of China, the Hong Kong Monetary Authority, the Saudi Central Bank, the Bank of Thailand, and the Central Bank of the UAE.[85] Built on a blockchain called the mBridge Ledger, the platform ensures compliance with jurisdiction-specific policies and legal requirements.

The Bank for International Settlements (BIS) Innovation Hub supported Project mBridge for the first 4 years, and in October 2024, handed over the management, deeming that the project had reached sufficient maturity to require no further assistance in coordinating its development (Reuters 2023).

85 Observing members include the following: Asian Infrastructure Investment Bank; Bangko Sentral ng Pilipinas; Bank Indonesia; Bank of France; Bank of Israel; Bank of Italy; Bank of Korea; Bank of Mauritius; Bank of Namibia; Central Bank of Bahrain; Central Bank of Brazil; Central Bank of Chile; Central Bank of Egypt; Central Bank of Jordan; Central Bank of Luxembourg; Central Bank of Malaysia; Central Bank of Nepal; Central Bank of Norway; Central Bank of the Republic of Türkiye; European Central Bank; International Monetary Fund (IMF); Hungarian National Bank; Monetary Authority of Macao; National Bank of Cambodia; National Bank of Georgia; National Bank of Kazakhstan; New York Innovation Center, Federal Reserve Bank of New York; Reserve Bank of Australia; Reserve Bank of India; South African Reserve Bank; and World Bank.

After pilot projects among participating central banks, selected commercial banks, and their customers in four jurisdictions, mBridge reached the Minimum Viable Product (MVP) stage, enabling real-value transactions and compatibility with the Ethereum Virtual Machine for deploying decentralized applications and smart contracts.

BRICS Pay

One of the promising initiatives in harnessing the transformative power of fintech to drive economic growth and financial inclusion is BRICS Pay, a unified payment system developed by the BRICS nations (Brazil, Russia, India, the People's Republic of China, and South Africa). BRICS Pay is aimed at creating a unified payment system that facilitates seamless transactions among the BRICS nations.[86] This system can serve as a model for CAREC, as it demonstrates how regional cooperation can enhance financial connectivity and efficiency. BRICS Pay enables smooth cross-border transactions, reducing the need for multiple currency conversions and lowering transaction costs. The system is designed to be interoperable with existing national payment systems, to achieve seamless integration and user convenience. BRICS Pay adheres to stringent security standards and regulatory requirements, ensuring safe and compliant transactions.

The BRICS Pay initiative provides a valuable model for regional payment systems, having shown the potential of fintech to drive economic growth and financial stability. BRICS Pay has the potential to challenge Western financial dominance and reduce reliance on the US dollar by fostering financial independence; however, it faces hurdles in terms of scalability, interoperability, regulatory compliance, and cybersecurity (Krause 2024).

CROSS-BORDER REGULATION AND COMPLIANCE

The emergence of new technologies championed by the private sector innovators seems to favor fintechs over traditional banks, at least for the time being. Generative AI provides immediate advantages and delivers significant productivity gains in the areas where fintech costs are centered: coding, customer support, and digital marketing (with improved targeting). As financial services become increasingly embedded in nonfinancial activities, fintechs need to ensure compliance and maintain strong partnerships to thrive.

A momentum for technical advancement is building due to an increasing awareness of the advantages of enabling fast, efficient, and real-time financial transactions through the harmonization of payment systems, such as those described in this chapter. Some innovations offer distinct promise because they offer financial cooperation as an alternative to undergoing cumbersome regulatory and technical harmonization. Where processes such as authentication are streamlined technically and simplified for consumer use, this paves the way to the incorporation of fintech into operations across a wide range of businesses.

One such example is OpenPayd, an innovative company in the United Kingdom (UK) that provides a gateway for embedded financial services globally. As a unique Banking-as-a-Service (BaaS) platform, OpenPayd allows businesses to integrate a wide range of financial services directly into their own platforms via a single, developer-friendly API (Williams 2024). This provides a scalable way for businesses to

[86] Beyond the founding members, BRICS has expanded to include Egypt, Ethiopia, Indonesia, Iran, Saudi Arabia, and the United Arab Emirates. CAREC economies Kazakhstan and Uzbekistan are among the partner countries, as are Belarus, Bolivia, Cuba, Malaysia, Thailand, and Uganda.

offer accounts, payments, foreign exchange, and other banking services as they grow, without having to become fully licensed banks. It also offers the potential to cover the cross-border instant payment needs of sophisticated international e-commerce platforms such as Lazada (Chapter 6).

After focusing on the client bases of digital asset companies, trading platforms, marketplaces, and other financial institutions, OpenPayd is now being approached by firms in completely different markets. The firm's head of banking and payments infrastructure, Barry O'Sullivan, said in an interview in 2024 that blockchain was among the areas the firm was assessing, especially for cross-border payments. He took the view that regulation and compliance around protecting end users will encourage growth if done well, but could discourage innovative technologies if regulatory standards were too difficult to meet (Williams 2024).

The Impact of Fintech on Regulation Frameworks

Improved fintech capability in CAREC would have a significant impact on regulation. As fintech companies have disrupted traditional financial services, regulators have had to keep up with the changes. Here are some of the ways that fintech has impacted regulation:

- **Increased maturity in the regulatory scrutiny.** Fintech companies will be subject to increased regulatory scrutiny, particularly in areas such as consumer protection and data privacy. Regulators are paying close attention to how fintech companies collect, store, and use consumer data, as well as their compliance with anti-money laundering (AML) and Know-Your-Customer (KYC) regulations.
- **Development of regulatory sandboxes.** Some regulators have created regulatory sandboxes, which allow fintech companies to test their products and services in a controlled environment with reduced regulatory barriers.
- **New regulatory frameworks.** Fintech has led to the creation of new regulatory frameworks, such as the Payment Services Directive (PSD2) in the European Union. It regulates payment services and provides a legal framework for open banking.
- **Collaboration between regulators and fintechs.** Regulators have recognized the importance of collaboration with fintech companies to ensure that regulatory requirements are met without hindering innovation. Some regulators have established innovation offices or regulatory sandboxes to facilitate this collaboration.

Overall, fintech has had a significant impact on regulation, prompting government authorities to adapt to new technologies and to come up with innovations of their own regarding approaches to regulation.

Compliance as Strategy

The regulatory advantages that fintechs have enjoyed over traditional finance are narrowing due to increased scrutiny and actions against fintech sponsors, particularly in areas such as Banking as a Service (BaaS) and cryptocurrency. Regulatory frameworks and standards governing or impacting the global fintech sector have come to the fore, although much still remains to be done to create a level and fair regulatory environment across all financial service providers. Fintechs also need to ensure compliance and maintain strong partnerships, as financial services become increasingly embedded in nonfinancial activities, with customer activities increasingly digitized across both the business-to-consumer (B2C) and business-to-business (B2B) sectors. Indeed, thriving fintechs will view compliance not as an obligation, but as a strategic advantage, necessitating a proactive approach to risk management and regulatory adherence. This strategic approach consists of preemptively assessing applicable regulations and proactively implementing industry-grade guidelines and controls, particularly in the critical areas involving financial crime, such as AML, KYC, and sanctions, as well as cybersecurity and fraud prevention (BCG and QED Investors 2024).

Shared Systems

Traditional banks are leveraging their customer data and engagement to counter fintech innovations, highlighting the need for fintechs to enhance their competitive edge through partnerships and compliance. Increasingly, opportunities for this are emerging from the Digital Public Infrastructure (DPI) ecosystem—a framework of shared digital systems that are secure, interoperable, based on open technologies, and designed to provide equitable access to public and private services on a society-wide scale (Hadda and Mukherjee 2024).

Although countries like India and Brazil have seen success with DPI, whether other nations can replicate this success will depend on their market context and infrastructure maturity (Box 9.1).

Box 9.1

Government Support for Comprehensive and Integrated Digital Public Infrastructure

Governments, especially in emerging markets, that implement a three-part Digital Public Infrastructure (DPI) ecosystem—made up of digital identification (ID), payments, and data exchange layers—have broadened access to financial services, spurring innovation and ultimately benefiting the public.

Many countries have tried to emulate the success of the two leading players in this domain: India's Unified Payments Interface (UPI) and Brazil's Pix. However, the limited success of these efforts reveals that isolated implementations of point solutions for digital identity or real-time payment systems do not suffice to foster widespread adoption. Instead, governments should lay out the set of interoperable protocols and put in place fundamental enablers from which innovation can occur.

For example, a real-time payment infrastructure is now commonplace, with more than 80 countries having one in some form.[a] But adoption has been lackluster in many markets, often owing to the presence of established alternative solutions and the absence of supporting DPI functionalities, such as directory services that are critical for fostering growth.

Where real-time payment has taken off is in markets where DPI has been comprehensively implemented. In India, for example, the number of monthly real-time payments has grown five times since 2022, from 2.6 billion to 13.3 billion.[b] The availability of an alias directory and Quick Reference (QR) codes on top of the real-time payment (RTP) infrastructure was critical to propelling innovation.

Where DPI has worked, government involvement had made a difference by setting out a broad vision for the infrastructure and established protocols and incentives for adoption by the private sector. Moreover, the success of DPI hinges on its comprehensiveness (including a digital identity, a directory, and supporting services) and on its full integration across systems; by contrast, siloed point solutions simply do not have the same impact.

continued on next page

Box 9.1 *continued*

How a Digital Public Infrastructure Enables Private Creators to Innovate

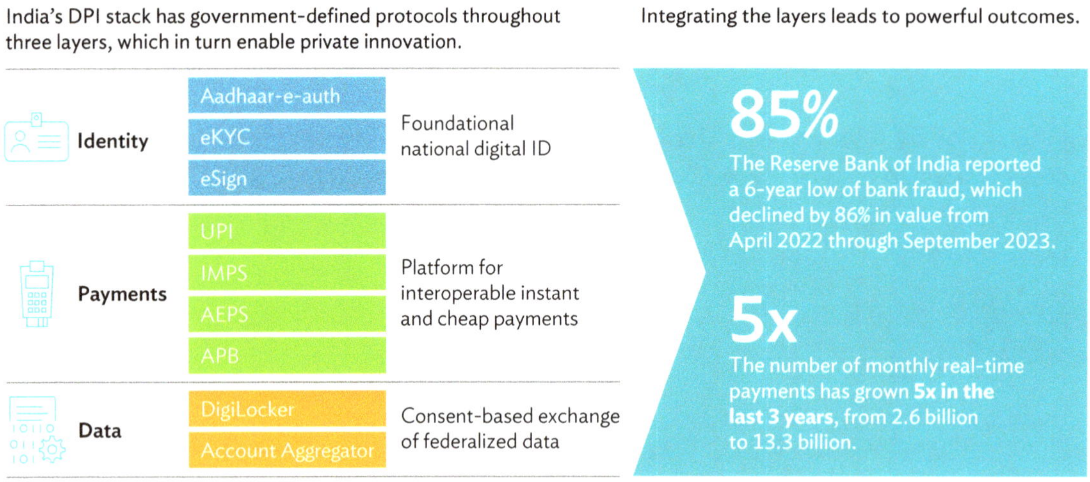

AEPS = Aadhaar Enabled Payment System, APB = Aadhaar Payment Bridge, DPI = Digital Public Infrastructure, eKYC = electronic Know Your Customer, eSign = electronic signature, ID = identification, IMPS = Immediate Payment Service, UPI = Unified Payments Interface.

Notes:

1. Aadhaar-e-auth (Aadhaar electronic authentication) is a digital process for verifying the identity of an Indian citizen by using their Aadhaar number.
2. DigiLocker is a secure cloud-based platform based in India that provides digital document storage and verification.

[a] Cook. 2021. Comparing India's UPI and Brazil's New Instant Payment System, PIX, CGAP.

[b] National Payments Corporation of India. UPI Product Statistics. https://www.npci.org.in/what-we-do/upi/product-statistics.

Sources: Authors' desktop research; Boston Consulting Group (BCG) analysis; company presentations to investors; National Payments Corporation of India; and UPI Product Statistics for 2024.

REGIONAL COOPERATION EXPERIENCES THAT ARE RELEVANT FOR CENTRAL ASIA

Chapter 8 highlighted the point that a range of foreign fintech firms have been welcomed into incubation spaces across CAREC. Besides this, firms originating in the region have developed strong markets beyond their home countries. For example, Georgia-based TBC Bank Group PLC has a presence in Uzbekistan; the National Bank of Georgia (NBG) operates at the sandbox stage in the regional treasuries market (UZCE 2024), while Tajikistan-based Alif Bank is among the financial service firms across the region that regard Uzbekistan as a market ripe for fintech growth (*FinTech Bulletin* 2023). Halyk Bank, OTP Bank, and Santander have also been invited to join the expanding fintech scene in Uzbekistan.

A mature framework for fintech regional integration improves collaboration and coordination between different systems across a specific group of nations with similar infrastructures (including internet penetration and quality), income levels, and readiness to adopt new technologies and financial instruments.

The exchange of information, technologies, and resources among companies operating in the region could be pegged to the framework to create a more streamlined and efficient financial ecosystem. All emerging fintech markets in CAREC could eventually enjoy key benefits from this integration. By creating a more connected and collaborative network, integration can increase access to financial services for individuals and businesses, with opportunities for start-ups to leverage their own skill sets and bring innovative solutions to market.

Fintech Opportunities from Regional Integration and Cooperation

These are

- cultivating partnerships continuously, to leverage capabilities;
- advancing financial inclusion programs, to bring more people into fintech realms;
- accelerating economic relief efforts, using fintech to help more people onboard payment platforms;
- empowering gig workers to use payment technologies that they would not have done before; and
- harnessing the Internet of Things (IoT), as more and more devices come to the market at affordable prices.

The potential for increased innovation and collaboration creates openings for engaged private sector players to develop innovative financial services in a more robust and dynamic financial ecosystem. The central components needed for national fintechs and finance sector players to realize these developments include improved interoperability, scale-up opportunities, and regulatory cohesion.

Useful cases for harmonizing interoperability have been highlighted in this chapter, along with the accompanying regional regulations. With regard to CAREC's emerging fintech markets, a solution for multilateral cooperation on real-time payments may exist in the form of a system similar to the Arabian Gulf System for Financial Automated Quick Payment Transfer (AFAQ), if the proper regulatory and protocol changes are adopted. AFAQ has adopted the latest technologies in a way that improves efficiency and reduces dependence on financial systems and external transfer networks. This is something that emerging fintech markets in CAREC could achieve through a phased-in adoption.

Collaborative Cohesion and Scaling Up

The standardization of cross-border regulations requires a great deal of collaboration among national and fintech-sector participants to create a regional vision incorporating diverse national regulatory trajectories. A step in the right direction at the initial stages would be the creation of working groups among the central banks or bank associations, to include a stocktaking of the standards employed in their national ecosystems and to work toward compatibility and interoperability through the piloting of tangible open-banking use cases. This may involve selecting two or three countries at the beginning, and engaging other emerging fintech markets throughout CAREC at a later stage. As to the future governance of the API ecosystem, oversight structures such as the Joint Regulatory Oversight Committee in the UK—composed of representatives from His Majesty's Treasury, the Competition and Markets Authority, the Financial Conduct Authority, and the Payment Systems Regulator—or the Southern African Development Community (SADC) Payment System Oversight Committee (PSOC) might prove useful models.

Turning to scale-up opportunities that involve a regulatory component and the potential to attract engaged private investors, some cases pertinent to cooperation-oriented countries in CAREC are found in emerging capital markets seeking to solve the "scale" problem by linking with exchanges in neighboring countries.

Various models have potential:

- **Completely integrated markets.** The Baltic nations (Estonia, Latvia, and Lithuania) have integrated their markets under the same IT system and NASDAQ ownership, whereby transactions are cleared and settled through a common central securities depository (CSD).
- **Overlapping ownership and IT systems.** The Central and Eastern European Stock Exchange Group provides access to the Budapest, Vienna, Ljubljana, and Prague stock exchanges, although the ownership of these exchanges vary and are sometimes interconnected. The group also uses some compatible IT systems.
- **Cross-border order routing and customer access.** The SEE Link is an automated order routing system designed to optimize the fulfillment process for e-commerce businesses in the Bulgaria, Macedonia, and Zagreb stock exchanges. Each market is stand-alone, clearing and settling its own trades. However, the system allows investors in these three countries directly access the other exchanges through local brokers.

These different models all pay homage to a realpolitik interest, in that each country wishes to have its own "stock market" as a national symbol. This may indeed limit the idea of a full regionalization of capital markets in Central Asia. A more promising focus might be on how the transactions executed on any one exchange are cleared and settled, and where the records of ownership are held (e.g., by CSDs). This "behind the scenes" aspect is little noticed and so, politically, could be a better avenue for approaching linkages to increase efficiency, reduce costs, and provide better financial plumbing for CAREC's emerging fintech markets.

This approach is also supported by these institutions overall, generating far more revenue than their exchange counterparts and actually holding assets in custody within the infrastructure (systemic importance). Here, two models are informative:

- **CSD network within the European Union.** Each EU member state operates its own CSD, which clears and settles trades in their counterpart exchanges and holds assets in custody. However, the regulatory framework for each CSD is *identical* to that of the Central Securities Depositories Regulation, a mandatory set of rules for each EU member. From a legal and regulatory perspective, this enables cross-border linkages.
- **Clearstream and Euroclear.** These entities are global custodial networks through which foreign investors can hold assets in a local market. They thus allow clearance and settlement for outside investors and represent an offshore linkage. They are not, however, a clearance and settlement operation for domestic participants.

In view of the above, the questions for the CAREC members when considering regional capital market linkages are as follows:

- Is your capital market infrastructure financially sustainable? In other words, could it survive and thrive based on the scale of your economy's corporate population? If not, would a profit-sharing arrangement with the infrastructures of other neighboring markets be acceptable?
- Would your country be willing to allow the exchange to retain local visibility, but clear and settle its transactions through a collective multimarket arrangement?
- If yes, is your market willing to adopt a regulatory framework governing clearance and settlement, record-keeping, and custody identical to that of other CAREC member countries?

If the answers to the above are positive, then the issues of IT compatibility disappear, as the various markets would be operating off the same platform.

If disagreements exist over where the common CSD records should be located, distributed ledger technology (DLT) may be part of the solution. If a country has national security concerns over the control of the population's securities records when the CSD is located outside the country, DLT would socialize the ownership and control. In this regard, fintech could break any resistance to the integration of CSD operations across the region.

If some or all of the member countries opt to explore the use of DLT as the backbone for cross-border CSD functionality, it may be possible to develop a prototype of a cross-border securities transaction system using blockchain technology to directly connect central banks and CSDs within ASEAN+3 (the Association of Southeast Asian Nations plus the People's Republic of China, Japan, and the Republic of Korea). A direct connection for processing cross-border securities transactions inside the region would represent a switch away from the current practice of clearing and settlement by a global network of custodians and correspondent banks in global centers in either the US or Europe.

Sowing the Seeds of Regional Cooperation

At this critical juncture in fintech development, the CAREC economies require a comprehensive framework to guide greater efficiencies in the digital economy. This framework encompasses five key areas for regional cooperation: institutional arrangements, regulatory oversight, infrastructure development, innovation support, and international collaboration. Developments in each area need to be designed to foster a robust and inclusive regional fintech ecosystem.

Fintech regulatory cooperation in the region has occurred in an ad hoc manner, with cases of actual bilateral regulatory cooperation being limited so far. While bilateral efforts involving Georgia were mentioned in Chapter 3, agreements between Kazakhstan and Uzbekistan have generated discussions on a geographic broadening and strengthening of fintech integration.

Bilateral cooperation has expanded into a broader regional initiative through a significant multilateral meeting in 2021 of financial regulators from Kazakhstan, the Kyrgyz Republic, Tajikistan, Turkmenistan, and Uzbekistan (AFSA 2021). A joint declaration laid out the intention to support cross-border economic initiatives in financial services and efforts to improve regulatory cooperation. The meeting emphasized the regulators' collective commitment to developing financial linkages and to creating an attractive environment for investors.

The Astana Financial Services Authority (AFSA) and Uzbekistan's National Agency of Perspective Projects (NAPP) established a comprehensive road map for enhancing cooperation (AFSA 2024). This strategic framework encompasses joint initiatives across capital markets, crypto markets, and the insurance sector, while facilitating collaboration on securities issuance, including green bonds and *sukuk*. The road map also explores opportunities for Uzbek companies to pursue initial public offerings (IPOs) through the Astana International Financial Centre (AIFC).

The partnership between the AFSA and NAPP extends to collaborative research on DLTs and the sharing of regulatory sandbox expertise. This joint effort focuses on testing innovative financial solutions across capital markets, crypto markets, and insurance sectors within a controlled regulatory environment.

Wider fintech collaboration in CAREC seems feasible, but the region is apparently not ready for actual integration and cross-border access. Challenges hindering progress include differences in regulatory frameworks for payment systems, banking operations, and digital assets. In addition, variability in internet penetration and quality across the region needs to be addressed, while disparities in economic development, income levels, and the states' willingness to adopt modern technology and financial instruments further complicate matters.

A regionwide approach has to start somewhere, however, and the Georgia-centered practical steps presented in this book will allow it to stand as a statement of intent to grow partnerships throughout the region. To find common ground for fintech solutions and deepen financial market interconnectedness, a multifaceted approach will be needed, one that is appropriate and phased in according to readiness for collaborative fintech adoption across the region. The approach should encourage interoperability by aligning legal and regulatory environments, which will require dialogue and engagement of financial regulatory bodies and other state institutions.

Back to the Middle Corridor

Chapter 3 laid the ground for the Middle Corridor as an approach that starts to stimulate open banking and the sandbox approach on a regional level. Fintech-enabled regional cooperation among the Middle Corridor countries—including Azerbaijan, the PRC, Georgia, Kazakhstan, and Turkmenistan, along with Türkiye—could serve as a new financial infrastructure enabler within a broader CAREC perspective.

In the context of trade development, the World Bank has suggested that the Middle Corridor could be reimagined as an economic corridor, which first and foremost would require the adoption of an institutional mechanism transcending country boundaries and a legal basis that would require agreement among decision-makers from different agencies, not just those involving transport (World Bank 2023). An institutional mechanism, the Coordination Platform for the Middle Corridor, was launched in October 2024. Supported by the EU, Central Asian countries, South Caucasus states, Türkiye, and major international financial institutions, the initiative focuses on promoting the corridor and prioritizing infrastructure investments. The EU plans to launch a regional transport program in 2025 to support these developments, addressing logistics, digitalization, and interoperability. Recent efforts to strengthen the corridor include the PRC's involvement in a joint venture with Kazakhstan, Azerbaijan, and Georgia aimed at improving cargo delivery and transport coordination (Huseynov 2024).

The Middle Corridor concept could evolve into an interesting fintech value proposition for other countries within the region. The potential for fintech-enabled regional cooperation throughout the Middle Corridor could be thought-provoking, even for those most skeptical about the real benefits of cross-country fintech cooperation. The identification of fintech-related enablers and actions under the Middle Corridor road map could be a starting point for the establishment of a cross-border sandbox, drawing in a wider range of regional authorities, and promoting common principles for open banking through relevant regional forums.

PRACTICAL STEPS TOWARD DEEPENING THE COLLABORATIVE SPIRIT

Two dynamics are at play in charting the steps needed to achieve the transformation of CAREC fintech markets into a community for regional cooperation. The first is to narrow the gap between well-stated intention and completed action. The second is to widen adoption, with a Middle Corridor core proposed as an initial focal point. The needed actions and responsible agents are laid out, in the context of Georgia, in Table 9.1.

Table 9.1: Actions and Responsible Institutions for Fintech Collaboration in Georgia

Pillar	Example of Actions	Responsible Entity
Institutional arrangements	Establish institutional arrangements to support Georgia's fintech strategy implementation (e.g., an interinstitutional fintech committee and working group, including operating rules and procedures).	NBG (lead) ISSSG, MOESD, DGA, GNCA, State Inspector's Service, National Security Council, and/or the Department of Information and Cybersecurity
Regulation, oversight, and supervision	Develop a staggered approach to broadening the scope of open banking to enable consent-based access to customer data across sectors.	NBG (lead) ISSSG, DGA, MOESD, Communications Commission (ComCom)
	Issue a call for evidence on P2P lending and securities crowdfunding to inform the development of a regulatory proposal.	NBG, MOESD
	Design a regulatory road map on crypto assets and crypto-asset services, with a focus on aspects of consumer and investor protection.	NBG, MOESD
	Undertake a review of the legal aspects of digital assets and tokenization.	NBG, MOESD
	Explore and operationalize uses of AI for fraud detection and prevention.	NBG, ISSSG
	Develop and implement internal supervisory-technology strategies (suptech).	NBG, ISSSG
	Establish appropriate cooperation mechanisms in the area of cybersecurity.	National Security Council (lead) NBG, ISSSG, DGA
	Expand the scope of cybersecurity supervision.	NBG
	Strengthen the framework for fraud management and product suitability.	NBG
Infrastructure	Design a system to enable a wide range of entities to use FPS platforms and provide overlay services.	NBG
	Evaluate the discharge of open banking arrangements and develop mechanisms to ensure inputs from a wide range of stakeholders.	NBG
	Promote technology-driven innovations by conducting early-stage experimentation of new technologies.	NBG
	Assess the feasibility of shared platform applications, such as those for SMEs lending and regulatory technology (regtech).	NBG, MOESD in cooperation with other authorities (depending on the application)
	Work with MOJ to roll out the digital identity wallet in the financial sector.	NBG, ISSSG, MOJ
Innovation support	Revise the sandbox access criteria to enable participation by unregulated entities.	NBG
	Evolve a "one-stop shop" system connecting sandbox entities to financial support.	NBG, GITA

continued on next page

Table 9.1 *continued*

Pillar	Example of Actions	Responsible Entity
International collaboration	Promote common principles for open banking through relevant regional forums.	NBG
	Work with other central banks and government authorities in the region to explore the establishment of a cross-border sandbox.	NBG, other central banks in the region
	Facilitate a "beyond-Georgia fintech ecosystem" to establish Georgia as a regional fintech hub for the "Middle Corridor" countries.	NBG
	Identify fintech-related enablers and activities under the Middle Corridor road map.	NBG, central banks of the Middle-Corridor countries

DGA = Digital Governance Agency, fintech = financial technology, FPS = fast payment system, GITA = Georgia's Innovation and Technology Agency, GNCA = Georgian National Competition Agency, ISSSG = Insurance State Supervision Service of Georgia, MOESD = Ministry of Economy and Sustainable Development, MOJ = Ministry of Justice, NBG = National Bank of Georgia, P2P = peer-to-peer, SMEs = small and medium-sized enterprises.

Source: National Bank of Georgia.

- **Institutional arrangements and governance.** The establishment of institutional arrangements is essential for fintech development. This includes creating a dedicated fintech committee or working group with clearly defined operating rules and procedures.
- **Regulation, oversight, and supervision.** A comprehensive regulatory framework should be implemented by means of several key initiatives. First, a staggered approach should be used to broaden the scope of open banking. Second, regulators should issue a call for evidence on peer-to-peer lending and securities crowdfunding to guide regulatory proposals. Third, a regulatory road map for crypto assets and services should focus on protecting consumers and investors. The framework should prioritize AI applications for fraud detection and prevention. In addition, cybersecurity cooperation needs enhancement through expanded supervision and strengthened fraud management, particularly for complex fintech products.
- **Infrastructure.** The development of a robust financial infrastructure requires several critical components. A cross-border financial payment system should be designed to accommodate various entities and support overlay services. Open-banking arrangements should be evaluated with input from diverse stakeholders. The feasibility of shared platforms for SME lending and regulatory technology should be assessed. Furthermore, the financial sector will require the implementation of a digital-identity e-wallet system.
- **Innovation support.** The innovation framework should be enhanced in two key ways: first, the cross-border regulatory sandbox should revise its access criteria to include unregulated entities; second, the framework should evolve toward a "one-stop shop" that connects sandbox participants with financial-support resources.
- **International collaboration.** This should focus on three primary areas: regional forums should promote common principles for open banking. Collaboration with regional authorities will be essential for establishing a cross-border sandbox. Finally, stakeholders must identify and develop fintech-related enablers and activities in the Middle Corridor.

The building of cooperation should focus on the user–client path, integrating fintech, retail, and traditional banking to improve the user experience. If demand exists for cross-border transfers or other operations in which individuals can quickly and seamlessly access reliable financial services, integration processes will advance more rapidly. The large volumes of cross-border trading, investments, P2P transactions, and other activities demonstrate the existence of such demand.

In the burgeoning area of e-commerce, for example, CAREC must reach a consensus on the CAREC Digital Strategy 2030. Endorsed by the CAREC Ministerial Conference in 2021, this strategy would be a crucial step toward the creation of the CAREC Digital Space, including a collaborative regional fintech community (CAREC Program, EAKPF, and ADB 2022).

The "eTrade for all" initiative, a global partnership led by the United Nations Conference on Trade and Development (UNCTAD), could significantly contribute to the development of the region's e-commerce ecosystem (Fredriksson 2021). Through the online platform (etradeforall.org), CAREC can access organizations that provide technical assistance and capacity building related to e-commerce.

For the CAREC region's emerging fintech markets to catch up with the global growth in B2C e-commerce, the following policies are proposed:

- Assess and monitor B2C e-commerce progress for both domestic and cross-border purchases.
- Educate stakeholders—consumers and micro, small, and medium-sized enterprises (MSMEs)—on the welfare benefits of B2C e-commerce.
- Arrive at a consensus among member governments regarding the promotion of a digital future for CAREC through regional-cooperation agreements.
- Include both fintech and e-commerce strategies in the CAREC Digital Future Road Map.[87]
- Expand the areas of cooperation and collaboration on B2C e-commerce beyond the CAREC region.

In all these areas for building cooperation, a phased approach might be necessary. It might start with the capital market, where companies planning to go public could consider issuing securities across different jurisdictions. In pure fintech terms, cross-border transfers could be explored. Effective cooperation would require an alignment among regulators, state digitalization and trade bodies, telecom companies, large banking structures, and key fintech firms.

Fostering Collaborative Dialogue on Harmonization

The Asian Development Bank (ADB), in collaboration with the CAREC Institute and regional stakeholders, has led efforts to advance fintech development through collaborative dialogue in the region. This is essential for harmonizing fintech regulations to ensure a consistent regulatory environment that reduces barriers to entry and facilitates cross-border operations.

Bringing together regulators, industry leaders, and policymakers would enable the sharing of best practices and innovative solutions. Through this knowledge exchange, CAREC economies could adopt and adapt

87 The CAREC Digital Future Road Map is part of the CAREC Digital Strategy 2030, which aims to create a common digital space for accelerating economic growth and digital transformation. The road map outlines five interconnected pillars: digital infrastructure, the digital economy, digital government, digital society (ensuring that digital transformation benefits all segments of the population), and digital security.

successful fintech models to their specific contexts. ADB's regional workshops and conferences serve as vital platforms for this knowledge dissemination.

Infrastructure development remains a critical component of fintech growth. Through collaborative efforts, countries could identify and bridge infrastructure gaps, ensuring that the region has the necessary digital foundation to support fintech innovation. ADB-hosted discussions have emphasized the importance of investing in digital infrastructure to improve connectivity and accessibility.

Collaborative dialogue could help in crafting policies that promote financial inclusion and ensure that fintech solutions are accessible to all segments of society. ADB's focus on inclusive digital growth underscores fintech's role in achieving broader economic inclusion.

To foster fintech development, ADB, the CAREC Institute, and their partners have organized several regional workshops. A notable example is the Regional Workshop on Fintech Development in the CAREC Region, held in Tbilisi, Georgia, in February 2024. This workshop invited experts and stakeholders to discuss fintech innovation strategies and regulatory harmonization.

Building a Mechanism for Consensus

Building a consensus among the various stakeholders and obtaining commitments from them to specific actions will require sustained dialogue. Even then, momentum is not guaranteed; the consensus would still need to be supported. The next steps through a multiyear, complex road map cannot be taken until regional agreement has been reached on the strategic goals. Although it is possible to outline suggested actions within each pillar of the strategic suggestions, which this book offers to policymakers, it is not yet possible to assign region-level responsibilities and time lines (i.e., to make tactical decisions) in the same way that it can be done within nations. That is because the CAREC countries have yet to accept and adopt a road map. However, the proposition carries tremendous potential.

Instead, a vision of the next steps will depend on what comes out of a pan-regional public–private dialogue platform, one that includes engagements with a wide spectrum of stakeholders. Such stakeholder engagement would help finalize the vision and transform the road-map proposals into a comprehensive action plan for taking fintech capacities to a qualitatively higher level.

The first step toward implementing the dialogue platform is to identify the stakeholders in the emerging fintech markets of the CAREC region (Figure 9.1).

At this stage, potential players in CAREC fintech ecosystems can be grouped into four categories: (i) regulators, (ii) trade associations and nongovernment organizations, (iii) private sector participants, and (iv) innovation drivers. These groups would provide the initial candidates for the dialogue platform, which should be expanded later based on feedback from the participants.

The following step would be the preparation of a communication action plan with the most important national stakeholders. After these stakeholders are identified, they must form a well-coordinated public–private partnership to address integration problems, which would inevitably mandate closer coordination and supervision of large groups with complex compositions. This is currently a challenge: although the dynamics of individual groups, forums, and organizations drive aggressive action plans, at the level where these plans are combined, large gaps will have to be filled by streamlining, concentrating, and orchestrating successful results.

Figure 9.1: Typical Key Stakeholders in Fintech Ecosystems

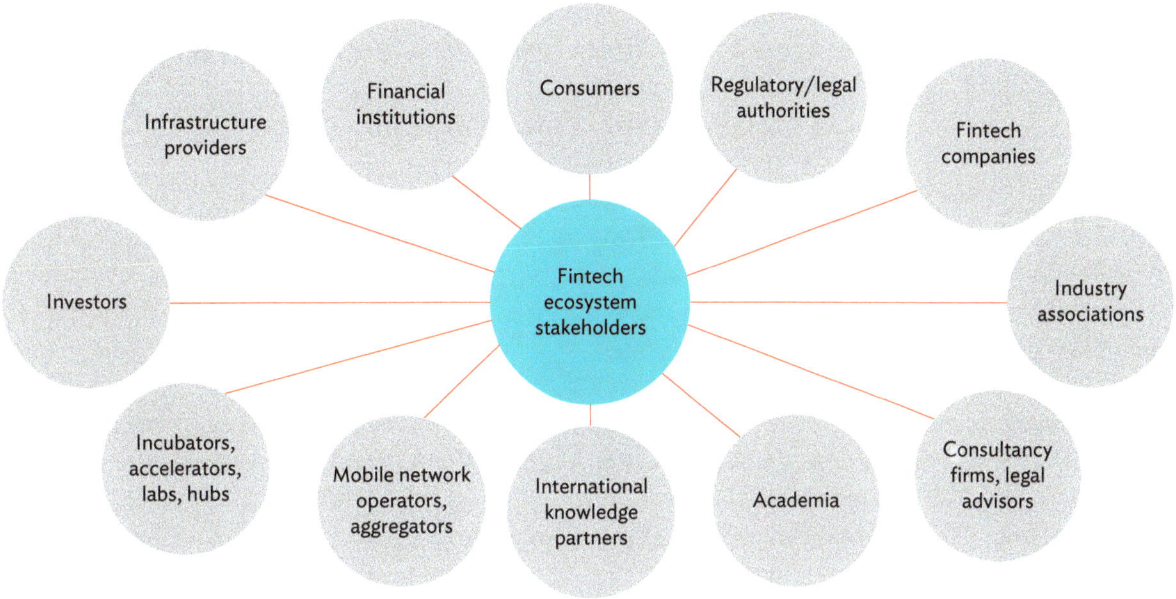

fintech = financial technology.

Source: Alliance for Financial Inclusion. 2020. *Creating Enabling FinTech Ecosystems: The Role of Regulators*. Special Report. p. 13. https://www.afi-global.org/sites/default/files/publications/2020-01/AFI_FinTech_SR_AW_digital_0.pdf.

In preparation for planned discussions, video calls or task-group visits to target countries would be a good way to inform key people about the goals that need to be achieved. These sessions could include a course (bespoke or otherwise) to help build their knowledge of fintech concepts and terminology. This would promote better communication at the discussions.

Next would come the launching of a "CAREC Fintech Policy Forum," and the formation of a secretariat to help drive the forum's progress and facilitate policy coordination and cooperation. The secretariat would act as a conduit for sharing important information, and its existence as an institution would enable it to continue promoting regional cooperation through regular meetings and new regional-integration initiatives. It would be remiss not to mention that the establishment of any regional institution for fintech cooperation would require qualified staff, so the CAREC member countries would need to secure executive support with technical competency.

When preparing the groundwork for the CAREC Fintech Policy Forum's public–private dialogue platform, the organizers could draw from the experience of those who have set up and run institutional public–private dialogue platforms in Georgia, Kazakhstan, the Kyrgyz Republic, and Uzbekistan.

The collaborative dialogue thus facilitated by ADB and its partners would be pivotal for advancing fintech development in the region. By harmonizing regulations, sharing knowledge, addressing infrastructure needs, and promoting financial inclusion, these efforts contribute to the creation of a robust and inclusive fintech ecosystem.

Closing Remarks

The CAREC region still has far to go before it can enable its economies and people to benefit from digital development. This book aims to show the benefits of a clear digital road map for establishing a collaborative regional fintech community. Losing the way would mean missing a clear and present opportunity to benefit from economies of scale; the acceleration of innovation through knowledge sharing; and the chance to spread the costs of technology development, as a way to deepen financial inclusion.

Harmonized fintech regulations and standards across CAREC would reduce the barriers to cross-border financial services and payments. They would facilitate trade, lower transaction costs, and enable businesses to operate more seamlessly across national borders. Crucially, the standardized digital payment systems and financial platforms described in this book could make it easier for SMEs—the backbone of the CAREC economies—to take part in cross-border commerce.

When technological infrastructure is shared and interoperable systems activated, the result is expanded market access. By pooling their resources and coordinating digital-infrastructure development, emerging fintech markets could create more robust and cost-effective financial networks than they could have done acting alone. These networks would be particularly valuable for reaching remote and underserved populations across the region's vast terrain.

Significant efficiencies could be gained when countries learn from each other's fintech market experiences and technical expertise. Another significant benefit from coordinated fintech development would be the strengthening of the region's position in global financial markets. Increasingly efficient capital markets, linked and made more accessible through fintech advances, would add capacity to the CAREC region's engines of economic growth.

A harmonized CAREC fintech ecosystem would be more attractive to international investors and financial institutions than fragmented national markets would be. It would help attract foreign investment and expertise, while giving the region's financial institutions better access to global markets.

REFERENCES

Asian Development Bank (ADB). 2016. *Financial Inclusion in the Digital Economy*. https://www.adb.org/publications/financial-inclusion-digital-economy.

Astana Financial Services Authority (AFSA). 2021. AIFC Develops Cooperation of Central Asian Financial Regulators. News release. https://afsa.aifc.kz/aifc-develops-cooperation-of-central-asian-financial-regulators/.

———. 2024. AFSA and the National Agency of Perspective Projects of the Republic of Uzbekistan Sign Roadmap to Enhance Cooperation. News release. 15 August. https://iac.aifc.kz/en/news/afsa-and-the-national-agency-of-perspective-projects-of-the-republic-of-uzbekistan-sign-roadmap-to-enhance-cooperation.

Bhattacharya, S. and B. K. Sachdev. 2024. Regulatory Challenges and Opportunities for Future Fintech and Green Finance. In V. Sharma et al., eds. *Blockchain's Transformative Potential of Financial Technology for Sustainable Futures*. Springer. pp. 103–122. https://link.springer.com/book/10.1007/978-3-031-70219-8.

Boston Consulting Group (BCG) and QED Investors. 2024. *Profits, Prudence, and Growth*. 2nd ed. BCG. https://web-assets.bcg.com/60/c1/4373568b4050a6f760808f828cf2/2024-fintech-report-june-2024-1.pdf.

Chai, H. Y. and Y. Rhee. 2024. *Fintech and Capital Markets Development and Integration in the CAREC Region*. Output 1c. CAREC Institute. https://estore.carecinstitute.org/wp-content/uploads/2024/02/ENG_Short-version_Fintech-and-Capital-Markets-Development-and-Integration_20240221_RHEE.pdf.

European Central Bank (ECB). 2017. The New TARGET Instant Payment Settlement (TIPS) Service. https://www.ecb.europa.eu/press/intro/mip-online/2017/html/201706_article_tips.en.html.

———. 2025a. Instant Payments Regulation. https://www.ecb.europa.eu/paym/integration/retail/instant_payments/html/instant_payments_regulation.en.html.

———. 2025b. Single Euro Payments Area (SEPA). https://www.ecb.europa.eu/paym/integration/retail/sepa/html/index.en.html.

European Commission (EC). 2025. EU Digital Identity Wallet Pilot Implementation. https://digital-strategy.ec.europa.eu/en/policies/eudi-wallet-implementation.

EC and EU Digital Identity Wallet. n.d.-a. About the Initiative. https://ec.europa.eu/digital-building-blocks/sites/display/EUDIGITALIDENTITYWALLET/About%2Bthe%2Binitiative.

———. n.d.-b. The Many Use Cases of EU Digital Identity Wallets. https://ec.europa.eu/digital-building-blocks/sites/display/EUDIGITALIDENTITYWALLET/The+many+use+cases+of+the+EU+Digital+Identity+Wallet.

European Council. 2024. Council Adopts Regulation on Instant Payments. Press release. 26 February. https://www.consilium.europa.eu/en/press/press-releases/2024/02/26/council-adopts-regulation-on-instant-payments/.

European Payments Council. n.d.-a. SEPA Payment Account Access. https://www.europeanpaymentscouncil.eu/what-we-do/other-schemes/sepa-payment-account-access.

———. n.d.-b. SEPA Timeline. https://www.europeanpaymentscouncil.eu/about-sepa/sepa-timeline.

European Union (EU). 2009. Regulation (EC) No. 924/2009 of the European Parliament and of the Council of 16 September 2009 on Cross-Border Payments in the Community and Repealing Regulation (EC) No. 2560/2001. https://eur-lex.europa.eu/eli/reg/2009/924/oj/eng.

———. 2015. Directive (EU) 2015/2366 of the European Parliament and of the Council of 25 November 2015 on Payment Services in the Internal Market, Amending Directives 2002/65/EC, 2009/110/EC and 2013/36/EU and Regulation (EU) No. 1093/2010, and repealing Directive 2007/64/EC. https://eur-lex.europa.eu/eli/dir/2015/2366/oj/eng.

———. 2021. Regulation (EU) 2021/1230 of the European Parliament and of the Council of 14 July 2021 on Cross-Border Payments in the Union. https://eur-lex.europa.eu/legal-content/EN/TXT/?uri=CELEX%3A32021R1230&qid=1749511867493.

Financial Stability Board (FSB). 2023a. FSB and IMF Outline Comprehensive Approach to Identify and Respond to Macroeconomic and Financial Stability Risks Associated with Crypto-Assets. Press release. 7 September. https://www.fsb.org/2023/09/fsb-and-imf-outline-comprehensive-approach-to-identify-and-respond-to-macroeconomic-and-financial-stability-risks-associated-with-crypto-assets/.

———. 2023b. *G20 Roadmap for Enhancing Cross-Border Payments: Consolidated Progress Report for 2023*. https://www.fsb.org/uploads/P091023-2.pdf.

FinTech Bulletin. 2023. Key Trends and Opportunities in Uzbekistan's Fintech Sector. 24 December. https://bulletins.bfconsulting.com/en/key-trends-and-opportunities-in-uzbekistans-fintech-sector/.

Gulf Payments Company. n.d. AFAQ. https://www.gulf-payments.com/en/our-services/.

Hadda, K. and A. Mukherjee. 2024. How Digital Public Infrastructure Can Support Financial Inclusion. Issue Brief. *Atlantic Council*. 21 October. https://www.atlanticcouncil.org/in-depth-research-reports/issue-brief/how-digital-public-infrastructure-can-support-financial-inclusion.

Hedman Law Firm. 2024. Expanding Cross-Border: Legal and Regulatory Challenges of Fintech. https://hedman.legal/articles/expanding-cross-border-legal-and-regulatory-challenges-of-fintech/.

Huseynov, V. 2024. Multiple Countries Strive to Enhance Middle Corridor Despite Challenges. *Jamestown Foundation*. 28 October. https://jamestown.org/program/multiple-countries-strive-to-enhance-middle-corridor-despite-challenges/.

International Organization of Securities Commissions (IOSCO). n.d. Key Regulatory Standards. https://www.iosco.org/about/?subsection=key_regulatory_standards.

ISO 20022 Payments. n.d. SCT Inst & TIPS: Introduction to TIPS. https://www.iso20022payments.com/sct-inst-tips/intoduction-to-tips/?.

KPMG. 2025. *Pulse of Fintech H2'24: Global Analysis of Fintech Funding*. https://kpmg.com/fintechpulse.

Krause, D. 2024. *The Future of Global Payments: BRICS Pay and the Evolving Financial Order*. https://papers.ssrn.com/sol3/papers.cfm?abstract_id=5043142.

Linklaters. n.d. Fintech and Payments Legal Outlook 2025. https://www.linklaters.com/insights/publications/legal-outlook/2025/fintech-and-payments.

Muratbekova, A. 2024. Digitalization in Central Asia: Progress and Potential. In E. Akilli, B. Güneş, and O. Güner, eds. *Digital Diplomacy in the OSCE Region: From Theory to Practice*. Springer. pp. 33–44.

National ITMX. n.d. Our Products and Services. https://www.itmx.co.th/product-and-service.

Reuters. 2024. BIS to Leave China-Backed Central Bank Digital Currency Project. 31 October.

Rosen, K. 2024. Real-Time Payments Must Go Truly Global to Unlock Further Growth. *IBS Intelligence*. 19 June. https://ibsintelligence.com/blogs/real-time-payments-must-go-truly-global-to-unlock-further-growth/.

Tink. 2023. Three Key 2024 Milestones in EU Payments Regulation. 21 December. https://tink.com/blog/open-banking/eu-payment-regulation-2024/.

United Nations Economic and Social Commission for Asia and the Pacific (UNESCAP). 2021. *Digital and Sustainable Trade Facilitation in Central Asia Regional Economic Cooperation (CAREC) 2021*. United Nations. https://www.unescap.org/sites/default/d8files/knowledge-products/CAREC_report_2021_0.pdf.

Uzbek Exchange (UZCE). 2024. The First Successful Deal Concluded by the Bank of Georgia on the Uzbek Government Securities Market. Press release. 20 June. https://uzrvb.uz/en/press-center/news-and-announcements/-the-first-successful-deal-concluded-by-the-bank-of-georgia-on-the-uzbek-government-securities-market.htm.

Williams, C. 2024. OpenPayd: At the Forefront of Consolidating and Exploring New Payment Innovations. *Payment Expert*. 28 June. https://paymentexpert.com/2024/06/28/openpayd-exploring-payment-innovation/.

World Bank. 2023. *Middle Trade and Transport Corridor: Policies and Investments to Triple Freight Volumes and Halve Travel Time by 2030*. https://www.worldbank.org/en/region/eca/publication/middle-trade-and-transport-corridor.

——. 2024. *Digital Progress and Trends Report 2023*. https://www.worldbank.org/en/publication/digital-progress-and-trends-report.

APPENDIX

Methodology for the Four-Pillar Indicators

This appendix details the selected indicators across the four pillars discussed in Chapter 1: finance, technology, capability, and regional cooperation. When indicators have come from third-party sources, such as the World Bank, their definitions and source links have been provided. In cases where the indicator has been created by the research team for this book, the definition and scoring methodology have been outlined.

Descriptions of Selected Indicators for Each Pillar in Chapter 1

Indicator	Description	Notes/Scoring Methodology	Source
	Pillar 1: Finance (10 indicators)		
Owned a financial institution account	Ownership of an account (single or joint) at a bank or another type of financial institution (% of population aged 15+ years)		World Bank Global Findex 2025
Used mobile money account	Use of a mobile money service in the past year		World Bank Global Findex 2025
Made or received digital payments	Use of mobile money, debit or credit card, or mobile phone to make a payment from an account; e.g., paying bills, sending or receiving remittances, receiving payments for agricultural products, receiving government transfers, receiving wages, receiving a public sector pension directly from or into a financial institution account or through a mobile money account (% of population aged 15+)		World Bank Global Findex 2025
Received wages into a financial account	Any money received from an employer in the past year in the form of a salary or wages for doing work, and received directly into a financial institution account (% of population aged 15+)		World Bank Global Findex 2025
Owned a debit or credit card	Ownership of a debit or credit card (% of population aged 15+)		World Bank Global Findex 2025

continued on next page

Appendix table continued

Indicator	Description	Notes/Scoring Methodology	Source
Made a utility payment using an account	Regular payments for water, electricity, or trash collection directly from a financial institution account or by using a mobile phone (% of population aged 15+)		World Bank Global Findex 2025
Firms using banks for investment capital	Percentage of firms using bank loans to finance purchases of fixed assets		World Bank Global Financial Development Database, 2021
Firms using banks for working capital	Percentage of firms using bank loans to finance working capital		World Bank Global Financial Development Database, 2021
MSMEs reporting a financial gap	Percentage of MSMEs that find it challenging to obtain credit		SME Finance Forum, 2025
Firms reporting finance as major constraint	Percentage of firms identifying access to and/or cost of finance as "major" or "very severe" obstacles		World Bank Global Financial Development Database, 2021
Pillar 2: Technology (Including Infrastructure) (6 indicators)			
Internet users	Measures the proportion of individuals using the internet		World Bank Global Financial Development Database, 2021
Mobile broadband subscriptions	Active mobile-broadband subscriptions per 100 inhabitants (i.e., the sum of standard mobile-broadband and dedicated mobile-broadband subscriptions to the public internet); covering actual subscribers, not potential subscribers, even though the latter may have broadband-enabled handsets		World Bank Global Financial Development Database, 2021
Fixed broadband speed	Measures the median fixed broadband download speed in Mbps		Speedtest Global Index, 2021
Fast-payment systems	Measures the existence and openness of the fast-payment system	0 = No fast-payment system 1 = Being developed/planned/ in consideration 2 = Yes, but only accessible by banks 3 = Yes, open to banks and nonbanks	Access Partnership, 2022

continued on next page

Appendix table continued

Indicator	Description	Notes/Scoring Methodology	Source
National digital identities	Measures the existence and use of a national digital ID system	0 = Electronic national ID card with biometric chip 1 = Planned national digital ID (online): ongoing/in process/ in consideration 2 = National digital ID (online): only for government services 3 = National digital ID (online): open ID for government + private sector innovation	Access Partnership, 2022
Adoption of and investment in emerging technologies	Including adoption of emerging technologies, investment in emerging technologies, robot density, and computer software spending		Network Readiness Index, 2024
Pillar 3: Capability (5 indicators)			
Laws relating to ICTs	Concerning laws relating to ICTs (1–7) (e.g., e-commerce, digital signatures, consumer protection)[a]		Global Information Technology Report, 2016
Adaptability of legal frameworks	Concerning a legal framework's adaptability to digital business models (1–7) (e.g., e-commerce, sharing economy, fintech)		World Bank GovData360, 2022
Fintech-focused regulations	Concerning specific regulations such as payments, e-money, and P2P that enable fintech innovation and growth	6 = Covers more than five aspects 4 = Covers two to five aspects 2 = Covers one aspect 0 = No regulatory framework or only in draft	Access Partnership, 2022
Fintech innovation initiatives	Gauging whether there are initiatives driving and supporting fintech (e.g., sandboxes, grants, fintech festivals, fintech innovation hubs)	6 = Yes, collaborative (public and private sector participation) 4 = Yes, driven by either public or private sector 2 = Planned 0 = No initiatives in place	Access Partnership, 2022
Digital skills	Digital skills among the population (1–7) (e.g., computer skills, basic coding, digital reading)		World Bank TCdata360, 2023
Pillar 4: Regional Cooperation (3 indicators)			
International commitments	Gauging whether the country or financial regulatory authority has committed to fintech cooperation through digital economy agreements, MOUs, or joint statements with other countries	6 = Yes, binding commitment through digital economy agreements and accompanying MOUs (with CAREC or non-CAREC countries) 4 = Yes, through MOUs, joint statements, cooperation agreements 2 = Planned/in discussion 0 = No	Access Partnership, 2022

continued on next page

Appendix table continued

Indicator	Description	Notes/Scoring Methodology	Source
Cross-border initiatives	Gauging whether there are cross-border initiatives to enhance interoperability in payments, enable e-invoicing, or facilitate harmonization of standards, to advance fintech	6 = Yes (more than two) 4 = Some (one or two) 2 = Planned/in discussion 0 = No	Access Partnership, 2022
Participation in regional and other international platforms	Gauging whether the country or financial regulatory authority is participating in regional or international platforms to drive cross-border fintech cooperation	6 = Yes, with central bank participation in multilateral platforms to support financial innovation (e.g., Global Financial Innovation Network); country participation in multilateral platforms to support digital financial inclusion (e.g., Alliance for Financial Inclusion); and country participation in CAREC-specific initiatives to support fintech innovation 4 = Some (one or two of the above) 2 = Planned (official statement) 0 = No	Access Partnership, 2022

CAREC = Central Asia Regional Economic Cooperation; fintech = financial technology; ICT = information and communication technology; ID = identification; Mbps = megabits per second; MOU = memorandum of understanding; MSMEs = micro, small, and medium-sized enterprises; P2P = peer-to-peer.

[a] Baller, S., S. Dutta, and B. Lanvin, eds. 2016. *The Global Information Technology Report 2016: Innovating in the Digital Economy*. World Economic Forum. https://www3.weforum.org/docs/GITR2016/WEF_GITR_Full_Report.pdf.

Limitations of the Approach

While indicators under the four pillars are selected from well-established global and international sources, where the data had been collected using rigorous survey methodology, several limitations of the indicator system exist:

- **Data availability.** There were data gaps for some of the emerging fintech markets among the Central Asia Regional Economic Cooperation (CAREC) member countries, including Tajikistan and Turkmenistan. Consistent data gaps also existed for some of the countries included in the benchmarking analysis, such as Brunei Darussalam. Research and insights from experts were used to support assessments on fintech progress and development in those countries.
- **Data comparability.** For some indicators, such as those measuring capital and financing constraints under Pillar 1, updated data were not available for some CAREC and benchmarking countries. This was due to delays in data collection and reporting from the external sources, impacting the level of comparability across countries and regions. Research and insights from experts were used to support assessments on fintech progress and development.
- **Scoring mechanism.** Where indicators to measure fintech progress did not exist, Access Partnership created them. While every effort was made to ensure that the scoring of indicators remained fact-based and objective, in some cases, limited information may have hampered correct assessments of countries.

www.ingramcontent.com/pod-product-compliance
Lightning Source LLC
Chambersburg PA
CBHW041753220926
51847CB00014B/183
* 9 7 8 9 2 9 2 7 7 4 8 9 9 *